LATINOS IN THE UNITED STATES

History, Law and Perspective

Series Editor

ANTOINETTE SEDILLO LÓPEZ
University of New Mexico
School of Law

Advisory Panel

Tobias Duran, Ph.D.
Cecelia M. Espenoza, J.D.
Paul Finkelman, Ph.D.
Christian Fritz, J.D., Ph.D.
F. Chris Garcia, Ph.D.
Placido Gomez, J.D., LL.M.
Richard Gonzales, J.D.
Emlen Hall, J.D.
Berta Hernandez, J.D.
Eduardo Hernandez-Chavez, Ph.D.
Victor Lopez, J.D.
Jose Martinez, J.D.
Margaret Montoya, J.D.
Michael Olivas, Ph.D., J.D.
Leo Romero, J.D., LL.M.
Christine M. Sierra, Ph.D.
Gloria Valencia-Weber, J.D.

A GARLAND SERIES

SERIES CONTENTS

VOLUME

3

CRIMINAL JUSTICE AND LATINO COMMUNITIES

Edited with an introduction by

ANTOINETTE SEDILLO LÓPEZ

GARLAND PUBLISHING, INC.
New York & London
1995

Library of Congress Cataloging-in-Publication Data

Criminal justice and Latino communities / edited with an introduction by Antoinette Sedillo López.
    p.   cm. — (Latinos in the United States ; v. 3)
    Includes bibliographical references.
    ISBN 0–8153–1772–7 (acid-free paper)
    1. Criminal justice, Administration of—United States.
2. Discrimination in criminal justice administration—United
States. 3. Hispanic Americans. 4. Latin Americans—United
States.   I. López, Antoinette Sedillo. II. Series.
HV9950.C7435 1995
364.973'08968—dc20   94–36051
                                             CIP

Printed on acid-free, 250-year-life paper
Manufactured in the United States of America

To my children, Victor Francisco and Graciela Raquel.
Esta colección es tu historia y tu herencia.

CONTENTS

Estrangement, Machismo and Gang Violence

Race and Juvenile Justice Processing in Court and
Police Agencies

No Comprendo: The Non-English-Speaking Defendant
and the Criminal Process

Socialization of Chicano Judges and Attorneys

INTRODUCTION

In recent years, the United States has faced increasingly disturbing crime statistics. Policy makers have proposed various reforms of the criminal justice system. Poor and minority people are most likely to be robbed, murdered or assaulted. They are also most likely to be arrested, convicted and imprisoned. Yet they are not adequately represented as policy makers and decision makers concerning criminal justice system reform. The results of the first trial of the police officers whose beating of Rodney King was captured on videotape brought into sharp focus the question of whether minority victims are taken seriously and whether minorities should have confidence in the criminal justice system. Minority communities have begun to challenge the criminal justice system.

The articles on criminal justice in this volume range from a review of the legal system's historical treatment of Latinos to contemporary critiques of the legal system and criminological research techniques. Latinos have been targeted by police and treated unfairly in the criminal process. Studies have shown that they have experienced disparate sentencing decisions. Language barriers further handicap many Latino criminal defendants. Further, criminological research has stereotyped and created negative images of Latinos. These images have influenced the objectivity of the research. As victims, Latinos have not seen hate crimes against them vigorously prosecuted. It is no surprise that empirical research demonstrates that many Latinos lack confidence in the criminal justice system. Finally, despite the emphasis on crime prevention in this country, there has simply been insufficient research and attention paid to the needs of the Latino community. Latinos need to make their voices heard on issues of criminal justice system reform that affect their communities.

Tobias Duran describes a political murder and the subsequent trial in Santa Fe, New Mexico, in the 1890s. He discusses Thomas Catron's possible involvement and subsequent disbarment proceedings against him. Anglo and Mexican political rivals increasingly used violence as response to conflicts. Duran considers the function of the rule of law in power relationships between Hispanic and Anglo residents of New Mexico.

Larry Trujillo criticizes criminological theory construction. He states that criminological research has created biased stereotypes and negative images of Chicanos. He traces the origins of the distorted images created during and after the Mexican-American War. Mexicans were stereotyped as having innate criminal tendencies as bandidos or outlaws. He describes outmoded theories of biological determinism and cultural deviance that influenced sociologists and psychologists. Trujillo demonstrates the obvious and subtle biased ideologies in their research methods and findings.

Hisauro Garza analyzes differential treatment by comparing the treatment of Chicanos and Anglos through each stage of the criminal process in Monterey County, California. Controlling for prior criminal record and current criminal charges, Garza analyzes data from 187 cases. He found a relationship between ethnicity and social class at every stage of the trial process. Garza found that when Chicano ethnicity and lower social class were both present the likelihood of negative differential treatment increases.

David Carter presents an exploratory study about the attitudes of Hispanics in Texas toward crime and the criminal justice system. He gives his perception of Hispanic cultural norms and values and then analyzes empirical data gleaned in response to questionnaires. He found that Hispanics in Texas feel "less safe" concerning crime than does the general population. Hispanics do not trust the police and do not feel that they have adequate police protection. Their evaluations of the police are lower than those of the general population. Yet they feel that the criminal courts are fair and just. Hispanics tend to possess a punitive rather than a rehabilitative attitude toward corrections.

Relying on the same data set, David Carter also studied Hispanic perceptions of police performance. He found that police did not meet Hispanics' expectations of them. When expectations were not fulfilled, Hispanics lowered their evaluations of police officers. He found that barriers imposed by linguistic and symbolic communication differences and a failure to understand each other's culture (including the police subculture) contributed to the distrust.

Alfredo Mirandé analyzes community and police conflict in a Southern California barrio. He chose this particular barrio because it was the site of a recent community-police confrontation and had a long history of community police conflict. It also seemed typical of an isolated southwestern barrio. He found that the

Chicano respondents supported the hypothesis that fear of crime correlated with support for increasing police power. The survey results only somewhat supported the hypothesis that fear of the police would be correlated with favoring the protection of civil liberties. The reason for the relatively weak support for the hypothesis was that Chicanos held very strong support for civil liberties, whether they expressed fear of police or not. The results also supported the hypothesis that fear of the police was correlated with a desire to limit police power.

Malcolm Holmes and Howard Daudistel compared sentencing of Anglo, Black and Mexican origin defendants in El Paso, Texas, and Tucson, Arizona. The greatest disparity of sentencing was observed in El Paso. Blacks and Mexican origin defendants were considerably more likely to receive a severe sentence than otherwise similar Anglo defendants. Minority defendants in Tucson were also more harshly sentenced. They theorize that differences in plea bargaining and the size of the minority population might affect the sentencing results.

Tanya Katerí Hernández writes of unconscious racism in prosecuting racially motivated violence. The Puerto Rican Legal Defense and Education Fund has documented a marked increase in racial violence against Latinos. Hernandez believes that bias crimes often elude prosecution because they are perpetrated by police officers, a group that prosecutors are reluctant to antagonize. Further, prosecutors themselves may suffer from unconscious racism that affects their decision making. She argues that current statutes are inadequate in addressing bias-related violence. She proposes carefully drafted statutes that reduce prosecutorial discretion in the decision to prosecute to ensure that bias crimes against members of all groups that experience irrational hatred are pursued.

Gary LaFree compared treatment of Hispanics and whites in Tucson and El Paso in pretrial release outcomes, convictions and sentencing. Like Holmes and Daudistel, he found greater disparities in El Paso. Hispanic criminal defendants received less favorable pretrial release outcomes, were more likely to be convicted in jury trials and received severer sentences. Other outcomes were not markedly different. He suggests that differences may be due, at least in part, to differences between established Hispanic citizens and less well-established Mexican-American citizens and Mexican nationals. Different outcomes might also be explained by different mechanisms for providing attorneys to indigent defendants and differential language difficulties in the two cities.

Bonnie J. Bondavalli and Bruno Bondavalli provide a summary of issues affecting Spanish-speaking criminal defendants. They express concerns about criminal justice issues such as data collection, community-police relations, language, inadequate correctional programming and treatment. They propose improved multicultural training of criminal justice officials.

Howard Erlanger challenges the myth that barrio cultural values condone violence. He concludes that while subcultural values of the barrio may differ from Anglo values, the barrio values do not require or condone violence. Rather, violent behavior may be a product of the way in which conditions limit expression of those values.

Dale Dannefer and Russell Schutt study bias in the juvenile justice system. They compare how Blacks, Hispanics and whites were treated in the juvenile justice system from police contact through sentencing. They found substantial bias in police disposition but less evidence of bias in court decisions. They also found severer court disposition for Hispanic juveniles than for Black juveniles.

Joan Bainbridge Safford looks at the problems of a non-English-speaking defendant in the criminal justice system. She outlines the scope of the problem throughout the country for the Spanish-speaking Puerto Ricans in the East and the Mexican Americans in California as found by the Civil Rights Commission study. Bainbridge Safford raises constitutional issues and discusses the need for professional interpreters and transcriptions of the interpretation.

F.V. Padilla considers the impact Hispanic judges and attorneys can have on the criminal justice system. He describes Mexican-American judges and attorneys from five southwestern states in terms of family background, ethnicity, religion, education, age and occupation. He finds that the Mexican-American attorneys he studied in the early 1970s tended to conform to the legal system rather than challenge it. He calls for increased representation of Mexican Americans in the criminal justice system.

The articles in this volume present disturbing information on Latinos and the criminal justice system. It is of vital importance that Latinos participate in attempting to improve the criminal justice system. Latinos' needs in terms of crime prevention, fair processes and freedom from bias must be addressed.

FURTHER READING

"El Chicano Y the Constitution: The Legacy of Hernandez v. Texas: Grand Jury Discrimination," 6 *University of San Francisco Law Review* 129 (1971).

Meadow, Arnold, Stephen I. Abramovitz, Arnold de la Cruz and German Otalora Bay, "Self-Concept, Negative Family Effect and Delinquency," 19 *Criminology* 434 (1981).

Romero, Leo M., and Luis G. Stelzner, "Hispanics and the Criminal Justice System," in *Hispanics in the United States: A New Social Agenda,* edited by Pastora San Jose Cafferty and William McCready. New Brunswick, N.J.: Transaction Books Rutgers, 1985.

Sandoval, Ruben, and Douglas R. Martinez, "Police Brutality: The New Epidemic," 8 *Agenda: A Journal of Hispanic Issues* 14 (1978).

Sotamayor, Marta, "Juvenile Delinquency—A Community Perspective," 9 *Agenda: A Journal of Hispanic Issues* 15 (1979).

U.S. Commission on Civil Rights, *Mexican Americans and the Administration of Justice in the Southwest.* Washington (March 1970).

Vigil, James Diego, "Group Processes and Street Identity: Adolescent Chicano Gang Members," 16 *Ethos* 421 (1988).

Zatz, Marjorie S., "Race, Ethnicity, and Determinate Sentencing: A New Dimension to an Old Controversy," *Criminology* 22 (1984).

FRANCISCO CHÁVEZ, THOMAS B. CATRON, AND ORGANIZED POLITICAL VIOLENCE IN SANTA FE IN THE 1890S

TOBIAS DURAN

POLITICAL CONFLICTS IN New Mexico during the last quarter of the nineteenth century frequently resulted in violence. As a recent study on violence has noted, New Mexico may have been "the only place in America where assassination became an integral part of the political system. . . ."[1] Several examples, in fact, illustrate this prevalent political violence: in 1884 Juan Patrón, Lincoln County leader, was murdered; in 1896 Albert J. Fountain, Doña Ana County politician, mysteriously disappeared; and in 1904, an unknown assassin shot and killed José Francisco Cháves, Valencia and Torrance County political boss.[2] Moreover, Lincoln and Colfax County battles and vigilantism in Socorro, Albuquerque, and Las Vegas added to this widespread discord.[3]

Although violence was a fact of life, the ambush in 1892 of popular Santa Fe County political leader Francisco Chávez, age 41, aroused unusual indignation and intensified existing strife. As one journalist wrote: "In the history of horrid crimes of the Southwest, . . . none was more dastardly, cold-blooded and fully predetermined. . . ."[4] The celebrated murder trial produced "sensation after sensation," implicating old-guard political veterans, and eventually led to the execution of four Mexicanos, suspected of being only part of larger conspiracies.[5] Another writer, Thomas Smith, chief justice of the New Mexico Supreme Court, added that the accused had pursued a "diabolical conspiracy of long standing," and pronounced the case a *"cause célèbre"* because of the "prominence of the deceased, . . . the notoriety of the criminals, . . . the complication and mystery

0028-6206/84/0700-0291 $2.00
© Regents, University of New Mexico

of the circumstances, and . . . the intense interest of the populace."[6]

Chávez, whom historian Ralph Twitchell described as a "powerful personality in the administration of political affairs," became a formidable foe of the Santa Fe Ring and "seemed to be on the verge of welding" widespread opposition to the powerful clique. Led by Republican boss Thomas Benton Catron, the ring illustrated the monopolistic tendencies of many American business concerns in the Gilded Age.[7] On the other hand, Chávez, former sheriff and party chairman of Santa Fe County, was a prominent Democrat, "the acknowledged leader of his party, and much the strongest man politically in the county."[8] Because of the "popularity and power" of Chávez, Supreme Court Justice Napoleon B. Laughlin concluded that the motive for his assassination was "political jealousy."[9]

Apparently, a series of episodes set the stage for the murder of Chávez. In March 1890, Faustino Ortiz, a Republican ward politician, mysteriously disappeared; several months later his body was found near the Máscaras arroyo in northwest Santa Fe. Although Francisco Chávez and Romulo Martínez, U.S. marshal from 1885 to 1888 and Democratic party leader, were charged with murder, the indictments were quashed.[10]

Five months later, Thomas Catron received a letter from one S. Davis stating that an acquaintance had attended a meeting the year before in which Democratic party leaders had planned to murder Catron and Faustino Ortiz. The informant said he would disclose names of persons involved and more details in exchange for a reward and protection, but Catron apparently rejected the offer.[11]

The following February, several shots were fired through the window of Catron's law office in Santa Fe. The *Santa Fe Daily New Mexican* reported that several unidentified men on horses had fired the shots, one of which struck J. Arturo Ancheta of Grant County, who was attending a meeting with Catron. Ancheta's wound was not fatal, and the gunfire struck no one else.[12]

The next day, a group demanded a full-scale investigation, and Catron introduced Council Bill 122, requesting funds to pay for the investigation. Arguing that Ancheta had been "shot while conducting business for the [territorial] Council," Catron persuaded legislators that public money ought to be used to bring the "culprits to justice." At the same time, Governor LeBaron Bradford Prince was authorized to hire a private detective to infiltrate "secret groups," who, according to Prince, were undermining public order.[13]

Catron was convinced he had been the prime target. The *Santa Fe New Mexican*, which Catron and the ring controlled, argued that past antagonisms had led to the shooting. Surely, the *New Mexican* reasoned, Ancheta was too young—he was serving his first term in the Assembly—to have gained such bitter enemies this early in his political career; so Catron must have been the intended victim.[14] Governor Prince agreed, dismissing the possibility of an attack on Ancheta.[15] Democrats and members of the Knights of Labor believed, however, that Ancheta had been the intended victim because of his opposition to legislation favoring the Santa Fe Ring.

Five months earlier the Knights of Labor had written to T. V. Powderly, national leader of the Knights, analyzing social conditions in New Mexico. The Knights accused Catron and his "cormorants" of "entrenching themselves behind technical forms of law in the possession of vast tracts of community grant land. . . ." These "community land thieves and public corruptionists," including leading lawyers, prominent politicians, and businessmen of different stripes, had used "corrupt and tyrannical practices to carry out their evil deeds." Cultivating "close relations with the all-powerful Spanish-Mexican rico class," the ring had "gained economic and political control throughout the Territory." Meanwhile, the "mass of the poor people" had been "systematically robbed by means of the courts and legal processes." The "clandestine and violent resistance" of the people was therefore an understandable response to the wholesale corruption in New Mexico. This letter from the Knights, who for a period of time united with *Las Gorras Blancas*, a San Miguel county-based organization fighting to retain their land, clarified their interpretation of the social context in which they believed political violence was taking place.[16]

Ring members countered, accusing the "Mexican Knights of Labor" of depredations and outrages.[17] According to Prince, a Pinkerton agent had "found that everywhere among the Mexican Knights there [was] the most bitter feeling against land-owners" and others thought to be opponents. The Knights and the White Caps, whom

3

the ring saw as the same, "constantly talk[ed] of killing," and one member even recommended "the knife instead of the pistol" because it was noiseless.[18]

In addition, the accusation continued, the "Mexicans" who had joined these groups were "very ignorant and excitable" and would be stirred up "to almost any deed of violence." Indeed, a "few dangerous demagogues" controlled these men, and together terrorized the region. The situation in New Mexico could "not be judged by American standards, as if the people were intelligent Anglo-Saxons, [for] here it [was] entirely different!"[19]

Two days after Ancheta was shot, Governor Prince wired James McParland of the Denver Pinkerton Agency, requesting an investigator. McParland sent agent Charles A. Siringo, alias Charles L. Allison and Charles T. Leon, to infiltrate the Knights of Labor and Las Gorras Blancas. Siringo later wrote he had been assigned the case because he knew a "little Mexican."[20] Governor Prince, Solicitor General F. O. Bartlett, and Catron were the only ones privy to Siringo's sleuthing, which was paid for by public funds.

Based on Siringo's information, McParland's initial report pointed a finger at Chávez. "From the little information" available, McParland wrote, "Catron was the target and sheriff Chávez is at the bottom of it."[21] Nearly three weeks later, McParland told Prince that the "Operative" (Siringo) should "cultivate Chávez's acquaintance" to secure pertinent information. In McParland's view the White Caps, the Knights of Labor, and the Democrats were all the same and to be treated as opponents.[22]

In April, Siringo wrote to Prince describing Nicanor Herrera as the "worst of the White Cap leaders" and as one who swore that Catron had "to die before the next election."[23] While Nicanor was "a fine looking specimen of the Mexican race," with "jet black wavy hair, reaching to his shoulders," he had a "fierce facial expression that portended evil to his enemies."[24]

Siringo also reported meeting a Mr. Donihue, married to a cousin of Herrera, and "a democrat and a warm friend of Chávez." Donihue attacked the ring and asserted that the territorial legislature should appropriate $20,000 "to hunt up the shooters" of Ancheta and place those funds in the hands of Sheriff Chávez.[25] On the other side, McParland wrote Prince a few days later that Herrera and his two

4

brothers intensely disliked Catron and that they knew "all about the assassination attempt."[26]

Siringo agreed with McParland's attempt to tie Chávez to the Knights of Labor. Noting that Chávez was the "master workman of the lodge here," Siringo revealed that Chávez wanted him to accompany Chávez "to the big K. of L. convention in Las Vegas on the 9th. . . ." Siringo concluded that "the sheriff and the gang" had planned the shooting.[27] The next day, Siringo added that he was "satisfied" Chávez and Pedro Delgado, a Santa Fe Democrat, were "at the bottom" of the plot; and he was convinced that they were planning another attack on Catron. Delgado had admitted that they were after Catron but would not reveal whether they would "have him killed or not. When I first questioned him about the shooting," Siringo wrote, "his actions convicted him in my mind."[28]

According to Siringo, Stanley Pardello, a member of the Knights, had admitted "that the shots were fired at Catron and that Ancheta was hit by accident." But, he added, there would be another try before the next election.[29] A week later McParland wrote to Prince that he was convinced that Sheriff Chávez had instigated the attempted assassination. In addition, Chávez's allies, the Garcias from Ojo de la Vaca, McParland continued, had "pretended to be Republicans and friendly to Catron for past favors he bestowed on them, but [their] friendliness [was] merely a pretext."[30]

The investigation by the Pinkertons ended in late July, Siringo admitting that he had failed to identify positively the men who had fired the shots. In his concluding report, McParland wrote Governor Prince:

> The country is certainly in a bad state, although it may not appear on the surface, but we have the inside facts. It is true that in all such cases there are a lot of blow hards, who never do anything but talk, but at the same time, they excite other people to commit crimes. I consider that the secret society of White Caps is traveling in [this] . . . direction in New Mexico.[31]

After the shooting of Ancheta in Santa Fe, several persons tried to gain Catron's favor. Elfego Baca, deputy U.S. marshall, offered his help, telling Catron of a conversation he had overheard leading him to believe there had been a plot to murder Catron. The motive apparently stemmed from Catron's opposition to certain legislation, but Baca did not elaborate.[32]

Another correspondent, Wilmot E. Broad, manager of the Tierra Amarilla Land Grant (which Catron owned and controlled), told Catron that two of his enemies, Refugio Martínez and Ramón Archuleta, had been in Santa Fe at the time of the shooting. Broad considered Martínez "loco and dangerous," and Archuleta, he said, was a member of the White Caps. Although the men became immediate suspects, no formal action was taken against them. Still another writer urged that a sizable reward be offered, which, as he put it, would scare "the murdering sons of bitches."[33]

But it was Thomas Branigan, a loyal Republican, who may have produced the most significant clue in the shooting. Branigan told Catron of a conversation he had overheard in an Albuquerque restaurant between Romulo Martínez, a Santa Fe County Democratic party leader, and several other men. Branigan said Martínez had bitterly cursed Catron, saying "he was damn sorry" for having dissuaded a man from killing Catron. Martínez had not mentioned names, but Branigan assumed the man was the same one who had opposed Catron's take-over of the Chama Land Grant.[34]

Meanwhile, two Democratic ward politicians in Santa Fe, Sylvestre Gallegos and Francisco Borrego, became embroiled in a dispute in the summer of 1891 that would help bring about the Chávez murder. When Borrego left the Democratic party and began collaborating with Catron, Gallegos denounced Borrego and challenged him to a fight. In the ensuing gun battle, Borrego shot Gallegos through the head, killing him instantly. Charged with murder Borrego stood trial, Catron serving as legal counsel and bondsman. Pleading self-defense, Borrego won acquittal. Following the trial, Borrego claimed Francisco Chávez had viciously assaulted him after the shoot-out, and he promised revenge on Chávez. Even before the trial Borrego had charged that on 28 December 1889 Chávez had brutally beaten him with a pistol.

The political violence reached an apex on 29 May 1892, when Chávez was gunned down. La Voz reported that Chávez and Atilano Gold left a bar in Santa Fe and started walking toward Chávez's home. After they crossed the Guadalupe bridge, shots rang out from behind a telegraph pole located inside the cemetery. Struck once, Chávez spoke his last words: "*Estos brutos me han asesinado*" (these brutes have assassinated me).[35] Three more shots also struck Chávez. Gold reported that other shots aimed at him had missed, but it soon became clear that Gold had taken part in the plot, persuading Chávez to leave the bar shortly before 10:00 p.m., and convincing him to walk his fateful route.[36]

A large group of people gathered immediately, demanding an investigation. Working with two bloodhounds from the penitentiary, investigators located two cartridges from a Colt .45 revolver and the footprints of two men, but they were unable to locate the persons who fired the shots. Later, an autopsy showed that a bullet from a Winchester rifle had pierced Chávez's heart. The investigation also revealed that on the day of his death Chávez had been fearful because, as he said, "*La gavilla anda tras de mi*" (the gang is after me).[37]

Catron was enroute to the Republican National Convention in Council Bluffs, Iowa, when he learned about the assassination. Miguel A. Otero, who was with Catron at the time, later recalled: "Mr. Catron appeared deeply interested and worried, remarking to me, 'these damn fools would never have done this had I been there,'" but Otero did not elaborate on Catron's cryptic comment.[38]

Four days after Chávez died, his ally Juan Pablo Domínguez confronted Borrego, whom he suspected of having been involved in Chávez's cold-blooded murder. In the ensuing shoot-out, Borrego killed Domínguez. Charged with murder, Borrego went on trial in the summer of 1893. Catron again represented him; again pleading self-defense, Borrego won acquittal.[39]

Finally, in January 1894, twenty months after Chávez's murder, Francisco Borrego and his brother Antonio, Lauriano Alarid, and Patricio Valencia were arrested on suspicion of first degree murder. A fifth suspect, Hipólito Vigil, was killed resisting arrest. The *Santa Fe New Mexican*, now under Democratic control, charged that former Governor Prince, a Republican, had protected the suspects by not pressing for an investigation during his tenure in office.[40]

On 14 January 1894, an exhaustive preliminary hearing began with Judge Edward P. Seeds presiding. Catron and Charles Spiess

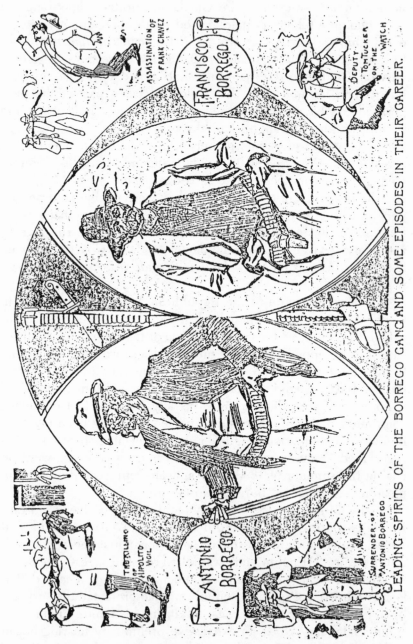

San Francisco Weekly Examiner, 11 March 1897, pp. 14–15.

represented Borrego, et al., and District Attorney Jacob H. Crist assisted by Napoleon B. Laughlin were the prosecutors. A witness for the prosecution, Juan Gallegos, soon revealed that in late 1891 Hipólito Vigil and the Borrego brothers, on orders from the Alliance League (which had organized to fight the Knights and Las Gorras Blancas) had urged him to help murder Chávez. For his participation he had been promised $700 from Catron and the lawyer's legal counsel in case trouble arose after the murder.[41]

After Chávez's death, Felix Martínez, editor of *La Voz del Pueblo* and a perennial foe of the ring, heightened his attacks on the ring and the Alliance League. Martínez encouraged young Mexicanos to struggle against oppression by urging them to fight against a man (Catron) who held "a whip in one hand and a bone in the other." "Where is the dignity in this?" *La Voz* asked. The main question of the day, the editor added, "is not one of political parties, but one of a struggle of honest people against monoplies and their gang of paid assassins. It is a fight against land thieves and those that steal the people's money." In the same issue, *La Voz*, drawing upon the testimony of Francisco Anaya, reported that Chávez had known of a plot by the Alliance League to kill him. A member of the League with Twitchell, Catron, Antonio Ortiz y Salazar, Hipólito Vigil, Francisco Borrego, and others, Anaya revealed that *Los Caballeros de Ley y Orden* (the Knights of Law and Order), another secret group aligned with the Alliance League, had been organized two years before to help carry out the underhanded designs of the league.[42]

Meanwhile Catron charged that the Democrats were trying to pin Chávez's murder on him and his confederates. Defending himself, Catron said he was a Mason and belonged to other benevolent societies; but these "secret societies," he continued, were to help "fallen brothers," the needy, and "widows and orphans." Then Catron added: "Democrats want the public to believe I am at the bottom of the Chávez murder. I will tell you a little secret. I miss Mr. Francisco Chávez more than the democrats do. He had pledged to support me for U.S. delegate. It was in my interest to protect him."[43]

In answer to Catron and his associates, the *Santa Fe Sun* asserted that the Alliance League had the gall to accuse the Knights of Labor "of destroying fences when they are the ones that secretly practice inquisition, condemning to death brutally and cowardly those that protest their abuse and thievery."[44] Alliance members, however, justified the league's existence as a self-defense measure against what they considered verbal and physical attacks of the Knights of Labor and Las Gorras Blancas.[45]

During these charges and countercharges, the suspects in the Chávez murder were bound without bond to district court in early 1894. Judge Edward P. Seeds, relying heavily on the testimony of Juan Gallegos, decided on a trial. Seeds also considered the testimony of Francisco Rivera, who had turned state's evidence and who said he had seen the defendants at the scene just before the murder. The defendants, meanwhile, insisted they were playing cards at the time, but they could not substantiate their alibi.[46]

A short while later, Catron received a letter from Juliana Chávez, the deceased's mother. The missive, which was later published in the *Santa Fe New Mexican* (8 March), was an attack on Catron and his alleged role in the murder of Francisco Chávez. Mrs. Chávez wrote:

> Mr. Catron, you are not above suspicion of knowing more about the assassination of my son than you have ever found it convenient to reveal, this suspicion is a natural one, the murderers as far as discovered are political partisans of yours, they frequented your office, were of the same society, sworn with you to mutually protect each other, you have always defended them in their commissions of crimes, you have gone on their jail bonds and thus turned them loose on the community to commit other murders. . . .[47]

The biographer of Catron claims that his enemies wrote the letter to embarrass Catron. Whether Chávez's mother wrote the letter is not clear, but evidently some people believed the accusations.[48]

After a delay of more than a year, the trial of Borrego et al., began in April 1895 during a special term of the Santa Fe District Court. By then Napoleon B. Laughlin, one of the prosecutors in the preliminary hearing, was a judge in the First Judicial District, so he disqualified himself, and Humphrey B. Hamilton, district judge for the Fifth District, was assigned to the widely publicized case. The trial continued for nearly six weeks at a cost of $5,000.

A long parade of witnesses appeared, and newspapers published blow-by-blow accounts. After bitterly contested proceedings, the jury on 29 May found the defendants guilty of first-degree murder, three years to the day after the assassination. The prosecution used the same damaging evidence presented in the preliminary hearings to prove its case against the defendants. Many years later attorney William Keleher called the trial "the most celebrated criminal case" after the treason trials of the Taos Revolt in 1847.[49]

The testimony of Juan Gallegos helped clarify events leading to the assassination of Chávez. He recounted a conversation with Hipólito Vigil on the first day of the 1890–91 Territorial legislature in which Vigil had said: "what we want is to kill Francisco Chávez." One day later when Gallegos met with Francisco Borrego and Vigil in a saloon near Catron's office Vigil told him, "compadre . . . we want to kill Chávez for his political views and we want you to do it because Chávez has a good deal of confidence in you. He will not mistrust you as he mistrusts us." Borrego then added:

> by killing Chávez there will not be a Democratic party and then we shall reign. Do you remember when I killed Sylvestre Gallegos? What have they done to me? Nothing. And they will not do anything to me. And why will they not do anything to me? Because I am clinging to the strong arm, which is Mr. Catron's. Besides being very rich, he is a very good lawyer; and for that you shall have a very good reward.[50]

In yet another meeting, Borrego told Gallegos:

> The reward is already ready to kill Chávez; as soon as you kill him Mr. Catron will deliver to you seven hundred dollars and in case they find out you are the one, Catron will help you out. Mr. Catron will defend you; and for this we shall have a regular meeting and in the regular meeting we shall appoint those who are to kill Chávez, and he who would not do it will have to suffer the consequences.[51]

Later, according to Gallegos, Vigil told him "this is the best place to kill Chávez [just past Catron's office], this is the best street to kill him." Then Vigil outlined the manner in which they would close in on Chávez and provide proper signals when Gallegos was to shoot. He promised Gallegos a good pistol and urged him to aim at Chávez's "thick" body. "We will take care of anyone who tries to go after you," Vigil promised.[52]

Gallegos testified that he led them to believe he had acceded to their request, but, upon reflection, he decided against participating in the plot and sent Chávez a note alerting him of the conspiracy. The note, which Gallegos identified during the trial, was found among Chávez's papers. Gallegos left New Mexico for a short period of time, fearing reprisal from the "Button Gang" for not cooperating, but returned to New Mexico to testify in the trial. According to the *San Francisco Weekly Examiner*, when Catron heard Gallegos testify, "a ghastly pallor spread over Catron's face, his jaw dropped and a look of fear came into his eyes." The reporter said Catron had collapsed soon after and was confined to bed with shingles.[53]

Francisco Rivera, who turned state's evidence, added other details to the assassination plot. He testified that he had gone to Hipólito's office on 23 May 1892 and that the four defendants were there: "I don't remember which one of them said 'they had called me to enter into an agreement to kill Chávez.' I hung my head down and did not answer a word."[54] Later that evening, Rivera continued, the four defendants and Vigil had met him at a local bar. Vigil gave him a pistol and said, "let's go."[55] When District Attorney Jacob Crist asked where they were going, Rivera replied: "We were going to lie in wait for Francisco Chávez and kill him."[56] Soon after, however, Rivera backed out of the conspiracy. Rivera also recounted that on the night of 29 May he had seen the four defendants and Vigil near the Guadalupe bridge just before 10:00 p.m. He described in detail where they were standing when he heard the gunfire that struck Chávez: "I remember that Francisco Borrego was behind the pole, with his back toward the chapel. The other four were in front of him. Three of the defendants had pistols and my namesake Francisco had a rifle—a Winchester. . . ."[57]

During the trial, several newspaper editors in the territory added to the controversy by asserting that Catron had been involved in some way in the murderous act. The *Eddy Current* said Catron had employed the assassins, while Kistler of the *Las Vegas Optic* wrote that if Catron had anything to do with the "gang of assassins" he was defending, he too should be on trial. The *Lordsburg Liberal* did not doubt the accused's guilt, but feared tremendous pressure would make conviction virtually impossible. The *Silver City Eagle* blamed prominent Republicans for the "premeditated murder," and the *Eddy Independent* noted a rumor persisted that a very important gentleman in the territory was implicated in the case.[58]

After the guilty verdict, the defense moved for a new trial and for arrest of judgment, but both were denied, and the defendants were sentenced to be executed on 10 July 1895. The case, however, was appealed on writ of error and reviewed by the New Mexico Supreme Court.

Before the highest court rendered judgment, however, Catron had to defend himself in formal disbarment proceedings against five separate and distinct charges of unprofessional conduct stemming from the trial. These charges against Catron and his defense contradicting the charges provide illuminating glimpses into the legal system of New Mexico in the 1890s.

First of all, Catron was accused of attempting to persuade Ike Nowell, a material witness for the prosecution, to change his testimony or not to testify. In the preliminary hearing Nowell testified that he had seen the Borrego brothers near the Guadalupe bridge just before the assassination. At the disbarment proceedings Nowell added that Catron had promised to defend Nowell in case he incriminated or perjured himself. The charge against Catron was dismissed by the court because the only two witnesses (Catron and Nowell) did "not appear before the court possessing equal credibility." In trying to encourage the court to reach such a conclusion, Catron produced witnesses who discredited Nowell, saying that he was a simple "hack driver," "a frontiersman," and accused him of drinking "too much whiskey." In addition, Nowell was warned in the streets and saloons of Santa Fe not to testify against Catron.[59]

Secondly, Catron was accused of inducing Porfiria Martinez de Strong to give false testimony in favor of the defendants. She testified that Fred Thayer, who worked for Catron, and two other men had gone to her home in Lamy at midnight and, leading her to believe they were deputies, took her to Catron's law office in Santa Fe where she slept and ate meals during the time she testified at the trial. When cross-examined by the district attorney, she said her previous testimony in the defendant's favor was untrue. She claimed her life had been threatened, that Catron's confidants had intimidated her under false pretenses. Charles Spiess, Charles Conklin, Thayer, and Catron all categorically contradicted her statements. The court dismissed this charge, concluding that "Porfiria was a very ignorant woman, who understood little English, . . . could not read nor write her own language," and possessed a "bad moral reputation."[60]

Next, Catron was charged with trying to "influence or improperly control" the testimony of prosecution witness, Max Knodt, a disinterested and impartial party. Catron allegedly gave Knodt a train pass to Fort Wingate to visit "a lady friend," who had been Catron's "servant," in exchange for improper testimony. This charge was also dismissed after Knodt was described as a poor man, "a foreigner with little education, who spoke broken English, very poor Spanish, bad German," and a "butcher by trade."[61]

The fourth charge accused Catron of attempting to persuade the mother (Mrs. Rosa Gonzáles) of two sons, who were material witnesses, to "get them away from court," to get them to change their testimony, or better still, not to testify. Gonzáles testified that Catron had asked her into his office and had offered to write a letter supporting her application for a pension as the widow of a war veteran. When she offered to pay Catron's legal fees for writing the letter, he refused payment, saying all he wanted was her cooperation in assisting his clients. She refused, stating, "I would not meddle in my sons' affairs—I do not dictate to my family." Catron then offered money to "induce her sons to testify in behalf of the Borregos, or not to testify against them."[62] Only Catron and Gonzáles were present during this verbal exchange, and Catron used this fact to his advantage. When he took the stand he "positively without hesitation, and without qualification wholly and absolutely denied her statement." The court said it was forced to believe Catron since Gonzáles' character was "such as to render her unworthy of credit." She was described as "a very old ignorant woman, in extreme straits of poverty and distress, and denominated by some of the impeaching witnesses as a 'procuress.'"[63]

Finally, Catron was accused of attempting to influence the testimony of Mauricio Gonzáles. Mauricio and his brother, Luis, also an important prosecution witness, were attacked as "unworthy of belief," as "ignorant, possessed of a certain degree of cunning, but of idle and dissolute characters, without any designated occupation." After their characters were undermined, this charge against Catron was also dismissed.

Justice Gideon D. Bantz, concurring with the majority opinion, asserted that accusations against Catron came from persons who did not "commend themselves to confidence, and [that] such testimony [could] not outweigh that of men of respectable reputation."[65] Justice Laughlin, in a dissenting opinion, argued that while leading persons and officials of the area would not accept the opinion of Catron's critics, largely because of their "lower-class status," he was convinced that this class had become "cognizant of the commission of crime, and expose[d] and furnish[ed] testimony for its detection and punishment."[66] Laughlin added that "the law protects with its mantle of mercy, alike, the rich and poor, the high and the low; and those four men now awaiting in solemn solitude . . . are just as much entitled to their lives as the respondent is to practice law at this bar."[67] Despite these legal controversies that plagued Catron, he survived, continuing to practice law, while the four defendants were hanged and Chávez was eliminated.

After the trial, Patricio Valencia and "Chino" Alarid confessed to their part in the murder, but they pointed to Francisco Borrego and Hipólito Vigil as most responsible for the assassination. While one scholar concludes that these men confessed voluntarily, some newspapers and the defense attorneys believed that the confessions were made to bring about pardons or less harsh sentences.[68]

After reviewing the case, the Supreme Court found no substantive errors in Judge Hamilton's lower court and affirmed judgment against the accused. The *New Mexican* agreed with the court's decision, proclaiming that "murder must be stamped out in fair New Mexico," and publishing the full text of the court's opinion written by Thomas Smith, chief justice, calling it a "learned, luminous and able" opinion. "The evidence of the court," Smith had argued, was "abundant to establish that the accused unlawfully, feloniously, willfully, and purposefully shot Francisco Chávez with a deliberate intention to take his life. . . ."[69] Execution was scheduled for 24 September 1896.

Catron went to great lengths to delay execution, appealing to

President William McKinley for reprieve, then to the U.S. Supreme Court for writ of *habeas corpus,* but to no avail. According to one commentator: "The persistent and able efforts of Catron and Spiess to save the criminals from the gallows became increasingly unpopular.[70]

Meanwhile, the Borrego brothers made a desperate attempt to escape from jail. Unsuccessful, they were subsequently transferred to the penitentiary and kept under close guard. Francisco Borrego confided to a fellow prisoner about a plot to kill Sheriff William P. Cunningham and Governor William T. Thornton if efforts to save him failed.[71] Efforts did fail, and Francisco and Antonio Borrego, Patricio Valencia, and "Chino" Alarid were executed on 2 April 1897. *La Voz* decried their deaths: "If it is true that the guilty were used, it is indeed a tragedy. It is sad for New Mexico that her sons should be used. Neo-Mexicanos must be more independent. Do not be misled by bárbaros who will ever force you to sacrifice your life."[72]

Strongly opposing the activities of Catron and the Santa Fe Ring, *La Voz* believed the four Mexicanos found guilty had become pawns of ring leaders to eliminate Chávez from the political scene. In short, *La Voz* interpreted Chávez's murder as part of broader political relationships in which violence as an extreme form of conflict played a central part.

Indeed, assassination in the last quarter of the nineteenth century in New Mexico did become a technique of political action; organized violence became an acceptable means of achieving specific goals. Conspirators planned and controlled a system of violence, and a perverse "logic" of political murder pervaded the territory. Assuming a "contagious" character, each violent episode stimulated other events in a chain partly motivated by retribution.[73] Violence was rationally conceived and implemented, and most victims knew in advance of the direct and severe means that could be used in the exercise of power. Generally, this violence was symptomatic of social problems stemming primarily from conflict over control of land and its resources.

Not surprisingly, Victor Westphall, the sympathetic biographer of Catron, blames the violence of the "Button Gang" on "the lower class members," on "the man on the street," on "those of limited privilege in social attainments," or on "the rank and file" like the Borrego brothers and other "bad" Mexicans.[74] Such untenable assumptions or conclusions, however, fail to grapple with more complex and appropriate questions.

The function of the rule of law in power relationships, for example, is such a question. These relationships are partially mediated by the logic, rules, and procedures of the law. Although the law, like other institutions, justifies existent class and race relations, it has an independent life, and sometimes appears to the powerful and to the powerless, to uphold standards of equity based on universal, logical criteria. In this case in the 1890s Catron and the class he represented played power games according to established rules, arrived at seemingly through consensus, but they made certain their interests were protected. When they blatantly abused the rules in order to maintain control, they risked losing the entire game. Paradoxically, when Catron was charged with unprofessional conduct, the rules of the game were further legitimated by the accusations against him, and the controlling forces consolidated their power to a greater extent because now "everyone knew that all were equal under the law." As an example of this sophisticated use of the law, Catron went on to become president of the New Mexico Bar Association, was elected U.S. delegate, and, in 1913, became one of New Mexico's first U.S. senators.

The rhetoric and rules of nineteenth-century New Mexico were not always a sham. At times, although infrequently, but often enough to maintain relative stability and continuity, the behavior of powerful cliques such as the Santa Fe Ring was modified and checked by law. This dimension of the rule of law convinced the powerless at least of its potential utility. They sensed that the law could be one alternative in their struggle for survival.[75]

NOTES

1. Richard Maxwell Brown, *Strain of Violence* (New York: Oxford University Press, 1975), p. 14.

2. For an account of Fountain's murder, see A. M. Gibson, *The Life and Death of Colonel Albert Jennings Fountain* (Norman: University of Oklahoma Press, 1965). The deaths of Patrón and Cháves have yet to be explained.

3. For a history of the Lincoln County War, see Maurice G. Fulton, *History of the Lincoln County War*, Robert N. Mullin, ed. (Tucson: University of Arizona Press, 1968). For a narrative of conflict in Colfax County, see Morris F. Taylor, *O. P. McMains and the Maxwell Land Grant Conflict* (Tucson: University of Arizona Press, 1979).

4. *Albuquerque Democrat*, quoted in *Santa Fe Weekly New Mexican*, 18 January 1894.

5. William Keleher, *The Fabulous Frontier: Twelve New Mexico Items* (Albuquerque: University of New Mexico [UNM] Press, 1962), p. 106.

6. Borrego v. Territory, 8 N.M. 446, 46 Pac. 349, affirmed 164 U.S. 612, 41 Law Ed. 572, 17 Sup. Ct. 182.

7. Ralph E. Twitchell, *The Leading Facts of New Mexico History*, 5 vols. (Cedar Rapids, Iowa: Torch Press, 1911), 2: 512; Robert Johnson Rosenbaum, "Mexicano versus Americano: A Study of Hispanic-American Resistance to Anglo-American Control in New Mexico Territory, 1870–1900 (Ph.D. diss., University of Texas at Austin, 1972), p. 279.

8. Catron, In re, 8 N.M. 275, 43 Pac. 724.

9. Catron, In re, 8 N.M. 275, 43 Pac. 724.

10. Territory v. Romulo Martínez, *et al.*, Santa Fe County, 2507.

11. S. Davis to Catron, 14 August 1890, Catron Papers (CP), 102, box 8, University of New Mexico (UNM).

12. *Santa Fe Daily New Mexican*, 6 February 1891.

13. *Santa Fe Daily New Mexican*, 6 February 1891.

14. *Santa Fe Daily New Mexican*, 6 February 1891. Until January 1894, pro-ring forces owned or controlled the *New Mexican*. At that time the newspaper changed ownership and became anti-ring and anti-Republican for several years until it again came under Republican control.

15. Prince to McParland, Prince Papers (PP), State Records Center and Archives (SRCA), Santa Fe, TANM, roll 116, frame 299.

16. *Las Vegas Daily Optic*, 22 August 1890.

17. "Statement with regard to New Mexico," "n.d.," PP, SRCA, TANM, roll 116, frames 826–29.

18. "Statement with regard to New Mexico," "n.d.," PP, SRCA, TANM, roll 116, frames 826–29.

19. "Statement with regard to New Mexico," "n.d.," PP, SRCA, TANM, roll 116, frames 826–29.

20. Charles A. Siringo, *A Cowboy Detective* (Chicago: W. B. Conkey, 1912), p. 116.

21. McParland to Prince, 20 February 1891, PP, SRCA, TANM, roll 121, frame 710.

22. McParland to Prince, 11 March 1891, PP, SRCA.

23. C. L. Allison to Prince, 4 April 1891, PP, SRCA.

24. Siringo, *Cowboy Detective*, p. 118.

25. C. L. Allison to Prince, 4 April 1891, PP, SRCA.

26. McParland to Prince, 8 April 1891, PP, SRCA.

27. C. L. Allison to Prince, 7 July 1891, PP, SRCA.

28. C. L. Allison to Prince, 8 July 1891, PP, SRCA.

29. C. L. Allison to Prince, 8 July 1891, PP, SRCA.

30. McParland to Prince, 15 July 1891, PP, SRCA.

31. McParland to Prince, 25 July 1891, PP, SRCA.

32. Elfego Baca to Catron, 7 February 1891, CP, 102, box 10, UNM.

33. M. W. Mills to Catron, 9 February 1891, CP, 201, box 10, UNM.

34. Thomas Branigan to Catron, 17 February 1891, CP, 102, box 10, UNM.

35. La Voz del Pueblo, 4 June 1892.

36. La Voz del Pueblo, 4 June 1892; Weekly New Mexican Review, 25 January 1894.

37. La Voz del Pueblo, 1 October 1892.

38. Miguel Antonio Otero, My Nine Years as Governor of the Territory of New Mexico, 1897–1906 (Albuquerque: UNM Press, 1940), p. 260.

39. San Francisco Weekly Examiner 11 March 1897.

40. Santa Fe Weekly New Mexican, 18 January 1894.

41. Santa Fe Weekly New Mexican, 25 January 1894. The Alliance League, also known as the Knights of Liberty and the "Button Gang" (so-called because of their buttons with emblems symbolizing fraternity), was organized ostensibly for mutual support and protection in reaction to the Knights of Labor and Las Gorras Blancas. The league boasted it had at least one hundred members including Catron, Ralph Twitchell, Max Frost, Charles A. Spiess, and other well-known Republicans and members of the Santa Fe Ring. A few Mexicanos like the Borrego brothers also belonged to the organization, frequently playing roles as henchmen (Victor Westphall, Thomas Benton Catron and His Era [Tucson: University of Arizona Press, 1973], p. 209).

42. La Voz del Pueblo, 15 October 1892.

43. Unidentified newspaper clipping, Frank Clancy Papers, Scrapbook I, SRCA.

44. Santa Fe Sun, 15 October 1892.

45. Westphall, Catron and His Era, p. 209.

46. Westphall, Catron and His Era, p. 226.

47. Juliana V. Chávez to Catron, 2 March 1894, CP, 102, box 21, UNM.

48. Westphall, Catron and His Era, p. 227.

49. William Keleher, The Fabulous Frontier, p. 106.

50. Juan Gallegos testimony, 8 May 1895, District Court, Santa Fe County, 2618, SRCA.

51. Gallegos testimony, District Court, Santa Fe County, 2618, SRCA.

52. Gallegos testimony, District Court, Santa Fe County, 2618, SRCA.

53. San Francisco Weekly Examiner, 11 March 1897.

54. Francisco Rivera testimony, District Court, Santa Fe County, 2618, SRCA.

55. Rivera testimony, District Court, Santa Fe County, 2618, SRCA.

56. Rivera testimony, District Court, Santa Fe County, 2618, SRCA.

57. Rivera testimony, District Court, Santa Fe County, 2618, SRCA.

58. Quoted in *La Voz del Pueblo,* 8 June 1895.

59. Catron, In re, 8 N.M., pp. 256–61, 292, 43 Pac. 724.

60. Catron, In re, 8 N.M., 309, 43 Pac. 724.

61. Catron, In re, 8 N.M., 264, 43 Pac. 724.

62. Catron, In re, 8 N.M., 300, 43 Pac. 724.

63. Catron, In re, 8 N.M., 312, 43 Pac. 724.

64. Catron, In re, 8 N.M., 312, 43 Pac. 724.

65. Catron, In re, 8 N.M., 273, 43 Pac. 724.

66. Catron, In re, 8 N.M., 316, 43 Pac. 724.

67. Catron, In re, 8 N.M., 321, 43 Pac. 724.

68. Arie W. Poldervaart, *Black-Robed Justice,* Publications in History, vol. 13 (Santa Fe: Historical Society of New Mexico, 1948), p. 156; Westphall, *Catron and His Era,* p. 229.

69. Borrego v. Territory, 8 N.M. 446, 46 Pac. 349, affirmed 164 U.S. 612, 41 Law Ed. 572, 17 Sup. Ct. 182.

70. Poldervaart, *Black-Robed Justice,* p. 159.

71. *Santa Fe New Mexican,* 11 September 1896.

72. *La Voz del Pueblo,* 1 June 1895.

73. See William J. Crotty, ed., *Assassinations and the Political Order* (New York: Harper and Row, 1971).

74. Westphall, *Catron and His Era,* p. 209.

75. See E. P. Thompson, *Whigs and Hunters* (London: Allen Lane, 1975), pp. 259–69.

"La Evolución del 'Bandido' al 'Pachuco' ":
A Critical Examination and Evaluation of
Criminological Literature on Chicanos

Larry D. Trujillo*

I. INTRODUCTION

Criminological theories that have dominated the field have moved many criminologists toward definitions of social reality which support the existing social order. The dominant theoretical trend, therefore, has been the development of social theory which addresses itself to social control. With this perspective in mind, it is apparent that the works of criminologists have benefited and will continue to benefit certain sectors of the society while neglecting, or working to the disadvantage of, other sectors. One group that has suffered at the hands of traditional criminological theory construction and its subsequent practice is the Chicano.

Criminological research has provided information and techniques for manipulating, controlling, and repressing Chicanos. In addition, criminological literature has helped to create myths, stereotypes, and negative images of Chicanos as "innately criminal," "natural thieves," "prone to lawlessness," etc. The purpose here is to critically examine and evaluate traditional criminological literature on Chicanos. The analysis traces the origins of the distorted image of the Chicano in the context of crime and criminality, and suggests the need for new analytical paradigms for the examination of criminological phenomena among Chicanos.

In a recent article on "The Incarcerated Mexican-American Delinquent," Professor Alvin Rudoff explains the high delinquency rate among Mexican-American youth as follows:

*Larry D. Trujillo received his B.A. and M.Crim. from the University of California, Berkeley in 1972 and 1973 respectively. He is currently a doctoral student at the School of Criminology, Berkeley.

There are several factors of the Mexican American culture that tend to impede the acculturation and treatment process and affect their background and personality. The family constellation is an unstable one as the father is seen as withdrawn and the mother as a self-sacrificing and saintly figure. The Mexican American has little concern for the future, perceives himself as predestined to be poor and subordinate, is still influenced by magic, is gang-minded, distrusts women, sees authority as arbitrary, tends to be passive and dependent, and is alienated from the Anglo culture. . . . unambitious, spurns achievement . . . is immature, rigid, restricted, fatalistic, has minimum self confidence and self direction and inefficient use of intellectual capacities . . . . are more seriously depressed than Anglo counterpart. . . . It is very tempting to assume the social problems of the Mexican Americans will be ameliorated with acculturation and assimilation. . . . (1971:11-14)

Thus, in one short article, Professor Rudoff manages, in the name of "objective" criminology, to perpetuate many of the myths and stereotypes that have been transmitted since the Mexican conquest. In making certain assumptions about the Chicano delinquent, he relies on the work of other social scientists—quoting from Sanders (1958), Kluckholm (1954), Lewis (1951), and Broom (1952). Studies by these social scientists have been severely criticized by Chicano social scientists for their racist and ethnocentric biases. The authors quoted by Professor Rudoff have often relied on the generalizations of other social scientists (Byram, 1919; McLean, 1926) whose work was often done without adequate examination, analysis, empirical observations of and sensitivity to the people researched. These social scientists, in researching the different aspects of the Chicano, have emphasized certain aspects while neglecting others. In Rudoff's case, as in many others, the aspects emphasized have, for the most part, been negative ones. Many criminologists, in writing about the Chicano, have advanced familiar theories that, although proposed to be "value free," have in reality been ideological in nature.[1] And as Thomas Szasz points out: "Familiar theories have a habit of posing sooner or later as objective truth" (1960:113). The theories introduced in these criminologists' writings (Bogardus, 1943; Heller, 1966) on the Chicano have been slanted towards the dominant societal value system and the maintenance of the status quo. The earliest criminological studies were blatantly biased; later works were much more sophisticated and subtle in their biases.

With this in mind it becomes clear that the criminological literature on the Chicano must be critically examined and evaluated. Attention will be focused on the period between 1848 when the Treaty of Guadalupe Hidalgo was signed, and 1943, the beginning of the era of the "pachuco." The major criminological schools of thought, the major ideologies and philosophies at the time, the political and social events occurring in the United States and in Mexico (when appropriate), and the influence these factors had on the various criminological works will be identified and discussed.

II. THE HISTORICAL CONTEXT: COLONIAL CAPITALIST EXPLOITATION[2]

A. *Justice Becomes a Mockery*

Under the Treaty of Guadalupe Hidalgo (1848) which concluded the war between the United States and Mexico, Mexico was compelled to cede one-half of her territory to the United States. Chicanos,[3] set apart by race, language, and culture, were not assimilated as full or equal citizens despite the formal guarantees that were made. Instead they were systematically oppressed as the expanding colonial capitalist economy demanded control of the rich mining, agricultural, and ranching lands, and the use of indigenous people as a cheap labor force.

These accomplishments were effected through legal means when possible and illegal means when necessary. Property rights were guaranteed by the treaty, but not protected by the American government. It was a period when "equal protection before the law" became a mockery to the Chicano people of the Southwest.

B. *The Rise of Racial Stereotypes*

Although the emergence of racial stereotypes occurred many years before the first criminological writings were to appear on Chicanos, it was the role of cultural and social differences between Chicanos and Anglos, the inability and reluctance of Chicanos to assimilate, and the stereotypic image that arose from conflicting cultures that were to provide the basic theoretical material in early criminological writings. With the vestiges from the war of slogans such as "Kill the Mexicans" and "Death to the greasers," a strong degree of Anglo nationalism and racism led to the development of racial stereotypes of Chicanos. As the early historian F. L. Olmstead points out:

> ... between our Texans and Mexicans there is an unconquerable antagonism of character, which will prevent any condition of order when the two come together ... the bigoted, childish and passionate Mexicans are considered to be heathens, not acknowledged as "white folk" (See: McWilliams, 1948:113).

The practice of racism and exploitation was prevalent well before the conquest but it is during the debates over expansion and the Mexican War that we can detect the emergence of particular race theories that were to justify the war, expansion, and the imperialist conquest of the Mexican people. It was during this time that John O'Sullivan, the editor of *Democratic Review,* coined the term "manifest destiny" and used it in his editorials, telling the American people that the entire continent should belong to them because they were a superior race. Concerning the Mexican territory, he said:

> The Anglo-Saxon foot is already on its borders. Already the advance guard of the irresistible army of Anglo-Saxon emigration has begun to pour down upon it. . . . A population will soon be in actual occupation of California, over which it will be idle for the backyard Mexico to dream of domination (Gossett, 1964:44).

This ethnocentric conception of the appropriateness and superiority of Anglo institutions and the correlating belief that all conflicting ways of life were necessarily bad or inferior became the predominant mode of thinking of the time.

C. The Creation of a Cheap Labor Force

Another point that usually is not dealt with at any length in the histories that have been written about the Chicano is the role of the American capitalist in the colonization[4] of the Southwest. Most histories either justify or are apologetic for the Anglos' treatment of the Mexican but few deal with the huge economic victory the conquest represented for American capitalists. During the 1850's and 1860's, large-scale cattle rings, public land stealing rings, and mining raids and seizures put the territory in the hands of a few rich capitalists. As Anglo colonists and speculators gained control (most often illegally) over the land and the livelihood of the independent Chicano farming and ranching villages, a new pool of cheap colonial labor was produced to work the fields and build the railroads that were essential to the early development of a national capitalist economy.[5] Leonard Pitt sums up the colonizing period as follows:

> . . . in a matter of months they [the Yankee imperialists] over-turned the old institutional framework, expropriated the land, imposed a new culture, and in the process exploited the labor of the local population whenever necessary (1971:113).

At this same time events in Mexico were having a major impact on the American economy. Benito Juarez' anti-slavery, anti-aristocracy, anti-political clericalism—War of Reform—had given way to the pro-industrialist, American-capital Diaz regime. Diaz was heavily influenced by the cientificos (positivists) who pushed an all-out assault on feudalism and tight relationship with American industry. American business collaborated with Mexican industrialists, causing a dependency relationship for Mexico.[6] Thus upon American prompting the Mexican economic thinkers encouraged immigration. The cheap labor provided by Mexico was needed by the capitalists in much greater quantities after the Chinese Exclusion Act of 1882.

As the capitalists accumulated their mass fortunes during this period, much violence and harassment were perpetrated upon the colonized Chicanos. As Hubert Bancroft indicates, "a high number of Mexicans were whipped, banished or hanged . . . it was almost a by-word in our midst, that none but the Mexicans could be convicted of a capital offense" (See: Pitt, ibid.:170). In the mines Chicano miners were being raped, pillaged and lynched by Anglo miners, with the "greasers' criminal conduct" cropping up as a justification for the Anglo miners to methodically exterminate the Chicanos. In the agriculture fields harassment, beatings and lynchings also became commonplace. If Chicanos rebelled against their oppression, as many did, greater repression at the hands of U.S. justice occurred. Police and military violence became a frequent way to preserve "law and order." When that wasn't enough vigilante committees were formed to take the law in their own hands.

The violence that was committed against the Chicano had to be justified. The vigilantes justified their actions in much the same way as the police do in the barrios today. They took the stance that they were the champions of law and order and were attempting to rectify conditions by demanding an "eye for an eye." Another justification was that the Chicanos' criminal nature had to be controlled; to Anglos every Chicano was a potential outlaw.

D. The Rise of the "Bandidos"

As the repressive actions became greater, some Chicanos began to form protective guerilla units. These events are important because they gave rise to the "bandido" image of the Chicanos with their "innately criminal behavior," which eventually found its way into the writings of many criminologists. The historians and social scientists have distorted both the reality and importance of the bandidos. By depicting them as murdering, throat-cutting, bloodthirsty, thieving outlaws, history has been distorted and untrue myths and stereotypes of the Mexican bandits have been perpetuated (Castillo and Camarillo, 1973:1-10). Pitt comments:

> Endless theories have arisen that refute, defend, or explain the bandidos. Outright bigots, of course, simply charge them with the "innate depravity" of Mexico and let it go at that (1971:171).

Rudolfo Acuna, a Chicano historian, suggests a different way of looking at the situation from most traditional historians:

> ... resistance also manifest itself in anti-social behavior. When the colonized (Chicanos) cannot earn a living within the system, as when they are degraded they strike out. The most physical way is to rebel (1972:113).

Eric Hobsbaum (1969), in a like vein, has made the argument that the bandit is a universal and unchanging phenomenon, and represents little more than a peasant protest against oppression, injustice and poverty. Eric Wolf (1969:144) has called the bandit a "primitive revolutionary." From this perspective, therefore, the "bandidos" were not "criminals" but fighters for freedom, and leaders of the Chicano peoples' struggle for liberation and self-determination.

Hence it was during this period that the racial stereotype of the "conniving Mexican outlaw" who is "naturally criminal" found its way into the American consciousness. This stereotype has been sustained through numerous movies, books, and television programs.[7] So today most people know of Joaquin Murieta and Tiburcio Vazquez and the era of banditry in California and the Southwest in the 1870's and 1880's, but few know of the brutal social, political and economic oppression that forced their emergence.

E. Violence Along the Border

The period 1908 to 1925 was characterized by violence along the border as Mexico was immersed in revolution.[8] It is estimated that between five hundred to five thousand Mexicans and Chicanos were killed (Morales, 1972:14). And just as law enforcement officials today suspect Chicano activists and militants to be in collusion with the Communists, Texas suspected Mexicans of partnership with the Germans during World War I. Social injustice suffered during this period can be examined on two fronts—the rural scene and the urban scene. Armando Morales points out:

> Brutal illegal assaults on Mexican Americans by law enforcement agencies condoned through passive indifference by judicial institutions continues in rural reas. Similarly, the urban scene reflects such incidents, but perhaps even more significant from the standpoint of destructively affecting far greater numbers of people for longer periods of time, formal social policy specifically directed at people of Spanish surname is established (Ibid.).

III. CRIMINOLOGICAL THEORY: MYTHS BECOME TRUTHS

A. Biological Determinism: It's in the Blood

The notion of the "bandido"[9] being innately criminal was not inconsistent with the general criminological thought of the time. In the first part of the 19th century criminality had been equated with sin, pauperism, and immorality, with a very heavy reformist attitude shaped by the Enlightenment, humanism, principles of democracy and religious ideas (Vold, 1958). But with the emergence, at the end of the century, of the popularity of the conservative Social Darwinism and individual-istic economics, the reformist notion was strongly challenged. Criminology became heavily influenced by the European positivists. In 1876 Cesare Lombroso wrote *The Criminal Man* which carried the theoretical claim of the "born criminal type." Lombroso rejected the notion of crime as a social phenomenon and began to identify it with physical characteristics or stigmata. The positivists used the methodology of the natural sciences, relying heavily upon biology. The emphasis of this school of thought on biological determinism was to become a popular explanation of the Chicano's criminal behavior.

At about this same time Herbert Spencer, in *The Man Versus the State* and other writings, was developing the concepts of "survival of the fittest" and "natural selection" in human evolution that eventually became the social theory of Social Darwinism. Spencer very freely talked of inferior races and in one letter suggested to a colleague that,

> Intermarriage [among the races] should be "positively" forbidden. It is a root question of biology. Animal breeders had long known that random intermixture of stocks could only lead to degeneration. And . . . had to look at the halfbreed in America to see the same was true of the human race (See: Gossett, 1964:151).

Race consciousness was also sharpened among the social scientists in this country about this time with the beginning of the Eugenics Movement. The Eugenicists believed feeblemindedness, criminality, and pauperism were strongly influenced by hereditary factors. Galton, a cousin of Charles Darwin, coined the word as well as the popular catch phrase "nature or nurture," which precipitated considerable controversy over the relationship between heredity and environment (Ibid.).

The social science literature that appeared around the turn of the century was in large part produced by Americans concerned with the "new" European immigrants who began to arrive in 1882 (Vaca, 1970:7). In their writings on the Chicano, one of the main problems criminologists addressed themselves to was how to control these "inferior people." The Chicanos' problem was much greater, however, than that of the new immigrants because they were faced with the ideology of Anglo superiority that in practice made it very clear there was no place for a person of color in the system as a free citizen and equal competitor.

Two of the groups that were most opposed to Mexican immigration were the Eugenicists and the labor unions; the Eugenicists claimed racial inferiority of the non-Anglo stock, and the labor unions objected to the lowering of wage scales by cheap foreign labor market. One of the most energetic racists of the time was E. A. Ross. He was a champion of the labor unions (denouncing laissez-faire individualism as "a caricature of Darwinism," invented to justify the ruthless practices of businessmen) and an advocate of immigration restrictions. Gossett in paraphrasing Ross's position on the immigration of Mexicans to the United States states:

> The energy and character of America was 'lowered by the presence in the South of several millions of an inferior race.' Ross concluded that the superiority of a race cannot be preserved without pride of blood and an uncompromising attitude towards the lower classes (Gossett, Ibid.:169).[10]

It was during this period another of our country's most active racists, Madison Grant, wrote *The Passing of the Great Race* in 1916, selling over 50,000 copies in the United States. Grant, the vice-president of the Eugenics Society and an official of the Immigration Restriction League, developed the theory of racial superiority of the Nordic race, with inferior races through miscegenation leading to inferior strains. He attempted to prove superior intelligence of the Nordic race and the notion that the "American" intelligence is declining due to racial mixture. Grant concluded that homogeneity of the superior Anglo could not be achieved by such processes as the "melting pot," since the inferior races would ruin the mix. John Stroddard about this time published *Stroddard's Lectures,* in which he stated that the key to 20th century world politics would be the relations among the races of mankind, and that the highest "scientific humanist" goal was to protect the Nordic race (See: Gossett, Ibid.:353-90).

It is interesting to note that in Mexico during this period Jose Vasconcelos, Secretary of Education, was writing of "La Raza Cosmica" (the cosmic race), stating the universalism of the Ibero-American race, having its origins in pluralistic Spain and equally pluralistic Mexico. He argued strongly against the pure race Anglo superiority concept. He felt that the Latin races through miscegenation were creating a more universal race that was desirable to a more peaceful civilization. He stated:

> The whole theory of one stock above another will have to be changed. The practice of putting the so-called lower races to work for the benefit of the superior will have to be abandoned or else the dominators will have to suffer from the revenge of the oppressed. The revenge is in the law of nature itself (1926:13).

With these modes of thinking emerging and gaining popularity we see works such as Henderson's *An Introduction to the Study of Dependent, Defective and Delinquent Classes,* Francis Galton's *Heredity and Crime* and many other studies attempting to prove inherent tendencies of crime.[11] It was a period when crime was related to individual factors with the dominant perspective being biological determinism. This period produced theories of criminal behavior based on phrenology, heredity, personal defects, and mental retardation. So the articles (Ross, 1923; Garretson, 1919) that were published discussing the Chicano and crime had as their basic theoretical perspective biological or racial determinism. They concentrated on the Chicano's behavior in terms of biological or racial weaknesses.

Chicanos were described as "lawless" or "criminal" because of their "Indian blood," "mental retardation," "low intelligence," and "feeblemindedness" which were all judged by Anglo I.Q. testing. They were seen as deviant because "such was their nature"; and their excellence for stoop labor was viewed as inherent because they did not aspire to land ownership.

Consequently, by the turn of the century, the idea of racial superiority had deeply penetrated nearly every area of social science. The superiority of the Anglo-Saxon race was fully documented and had immense philosophical and scientific backing. And because Chicanos were seen as "inherently criminal," the injustice and repression they faced at the hands of the United States system of justice became justified.

B. The Chicago School: Sophisticated Social Darwinism

In the 1920's and 1930's the attempt of the social scientists was to understand those characteristics of the Mexican and Chicano that uniquely marked them as different from the American population. Criminologists[12] concerned themselves with the question of why Chicanos had a markedly higher crime rate than the general population. In searching for an answer, urbanization, immigration, population growth, culture, and family patterns were some of the areas explored. This was a period in criminology when, although biological determinism was still very popular, sociological criminology was beginning to emerge. As Quinney notes, the basic ideology of this period was pragmatism, institutionalism, behaviorism and economic determinism (1970:66).

At the University of Chicago, Park, Burgess, Thrasher and others formed the core of the Chicago School of Criminology. The orientation of the leaders of the school was a sophisticated kind of Social Darwinism. They regarded social deviance as a pathological but natural phenomenon, part of the "web of life," just as a weed is a natural but undesirable part of a garden. The method of investigation involved field studies of social deviants, e.g., prostitutes and juvenile gangs, in their natural environment with "participant observation" by the investigator. Although these studies did not specifically deal with the Chicano, their theoretical perspective and method of investigation were used by later sociologists and criminologists (Bogardus, 1943; Lewis, 1951) who wrote about the Chicano and crime. The major concerns that found their expression in criminology centered around: (1) the desirability of the Mexican immigrant; (2) the problems faced in attempting to assimilate Mexican immigrants into the American way of life; and (3) the causes of high crime rates, juvenile delinquency, and arrests in the Chicano community.

The major theoretical theses (Vaca, 1970) that served as causal explanations for these conditions also took three main perspectives: (1) biological determinism: "it's in the blood" inherent criminality theory still maintained a degree of acceptability and popularity; (2) cultural determinism: a perspective with the thesis that it was the inadequacy of the Chicano's culture that led to crime. Like biological determinism, cultural determinism afforded scientific evidence to place the blame for Chicano crime upon the shoulders of Chicano individuals instead of on the society. It was felt that the ills plaguing Chicanos were due to their "psychological selves" caused by the traditional culture of Mexico. The third and final thesis (3) was environmental determinism: this perspective postulated that the causes of social problems of Chicanos are attributable to the economic and social problems of American society; thus the call for liberal reforms of the system.

IV. A CRITIQUE OF THE STUDIES

A. The Sociological Perspective

Samuel Bryam wrote one of the first sociological studies on the Chicano. His concern was with the social characteristics of Chicanos that somehow made them different from other Americans. Bryam notes that:

> As to be expected under the circumstances, the proportion of criminals among the Mexicans is noticeably greater than among the other foreign born or among the natives (1919:727).

He goes on to show that in Los Angeles County, California, the Chicanos comprised 11.4 percent of the total number of persons charged with felonies, while their general population was only 3.6 percent in 1907. In Arizona, he goes on, where the proportion of Chicanos to the total population was greater than in Los Angeles, a correspondingly large proportion of inmates of various penal institutions was of this race (Ibid.:729). Bryam's final analysis of the desirability of Mexican immigrants is:

> . . . it would be recognized that although the Mexicans have proved to be efficient laborers in certain industries, and have afforded a cheap and elastic labor supply for the south-western United States, the evils to the community at large with their presence in large numbers almost invariably brings many more than overbalance their desirable qualities (Ibid.: 730).

An example of a sociological treatment of the concern with the assimilation of the Mexican into the American society is R. E. Dickerson's study, "Some Suggestive Problems in the Americanization of Mexicans" (1919). Dickerson felt that Mexicans could become good American citizens if given the proper chance, but that American society in many ways blocked their mobility. On the characteristics of the Mexican he states:

> There is an unusual eagerness and desire for self-development, almost any opportunity that promises helpfulness is eagerly seized upon. There is a great deal of respect for authority and achievement which makes Mexican boys as a whole better disciplined and more readily controlled (See: Vaca, Ibid.:16).

It is not surprising that during this period when the foundations and formulations of social control theory were at their peak that the ability of any group to be easily controlled would be seen as a positive trait.

Some liberal sociologists and criminologists did point towards the conditions of the system as the cause of the Chicano's problems but none took issue that it was the capitalist system itself (with its racist/exploitative nature) that was at fault. And while some mildly condemned the capitalists none suggested that they be moved from power and the capitalist machine disbanded. Repeatedly, these social scientists argued that Chicanos, because they suffered from poor education, income, housing and other necessities, often fell into criminal activities, thus overtaxing the law enforcement system.

Other sociologists (Humphrey, 1941; Tuck, 1946) blamed all the social ills that plagued Chicanos on their Mexican culture. Mexicans, they argued, because of their culture, are lazy (living in mañana-land), shine on responsibility, lack competition, and enjoy savoring life with rest and leisure. With these stereotypes in hand these authors go on to make the logical conclusion that the Mexican immigrant is naturally deviant. Or, as Norman Humphrey states:

> But what is conceived to be normality in American life is culturally defined, and its form and content are conditioned by cultural values. ... [The solution] ... we must rehabilitate these deviants with "new" and "desired" cultural values (Ibid.:54).

B. The Psychological Perspective

About this time a barrage of psychological studies on intelligence began to appear. Lewis Terman (See: Gossett, 1958:171) perfected the Stanford-Binet scale of intelligence, and a group of psychologists introduced the proposition that intelligence was largely hereditary, only minimally influenced by environmental conditions. Chicano children became one of the primary test groups for these social scientists.[13] Once they were satisfied that Chicano children were intellectually inferior, mentally retarded or feeble-minded, they went on to "scientifically prove" other personality traits that supposedly resulted from this low mentality. One of their most popular conclusions was a propensity for criminal behavior.

The theoretical base for the argument of the high relationships between mental retardation and crime had been set down years earlier in Henry Goddard's Kallikak Family (1912), Richard Dugdale's The Jukes (1910), and Charles Goring's The English Convict (1913). Later in another book on the subject, Goddard concluded:

> It is no longer to be denied that the greatest single cause of delinquency and crime is low grade mentality (1920:74).

During World War I the many Chicanos entering the service did very poorly on the army intelligence testing. And as The Report on Crime and the Foreign Born indicates, criminologists tried to establish a causal relationship between the mental retardation of those recruits and the large number of Chicanos who were in the jails and prisons across the Southwest (1931:76). Another psychologist, R. M. Yerkes, suggested "that those who were identified with the psychological service in the United States Army in the course of World War I have claimed that recruits who were Nordic blood were of superior intelligence" (See: Barnes, 1959:121). In this study, like most others of the time, no mention was made of the cultural skewedness (Anglo) of the test, or the fact that it was in English at a time when many Chicanos' primary language was Spanish. As with the sociologists, the psychologists seemed to be divided in their theoretical persuasions between perspectives of biological determinism—low intelligence was racially inherited; cultural determinism—the Mexican culture as inferior; and outside forces, e.g., the school system, lack of bilingual/bicultural tests, and environmental forces.

C. The Government Commissions

In the early 1930's two major governmental reports appeared that had a detailed analysis of the roles of Chicanos in the society and their relationship to crime and the criminal justice system. The first of these was the Governor Young Report, *Mexicans in California* (1930). The section of this report that dealt with crime and delinquency in the Mexican population was basically a statistical breakdown of the Mexican crime rates. It showed such things as the arrest rates (Mexicans and Mexican Americans 15.5%, Whites only 4.6% of the total population of the state), numbers by race in state institutions, and comparisons of crime rates to other races. The report also indicated that in the area of juvenile delinquency, the administrators of the two main correctional schools for boys were sharply concerned about the rapid increase in the number of Mexican boys committed. It was also mentioned that the institutions indicated a decidedly lower rate of intelligence for Chicano boys. Those sent to prison were most inclined to commit violations of the Poison Act (narcotics), and carrying and/or assault with a deadly weapon, pointing out they rarely commit forgery—"which is to be expected among people having a high illiteracy and little familiarity with banking" (Ibid.:201). The report had a very shallow theoretical base and presented no real analysis of the problem. The few assumptions it did make were not supported by any empirical data. The method of collecting the statistics and the sources of the data leave one very skeptical about the general veridicality of the report. The authors of the report in their conclusion stated:

> It is not possible to draw any close comparison of the incidence of crime among the Mexican population as compared to the general population. It would appear to be very high but the comparison is

affected by the fact that more men than women have entered the country and the age distribution gives a large proportion of Mexicans in the age groups most commonly found in prison. Police officials generally state greater tendency among arrested Mexicans to plead guilty to charges and the common inability to extended defense and appeal cases, both undoubtedly increase the apparent crime among Mexicans (Ibid.: 205).

The following year the National Commission on Law Observance and Enforcement *(Wickersham Report)* came out with a special report on *Crime and the Foreign Born* (1931). The early studies of the Wickersham Report showed that Chicanos were regarded by members of the dominant racial group as "a bad lot," as well as a "natural" thieves who had no "idea of private property" (1931:ix). But as Max Handman, one of the researchers for the report, states:

> There is no evidence to show that the Mexican runs afoul of the law any more than anyone else, and if the complete facts were known they would most likely show that he is less delinquent in Texas than the non-Mexican population of the same community (Ibid.:245).

In the larger report three separate reports were presented by Dr. Paul Taylor, Dr. Max Handman, and Paul Warmhuis, supposedly all experts on Mexican-American relations.[14] Professor Taylor gives a sort of introductory overview to the report.[15] He surveyed several cities throughout the Southwest attempting to measure how the people felt about Chicanos and crime. The study showed the general population believed that Chicanos were "lawless" and "criminal," more so than the facts warranted. All the problems that faced Chicanos in 1971 were discussed in this 1931 report (Civil Rights Report, 1971): police deployment is heavier in Chicano areas; arrest rates are higher; illegal practices and biased discretion are common; failure to make bail, hire lawyers, pleas of guilty prevail; and language barriers for Chicanos, racism, discrimination and class exploitation are common experiences of the Chicano in relation to the criminal justice system. Once again these statistical data are very questionable and confusing. In the charts presented, with a breakdown of arrest rates, different nomenclature is used. One chart may read "American of Mexican descent," another, "White of Spanish descent," and still another, "red." There was little consistency in the findings.

Professor Handman (1931), in his report, begins by attacking the biological determinist position. He states:

> ... the moment we throw the notion of national traits into the realm of biological determinism we are confronted with the statement that

34

the Anglo does not commit as much crime as the Mexican because his instinct is not prone to criminality. The difference between Mexican and Anglo instinct is not due to the fact that the Mexican has certain chromosomes which make him innately criminal, therefore the tautological statement that the reason the Mexican commits more crimes is because he is Mexican and not an Anglo (Ibid.:255).

Professor Handman, although denouncing biological determinism, does not reject the ideology that the fault rests with the individual Chicano; he simply replaces biological determinism with cultural determinism. This is shown in his statement:

> ... to Mexicans fighting is culturally approved form of gaining superiority. .... the result is that aggravated assault is common among Mexicans, not because they are inherently aggressive but because they live in a certain cultural stage, where fighting is approved (Ibid.:257).

But even in denouncing biological determinism we find in his work the following statement:

> ... when a string of Garcias, Sanchezs, Ramirezs are before you day in and day out the Jones and Smiths are apt to fade from your memory and the brown-skinned Mexican with his dumb and speechless stolidity is apt to linger for a long time and give you a conviction that you have been doing nothing but trying Mexican cases (Ibid.:258).

Paul Warnhuis (1931) in his report, "Crime and Criminal Justice Among Mexicans in Illinois," shows very clearly how law enforcement and the general public stereotype Chicanos as "lawless" and as "bandits." He also suggests that because of racism the Chicanos are more often victims of the "third degree" than other prisoners. Warnhuis' report is more of a descriptive analysis aimed at inspiring moral outrage. It has very little theoretical substance to it. And even though he denounces some of the stereotypes, he perpetuates others by giving a monolithic analysis of the Chicano: they are peace loving; alcohol is part of their diet; they have male-dominated households; and are illiterate (Ibid.:277).

Overall, these reports were much more sympathetic to the Chicano's plight with the criminal justice system, pointing out many of the injustices perpetrated upon them by the system. All the reports were liberal analyses of the problem in that they all concluded that reforms need to occur in the system to make it more equitable for Chicanos, but all changes and reforms were seen as workable within the system.

D. The Structural Functionalist

The late 1930's saw a brief re-emergence of the phrenology school of criminology. The continuing influence of Lombroso's substantive theory was found in the works of E. A. Hooten at Harvard, the Gluecks and William Sheldon, although they presented their analyses in a much more sophisticated fashion. Their works, of course, were well received by the racists who wanted to eliminate the "inferior" brown race.

But even more important to this period was the rise of the functionalist school of criminology, for its major theoretical paradigm is used to this day to explain the phenomenon of crime as it relates to the Chicano. Robert Merton, in *Social Theory and Social Structure* (1957), tried to account for the appearance in crime statistics of lower-class people in a greater proportion than people from the middle and upper classes. He reasoned that Americans are taught that in our land of promise, everyone can succeed—in fact, everyone must succeed, find happiness and gain security. We are told we are "all equal from the starting line," (to use a phrase common to conservatives), and that those who work hard and persevere will succeed. Merton argues that lower-class people, who have absorbed the ideology of success and equality but find hard work is not always enough, are blocked from upward mobility, become frustrated, and are more likely than others to turn to crime in an effort to get ahead.

Albert Cohen, another functionalist, adds to Merton's paradigm the concept of the "delinquent subculture" (1955). Cohen makes the assumption that working class boys revolt against the attempted imposition of a middle-class life style and middle-class values by becoming delinquent. The basic assumption of the Mertonian paradigm that the delinquent Chicano, for example, strives for pecuniary success and middle-class values, and if blocked turns to crime and makes it as a criminal—has not proved to be empirically valid. But the paradigm has been used repeatedly to explain the Chicano delinquent and criminal (Heller, 1966).

E. Criminologists and the Pachuco Phenomenon

As was previously mentioned, the 1940's saw the rise of the "pachuco." Several students of the period, (Acuña, 1972; McWilliams, 1948) claim that the so-called "Pachuco Riots" and "Pachuco Gangs dedicated to crime" were created by newspapers anxious for copy. The headlines detailed stories of "Chicano hoodlums" immersed in crime and subversive activities. This sensationalizing not only opened all Chicanos to nativist and racist attacks but also created another myth of the "criminality" of Chicanos. With the new concern about the "pachuco," social scientists soon began to explain the phenomenon. Psychiatrists had a field day explaining the "pachuco's" style as symbolic of the disorganization of a discriminate group.

Sociologists also attempted to explain the Chicano gangs. Emory Bogardus in "Gangs of Mexican American Youth," (1943) presented a kind of multi-factor set of causal explanations of the gang behavior of Chicano youth. The summary of his analysis is the following: gang behavior is due to unemployment (economic determinism); low intelligence due to inbreeding (biological determinism); growing up in neighborhoods that are (by Anglo standards) culturally deprived (cultural determinism); and discrimination (society's fault). His theoretical perspective is quite contradictory.

In another article, "Pachucos in the Making," George Sanchez suggests "the seeds of the problem of the Mexican 'crime wave' were sown a decade before by unintelligent educational measures, discriminatory social and economic practices, by provincial smugness and self-assigned 'racial' superiority" (1943:61). Sanchez, in a very systematic but somewhat apologetic fashion, shows that the blame is on the greater society, not the Chicano gang. He concludes in his article:

> The pachuco is a symbol not of guilt of an oppressed "Mexican" minority but a cancerous growth within the majority group which is gnawing at the vitals of democracy and the American way of life. The Pachuco and his feminine counterpart, the "cholita," are spawn of a neglectful society—not of the product of a humble minority people (Ibid.:11).

Thirty years have passed since the riots, but the blood has not been washed from the pavement of Los Angeles.

F. The Struggle for Better Conditions

In the 1930's as the social scientists were busy writing of the Mexican immigrant's role as passive, having no control over his/her political life in the barrio, Chicano unions and labor leaders were engaged in some of the bloodiest strikes for better conditions and wages ever staged in this country. McWilliams states,

> ... with scarcely an exception, every strike in which the Mexican American participated in the border lands in the thirties was broken by the use of violence and was followed by deportation (1948:153).

The philosophy of confrontation by Mexicans was not new to the labor strikes but can be traced to the early days of the revolution and the early United States among the bandidos. And as Octavio Romano points out, "On different occasions the confrontationist philosophy has been self-deterministic, protectionist, nationalistic, depending on and reacting to the surrounding circumstances" (1971:84).

G. The Rise of the Pachucos

While Chicanos became highly-decorated heroes of World War II, the home front was somewhat different. Once the Japanese were safely locked away in concentration camps, the media began a series of attacks on the Chicano community. Mexican crime and Mexican "pachucos" suddenly became a problem. Racism and repression against the Chicano[16] came to a climax in the so-called "Zoot suit" or "Pachuco" riots in 1943. The police stood by and watched servicemen come in and beat up the "zoot suiters." One Los Angeles newspaper was quoted as saying:

> It's too bad the servicemen were called off before they were able to complete the job . . . Most of the citizens of the city have been delighted with what's going on (See McWilliams, 1948:250).

And to get an idea of how the Los Angeles law enforcement felt about the incident, Officer Ayres of the Los Angeles Sheriff's Department is quoted by McWilliams as saying:

> . . . the criminality of teenage Mexican Americans is due to inferior genetic and cultural factors . . . Mexicans are more prone to kick an adversary who has been knocked down in a fight whereas an Anglo youth would be more inclined to fight fair (Ibid.)

The police saw the "pachucos" as enemies of the state working hand-in-hand with the Germans to destroy America, while the "pachucas" were merely cheap prostitutes infected with venereal disease and addicted to marijuana (Ibid.:251).

V. CONCLUSION

In surveying the criminological literature on Chicanos one thing becomes clear: criminologists have developed paradigms that are ideological in nature while attempting to conceal their biases in "value free" or "neutral" criminology. Also, as has been shown, the few criminologists who have written on the Chicano have for the most part perpetuated racist and ethnocentric myths and stereotypes. Through misrepresentation and often ignorance they have succeeded in de-emphasizing the very real problems of the Chicano in a racist society. After reading through the social science literature on Chicanos, Octavio Romano, for example, observes that the Chicano is viewed basically as

> . . . fatalistic, resigned, apathetic, traditional, emotional, impetuous, volatile, affective, non-rational, irrational, non-goal oriented, uncivi-

lized, primitive, unorganized, uncompetitive, uncooperative, retarded, under-achiever, under-developed, criminal, apolitical, apathetic and just plain lazy (1967:7).

These labels, although many are contradictory, are all negative. The racist and widely-accepted concepts and labels concerning Chicanos advanced in the name of social science show clearly the need for a new, more sensitive perspective, a Chicano perspective. Romano states in summing up how traditional social scientists have looked at Chicanos:

> ... the Mexican Americans are the generators of their own problems. Consequently, they are their own worst enemies ... (Ibid.:10).

This thesis of Chicanos being their own worst enemies, being victims of fate, being passive apolitical beings, serve racist criminologists in their explanations of why Chicanos suffer injustice at the hands of the criminal justice system. It is because they are too "passive" to do anything about it, and therefore "it is not our fault." A different perspective would show clearly that Chicanos, for well over one hundred years, have been demanding justice and equality within the United States system of justice, but because of class exploitation, racism, and indifference, those in power have ignored their pleas (Morales, 1972:6).

The development of new paradigms for research and analysis that will deal directly with the problems of racism, exploitation, and the injustices that confront the Chicano community is a vital need. It is therefore of primary importance that we begin to think of new methods and new theories that will work towards the liberation of Chicanos in this society. José Munoz sums this up as follows:

> As the whole world is in crisis, it is my conviction that the philosopher cannot cross his arms and remain locked up in his ivory tower viewing with indifference all that occurs around him. He must take a position. He must decide to take part in the struggle; not necessarily in a military sense, but in the field of ideas, orienting and seeking solutions to our problems according to his knowledge and understanding (1970:15).

FOOTNOTES

1. See Octavio Romano, "Anthropology and Sociology of the Mexican American: The Distortion of History," *El Grito*, II, No. 1 (Fall, 1968), pp. 13-26; Deluvina Hernandez, "Mexican American Challenge to a Sacred Cow," (March, 1970), Los Angeles, Chicano Cultural Center, University of California; Raymond Rocco, "The Chicano in the Social Sciences: Traditional Concepts, Myths and Images," *Aztlan*, (Fall, 1970), Vol. 1, No. 2; Carlos Munoz, "Toward a Chicano Perspective of Political Analysis," *Aztlan*, (Fall, 1970), Vol. 1, No. 2; Nick Vaca, "The Mexican American in the Social Sciences," *El Grito*, (Spring, 1970), Vol. III, No. 3.

2. The term "Colonial Capitalism" is used to emphasize the point that the Chicano in the United States has faced a dual oppression—that of race and class. To analyze this duality it

is essential to examine both colonial (rise of internal colonialism) and capitalist (rise of monopoly capitalism) structures from which racial and class oppression stem. This point is clarified by Bailey and Flores (1973:150):

> It is our belief that colonial expansion by which the U.S. absorbed vast territories paved the way for incorporation of its non white colonial labor forces. This contributed in turn to the accelerated process of capitalist accumulation necessary for the development of modern capitalism. It is our contention that not only did internal colonialism and monopoly capitalism develop concurrently, but that both processes are intimately interrelated and feed on each other. At the same time that the utilization of non-whites as a controlled, colonized labor force contributed to the development of the U.S. as the major metropolis of the international capitalist system, the attendent class system in the U.S. provided a means of reinforcing a racially and culturally defined social hierarchy.

3. Most Americans at this time, as is true today, regarded the Mexicans as Mexicans irrespective of nativity. This becomes confusing in reading the history and the social science literature for authors often say Mexican when they are talking about Chicanos. In this paper the term "Mexican" will be used when talking about non-native born, non-American citizens, migrants from the mother country Mexico.

4. As Blauner points out in *Racial Oppression in America* (New York: Harper and Row, 1972), colonial conquest and control have been the cutting edge of Western capitalism in its expansion and penetration throughout the world. Yet capitalism and free labor as Western institutions were not developed for people of color: they were reserved for white people and white societies.

5. This period of history saw bankers, lawyers, and politicians along with other capitalists dividing up the huge land grants, originally owned by the Mexicans and Californians. The state legislature worked hand-in-hand with the capitalists, setting up land commissions which either taxed the Mexican landowners out of existence or bled them by the high cost of litigations imposed by the Land Law of 1851. See Carey McWilliams, *Factories in the Field* (Boston: Little Brown, 1934), and *Ill Fares of the Land* (Boston: Little Brown, 1942). McWilliams also describes in vivid detail how the camps where the Mexican miners were living with their families were attacked and destroyed by the "Fortyniners" who then proceeded to "rush" the survivors back to Mexico.

6. The United States had over $2 billion invested in Mexico. With such a hold on the Mexican economy the U.S. capitalist could, through manipulation of the Mexican economy, keep the country underdeveloped.

7. This has been further portrayed by racist advertisers with their "Frito Bandito" and other similar characters that bring the image of the Mexican as "natural criminal" and "lawless" into the homes of millions of Americans. For a very good detailed analysis of how this racism works on the minds of millions through the media portrayals see: Thomas Martinez, "Advertising and Racisim: The Case of the American Mexican" (1971).

8. McWilliams exposes the feelings of law enforcement in these strikes when he quotes a Kern County sheriff as saying: "We protect our farmers here in Kern County. They are our best people. . . . They keep the country going. . . . But the Mexicans are trash. They have no standard of living. We herd them like pigs" (1948:154).

9. The Pachucos (male) and Pachucas (female) were mostly Chicano youth (ages 13-17) who belonged to barrios or neighborhoods. The boys wore drapes or zoot-suit uniform and tattooed a cross with three dots just above their left thumb. The girls wore black huaraches, short black skirts and high pompadours. They spoke Calo the barrio mixture of Spanish and

English. Dr. Octavio Romano (1971:84) has called the Pachucos the first truly separatist movement. Rudolf Acuna (1972:201) using the colonial analogy describes the Pachuco phenomenona: ". . . understandable within the context of the colonial experience, where dress and language distinguishes the colonized from the colonizer, and where the difference is emphasized as the former confronts his oppression . . ."

10. Ross also warned the Anglo-Saxon race that it was committing "race suicide" through low birth rates. He went on to say that the vertical rays of the sun caused enormous sexual appetites of brown-skinned people of the South. A good detailed analysis of what Ross really thought of the Mexican people is presented in Edward Alsworth Ross, *The Social Revolution in Mexico* (1923).

11. An exception to biological determinism was William Bonger, *Criminology and Economics* (1916). He concluded that poverty creates crime and furnishes the motive for it because capitalist structure of society is responsible for innumerable conflicts. He blamed capitalists for racial genocide. All crimes were natural acts inspired by the capitalist system.

12. See, for example: Edwin Banford, "The Mexican Causal Problem in the Southwest," *Journal of Applied Sociology*, July-August, 1924; Charles Thompson, "Mexicans—An Interpretation," National Conference of Social Work, 1927; Robert McLean, "Mexican Workers in the United States," National Conference on Social Work, 1928; Emory Bogardus, "Second Generation Mexicans," *Sociology and Social Research*, 13: 275-283 (1941); Norman Humphrey, "The Concept of Culture in Social Case Work," *Sociology and Social Research*, September, 1941. Also see Earl Sullenberg, "Mexican Population of Omaha," *Journal of Applied Sociology*, May, 1924; Helen Walker, "Mexican Immigrants as Laborers," *Sociology and Social Research*, 13: 55-62.

13. See for example: Kimbal Young, "Mental Differences in Certain Immigrant Groups," *University of Oregon Publications*, Vol. 1, No. 11, 1922; D. K. Garretson, "A Study of Causes of Retardation Among Mexican Children in a Small Public School System in Arizona," *Journal of Educational Psychology*, 19: 31-40; Thomas R. Garth, "A Comparison of Intelligence of Mexican and Mixed and Full Blood Indian Children," *Psychological Review*, 30: 388-401; H. T. Manuel, "The Education of Mexican and Spanish Speaking Children in Texas," University of Texas (1930); George J. Sanchez, "Group Differences and Spanish-Speaking Children—A Critical Review," *Journal of Applied Psychology*, 16: 549-583; Nick Vaca (1970) for a critical review of psychological perspectives on the Chicano.

14. Paul Taylor was professor of economics at U.C. Berkeley and author of many articles on scientific aspects of human migration, Mexican labor, and immigration. Max Handman was professor of economics at the University of Texas and specialized in prison labor and problems of Mexicans in the Southwest. And Paul Warnhius was representative of the Presbyterian Home Mission Board in the Southwest, having humanitarian interest in the Mexican people's problems.

15. One of the most interesting sections of the report was on drug use among Mexicans. The report states: "California is vitally interested in the traffic in marihuana . . . its use is widespread throughout southern California among the Mexican population . . . usually smoked as a cigarette causing exaltation and a feeling of physical power; but if continued the drug develops a delirious rage, causing the smoker to commit atrocious crimes. The report specified two groups that were feared for carrying dangerous drugs as they migrate: the Chinese in San Francisco (opium) and the Mexican in Los Angeles (marijuana) (205).

16. The Chicano to most criminologists has been a "silent" or "forgotten" minority or referred to as one of the "other" oppressed minorities. This is clearly shown by the fact that the author found only eighteen articles dealing with criminology written about the Chicano in

the first forty years of this century (compare this to over 500 articles annotated by Professor Savitz on blacks and crime).

REFERENCES

Acuna, Rudolfo
   1972 Occupied America: The Chicano's Struggle Toward Liberation. San Francisco: Canfiel Press.

Bailey, Ronald and Guillermo Flores
   1973 "Internal Colonialism and Racial Minorities in the U.S.: An Overview." Structures of Dependency. Edited by Frank Bonilla and Robert Girling. Stanford University Institute of Political Studies.

Barnes, Henry and Negley Teeters
   1959 New Horizons in Criminology. Princeton: Princeton University Press.

Bogardus, Emory
   1943 "Gangs of Mexican American Youth." Sociology and Social Research (September).

Bonger, William
   1916 Criminology and Economics. Boston: Little, Brown and Company.

Broom, Leonard and Eshref Shevsky
   1952 "Mexican Americans in the United States: A Problem in Differentiation." Sociology and Social Research, Vol. 36:153-58.

Bryam, Samuel
   1919 "Mexican Immigrants in the United States." Survey, Vol. 28:726-30.

Castillo, Pedro and Albert Camarillo
   1973 Furia y Muerta: Los Bandidos Chicanos. Los Angeles: Aztlan Publications, Monograph No. 4.

Civil Rights Report
   1971 Mexican Americans and the Administration of Justice in the Southwest. U.S. Commission on Civil Rights. Washington, D.C.: Government Printing Office.

Cohen, Albert
   1955 Delinquent Boys: The Culture of the Gang. Glencoe, Illinois: The Free Press.

Dickerson, R. E.
   1919 "Some Suggestive Problems in the Americanization of Mexicans." Pedagogical Seminary (September).

Dugdale, Richard
   1910 The Jukes. New York: Putnam's.

Gamio, Manuel
   1971 The Life Story of the Mexican Immigrant. New York: Dover Publications.

Garretson, D. K.
   1919 "A Study of Causes of Retardation among Mexican Children in a Small Public School System in Arizona." Journal of Educational Psychology, Vol. 9:31-40.

Goddard, Henry
1920 Human Efficiency and Levels of Intelligence. Princeton: Princeton University Press.

Goring, Charles
1913 The English Convict: A Statistical Study. London: Stationary Office.

Gossett, Thomas
1964 Race: The History of an Idea in America. New York: Schoken Books.

Handman, Max
1931 "Preliminary Report on Nationality and Delinquency: The Mexican in Texas." Report on Crime and the Foreign Born, Vol. 11.

Heller, Celia
1966 Mexican-American Youth: Forgotten Youth at the Crossroad. New York: Random House.

Hobsbaum, Eric
1969 Bandits. London: Weidenfeld and Nicholson, Ltd.

Humphrey, Norman
1941 "The Concept of Culture in Social Work." Sociology and Social Research (September).

Kluckholm, Clyde
1953 Personality in Nature, Society and Culture. New York: Alfred A. Knopf.

Lewis, Oscar
1951 Life in a Mexican Village. Urbana: University of Illinois Press.

Manuel, H. T.
1930 "The Education of Mexican and Spanish-Speaking Children in Texas." University of Texas publication.

Martinez, Thomas
1971 "Advertising and Racism: The Case of the Mexican American." Berkeley: Quinto Sol publication.

McWilliams, Carey
1934 Factories in the Fields. Boston: Little, Brown and Company.
1948 North From Mexico. Boston: Little, Brown and Company.

McLean, Robert
1926 That Mexican. New York: Flemming Revell Company.

Merton, Robert
1957 Social Theory and Social Structure. Glencoe, Illinois: The Free Press.

Mexicans in California
1930 Governor Young's Mexican Fact Finding Committee. San Francisco.

Moquin, Wayne (ed.)
1971 A Documentary History of the Mexican American. New York: Bantam Books.

Morales, Armando
1972 Ando Sagrando. Compton, California: La Perspectiva Press.

Munoz, Carlos
1970   "Toward a Chicano Perspective of Political Analysis." Aztlan, Vol. 1, No. 2.

National Commission on Law Observance and Enforcement
1931   Report on Crime and the Foreign Born. Washington, D.C.: U.S. Government Printing
       Office.

Pitt, Leonard
1971   The Decline of the Californios. Berkeley: University of California Press.

Quinney, Richard
1970   The Problem of Crime. New York: Dodd, Mead and Company.

Romano, Octavio
1967   "Minorities, History, and the Culture Mystique." El Grito, Vol. 1, No. 1.
1971   Voices. Berkeley: Quinto Sol publication.

Ross, Edward
1923   The Social Revolution in Mexico. New York: The Century Company.

Rudoff, Alvin
1971   "The Incarcerated Mexican American Delinquent." Journal of Criminal Law, Crim-
       inology and Police Science, Vol. 62:224-38.

Ruiz, Eduardo
1963   The Mexican War: Was It Manifest Destiny? New York: Praeger Press.

Sanchez, George
1943   "Pachucos in the Making." Common Ground (Autumn).

Sanders, F.
1958   "English-Speaking and Spanish-Speaking People of the Southwest." Social Perspec-
       tives on Behavior. Edited by Stein and Cloward.

Szasz, Thomas
1960   "The Myth of Mental Illness." American Psychologist, Vol. 15, No. 2.

Taylor, Paul
1931   "Crime and the Foreign Born: The Problem of the Mexican in Texas." Report on the
       Foreign Born, Vol. 11.
1930   "More Bars Against Mexicans." Survey Graphic (April).

Tuck, Ruth
1946   Not With Fist. New York: Harcourt, Brace and Company.

Vaca, Nick
1970   "The Mexican American in the Social Sciences, 1912-1970." El Grito, Vol. 3, No. 3.

Vasconcelos, José
1963   A Mexican Ulysses. Bloomington: Indiana Press.

Vold, George
1958   Theoretical Criminology. New York: Oxford University Press.

Warnhuis, Paul
    1931   "Crime and Criminal Justice Among Mexicans in Illinois." Report on Crime and the
           Foreign Born, Vol. 11.

William, Kirk
    1931   "Culture Conflicts in Mexican Life." Sociology and Social Research (March).

Wolf, Eric
    1969   "On Peasant Rebellions." International Social Science Journal, Vol. 21, No. 2.

Administration of Justice: Chicanos in Monterey County

Hisauro Garza

Differential treatment in the administration of justice has been examined by various authors dealing with *specific* areas or stages of the entire process of justice administration from the police to examinations of the trial process and various types of case dispositions.[1] These writings have in some measure touched on the function of *race* in judicial differential treatment. However, none of the above have dealt with the subject of differential treatment (1) in terms of functions of both *race* or *ethnic group* and *social class,* nor has (2) a comprehensive examination of this judicial partialism been made in terms of the various stages in the arraignment to disposition process in the courts.

The present paper deals with differential treatment process in the court-trial structure on a comparative basis by summarily examining two groups—Chicanos and Anglos—throughout the various decision stages in the trial process. It is posited that differential treatment exists generally as a consequence of the dominant-subjugated group context, and more specifically as a result of discrimination.

Paper delivered at the Southwestern Social Science Association's Annual Meeting, March 30–April 1, 1972, in San Antonio, Texas.

137

The institution here examined, the court, is one that is largely under the control of the dominant group, Anglos, with only a token representation of ethnic minorities. This dominant group is constituted basically of representatives of the *middle* or *upper* class. Thus, the hypothesis here is that a differential treatment exists which is functionally related to *ethnic* and *class* variables, i.e., that a negative differential treatment will most often, other things being equal, be incurred by those persons processed through the court that are either ethnically and/or class-wise different from those who make the decisions in the various stages of the court-trial process.

A further underlying assumption is that there exist perceptual differences in this dominant-subjugated relationship which are based on ethnic group membership and on social class position. Thus, there exists a certain systematic or categorical evaluation based on these perceptions which is functional in the various decision-making stages of the trial process.

The attempt here is to measure the extent of differential treatment in these trial stages, and to measure the extent to which variances in treatment can be accounted for by the *ethnic* variable and to what extent these can be accounted for by the *social class* variable, and to what extent by a combination of the two.

The indicators for one of the independent variables, the *ethnic* variable, are Spanish and English surname; and for *social class,* education and occupation. In addition, prior criminal record is controlled and measured.[2] The dependent variables are the following: (1) bail; (2) release on own recognizance; (3) entry of plea (guilty or not guilty); (4) convicted status; (5) time in jail at time of Probation or Pre-Sentence Report; (6) outcome of case (guilty or not guilty); (7) recommendation of probation officer; (8) granting of probation; (9) length of probation; (10) jail commitment; (11) length of jail commitment; and (12) prison sentence.

Procedures and Techniques of the Study

It became clear at the outset of the research that certain key variables should be controlled in order to interpret the data. A selection was made of a specific offense that could be held constant, had a high occurrence frequency among both groups, is a felony offense (since these are automatically after conviction, referred to the probation department, and therefore have either a Probation or Pre-Sentence Report with various kinds of information needed for this study), and did not bring about compounded charges. For this reason it was decided to avoid such offenses as narcotics or health and safety violations which have the highest occurrence frequency of all offenses in Monterey County and in the State of California.[3]

Second degree burglary was selected as the offense on which to measure judicial imbalance. This offense can be complicated since, for example, a defendant can be charged also with burglary and possession of stolen property at the same time. This gives the prosecution the upper hand, since it can usually get a guilty plea to at least possession of stolen property (the lesser charge) from the defendant. The prosecutor is in a better bargaining position. There are, also, other cases (none included here) for example, in which a burglary committed allegedly included a personal check which the defendant allegedly counterfeited. This tends to increase the various charges in the "bill of indictment." However, all of the cases included in the present study consist *only* of those cases that are: (1) simple second degree burglary; (2) not charged with two or more counts of burglary; (3) male defendants over twenty-one years of age; (4) did not possess ulterior factors, such as the defendant being a narcotics addict or alcoholic; and (5) clearly Spanish or English-surnamed defendants. The total number of cases (N = 187) consists of a purposive sample, of 68 Chicanos (36.4%) and 119 (63.6%) Anglos.

All (felonies) i.e., rape, burglary, robbery, murder, etc., are "held to answer" in superior court. This analysis is thus concentrated in the superior court records. Every aspect of this study is based on the burglary case files for 1960–61, 1964–65, and 1969–70, covering a total of six of the ten years from 1960 to 1970.

The Salinas (the capitol of Monterey County where the superior court and the records for this study are located) public defender system was started in June of 1969. This analysis reflects this for part of the 1969 and all the 1970 data, although about five to ten burglary cases which began in 1970 were excluded because these were still in progress at the time of the gathering of the data. Moreover, in 1969, a "branch court" of this superior court was started in Monterey (city), California. As a result, the figures for 1969–70 reflect this, since those cases arising in that area and tried in that court are *not* included here.

It should be pointed out at this point that the total number of each of the two groups is in no way representative of their respective populations in the county and that no attempt has been made to do so. These 187 cases are merely those that fulfilled the selection criteria. Equally, it is pointed out here that income data was unavailable and therefore is *not* included in the operationalization of *social class.*

Findings

Differential treatment is noted, in varying degrees, in each of the five major categories of the court-trial process. What stands out is the difference which remains even when controlling for prior criminal record. So-called *legal decisions* at each of these five stages are influenced by *extra-legal* factors, namely ethnic group membership, and social class position. Although *social class* does *not* appear as significant as does *ethnic group*, it is nonetheless significant in some of the five stages as will be pointed out in the following summary of findings.

Bail and Own Recognizance. No significant difference is discovered in the proportion of Anglos and Chicanos that were allowed to post bail. This is the case also when bail is examined by the social class indicators—no differences. Negative differential treatment is noted for release on defendant's own recognizance (O.R.). Chicanos are less apt to be released on O.R. No noticeable differences exist when the cases are examined by *social class* indicators. The assumption was that *lower class* (poor) defendants would not be viewed as candidates for pre-trial release on this basis because their "recognizances" might not appear to the court elite as sufficient for showing up in court at the time of trial as perhaps their higher social class counterparts.

Entry of Plea. Some of the things that stand out in regards to the entry of plea stage are that: (1) Chicanos are more apt to enter pleas of guilty; and (2) Chicanos with prior criminal records of two or more prior felony offenses have a greater likelihood of pleading *guilty* (this is above and beyond the fact that a much higher number of *all* the cases *with* prior criminal records plead guilty when compared with those *without* like records); and (3) no noticeable variations or negative differential treatment at this stage occurs when examined for social class indicators. This stage of the plea entry, in terms of social class indicators, shows a "reverse" differential treatment. Such result does not support the hypothesis of association between lower social class and negative differential treatment since defendants having *higher social class* positions do *not* receive more favorable treatment but, on the contrary, *do* enter *guilty* pleas most often.

In addition, of those cases pleading *not guilty,* Chicanos have a much higher rate of *not guilty* case outcomes when compared to their Anglo counterparts also pleading *not guilty.* This point is very important because, as will be illustrated in the following section on pre-sentence incarceration that Chicanos serve longer pre-sentence jail terms, Chicanos are often victims of this pre-sentence incarceration in spite of being legally innocent.

Pre-Sentence Incarceration. When the length of pre-sentence jail incarceration is dichotomized into those cases serving from zero to thirty-nine days and those serving from forty days and over in jail, it is found that Chicanos have a much greater likelihood of serving longer pre-sentence "terms" as shown in Table 1. These terms are measured by the total time served at the time of the preparation of the Probation or Pre-Sentence Report.

Table 1
**Time in Jail at Time of Probation or
Pre-Sentence Report for Chicanos and Anglos**

Time in Jail	Chicanos		Anglos	
0–39 days	(27)	47%	(64)	70%
40 days and over	(30)	53%	(27)	30%
	(57)	100%	(91)	100%

Note: This represents only 147 cases of the total N of 187, since time in jail data was available for these cases only.

Social class also appears as very significant in determining the severity of pre-sentence "terms." *Lower social class* defendants, as measured by formal educational attainment and occupation, have a significantly greater likelihood of spending *more* time in jail before final case disposition.

Probation. In this phase of the analysis the focus is on whether or not there exists negative differential treatment in the dispositions of the cases through the granting of probation and also in the length or severity of this probationary period. All convicted defendants in California are legally eligible for probationary release, and at the proper time during the trial are referred to the probation department of the county for a thorough investigation of the defendant's background, arrest history, convictions, employment history, marital status, etc. This investigation is then presented to the court as either a Probation (if the defendant is being considered for probation) or as a Pre-Sentence Report (if the defendant is to be sentenced or his case disposed of in some other manner).

The ethnic variable does *not* support the hypothesis of negative differential treatment in the granting of probation. In this instance, Chicanos are more apt to receive probation than Anglos. Green discovered quite the opposite in his Pennsylvania study.[4] He found that the major difference between the case dispositions of Blacks and Whites was at the stage of probation, where almost twice as many Anglos as Blacks were granted probation releases. The present examination does *not* support this conclusion. The same differential holds when analyzing the length of probation, Chicanos receive shorter periods of probation. Again, this differential also holds when controlling for prior criminal record.

This finding of "better" treatment of Chicanos is inconsistent with the findings in the overall study and with data from other related areas of the study. For example, Chicanos have a much higher representation in the *lower social class* category i.e., less education and lower status occupations, and it is found that *lower class* defendants are more apt to not be granted probation. Yet Chicanos appear as more likely candidates for being granted probation! Another inconsistency in this regard is that probation officers view farmworkers as "nomadic," "transients," "transitory," "migratory," or as "poor risks" for probation because of unstable residence as a consequence of having to migrate or move after the crop harvesting seasons. Most of the Chicanos in this study are farm workers. Yet again, Chicanos appear as faring much better than Anglos in being granted probation! This area deserves further research to clarify these apparent contradictions.

With regards to *social class* indicators, as mentioned earlier, lower class defendants are *less likely* to be granted probation. In this case, probation officers most often recommend incarceration as opposed to probation. Similarly, *social class* indicators appear as quite significant in the length of probation, where *lower class* defendants are much more apt to receive longer periods of probation.

Convicted Status. Convicted status, whether of a *felony* or of a *misdemeanor,* was also assessed for differential treatment on the basis of *ethnic* and *class* variables.

When convicted status is examined for both groups, it is found that *no* variations exist among each of the groups. In other words, the ethnic variable does *not* hold at this stage of measurement, since as many Chicanos as Anglos are apt to receive either *felony* or *misdemeanor* convictions. The same result of non-variance appears when measuring by *social class* indicators. Thus, this stage does not support the hypothesis of negative differential treatment according to *ethnic* group membership and according to *social class* position.

In controlling for prior criminal record, only a slight variation exists in which Anglos receive more felony convictions. However, the major difference is observed for cases *without* prior criminal records. In this instance, Chicanos are much more apt to receive felony convictions by a much greater margin over Anglos. What this possibly indicates is that convicted status is *not* dependent on prior criminal record as far as Chicanos are concerned, or at least *not as dependent* as in the Anglo cases.

County Jail. When the data is examined for county jail dispositions, it is found that Anglos are more apt to receive county jail *commitments*. However, quite large variances are observed when examining the *length* or *severity* of these jail commitments. In this respect, Chicanos are more likely to serve longer jail sentences. This supports Lemert's Los Angeles County study in which he concludes also that Chicanos serve longer sentences.[5] On examining prior criminal record, it is observed that this has greater effect on receiving county jail commitments for Anglos. Only slight differences are observed when measuring county jail commitments by *social class*. However, social class differentiation appears as very significant when examining the *length* of these jail commitments. *Lower class* defendants who receive jail dispositions are apt to serve longer sentences.

Prison. The last stage of the court-trial process selected for testing of the hypothesis is prison sentence. No differences in prison dispositions are observed by *ethnic* group alone. However, past criminal records are very functional in whether or not prison is the final outcome of the case. Chicanos with prior criminal records have a greater likelihood of receiving prison sentences.

The analysis at this phase of the judicial machinery does not substantiate entirely Green's findings that there is very little difference in prison sentences as a consequence of "race," since even though he states that it is the defendant's prior criminal background that a prison sentence hinges on, analysis indicates that the combination of a Chicano defendant with a prior criminal record increases the likelihood of a prison sentence far more than for Anglos with the same background.[6] This analysis does, however, support his conclusion that prior criminal record has the greatest *single influence* in prison dispositions.

Only slight variations are observed in prison case dispositions when measured by *social class*. Again, at this stage in the trial process, *social class* plays a very significant role, giving functional primacy to prior criminal record i.e., again prior criminal record has a greater effect in prison case dispositions when coupled with a *lower class* defendant.

Results and Conclusion

The data in the present analysis sheds light in a few little-studied areas so that inferences can be made. One thing that became clear as the research proceeded to this conclusion, is that there exists a relationship between the ethnic and social class indicators i.e., surname, education, and occupation, to the judicial decisions or dispositions at every stage of the trial process. This direct relationship gradually decreases as the judicial decisions get greater or "more serious" i.e., own recognizance to entry of plea, plea to probation, probation to county jail, county jail to prison. As these decisions "increase" from *lower order* to *higher order* there tends to be less correlation with the *ethnic* and with the *social class* indicators, and prior criminal record assumes a greater role or influence.

The results indicate that the *ethnic* variable is much more correlated with the *lower order* judicial decisions or stages where greater freedom for discretion exists i.e., own recognizance, plea, and pre-sentence jail. Chicanos at these stages fare worse than their Anglo counterparts. Thus, the ethnic variable is of primary importance or influence at these stages. Both the ethnic and social class variables correlate with differentials in treatment at the county jail commitment phase and with length of jail sentence. With respect to prison case dispositions, the ethnic and social class variables become less significant as prior criminal record assumes the primary influence in prison sentences.

Overall, the results support the hypothesis of differential treatment as measured by ethnicity and by social class, with ethnicity being the more significant of the two. However, another finding is that when the ethnic variable (in this case Chicanos) exists in combination with *lower class* status, or with prior criminal record, the probability of negative differential treatment increases. If the defendant is a Chicano he faces a certain likelihood of negative treatment, if he is also of a lower class status this likelihood increases, if he is of a lower class status and has a prior criminal record this likelihood becomes even greater! Thus the assumption that our courts discriminate against the ethnically different and against the poor is not an ill-founded one. *Extra-legal factors* (perhaps even rationalized and incorporated within the scope of legality itself) appear as significant influences in so-called *legal decisions* which negatively affect some defendants.

Notes

1. For justice administration focusing on police, see Kadish, 1962; Skolnick, 1966; LaFave, 1965; and Goldstein, 1960. For examinations of case dispositions, see Sellin, 1935; Lane, 1941; Lemert, 1948; Green, 1961; and Bullock, 1961.

2. Prior criminal record is controlled and measured for both groups. Two or more prior felony offenses have been used as the criteria for prior criminal record. Also, a natural check occurs in the total sample, since both groups have approximately the same proportional representation of those cases with prior criminal records (100) as they do in the total study sample i.e., of the 187 cases in the entire sample, 36.4% are Chicanos and 63.6% Anglos, while of the 100 cases with prior criminal records 39% are Chicanos and 61% Anglos.

3. State of California, *Reference Tables: Superior Court Prosecutions* (Sacramento, California: Bureau of Criminal Statistics, Department of Justice, Division of Law Enforcement, 1969), pg. 5.

4. E., Green, *Judicial Attitudes in Sentencing* (New York: MacMillan and Co., 1961), pg. 56.

5. E.M. Lemert and Judy Rosberg, *Administration of Justice to Minority Groups in Los Angeles County* (Berkeley, California: University of California Press, 1948), pg. 12.

6. Green, op. cit., pg. 62.

Bibliography

Bullock, H.A., "Significance of the Racial Factor in the Length of Prison Sentences," in *Crime and Justice in Society*, R. Quinney, ed., Boston: Little, Brown and Company, 1969, pp. 417–429.

Goldstein, J., "Police Discretion Not to Invoke the Criminal Process: Low-Visibility Decisions in the Administration of Justice," in *Delinquency, Crime and Social Process*, D.R. Cressey and D.A. Ward, eds., New York: Harper and Row, 1969, pp. 166–184.

Green, E., *Judicial Attitudes in Sentencing*, New York: MacMillan and Co., 1961.

Kadish, S.H., "Legal Norm and Discretion in the Police and Sentencing Process," *Harvard Law Review*, Vol. 75, (1962), pp. 904–931.

Lane, H.E., "Illogical Variations in Sentences of Felons Committed to Massachusetts State Prisons," *Journal of Criminal Law and Criminology*, Vol. 32 (1941).

LaFave, W.R., "Noninvocation of the Criminal Law by Police," in *Delinquency, Crime and Social Process*, D.R. Cressey and D.A. Ward, eds., New York: Harper and Row, 1969, pp. 185–208.

Lemert, E.M. and Judy Rosberg, *Administration of Justice to Minority Groups in Los Angeles County*, Berkeley, California: University of California Press, 1948.

Skolnick, J.H., *Justice Without Trial*, New York: John Wiley and Sons, Inc., 1966.

Sellin, T., "Race Prejudice in the Administration of Justice," *American Journal of Sociology*, Vol. 41, (1935), pp. 212–217.

State of California, *Reference Tables: Superior Court Prosecutions*, Sacramento, California: Bureau of Criminal Statistics, Department of Justice, Division of Law Enforcement, 1969.

Journal of Criminal Justice, Vol. 11, pp. 213–227 (1983)
Pergamon Press, Printed in U.S.A.

HISPANIC INTERACTION WITH THE CRIMINAL JUSTICE SYSTEM IN TEXAS: EXPERIENCES, ATTITUDES, AND PERCEPTIONS

DAVID L. CARTER

Department of Criminal Justice
Pan American University
Edinburg, Texas 78539

ABSTRACT

This is an exploratory study of Hispanics in Texas examining attitudes toward crime and the criminal justice system. The study focuses on cultural determinants among Hispanics as affecting attitudes and behaviors and identifies differences between Hispanics and other population groups. The article provides a background of general cultural dynamics which can affect human relationships and then examines specific characteristics of the Hispanic culture. Among the significant findings are that Hispanics in Texas (1) feel "less safe" concerning crime than does the general population, (2) do not feel that the police can reduce the incidence of crime, (3) feel they have inadequate police protection, (4) evaluate the police generally lower than does the general population, (5) feel that the criminal courts are generally fair and just, and (6) possess a strong punitive—rather than rehabilitative—attitude toward corrections. The article presents a critical summary of the methodology and findings of an extensive research project.

Cultural variation between groups in a heterogeneous society tends to influence group attitudes toward and experiences of various social institutions. This same variation may influence the perspective of each cultural group to social problems and relationships between man and society. Studies examining the interaction of culture with perceptions and attitudes toward criminal justice are relatively limited. A review of the literature indicates that the cultural research which has been done is almost exclusively limited to the experiences of black Americans with the criminal justice system and has left a near void in the literature with respect to Hispanic Americans.[1] In recent years Hispanics have voiced protests claiming that they are victims not only of disproportionate criminality but also of the criminal justice system (Bonilla, 1980). It may appear a priori that these claims are valid; however, little empirical evidence exists to support or deny these positions. Therefore, this article will present a summary of findings from an exploratory empirical research project examining Hispanic attitudes toward the criminal justice system in Texas.

STATEMENT OF THE PROBLEM

A premise which underlies our system of justice is that the government, through its administrative agencies, must be responsive to the public. This means that in the ideal sense there must be an understanding of human dynamics within subgroups of the population; empathy with respect to customs and social relationships; and conceptual familiarity with thought processes, attitude development, and behavioral responses to various stimuli. If these variables are not recognized at an operational level, the criminal justice system will not be responsive to the various publics it serves nor will it be able to establish effective two-way communications with those publics. This situation becomes aggravated when values and norms of one culture are applied to an alternate culture. The result is conflict along with an associated state of confusion between "ideals" of the system and "operational realities" in the administration of justice. Confusion exists because without an understanding of cultural dynamics, conflicting responses to a situation cannot be approached in a rational manner. That is, the criminal justice system procedurally operates on an artificial assumption of cultural consistency rather than recognizing differential traits.[2]

The researcher maintains that this condition becomes exacerbated when the mainstream Anglo-American values of law and social interaction are applied to Hispanics. Significant variations in interpersonal relations, family, and values exist between these cultures which, if not recognized, may lead to both conflict and a lack of responsiveness on the part of the criminal justice system. In turn, this contributes to diminished service delivery, increased hostility, and a mutual distrust between Hispanics and the criminal justice system. This research project addresses this discord and selected variables which contribute to it.

PURPOSE OF THE STUDY

This study examines the experiential relationship between Hispanics and the criminal justice system in Texas through the use of validated survey research methods. Specifically, the researcher has (1) identified factors which relate criminal victimization, perceptions of crime trends, and fear of crime among Hispanics; (2) defined the research population's experiences with the criminal justice system; (3) determined the research population's evaluations of the police and attitudes toward courts and corrections; and (4) identified common variables between these constructs which profile Hispanic relationships with the criminal justice system.

Victimization, Crime Trends, and Fear

Victimization among Hispanics has been examined in nine different offense categories: (1) aggravated assault, (2) attempted assault with weapon, (3) attempted assault without weapon, (4) attempted robbery, (5) burglary, (6) larceny, (7) larceny from motor vehicle, (8) personal larceny with contact, and (9) robbery. These categories were selected on the basis of their comparability to the National Crime Survey (NCS) results. The data gathered identified the incidence, characteristics, and subsequent interaction with the criminal justice system experienced by Hispanics in these crime categories.

Perceptions of crime trends was a subjective evaluation by respondents regarding their belief of whether crime had increased, decreased, or remained about the same within their neighborhood and nationwide. The respondents' fear of crime was evaluated on the degree of safety from crime that they felt and the reasons why fear existed.

Experiences with the Criminal Justice System

Data were gathered to define the specific nature of experiences the research population had with the criminal justice system in Texas. This included a primary emphasis on relationships with the police (e.g., reporting crime, arrests, traffic contacts, disputes, and other called for services) and secondary emphasis on relationships with the courts and corrections.

Primary emphasis was given to the police for two reasons. First, the police are the most overt symbol of the criminal justice system. Hence, experiences with the police influence systemwide perceptions and attitudes. Second, more people have contact with the wide array of police services than with other system components. Although systemwide experiential data were gathered, the research plan presumed that the greatest abundance and most reliable data would be law enforcement oriented.

Evaluations of the Police

Evaluative information was gathered on the police from the research population on both an experiential and nonexperiential basis. Information on expectations of police performance and satisfaction with performance was also gathered from those respondents who indicated that they had some form of police contact.

Attitudinal data were solicited from the sample members regarding their perceptions of "fairness" of the criminal courts and the purpose and effectiveness of correctional alternatives. These variables were particularly constructed to evaluate perceptions of the criminal justice system as a whole.

THE CULTURAL ENVIRONMENT

Fundamental to the understanding of Hispanics and their attitude toward the criminal justice system is a conceptualization of the Hispanic culture. It was expected that the Hispanic culture instilled differential attitudes toward crime and justice compared to those attitudes found among the general public. The legal system of this country is based upon Anglo-American values, norms, and a sense of "rightness." In that basic disparities exist between traditional Anglo-American and Hispanic cultures it may be reasonable to assume that any disenchantment and conflict with the criminal justice system by Hispanics may be founded upon cultural variables. In this

regard, the writer presents a summary examination of culture followed by a discussion of Hispanic culture. It is argued that selected cultural traits may be initiators of conflict between Hispanics and the criminal justice system.

An Overview of Culture

Essentially stated, culture is social heredity—the total legacy of past human behavior effective in the present representing the accumulation through generations of the artifacts, knowledge, beliefs, and values by which men and women deal with the world (Williams, 1965). In general, culture exists at five levels: social, psychological, biological, chemical, and physical (Feibleman, 1968). Although these five levels are systemic, it is the social level that has the greatest importance for the present topic. Those sociocultural characteristics which have the greatest propensity for interaction with the criminal justice system are *norms* and *institutions*.

A "cultural norm" is a specific prescription of behavior in a given situation (Hiebert, 1976). Cultural norms include both cultural goals and the approved means for attaining those goals. It should be noted that there are various gradations of norms, such as cognitive norms (a technical or prescriptive standard), conventional norms (etiquette, protocol), aesthetic norms (standards of taste, beauty), and moral norms (strict standards of acceptable behavior, "cultural laws") (Keesing, 1976).

If cultural norms dictate a course of action in a given situation which is not congruent with the institutional response to a situation, one may well experience a source of conflict which leads to disintegrating attitudes and perceptions and poor experiences. What may be acceptable behavior in one culture may be unacceptable in another. If the cultural environment is a formal institution (e.g., the criminal justice system) conflict may arise.

Institutions are formalized norms which are: (1) widely known, accepted, and applied; (2) widely enforced by strong sanctions which are continuously applied; (3) based on revered sources of authority; (4) internalized in individual personalities; (5) inculcated and strongly reinforced early in life; and (6) objects of consistent and prevalent conformity (Williams, 1965).

In a homogeneous society, such as Japan, institutional norms permeate virtually every portion of society, providing unified standards of behavior with minimal conflict. However, in a heterogeneous society, as found in the United States, institutional norms exist at two basic levels: formal institutions and informal institutions. Formal institutions are those which are sanctioned by law and represent the operational methods required for the society to be perpetuated. Informal institutions represent norms of an ethnic or communal group which are culturally based and may or may not directly conform to the standards of formal institutions.

These cultural pockets exist throughout the United States whether one examines the mountain people of Appalachia, Chinatown of San Francisco, the various tribes of Native Americans, or Hispanics of the Southwest. The significance of cultural conflict has important bearing on present-day social thinking inasmuch as modern existence implies living in close contact with peoples whose ways of life are different. As noted previously, the nature of American society, with its numerous subcultures, carries with it the conditions for human stress and tension as a product of cultural contact. Often what occurs under conditions of cultural contact is that the incoming group fails to understand the way of life of the existing population or makes demands on its group members for which cultural solutions are lacking. The original population comprehends no more clearly the institutions of the incoming groups, all of which leads to stress situations and, very likely, conflict (Wright and Phillips, 1979).

Cultural contact and cultural relativity have unique implications for the criminal justice system—one responsibility of which is to enforce formal institutional norms and resolve cases of human tension and stress. This points to the fact that normative conflict, in reality, does not occur at the cultural level; rather it exists on the individual level between persons of differing cultural perspectives.[3]

Culture may also interact with the criminal justice system at the psychological level, although the degree of direct interaction does not reach the degree of importance it does at the social level. Moreover, cultural psychology manifests its interaction with the criminal justice system via the social level. It should be noted, however, that intracultural disparities of social conventions are largely influenced by differential norm interpretation at the psychological level (Anderson, 1976).

To summarize the general dynamics of culture one finds that culture has seven basic characteristics:

1. It is learned from observation of behavior.
2. It exists before and beyond one's lifespan.
3. It is acquired by individuals and manifested in their behavior.
4. It dictates social behavior of both the group and individuals although such dictation is generic rather than exclusive.
5. It includes rules or designs (norms) for obligatory, approved, permitted, disapproved, and forbidden actions.
6. It establishes relationships between individuals (status) and sets forth the rules of interaction of those relationships (roles).
7. It is never completely static and uniform (Williams, 1965; Feibleman, 1968; Kupferer, 1971; Kaplan and Manners, 1972).

This writer contends that presumptions about a given cultural group's relationship with a social institution (i.e., Hispanics and the criminal justice system) must be predicated upon a fundamental understanding of cultural variables. Thus, the following discussion of the Hispanic culture must be viewed in light of these general cultural precepts.

The Hispanic Culture

The Hispanic culture does not encompass a single group of people with completely homogeneous traits, norms, or characteristics. Hispanics, for the purpose of this study, are persons of Spanish ancestry or culture from the various Latin American countries, predominantly Cuba and Mexico, regardless of race (U.S. Bureau of Justice Statistics, 1981). This definition is based upon the characteristics of the dominant Hispanic population in Texas, which this study examined. Although country of ancestral origin varies, there are a significant number of cultural similarities which classify these groups into a single category. These similarities are discussed to develop a group Hispanic profile.

Interpersonal Relations.[4] There are numerous elements of the Hispanic culture which can provide important insight into the understanding of acculturated behavior. By examining these elements and projecting them into situations involving crime and justice, understanding may be developed regarding perceived disparities in the Hispanic relationship with the criminal justice system.

The first element of interpersonal relations is familial roles and norms. The Hispanic family continues to play a central role in the organizations of social relationships between group members. For example, Sundays and other nonworking days are usually devoted to visiting relatives, to the extent that social relations are largely subsumed under kinship relations. The nuclear family remains an important element among Hispanics.

The preservation of authority survives within the family structure as a central element in familial relationships. There is not the "equality" of the sexes as it is known in the dominant American culture. The male and female role are defined early in life and are marked with the father as the central figure of authority. The Hispanic wife is of secondary position to the husband, but as a mother she becomes the most important member of the family.

An interesting element in the Hispanic culture is generosity and the reciprocity of amenities. For example, the immediate proffering of food and drink is institutionalized among Hispanics. Similarly, spontaneous giving is a pervasive pattern among Hispanics in a manner closely akin to that of Oriental cultures. This spontaneity tends to become submerged in a system of fixed reciprocity.

The elements of interpersonal relations can provide important insight for the interpretation of Hispanic attitudes toward the criminal justice system. For example, the arrest of a Hispanic father may be seen as an attack on the authority figure which must be resisted in order for status to be maintained. Relationships alone, however, do not aptly describe the complete cultural profile of the Hispanic. Interpersonal relations are, in fact, interactive with the basic "cultural personality."

Cultural Personality of the Hispanic. There are at least four basic components of the Hispanic personality. The first may be designated as a "personalistic" sense of loyalty and obligation (Erlanger, 1979). The key element of this component is the emphasis placed on concrete personal relations to develop significant loyalties and obligations among friends and relations. These loyalties and obligations

> are identified with the self in a possessive and protective sense so that they constitute an integral part of the "front" the [Hispanic] presents to the world, so that their fate (their treatment by others, their general welfare) is bound up with that of the self and the "honor" [and] . . . pride [the Hispanic] feels compelled to protect. (Simmons, 1962:109–110)

Any attempt by an "outsider" (e.g., the criminal justice system) to share or dispel loyalties and obligations is interpreted as an attack upon the self, and hence, the honor of the individual. Should this occur, some form of reciprocation or perhaps defense of the honor must result.

A second personality component, which is indirectly related to the first, is extreme sensitivity to insult (Lampe, 1978). The failure to reciprocate for a gift or to recognize one's honor, obligations, and loyalties all point to personal insult for which forgiveness may never come.

The Hispanic adult (male and female), who was reared in a child-centered culture, will tend to have feelings of self-importance and will take himself or herself quite seriously (Miller, 1978). The indulgence and protectiveness one receives during childhood (and which often continues into early adulthood) has definite advantages; however, this behavioral norm does not develop a high resistance to later life situations in which the individual's favorable self-concept may be questioned by those who are not committed to feel indulgent or protective toward him or her (Miller, 1978). Similarly,

> the inflated sense of *machismo* (masculinity) . . . helps to build the feelings of self-importance and . . . is fostered by the favored position of the male. . . . [Machismo is] seldom challenged until the individual emerges from the environment dominated by the socializing agents and is confronted in non-cultural situations. (Simmons, 1962:114)

Insults directed by "outsiders" against one's family and friends are received as directed at the self and are deeply resented, as are insults directed against any other individual or thing which has been personalized (Erlanger, 1979). This sensitivity to insult can manifest itself in many ways related to crime and justice. For example, to be victimized is viewed as an insult to the person and the family. The personalistic nature of the insult and the disrespect for one's honor implicit in the victimization may well stimulate the individual to react on a personal basis (e.g., revenge) rather than to report the offense to the police and use the formal structure of the criminal justice system.

A third personality component may be labelled as submissiveness or passivity (Lampe, 1978). It should be noted, however, that although submissiveness is inherent in the Hispanic personality, there are important limitations to this trait since

aggression is manifest in certain types of situations (Simmons, 1962). Passivity refers to withdrawal as a reaction to various situations rather than a hostile impulse to strike back and hurt the offender in return. The Hispanic's refusal to acknowledge another party is a "returned insult." This form of submissiveness has a distinct meaning to other Hispanics. It is when the "returned insult" is not recognized (usually by non-Hispanics) that aggression or hostility becomes the reaction (Simmons, 1962).

In the case of the Hispanic male, *machismo* has been elevated to a degree of prominence, and is a need to "prove" one's masculinity. In such cases the individual's sense of honor is heightened and overt aggressive retaliation against the frustrative agent is not only expected but required if the individual is to maintain his honor and reputation (Erlanger, 1979).

The fourth personality component may be described as "immediate dominion." This refers to the Hispanic characteristic of being predominantly oriented to immediate situational factors by reacting in accordance to the situation's initial impact on the individual with minimal regard for the ultimate consequences of those actions (Simmons, 1962; Segade, 1978). The immediate dominion characteristic indicates the Hispanic's tendency to respond spontaneously to the stimuli of a situation in such a way as to maximize a dramatic effect; it does not mean the Hispanic is opportunistic or insincere in his or her efforts (Segade, 1978). To seize upon an opportunity to make a histrionic gesture and attempt to outdo another is inherent in this personality component.

These characteristics, which are not consistent with the dominant Anglo-American culture, can produce conflict on both the individual and systemwide level which leads to a dysfunctional relationship between Hispanics and the criminal justice system. In essence, criminal justice officials—who are generally members of the dominant social group—fall prey to many of the stereotypes associated with the Hispanic culture: (1) confusing lingual differences with lack of intelligence, (2) viewing passivity as laziness, (3) confusing the trait of immediate dominion with self-centeredness and/or un-truthfulness, (4) interpreting sensitivity to insult as being short-tempered, (5) viewing *machismo* as conceit, and (6) interpreting the maintenance of the cultural status quo as "un-American" (Lampe, 1978; Salcedo, 1955; Simmons, 1962; Erlanger, 1979).

Understanding the nature of Hispanic culture is fundamental to problem solving when conflict occurs between Hispanics and the criminal justice system. Moreover, if the criminal justice system is to be responsive to Hispanic problems and needs, that is, to "understand that there are many stress factors facing Hispanics in a strange culture" (Somers, 1982), there must be a point of reference from which one may intermix the formal institutions of crime control and justice with the attributes of Hispanic culture.

METHODOLOGY

Data for this project were collected through the use of rigid survey research methods. Care was taken in instrumentation, sampling, and analysis to maintain internal and external validity. Since the project was exploratory research the author employed conservative interpretations and analysis to strengthen reliability. Space limitations prohibit a detailed description of the methods employed; thus the following discussion provides an overview of research methods.

Instrumentation was developed through a series of item development and pretest stages. The questions were generated following a review of extant literature on general attitudinal research, cultural research, and criminal justice research on public opinion. Based on the literature review, questions were developed to collect the desired data in both a valid and reliable manner. After a careful review and revision of the pool of questions, the test items were placed in questionnaire form for pretesting.[5]

To enhance the instrument's validity, a purposive sample for the pretest was selected to include Hispanics of different educational backgrounds, ages, sex, and socioeconomic status. Preliminary analysis for validity and reliability was performed on each item and questions found to be ambiguous, unclear, or noninformational were eliminated or modified. A second purposive sample reviewed the amended instrument and refinement was made in both the survey questions and the organization of the questionnaire.

After the final survey format and questions were solidified a Spanish language version was prepared by an experienced Spanish linguist and designed to allow for cultural variations of the Spanish language as found in Texas. This version of the survey was also pretested among purposive samples in a method similar to the English version.

A random probability sample of 500 persons with Spanish surnames was drawn from the Texas Department of Public Safety's file on persons holding current driver's licenses and official identification cards in the state of Texas. The author recognizes the external validity issues involved in this sampling method; however, sufficient controls were employed to minimize threats to generalizability of the results. While the use of this sampling frame omits those persons who do not possess a driver's license, this number does not appear to be significant in relation to the total population.[6] Moreover, the combination of a high return rate (which is a product of rigid methodology and follow-up) and an extremely close resemblance of the respondents' demographic characteristics to the characteristics of the known Texas population permits generalization of the findings to the entire survey population. It must nonetheless be recognized that there is no absolute control to ensure that sample members are completely representative of the Texas Hispanic population. Generalizability has been assumed after reviewing all of the control factors.

The methodology involved five mailings to the sample. The first was an announcement postcard sent one week before the first survey instrument was mailed. The second mailing was the survey package, which included both the English and Spanish

220 DAVID L. CARTER

questionnaires, a preaddressed, postage-paid return envelope, a letter explaining the purpose and use of the requested information as well as guaranteeing confidentiality, and a pencil to use in completing the questionnaire. Two weeks after the survey package mailing a reminder postcard was sent to nonrespondents. After another two weeks a second complete survey package was mailed to nonrespondents, followed two weeks later with the final reminder postcard.

These procedures produced a total response rate of 71.2 percent ($N=356$) with a usable response rate of 62.4 percent ($N=312$). Of the 44 returns not used, 26 were returned for no forwarding address, 6 were received after the cut-off date, 5 respondents returned the instrument refusing to answer it, 4 members of the sample were deceased, and 3 returns were rejected due to inappropriate completion of the instrument.

Characteristics of the Respondents

The data show that the respondent attributes closely resemble those known attributes of Hispanics in Texas (LULAC, 1978). Further comparison of demographic characteristics to census data (U.S. Bureau of the Census, 1981) reinforce the assumption of a representative sample. Although the proportion of male respondents (67 percent) was slightly higher than that in the estimated Hispanic population, this difference is not significant. The modal age group was 41–50 with 56.8 percent representing the 31–60 group or middle age. The significant majority (71.2 percent) of respondents was married and 70.8 percent had children, with a mean of 2.8 children per family, which is slightly higher than the general population average.

In examining education, the results show that a mode of 24 percent of the respondents had a high school education or its equivalent, which is approximately 4.5 percent below the total Texas population education level. More significantly, the data indicated that 45.2 percent of the Hispanic sample possessed less than a high school education

compared to 19.5 percent of the total Texas population. The median family income of respondents was in the $12,000–12,999 range, which is at the borderline poverty level for a family of four.

Most (76.3 percent) responding sample members live in a house, with 78.3 percent residing in an urban area.

FINDINGS

Eleven hypotheses were tested in this study addressing attitudinal and behavioral variables of respondents in four generic subject areas: (1) perceptions of crime trends, (2) fear of crime, (3) respondent behavior related to crime, and (4) evaluation of the local police. Additionally, comparisons were made, when possible, to the National Crime Survey findings in the above four categories. It should be noted that inferential comparisons cannot be meaningfully made between the present study and the NCS (or other studies) because of inherent differences in data. As a result, comparisons are made on a descriptive and a priori basis.

As noted previously, there is a virtual void in the literature concerning Hispanic relationships with the criminal justice system. As a result, the author is compelled to give an overview of the findings from this study. Future works will focus in detail on selected findings of this project, notably in the areas of (1) Hispanic relationships with the police and (2) fear of crime.

Hypotheses Results and Related Data

The first hypothesis examined the influence of local police evaluation on the respondents' perception of increased neighborhood crime trends. The findings indicate that regardless of how proficient or "good" the Hispanic public perceives the police to be, this conceptual image will not significantly affect its perception of crime trends ($\chi^2=17.068$, $df=6$, $p<.001$, $V=.169$). Thus, the public image of the incidence of crime is independent of its police evaluation.

Next, perception of increased crime trends nationwide was measured as being influenced by criminal victimization. The data revealed that there was no dependence between these variables ($\chi^2=2.899$, $df=2$, $p<.001$, $V=.099$). However, the third hypothesis tested the influence of victimization on perceptions of neighborhood crime and produced significant results ($\chi^2=26.725$, $df=2$, $p<.001$, $V=.303$). Hence, the null hypothesis was rejected in that the perception of neighborhood crime trends is significantly dependent on whether or not one was a victim of a crime.

The fear of crime hypothesis tested the impact of sex and victimization as independent variables which affect fear. The findings show that sex and fear of crime are, in fact, dependent on each other ($\chi^2=18.258$, $df=2$, $p<.001$, $V=.245$). However, criminal victimization and fear of crime are independent ($\chi^2=6.498$, $df=1$, $p < .001$). This result is somewhat surprising in that one would intuitively assume that victimization would affect fear just as it affects crime trend perceptions at the neighborhood level. Nonetheless, the data do not bear this out. It is interesting to note that the findings of this hypothesis are consistent with those of the NCS.

The sixth hypothesis produced a finding which indirectly supports the victimization/fear result. When testing the dependence of respondents changing their behavior to avoid crime on the independent variable, victimization, these variables were found to be independent of each other ($\chi^2=7.919$, $df=1$, $p <.001$). Once again, this is contrary to what one would expect a priori; however, it does appear that victimization alone does not cause Hispanics in Texas to change their behavior in order to prevent future crime.

Further analysis on respondent behaviors did show significant levels of dependence. Perception of safety in one's neighborhood during the day ($\chi^2=56.461$, $df=3$ $p<.001$, $V=.431$), perception of neighborhood safety at night ($\chi^2=52.612$, $df=3$, $p <.001$, $V=.418$), and perception of neighborhood crime trends ($\chi^2= 14.862$, $df=2$, $p<.001$, $V=.224$) all produce a high level of depen-

dence with respondent behavior. Thus, the interesting inference from these hypotheses is that, although victimization does not cause a behavioral change, respondent perceptions of the probability of victimization will cause some form of behavioral change for the expressed purpose of preventing crime.

The final areas of hypothesis testing addressed respondent evaluation of the police. The results show that there is not a significant level of dependence between feeling safe in one's neighborhood at night (as the dependent variable) and evaluation of the local police ($\chi^2=13.415$, $df=9$, $p< .001$, $V=.121$) and the county sheriff ($\chi^2=20.788$, $df=9$, $p <.001$, $V=.152$) (as independent variables). Thus, one may conclude that the Hispanic public does not feel the police, regardless of how "good" they are perceived to be, are able to significantly affect criminal incidence. Perhaps one of the more surprising elements of these hypotheses was that the evaluation of the county sheriff produced a higher level of interaction with the dependent variable than did the local police evaluation.

It should be recognized that the results of hypothesis testing for the present study are best viewed as pointing to potential relations between Hispanics and the criminal justice system. Without previous research to serve as a comparative standard, it must be assumed that the present findings are externally valid, at least until further investigations are accomplished.

Selected Data Comparisons to Other Research

Several salient areas of investigation by the NCS were addressed by the present study to compare Hispanic responses with those of the general public. (See Table 1 for a summary of these selected variable comparisons.) These comparisons are predominantly descriptive and, because of basic methodological differences, should not be viewed as conclusive. Nonetheless, the findings represent some interesting observations concerning the relationship of Hispanics with crime and justice.

222   DAVID L. CARTER

TABLE 1

SELECTED COMPARISONS OF RESEARCH RESULTS

	NCS* %	Present Study (Hispanics) %
Victim-Perceived Increase in Neighborhood Crime	49.0	79.0
Feeling of Safety in Neighbor- hood during Day	53.0	42.6
Feeling of Safety in Neighbor- hood during Night	18.0	12.0
Belief That People in General Have Changed Activities to Avoid Victimization	82.0	76.6
Belief That People in Neighbor- hood Have Changed Activities to Avoid Victimization	56.0	62.5
Respondent Has Changed Activity to Avoid Victimization	48.8	58.0
Victims Rating Police as Good	40.0	19.2

*(LEAA, 1979)

With respect to crime trends the NCS found no significant response variations regarding perceived crime rates when examined on demographic variables (Garofalo, 1977). The findings of the present study are consistent with NCS in this regard. When examining the perception of increased neighborhood crime dichotomized on victims/nonvictims, the NCS found that 49 percent of the victims perceived a crime increase, while the present study found 72 percent of the Hispanic victims perceived an increase in neighborhood crime.

On the variable of fear of crime both studies found that people in general feel less threatened by crime when they are close to home than when they are in another neighborhood. When viewing safety as a variable, 53 percent of the NCS sample and 42.6 percent of the Hispanic sample felt very safe being out alone in their neighborhood during the day, and 18 percent and 12 percent,

respectively, felt very safe being out alone in their neighborhood at night. Although statistical significance cannot be stated, an observation of the data permits one to conclude that Hispanics feel somewhat less safe from crime than does the general public.

Eighty-two percent of the NCS respondents and 76.6 percent of the Hispanics expressed the belief that people in general have changed their activity to avoid victimization. Further examination of the behavioral variables found that 56 percent of the NCS respondents believed that people in their neighborhood had changed their activity because of crime.

When asked if the respondents had personally changed their activity to avoid crime, 51.2 percent of the NCS respondents answered no; however, only 42 percent of the Hispanic respondents answered no. This finding suggests that a significant difference

66

TABLE 2

PERCEPTIONS OF FAIRNESS OF CRIMINAL TRIALS

	N	%	Cumulative Percentage
Very Fair	48	15.4	15.4
Generally Fair	166	53.2	68.6
Somewhat Unfair	54	17.3	85.9
Very Unfair	13	4.2	90.1
No Response	31	9.9	100.0

between the populations may exist and warrant further investigation. Further examination of this variable showed that 49 percent of the NCS and 76.4 percent of the Hispanic victims compared to 44 percent and 55.1 percent of the respective nonvictims who had changed their activity. Once again, the differences appear to be significant and should be studied in future research. In general, the findings on respondent behavioral changes support the conclusion that Hispanics feel less safe than the general population.

NCS evaluations of the police found that 54 percent of the white[7] respondents evaluated the local police as good while 25 percent of the black NCS respondents evaluated the police as good (LEAA, 1979). The present study found that 27.6 percent of the Hispanics gave the police a good evaluation, which appears to produce another difference worthy of further study. The NCS also found that 40 percent of the victims rated the police as good compared to 19.2 percent of the Hispanic victims. Once again, a researchable difference appears to exist.

No directly comparable findings on perceptions of the courts can be stated; however, one may generalize those results which have been examined and infer that Hispanics feel that the criminal courts are generally fair (see Table 2).

Some comparisons can be made between the study by Teske and Powell (1978) and the present study on the perceptions of corrections. Both studies found that 34

percent of the respondents believed that the main purpose of prisons was punishment. However, another 34 percent of Teske and Powell's respondents perceived the main purpose of prison as rehabilitation compared to 12.8 percent of the Hispanic respondents. With respect to probation and parole, Teske and Powell found that 13 percent approved of probation for serious crimes and 46 percent approved of parole for those convicted of serious offenses. This is compared to 7.7 percent and 17 percent of the Hispanic respondents on the same question, respectively. Some significant differences appear to exist which require further examination.

This comparative analysis has permitted some preliminary conclusions in areas collateral to the primary focus of investigation. Moreover, important areas of apparent significant difference have been identified and recommendations made for future study. The reader should note that any differences found in the comparison of studies may be influenced by time and other threats to validity and may not be exclusively attributable to attitudinal differences.

Examination of Projected Collateral Results

Based upon suspected cultural influences, some findings which were not specific to the hypotheses but were of interest were projected. First, it was projected that the ethnocentric nature of the Hispanic culture would lead respondents to perceive that

TABLE 3

RESPONDENTS' PERCEPTIONS (EVALUATIONS) OF LAW ENFORCEMENT

Factors*	Local Police %	County Sheriff %	Department of Public Safety %
More Police Officers Are Needed	46.5	33.0	33.0
More Money Needed for Police Equipment	23.1	18.3	16.3
Patrol and Investigate More	55.8	40.7	26.3
Improve Response Time	42.6	29.2	19.9
Improve Training	34.9	30.4	17.3
Be More Courteous	37.2	30.4	21.8
Keep Politics out of the Job	29.8	30.8	19.2
Don't Discriminate	38.8	28.8	28.2
More Traffic Control	22.1	16.7	19.6
Better Allocation of Officers	51.0	30.4	33.3
Officers Need College Education	17.6	15.1	9.6

*Factor categories listed in this table are abbreviated. In the questionnaire the categories were worded for easy understanding by the layman.

most crime in their neighborhood was committed by outsiders. This appears to be marginally true, although closer examination of the variables must be made for conclusive results to be identified.

With respect to fear of crime, it was projected that Hispanics would be overall more fearful of criminal victimization as an artifact of the deterioration of social relationships, with Hispanic males being less fearful because of the impact of *machismo*. The data show, based on analysis of the safety variables, that Hispanics are, in fact, more fearful of victimization than the general public. However, a surprising result is that males expressed a fear of crime twice as frequently as females (66.3 percent versus 33.7 percent). There is no readily apparent explanation of this finding.

The next expectation was that Hispanics living in urban areas at their present address for less than two years would view their neighborhood as unsafe as a product of unfamiliarity and a breakdown in cultural continuity. It appears that this is not the case, with 62 percent of this group expressing a feeling of safety. It was further projected that (1) Hispanics would perceive

TABLE 4

RESPONDENTS' ATTITUDES TOWARD CORRECTIONS

	Yes		No		No Response	
	N	%	N	%	N	%
Favor Probation* for Serious* Offenses	24	7.7	274	87.4	14	4.5
Favor Probation for Nonserious* Offenses	215	68.9	81	26.0	16	5.1
Favor Parole* for Serious Offenses	53	17.0	242	77.6	17	5.4
Favor Parole for Nonserious Offenses	230	73.7	67	21.5	15	4.8
Feel Prison Rehabilitates*	84	26.9	199	63.8	29	9.3

*Terms were operationally defined for respondents.

a crime rate increase consistent with that of the general public and (2) the respondents' overall evaluation of the police at all levels would be generally favorable based upon the Hispanic respect for authority. However, in contrast to NCS data, Hispanics rate the police relatively lower than does the entire white population.

An expectation in the area of behavioral change was that older respondents would exhibit little change in behavior to prevent crimes based upon cultural values of authority and respect. Cross-tabulations on age and activity change yield no clear result. A relationship between activity and age may exist but is not statistically significant in the present data.

The Hispanic culture shows a strong respect for education, a high level of involvement in political affairs, and a sensitivity to discrimination. This led to the projection that these areas would be identified by respondents as being of the greatest importance for local police improvement. Although each variable showed a relatively strong response, the greatest improvement needs for local police were identified as (1) the desire for police to patrol and investigate more and (2) the desire for a better allocation of police personnel. The inference from this finding is that Hispanics feel they receive inadequate protection from the police. This is supported by the fact that of

those respondents indicating a fear of crime, 98.8 percent cited inadequate police protection as a primary reason. (Table 3 specifies the percentage of respondents indicating improvement areas for local police, county sheriffs, and the Department of Public Safety.[8])

Finally, the researcher projected that Hispanics would possess a generally conservative (or punitive) attitude toward corrections because of the authoritarian influence, a strong sense of "rightness," and the Napoleonic nature of arbitration found in Hispanic relationships. Previous discussions of corrections in this article appear to affirm this expectation. (Tables 4 and 5 provide summary data results on corrections related variables.)

SUMMARY

In developing this study the researcher conducted an extensive literature review and found that virtually no empirical research had examined the relationship of Hispanics with the criminal justice system. Thus, the present study was inherently exploratory, requiring an investigation of cultural variables as they may be related to critical variables of crime and justice. As a result, it was just as important to identify true issues as it was to explain relationships

TABLE 5

WHAT DO YOU FEEL IS THE MAIN PURPOSE OF PRISON?

	N	Male %	Female %	Total %	Cumulative Percentage
Punish	106	26.0	8.0	34.0	34.0
Rehabilitate*	40	9.0	3.8	12.8	46.8
Incapacitate*	134	26.5	16.4	42.9	89.7
Other	22	4.8	2.3	7.1	96.8
No Response	10	2.1	1.1	3.2	100.0

*Terms were operationally defined for respondents.

between variables. To understand any problem one must have a genesis; this is the nature of exploratory research.

In general, the findings indicate that attitudinal and behavioral differences concerning criminal justice do exist between (1) Hispanics and the general population and (2) Hispanics and other ethnic minorities. It appears that these differences are based in cultural variables which become compounded when minority group members become socialized in the dominant society. The practical impact of these phenomena, although not totally clear, indicates that there are significant problems within the administration of justice involving Hispanics which could be remedied through cultural understanding and adjustment. The findings further indicate that applying cultural values of other groups to the Hispanic population will result in increased conflict and a deterioration of the Hispanic perception of equity in justice administration.

ACKNOWLEDGMENTS

This research project was funded by a grant from the Pan American University Faculty Research Council.

NOTES

[1] This is based on traditional library research, a computer search of the Bibliographic Reference Service files (which includes Books in Print, Dissertation Abstracts, ERIC, Psychological Abstracts, and the Social Science Citation Index) and seven key word searches of the NCJRS data base. Using these sources, in excess of 1.6 million interdisciplinary documents were searched with only seven sources identified as being related to Hispanics and the criminal justice system.

[2] Two collateral points are worthy of note at this point: (1) Differential operational procedures (of a formal nature) in criminal justice may bring to issue legal questions of equal protection. Thus, the author is maintaining that responses to cultural differences must actually be performed on an individual basis as a product of inculcated training on cultural dynamics. (2) The criminal justice system already performs differential responses—informally—based on social characteristics. For example, it is likely that the lower socioeconomic group public inebriate will be arrested while his middle- or upper-class counterpart will be taken home.

[3] This is not to infer that intracultural conflict is nonexistent. The present discussion is solely concerned with intercultural conflict as a basic element of disparity between various social groups and the criminal justice system.

[4] The material in this section is extrapolated from a variety of sources (Schoen, 1978; Simmons, 1962; Lampe, 1978).

[5] Limited copies of the copyrighted questionnaire are available for inspection on request.

[6] Not only was the driver's license file the best available statewide sampling frame, but the file parameters are also a strong indicator of reliability. According to the Department of Public Safety, the files have in excess of 10.5 million subjects which represents approximately 94 percent of all Texas residents over age 15 who are eligible to possess a driver's license or state identification card.

[7] The reader should note that the NCS classified all Hispanic sample members as "white" rather than in the "black and other" ethnic category.

[8] As can be seen from the overall data on the police, these findings appear to have significant implications. A second article is in preparation examining the findings of this project as specifically related to law enforcement.

REFERENCES

Anderson, R. (1976). *The cultural context: An introduction to cultural anthropology.* Minneapolis: Burgess Publishing Company.

Bonilla, R. (1980). Public Address by National President, League of United Latin American Citizens, Pan American University.

Erlanger, H. S. (1979). Estrangement, machismo, and gang violence. *Soc. Sci. Q.* 60 (September): 235–248.

Feibleman, J. (1968). *The theory of human culture.* New York: Humanities Press.

Garofalo, J. (1977). *Public opinion about crime.* Washington, DC: National Criminal Justice Information and Statistics Service.

Hiebert, P.G. (1976). *Cultural anthropology.* Philadelphia: Lippincott.

Kaplan, D., and Manners, R. A. (1972). *Culture theory.* Englewood Cliffs, NJ: Prentice-Hall.

Keesing, R. M. (1976). *Cultural anthropology: A contemporary perspective.* New York: Holt, Rinehart, and Winston.

Kupferer, H. J. (1971). *Culture, society and guidance.* Boston: Houghton Mifflin.

Lampe, P. E. (1978). Ethnic self-referent and the assimilation of Mexican Americans. *Intl. J. of Comp. Sociol.* 19 (December): 259–270.

Law Enforcement Assistance Administration (LEAA) (1979). *The police and public opinion.* Washington, DC: National Criminal Justice Information and Statistics Service.

League of United Latin American Citizens (LULAC) (1978). *A description of Latin Americans in the United States.* Mimeo.

Miller, M. (1978). Variations in Mexican American family life. *Aztlan* 9: 209–231.

Salcedo, C. (1955). *Mexican-American socio-cultural patterns: Implications for social casework.* M.A. thesis, University of Southern California—Los Angeles.

Schoen, R. (1978). Toward a theory of the demographic implications of ethnic stratification. *Soc. Sci. Q.* 59 (December): 468–481.

Segade, G. V. (1978). Identity and power: An essay on the politics of culture and the culture of politics in Chicano thought. *Aztlan* 9: 85–100.

Simmons, O. (1962). *Anglo-Americans and Mexican-Americans in south Texas.* New York: Arno Press.

Sommers, A. (1982). Improving human relations between the Hispanic community and law enforcement. *Police Chief* 69 (March): 32–33.

Teske, R. H. C., and Powell, N. (1978). *Texas Crime Poll—1978.* Huntsville, TX: Texas Criminal Justice Center.

U.S. Bureau of the Census. (1981). *Statistical abstract of the United States.* Washington, DC: U.S. Department of Commerce.

U.S. Bureau of Justice Statistics (BJS). (1981). *The Hispanic victim.* Washington, DC: U.S. Government Printing Office.

Williams, R. M. (1965). *American society: A sociological interpretation,* 2nd ed. New York: Alfred A. Knopf.

Wright, G. N., and Phillips, L. D. (1979). Cross cultural differences in the assessment and communication of uncertainty. *Cultural Anthropology* 20 (December): 845–846.

Journal of Criminal Justice, Vol. 13, pp.487-500 (1985)
Pergamon Press. Printed in U.S.A.

HISPANIC PERCEPTION OF POLICE PERFORMANCE: AN EMPIRICAL ASSESSMENT

DAVID L. CARTER

School of Criminal Justice
Michigan State University
East Lansing, Michigan 48824

ABSTRACT

This exploratory study examines relationships between the police and Hispanics in Texas. Specifically, data were collected on Hispanic evaluations of police performance, expectations of police performance, and overall satisfaction with the police. A sample of 500 Hispanics throughout the state of Texas were surveyed on their experienced and perceived relationships with three levels of police agencies: local (municipal) police, sheriff's officers, and the state's Department of Public Safety. Findings are reported based upon overall ratings of the police, victim-related data, and data from individuals who had any form of contact with the police. Significant findings show that any form of contact with the police appeared to lower the rating of police performance. This appears to be a product of the interaction between high public expectations and qualitatively poor police performance. Further findings indicate that an increase in the fear of crime among Hispanics lowered evaluations of local police. Similarly, victimization lowered the evaluation of local police, the county sheriff, and the Department of Public Safety. Hispanics also perceived that officers have a "bad attitude," that the police need to patrol and investigate more, that response time should be improved, and that there should be less discrimination against Hispanics. These findings appear to be largely influenced by ineffective communication (both symbolic and linguistic) and cultural conflict.

INTRODUCTION

Police relationships with minority groups have become a controversial enigma characterized by accusations, on the part of both law enforcement officers and the public, of misfeasance. Minority groups have complained that the police provide them with inadequate protection and service, expose them to harrassment and verbal abuse, and treat them in a different manner from other groups. Minorities have also claimed that they are more likely to be physically abused by the police than are members of the dominant society (Radelet, 1980). Conversely, the police tend to believe that minority groups target law enforcement personnel as a readily available symbol of "oppression by a white power structure" (Joyner, 1977:112). Thus the police feel they are often accused of prejudicial and discriminatory actions that should more appropriately be directed toward other elements of government.

Since 1961 the United States Commission on Civil Rights has explored police-minority relations extensively in multiple investigations. The Commission's findings show various forms of discrimination against minorities, ranging from disproportionately low levels of minority employment in police departments to slower police response times in minority areas and inadequate police services in minority neighborhoods (U.S. Commission, 1981).[1] In its report *Equal Protection in the South* (1965), the Commission found that officers used the power of their office to harrass minority group members no matter what the provocation. In the 1967 report *A Time to Listen . . . A Time to Act*, this finding was followed by the observation that minorities feel the police do not treat minority group members as human beings entitled to respect and dignity. This point, as well as the direct inference of discrimination, was clearly made by the Commission when it stated

> . . . a common belief [in minority areas] is that police officers regard their role as one of protecting the white population from the residents of the slum . . . a zoo keeper attitude is maintained toward the residents of the community. (U.S. Commission, 1967:24)

In its report *Justice,* the Commission discussed the issue of prejudice and proposed that "a policeman who 'hates' a particular minority group has a built-in motive for treating its members with special severity" (1961:84). This sentiment was expressed again, with specific reference to Hispanics, when the Commission stated:

Mexican-American citizens are subject to unduly harsh treatment by our law enforcement officers . . . they are often arrested on insufficient grounds, receive physical and verbal abuse, and [receive] penalties which are disproportionately severe. (1970:1)

The validity of this assertion may be questioned in light of the recent study by Petersilia (1983). She found that blacks and Hispanics were given longer sentences, and were incarcerated longer, than whites mainly as a result of the information judges and

parole officers use in determining sentences and release eligibility rather than because of a conscious prejudice against minorities. Furthermore, Petersilia's study found, through comparisons of the arrest, prosecution, and conviction processes, that the criminal justice system treated different racial and ethnic groups similarly. These findings are significant in light of related research in the area as well as the Commission's investigations.

Throughout various hearings, investigations, and reports, the underlying theme of the Civil Rights Commission's findings is that the police have not learned enough about minority group culture. Both the attitudes and the behavior of the police are based on stereotyped perceptions of minorities that are reflected in minority-group members' similarly distorted perceptions of the police. The existence of discrimination and distrust on the part of police and minority groups towards each other can have far-reaching effects: "A single occurrence or a perceived pattern of discrimination or unjustified use of force can have a powerful, deleterious effect on [police-community relationships]" (U.S. Commission, 1981:v).

THE PROBLEM

As a result of the apparent alienation between the police and minorities characterized in the Civil Rights Commission's findings, this study examined empirically one specific minority group's attitudes toward, and relationships with, the police. Hispanics were selected as the group to be studied because of the relative paucity of information on their relations with law enforcement. Moreover, given the increased dominance of Hispanics as a political force and the higher visibility of Hispanics in our society, the results of this study could serve as baseline data for future comparative research.

Mandel (1979) noted that Hispanics and Hispanic culture have been neglected by the criminal justice system. Not only have Hispanics been largely ignored by criminal justice research; official statistics rarely report data that is specifically stratified in terms of Hispanic ethnicity. The rationale for not distinguishing Hispanics from the dominant population is that Hispanics are not a separate race. Nonetheless, one must recognize that the ethnic characteristics embodied in language, name, culture, and appearance create the same minority group dynamics found in racial distinction. The importance of understanding police-Hispanic relations is to reduce the barriers imposed by culture and language while concomitantly increasing responsiveness and service delivery by the police (Sommers, 1982). Overcoming these barriers by establishing open lines of communication and cultural awareness can have, as found in Houston, a positive effect on police service delivery in the Hispanic community (Quintanilla, 1983).

The current study is largely exploratory; therefore, an important aspect of the research was to identify problems in Hispanic-police relations. While some variables were selected intuitively for testing, others were a result of extending Hispanic cultural dynamics that might conflict with police officer norms. A significant element of this study was to understand culture and its role in interpersonal relationships.

A previous article (Carter, 1983) provided a detailed discussion of culture, with specific attention to Hispanic cultural characteristics. To avoid reiteration, suffice it to note that expectations of formal institutional productivity (such as police performance) by the Hispanic public are based in cultural norms. Since institutional norms are typically consistent with those of the dominant society, they thereby conflict with Hispanic expectations.

This article explores the cultural expectations of Hispanics that are related to the police in order to determine points of conflict (or, at least, perceived conflict). It is maintained that what conflict exists is a product of (1) conflicting role definitions and (2) different expectations, as defined by cultural determinants. If this premise is

true, then problems in police-Hispanic relations may be largely contained through awareness/informational strategies rather than through operational changes.

Because of this study's exploratory nature, comparisons, per se, to previous research cannot be made. The focus here is on previous research on the attitudes of the dominant population toward the police, thus enabling the identification of distinctions between the dominant group and Hispanics.

LITERATURE REVIEW

The President's Commission on Law Enforcement and Administration of Justice (1967) stated that a lack of public confidence in law enforcement agencies tends to interfere with recruiting, diminishes the enthusiasm of officers about doing their job well, and may lead officers to leave police work. Further, if the public's evaluation of the police is low, not only police attitudes and values are affected, but also citizen cooperation throughout the criminal justice process.

Most members of the public have little contact with the courts or with correctional agencies. However, the public's relationship with the police is somewhat different. Of all criminal justice agencies, the public has the most frequent contact with the police. The reasons for this are that the police are the most widely dispersed, most readily accessible, and most visible agents of the criminal justice system. Additionally, portrayals of the police on television and in motion pictures in the past decade have not only heightened awareness of the police service, but also shaped public opinion (Schaefer, Vanderlook, and Wisnoski, 1979).

Public attitudes toward the police are further shaped and

> . . . complicated by unrealistic expectations of what the police can do. Each citizen expects the police to meet many goals, according to his or her own value system and understanding of what the police can and should do. (Couper, 1983:4)

Since value systems are strongly influenced by cultural determinants, expectations of police behavior may be significantly more diverse for Hispanics—or any other culturally distinct group—than the police, who predominately consist of, and are administered by, members of the dominant society, anticipate.

Overall, most research shows that people rate the police rather highly, even though they believe there may be room for improvement (cf., Carter, 1983; Teske et al., 1982; Figgie Report, 1980; Scaglion and Condon, 1980; Schaefer, Vanderlook, and Wisnoski, 1979; Peek, Alston, and Lowe, 1978; Munn and Renner, 1978; Garofalo, 1977; LEAA, 1977). For example, the National Crime Survey (NCS) data of the Impact Cities Program found that 82 percent of the respondents believed the police were doing either a good or an average job (Parisi et al., 1979). Similarly, the Figgie Report (1980) indicated that 84 percent of the American public had a high confidence in the police. White and Menke (1982) also found that the police had a positive community image with a significant number of people, who indicated that they felt the police were honest and competent.

Findings such as these are cited in the literature quite frequently. However, closer examination of the issue, based upon the impact of intervening variables, is warranted. Both the Figgie Report and NCS findings show that significant differences exist between racial groups in terms of their evaluations of police performance. According to the NCS, the proportion of whites who evaluated police performance as good was more than twice the proportion of blacks who did so (54 percent versus 25 percent—see Parisi et al., 1979). Although the results are not as dramatic, a Harris Survey found that 65 percent of white respondents rated police performance as positive, compared to 52 percent of the black respondents (Flanagan and McLeod, 1983). This is significant in light of Decker's (1981:85) finding that "the variable of race should be underscored . . . because it has been determined to be the most important

variable [affecting attitudes toward the police]." Schuman and Gruenberg (1972) expanded on this idea by observing that the interaction between race and neighborhood is important in explaining public attitudes. This is supported by Jacob (1971), who found that the "neighborhood culture" significantly influenced evaluations of the police. Walker et al. (1972) add another element to this phenomenon by proposing that the nature of police contacts, especially frequent involuntary contacts between blacks and the police, tends to lower satisfaction with police performance.

Mirande (1981) discovered that Mexican-Americans actually feared the police; this is an interesting finding, considering a study by Carte (1973:200) that indicated respondents "wished the police [would] conform more closely to middle-class standards of education and appearance." Would Hispanics prefer the police to be "more middle class," and would this reduce their fear of the police? If so, this may be an indicator of assimilation. Carte's results may look different, however, if a stratified racial population is examined. Peek, Alston, and Lowe (1978) reinforce the position of this study by stating that contradictory findings may be the consequence of sampling different publics. This does not mean that the findings are "inaccurate"; rather, it points to the necessity of conducting research on various groups.

A study by Parks (1976) found that for citizens who evaluated the police negatively, dissatisfaction with police response time was a primary variable in their overall dissatisfaction. Similarly, the Kansas City Police Department's Response Time Analysis Study (1977) identified two variables relating citizen satisfaction to police response time. The first variable was the amount of time between the discovery of the crime/incident and the reporting of the offense to the police by the victim. The Kansas City study found evidence that victims began expecting the police to arrive after they had decided to call the police but before the actual call was made. The impact of this tendency on public expectations of response time appears to be negative as well as largely uncontrollable.

The second variable was public perception of elapsed time. According to the Kansas City response-time data, in most cases the person who called the police perceived the response time to be longer than it actually was. This phenomenon was particularly evident in high-tension situations and/or when the incident was a personal crime. The effect of the above two variables is compounded because they are completely beyond the control of the police. Concerning racial variables, although, overall, whites were more satisfied with the police than were "blacks and others," white respondents were more strongly influenced by response time than were black respondents. Hispanics have indicated that they receive inadequate police protection and poor response to calls (Mirande, 1981). Thus the influence of response time on Hispanic attitudes toward the police must be examined.

Examining citizen evaluations of the police using the generic variables of victims/ nonvictims, the NCS found that nonvictims were only slightly more likely than victims to view the police as doing a good job (46 percent versus 40 percent) and were less likely to rate police performance as poor (10 percent versus 16 percent) (LEAA, 1979; 1977). Closer examination of victims who have suffered face-to-face confrontations with offenders tends to reveal more critical attitudes about police performance (Parisi et al., 1979; Garofalo, 1977; LEAA, 1977). In a related vein, however, Mirande (1981) found that the fear of crime among Hispanics led to increased support for police power. Perhaps this is, in part, a product of the fact that, proportionally, Hispanics are more frequently the victims of personal crimes than is the general population (Bureau of Justice Statistics, 1981).

Parks (1976) found that victims' satisfaction with police perfomance could be enhanced if the police officer took some form of action at the scene of the crime:

The findings indicate a *marked* increase in satisfaction when the police take some positive actions. Filling out a report results in satisfaction for 80 percent of the respondents. Further actions, such as questioning a suspect, checking the premises, and recovering stolen property [where relevant] result in even higher percentages of satisfied respondents. (1976:315)

Indirectly related to this need for action, Scaglion and Condon (1980) found that respondents who had spoken with police officers in an informal, but official, way (such as asking for directions or information) reported having satisfactory contacts and tended to have a better opinion of police than those not having such contacts. Interestingly, those individuals who had friends or relatives who were police officers were *not* inclined to be less critical of police than those who did not have such connections with the police (Scaglion and Condon, 1980). Scaglion and Condon found, thus, that citizen evaluation of the police appears to be most affected by actual contact with a uniformed officer in an official or semi-official capacity.

In addition to improving response time and taking some form of action in response to a victimization, other recommendations for improvement of the police service have been consistently identified. Carte (1973), Chackerian (1974), and Munn and Renner (1978) all found public recommendations for improvements such as detachment from politics, better police training, better use of technology, better management, increased educational standards, and a desire for the police to be more representative of the communities they serve. Findings have also indicated that segments of the community, which are delineated almost exclusively on racial lines, believe that the police must end discrimination against minorities if any improvements are to be realized. A 1977 Louis Harris poll (Parisi et al., 1979) found 67 percent of the blacks surveyed felt that blacks were discriminated against by the police. Similarly, Morales (1972) found that over half of his Mexican-American respondents believed that discriminatory police practices occurred in their neighborhoods. A closer examination of this issue by the

NCS indicated that respondents in the middle-income ranges were most likely to view the police as discriminatory, whereas respondents in the lowest and highest income levels tended to give the police a more favorable rating (Parisi et al., 1979; Garofalo, 1977). Interestingly, however, another study found that police did not feel they discriminated in their working decisions (Carter, 1984). Rather, they expressed the belief that officers generally made a concerted, conscious effort to avoid even the appearance of discrimination.

Staples (1972) maintains that the black attitude toward the police is based upon the "racist fabric of white America which has denied blacks a basic humanity . . . and equal justice under the law." It is asserted in this article that the empirical evidence does not support this position, in that the evidence fails to explain the relatively favorable attitudes toward the police by low- and high-income blacks. Rather, an alternate view, presented by Chackerian (1974), may more accurately explain the parameters of both black attitudes and general public evaluations of the police:

> The public's evaluation of the police [may] be explained in terms of the public's very general sentiments about government. . . . Evaluation of law enforcement may less reflect a specific determination of enforcement effectiveness and equity than a very diffuse sense of access to government. The feeling that government is remote and that officials are corrupt may be more important for one's evaluation of the police than the crime rate, arrest rate, or police observance of due process. (1974:142)

Munn and Renner (1978), noting the problems of measuring citizen evaluation of the police, suggested that such evaluations should be made on three levels. The first level is *public differentiation,* which refers to the possibility that different segments of society may evaluate the police in different ways. It is reasonable to assume that if there are extensive differences between identifiable groups within the public, such groups' perceptions and evaluations of the police will differ. The second level is the *nature of*

the differences between the views of various segments of the public. Because the police role covers a wide range of activities, it may be necessary to differentiate between various aspects of the police role. In this regard, Roberg (1976) observes that the police provide service to different publics; therefore, perceptions of "what the police do" vary greatly.[2] The third level deals with whether negative public evaluations of the police reflect differences in *beliefs about actual police roles* or whether these criticisms are emotional in nature, arising out of individuals' reactions to contact with the regulatory power of the police, as suggested by Brooks and Friedrich (1970). Munn and Renner (1978) contend that this difference is important, in that (1) negative evaluations interact with the role itself and with the performance of the role and (2) the negative evaluation is a result of the police fulfilling negative public expectations. On a related point, Whitaker et al. (1982) found that the public's expectations of the police included, specifically, freedom from fear of crime, more police presence, and civility in police behavior. While the latter two points are reasonably attainable, the abolition of public fear of crime is probably unrealistic.

The literature indicates, as one might expect, that ethnic identification produces different attitudes on various issues. For example, Bell (1983) suggests that the police and the public have distinct forms of prejudice that are affected by social distance, friendliness, and dissimilarity. These variables are substantially influenced by cultural determinants. The paucity of available research on Hispanic attitudes toward the police points to a significant void in the existing literature that must be filled if comprehensive understanding of public attitudes toward the police is to be achieved.

One contention of the present study is that both cultural norms and institutions may predicate attitudes and behavior in all forms of social interaction, including interaction involving crime and justice. The parameters of Hispanic culture, it is argued, significantly influence attitudinal variables and, consequently, interpersonal relationships.

METHODOLOGY

This study employed survey research methods, using a random probability sample of 500 Hispanic Texas residents. While it would have been desirable to collect data from a nonHispanic control group for comparison, this was not possible, given the parameters of the project's grant. Moreover, in order to ensure a representative sample of Hispanics in Texas, it was essential to focus on a large, exclusively Hispanic N-size, due to the nonproportional geographic distribution of Hispanics throughout the state. The sampling method used here ensured proportional Hispanic representation by geographic region. This is an important factor, in that Hispanic attitudes vary with respect to the cultural norms of the geographic location in the state (Carter, 1983).

The questions developed for the survey instrument were generated and validated through an evaluation of attitudinal and cultural research and through review of the extant literature. The questions were carefully reviewed and then selected for use in pretesting the survey instrument. A purposive sample for the pretest was selected; it included Hispanics differing in educational background, age, sex, and socioeconomic status. A preliminary analysis for validity and reliability was performed on each item, and questions found to be ambiguous, unclear, or noninformational were eliminated or modified. A second purposive sample reviewed the amended instrument, and both the survey questions and the organization of the questionnaire were refined.

After the final survey format and questions were solidified, a Spanish-language version was prepared by an experienced linguist. This version was designed to allow for both geographical and cultural variations in the Spanish spoken in Texas. This version of the survey was also pretested among purposive samples, using the same procedures employed in validating the English version.

A systematic random sample of 500 persons with predefined Spanish surnames was drawn from the Department of Public Safety's computerized file of people holding current driver's licenses in the state of Texas. While use of the driver's license file as a sampling frame omits individuals who are not licensed drivers, the procedure does provide a reliable method of acquiring a true random sample of Texas adults. The combination of a high return rate and a comparison of the respondents' demographic characteristics with the known characteristics of the state's population permitted generalization of the findings to the entire survey population of Hispanics in Texas.

The survey methods employed here involved five mailouts to the sample. The first was a pre-announcement postcard sent one week before the first survey instrument was mailed. The second mailout was the survey package, which included a copy of both the English and Spanish questionnaires, a pre-addressed, post-paid, return envelope, a letter that explained the purpose of the survey and the use to which the requested information would be put and that guaranteed anonymity, and a pencil for use in completing the questionnaire. Two weeks after the survey package was mailed, a reminder postcard was sent to nonrespondents. After another two weeks a second survey package was mailed to nonrespondents, which was followed two weeks later with the final postcard.

Through the use of these procedures, a total response rate of 71.2 percent ($N = 356$) was attained, with a usable response rate of 62.4 percent ($N = 312$). Of the 44 returns not used, 26 were returned due to no forwarding address, 6 were received after the cut-off date, 5 respondents returned the instrument but refused to complete it, 4 members of the sample were deceased, and 3 returns were rejected by the researcher due to inappropriate completion of the instrument.

Characteristics of the Respondents

The data show that respondent attributes relate very closely to the known attributes of Hispanics in Texas (League of United Latin

American Citizens, 1978). Although the proportion of male respondents (67.6 percent) was slightly higher than that in the estimated Hispanic population, this difference is not significant. The modal age group was 41–50, with 56.8 percent representing the 31–60, or middle-aged, group. The significant majority (71.2 percent) of the respondents were married, and 70.8 percent had children, with a mean of 2.8 children per family (slightly higher than the general population average).

In terms of education, the results show that a mode of 24 percent of the respondents had a high school education or its equivalent, which is approximately 4.5 percent below the total Texas population. More significantly, the data indicate that 45.2 percent of the Hispanic sample possessed less than a high school education, compared to 19.5 percent of the total Texas population. The median family income of respondents was in the $12,000–12,999 range, which is at the borderline poverty level for a family of four.

The majority (76.3 percent) of responding sample members lived in a house, with 78.3 percent residing in an urban area.

RESULTS

The data analysis, employing both descriptive and inferential statistics, produced a variety of interesting findings. Although not all correlations reflected statistically significant relationships, a number of defined trends emerged. These trends are noted with the caveat that any findings suggested from this data are implied a priori, through an extrapolation of the trends.

Results are presented in three categories that are consistent with the issues discussed in the literature review. These categories include: (1) general ratings of the police by Hispanics, (2) victim perceptions and attitudes related to the police, and (3) evaluations and expectations by respondents who had had some form of contact with the police. The reporting of any spurious corre-

lations was carefully avoided in the data analysis. Since chi-square is not a robust statistic, each significant relationship was examined for the influence of antecedent and intervening variables. Similarly, variables in significant findings were assessed to avoid conclusive statements based on symmetric relationships.

A description of some general findings provides an intuitive sense of respondent attitudes. Overall, 46.4 percent of the sample indicated a belief that the crime rate had increased over the past three years; only 7.6 percent felt the crime rate had decreased. Twenty-seven percent of the sample reported that they had been a victim of either a crime against their person or a crime against property in the past year, with only 35.8 percent indicating that they had reported the offense to the police. Other forms of official interaction with law enforcement agencies included traffic-related contacts (56.1 percent), disturbance-related contacts (17.9 percent), and arrest for an offense other than traffic (4.9 percent). Of this group, 44.7 percent described officer attitude as "good," with 20 percent reporting a "bad" attitude. With respect to the relationship between the incidence of crime and the police, the data indicate a significant association between a perceived inadequacy in police protection and fear of crime ($X^2 = 20.788$, $df = 9$, $p < .01$, $V = .252$).

Rating the Police

In order to elicit different attitudes, the study stratified the police on three levels: local (municipal) police, county sheriff's officers, and the Texas Department of Public Safety (DPS), which embodies various state policing functions, including the highway patrol. The sample was asked to rate each of these agency levels with respect to quality of job performance. From the results depicted in Table 1, one may assume that the agency with which most individuals had the highest contact (local police) received the lowest ratings.[3] This may imply that, in general, the public's attitudes toward the police are good until it has experience with the police. If

TABLE 1

RATING OF JOB PERFORMANCE BY AGENCY

Rating	Local Police	Sheriff	DPS
Good	29.4%	35.3%	57.9%
Average	55.6%	52.9%	39.4%
Poor	15.0%	11.8%	2.7%

ratings of police performance go down after police contact, this may be due to the interactive effect of poor police performance and unreasonably high public expectations of police performance. An intervening influence may also be that state agencies are perceived as being more highly competent than the local police or sheriff's officers.

The evaluation of local police was negatively associated with fear of crime; this implies that an increase in the fear of crime does tend to lower the performance ratings of local police ($p < .01$). Similarly, victimization was negatively associated with the evaluation of local police ($p < .005$), the county sheriff ($p < .005$), and the DPS ($p < .05$). The inference here is that with victimization, Hispanic evaluation of police performance decreases. These findings are particularly noteworthy in light of the previously reported association between fear of crime and a perceived inadequacy in police protection. However, there does appear to be a paradox in these findings.

If the public perceives an increased crime rate, the fear of crime will concomitantly rise. One may also assume that increased concern about victimization will produce a stronger desire for more police protection and, consequently, higher expectations of performance. All of these factors interact to produce a lower evaluation of police performance. If the police increase operational tactics to control crime (e.g., more proactive patrol, stopping more cars and persons, etc.), contact with the public will increase, which again lowers police evaluations. Assuming that this logic is valid, a remedy for the problem of poor evaluations of the police

might focus on long-term communications between the police and Hispanics, along with control of the quality of police contacts.

Both the literature review and the data suggest that Hispanics feel improvements are needed in police service in order for performance ratings to increase. When queried specifically on this issue, respondents clearly indicated areas where they felt improvement was needed. As indicated in Table 2, Hispanics expressed desires for (1) more patrol and investigative activity, (2) better personnel deployment, (3) enhanced response time, and (4) less discrimination against Hispanics.

The first two items (along with other findings in the study) indicate clearly that Hispanics desire the police to be more visible. Such a desire is probably influenced by the "security blanket effect"; however, the respondents were quite adamant in their belief that they were being discriminated against by the police agency, a belief evidenced by their perception that officers were not assigned to Hispanic neighborhoods. Once again, a tautology surfaces: the perceived underassignment of officers to Hispanic areas feeds the fear of crime, which in turn lowers the evaluations of the police.

The dynamics of response-time in this study are operationally the same as those reported in the literature review. That is, the expectations of response time and psychological time displacement interact to reduce evaluations of the police. Concerning the issue of discrimination, Hispanic responses indicated that this was another important area where improvement was needed. More dramatic than the data results were the qualitative findings provided in comments on the survey instrument. A preponderance of these comments addressed discrimination problems associated both with the police and with the total criminal justice process. Interestingly, a qualitative analysis of the comments indicates that the police may receive criticism for discrimination that should more accurately be directed toward the criminal justice system in toto.

TABLE 2

PRACTICES THAT POLICE AGENCIES COULD EMPLOY
TO PROVIDE BETTER SERVICE TO THE PUBLIC

| | Agency | | |
Improvement Practices	Local Police	Sheriff	Department of Public Safety
Patrol/investigate more	59.3%	49.8%	31.6%
Better personnel deployment	54.3%	37.2%	40.2%
Enhance response time	45.3%	35.7%	23.9%
Avoid discrimination	41.3%	35.3%	34.0%
Be more courteous/concerned	39.6%	37.2%	26.3%
More training	37.2%	37.2%	20.8%
Keep politics out of policing	31.4%	37.6%	23.2%
More college education	18.8%	18.4%	11.6%

Victims and the Police

The victim-police relationship can be tenuous, particularly if victims have expectations the police do not fulfill. Most expectations by respondents centered around aspects of the investigation of the incident in question (see Table 3). It is noteworthy that significant proportions of Hispanics ex-

TABLE 3

PERFORMANCE EXPECTATIONS OF
POLICE BY VICTIMS

Expectation	Percentage
Police would take a report	85.4
Ask questions about crime	75.6
Crime scene investigation	56.1
Conduct follow-up investigation	56.1
Ask questions in neighborhood	56.0
Take fingerprints	48.8
Property would be recovered	41.5
Suspect would eventually be caught	34.1
Provide general aid/assistance	31.7
Immediately arrest suspect	26.8

pected the police to take fingerprints at the scene of the crime (48.8 percent) and anticipated that stolen property would be recovered (41.5 percent). Given the nature of these variables, it seems reasonable to question the impact of the entertainment media on socializing the public toward performance expectations.

A number of substantive findings were identified through analysis of the data related to victims who had not reported the crime to the police. Nonreporting victims indicated that a significant reason for not calling the police was the belief that the police would do little or nothing to resolve the criminal incident ($r = .511, p < .001$). This implies that victims have a low expectation of police performance and suggests, given previously reported findings, that the victimization experience may reduce expectations of police performance. If this is the case, it is reasonable to assume that victimization also reinforces the perception of inadequate police protection, leading to lower performance evaluations.

Nonreporting victims indicated further that they expected that reporting the crime would involve a great deal of paperwork and time that would not have any effect in terms of resolving the crime ($r = .709, p < .001$). An interesting research question to follow up this finding is the relationship of personal value systems to the variables of social justice, attachment to tangible personal assets, and quality of life. It is intuitively presumed here that Hispanics give the highest value to quality of life, due to the high degree of ethnocentrism characteristic of the culture. This presumed strong commitment to family would mean attaching a lower value to the more global concern of social justice and thus may help explain a lowered sense of responsibility toward reporting crime.

Other findings dealing with victims indicate that crimes were not reported due to bad previous experiences with the police ($r = .333, p < .001$) and because respondents simply did not believe that the police had the ability to handle the crime ($r = .356, p < .001$). Moreover, a series of related questions showed a consistent tendency for Hispanic victims to fail to report crimes because they "did not feel it was worth it"($r = .495, p < .001$). These results all have important implications for cultural/communicative interaction concerning expectations about police behavior as well as for the value attached to social justice, as discussed earlier.

Concerning the reasons for not reporting crimes to the police noted in Table 4, several interesting, although not statistically significant, results can be noted. Nearly 11 percent of the respondents indicated fear of the police, 8.1 percent did not report the crime for fear of criminal revenge, and 5.4 percent were advised not to call the police by a friend or relative. The fear of police variable is consistent with the Mirande (1981) finding reported in the literature review. Such a fear, one may presume, has its foundation in social discrimination and cultural conflict. The fear of revenge may be a product of the higher personal-crime rate among Hispanics, as compared to the dominant population (Bureau of Justice Statistics, 1981), as well as of the frequent familiarity between offender and victim. Finally, the advice of friends/relatives not to call the police may be influenced by the strong ethnocentrism and cultural homoge-

TABLE 4

REASONS GIVEN BY VICTIMS FOR NOT REPORTING CRIMES

Reason	Percentage
Police would do little or nothing	43.2
Time involved in paperwork and questioning not worth effort	32.4
Police unable to handle situation	21.6
Previous experience with police was bad	16.2
Did not want to bother police	10.8
Afraid of police	10.8
Fear of revenge by criminal	8.1
Friend/relative advised not to call police	5.4

neity of Hispanic communities. Victimization may be viewed as a personal affront to be dealt with by one's family, and calling the police may be seen as resulting in the involvement of an external element that is inconsistent with cultural determinants.[4]

Those victims who did report crimes had prescribed expectations of police behavior that were not fulfilled. Notable significant correlations between reported victimization and unfulfilled expectations included the belief that police would take fingerprints ($r = .222, p < .001$), that officers would conduct a crime-scene search ($r = .261, p < .001$), and that stolen property would be recovered ($r = .221, p < .001$). When expectations were not fulfilled, both general evaluations of the police and satisfaction levels with the police decreased.

Reporting victims also indicated dissatisfaction with the police due to slow response times ($r = .207, p < .001$) and inadequate investigations ($r = .183, p < .001$). Both of these findings supported the contention of these victims that they received inadequate protection from the police.

Evaluation and Expectations by Respondents Who Had Contact With the Police

The results show that 41.6 percent of the respondents had had some "contact with the police." Contact refers to any direct encounter with a police officer in his/her official status. Of the individuals who had contact with the police, evaluations of the local police were significantly affected by the perceived adequacy of the officers' investigations ($r = .112, p < .05$). The term *investigation* applies here to any type of incident (e.g., crime, traffic, disturbance) and entails the public expectation of a reasonably comprehensive investigation. Evaluations were also significantly related to officers' bad attitudes toward the public, as perceived by the public ($r = .105, p < .05$). The findings indicate that respondents actually perceived that the police made situations worse ($r = .126, p < .01$).

While each of these findings is statistically significant, they are not highly robust. Nonetheless, they indicate important problems in police-Hispanic relationships that need to be recognized. Particularly in the case of the latter two findings, it may be inferred that problems concerning attitude and the handling of situations have important communication-related and cultural implications.

Other reasons for Hispanic dissatisfaction are enumerated in Table 5. It is particularly striking that in each category of dissatisfaction the percentage of individuals involved is relatively high. Once again, it may be assumed that dissatisfaction is either a product of, or aggravated by, communication problems and different cultural expectations. If individuals who had contact with the police were dissatisfied, the next logical step is to determine what was expected.

Data were gathered on a number of direct expectations of police performance, ranging from the taking of a report by police to apprehension of the suspect. Although there were no statistically significant correlations between expectations and officer behavior, a trend did develop. Nearly all expectations were negatively correlated

TABLE 5

PERSONS WHO HAD CONTACT WITH POLICE AND WERE NOT SATISFIED: REASONS FOR DISSATISFACTION

Reasons	Percentage
Inadequate police investigation	58.8
Poor evaluation of situation by officers	54.9
Response time too slow	43.1
No follow-up investigation	43.1
Officer had bad attitude	41.1
Police should have done more	39.2
Suspect was not caught	37.3
Property not recovered	29.4
Officer made situation worse	21.6
Police could not provide any help	21.6
Police did nothing	15.7

with police contact. This trend implies that as contact with the police increases—regardless of the nature of the contact—expectations for the police decrease. Perhaps this is indicative of cultural conflict, in that each group (the police and Hispanics) have, as a product of socialization, predefined behavioral patterns with which they expect the opposing group to conform. When conformity does not occur, expectations are lowered, while contempt for the opposing group increases. These dynamics apply to any relationship between a social group and the police. However, this problem is pronounced when a culturally distinct social group is involved.

Overall, the data in Table 6 show low expectations for police behavior in situations that involve more than the handling of an immediate crisis or incident. It is noteworthy that over a quarter of the respondents did not expect the police to do anything. Similarly, less than a third expected the police to provide any type of solution. These results suggest a deterioration of the already troubled police-Hispanic relationship.

TABLE 6

EXPECTATIONS OF POLICE BEHAVIOR BY
RESPONDENTS WHO HAD SOME FORM OF
CONTACT WITH POLICE

Expectation	Percentage
Problem would be solved	30.0
Police report would be filed	26.8
Nothing/did not expect police to do anything	26.0
Police would contact you later (follow-up)	23.5
Suspect would be caught	21.1
Police would provide advice	17.8
Suspects would go to trial	17.0
Property would be recovered	13.8

CONCLUSIONS

Throughout this study, a recurring finding surfaced: Hispanics had expectations of police behavior that were not being met. These expectations appear to be an interactive product of diminished police performance and unrealistically high performance standards. When expectations were not fulfilled, evaluations of the police declined. Impeding any remedial strategies for these problems are the barriers imposed by (1) linguistic and symbolic communications and (2) cultural distinction. These barriers are indicated throughout the cumulative findings reported in this article and are supported by Carter's (1983) findings on the influence of Hispanic culture.

There appears to be a general lack of knowledge on the part of both the police and Hispanics about each other's culture (including the "police subculture"). Whereas true cooperation between both groups should be a desired goal, a realistic goal for achieving a functional relationship is accomodation. Even accomodation requires active strategies, imposed by the police leadership, to educate both police officers and the Hispanic public. The objective each group should strive for is reciprocity through knowledge rather than dominion through assertion.

ACKNOWLEDGEMENT

This research project was funded by a grant from the Pan American University Faculty Research Council.

NOTES

[1] One significant problem with the findings from the various reports of the U.S. Commission on Civil Rights is that they are based on witness testimony, not empirical assessment. Thus the opportunity for bias certainly exists in the findings.

[2] A finding by Schaefer et al. (1979) indicated that the influence of television developed the perception of the police as "law enforcers" rather than as "service" providers. This perception was most notable among middle-class respondents.

[3] While it may be argued that citizens have the most contact with the DPS, due to traffic enforcement, this was not the case in this study. Citizen contact with local police was most frequent, over the widest array of circumstances—particularly for lower socioeconomic-level citizens. Moreover, in Texas DPS officers are "spread thin," patrol major traffic arteries, and maintain a low profile.

[4] For a specific discussion of these cultural characteristics, see Carter (1983: 217–18). As noted there, in Hispanic culture believes that "any attempt by an 'outsider' to share or dispel loyalties and obligations (e.g., such as calling the police after victimization) is interpreted as an attack upon the self, and hence, the honor of the individual" (1983: 217).

REFERENCES

Babbie, E.R. (1973). *Survey research methods.* Belmont, CA: Wadsworth Publishing Company.

Bell, D.J. (1983). Police attitudes: Based on beliefs or race? *Police Studies* 6:21–26.

Brooks, W.D., and Friedrich, G.W. (1970). Police image: An exploratory study. *J Comm* 20:370–74.

Bureau of Justice Statistics. (1981). *The hispanic victim.* Washington, D.C.: U.S. Department of Justice.

Carte, G.E. (1973). Changes in public attitudes toward the police: A comparison of 1938 and 1971 surveys. *J Police Sci Adm* 1:182–200.

Carter, D.L. (1983). Hispanic interaction with the criminal justice system in Texas: Experiences, attitudes, and perceptions. *J Crim Just* 11: 213–27.

——— (1984). Police brutality: A model for definition, perspective, and control. In *The ambivalent force*, 3d. ed., eds. A. Niederhoffer and A. Blumberg. Hinsdale, IL: Dryden Press.

Chackerian, R. (1974). Police professionalism and citizen evaluations: A preliminary look. *Public Administration Review*, March/April, 141–48.

Couper, D. (1983). *How to rate your local police.* Washington, D.C.: Police Executive Research Forum.

Decker, S.H. (1981). Citizen attitudes toward the police: A review of past findings and suggestions for future policy. *J Police Sci Adm* 9:80–87.

Figgie Report on fear of crime : America afraid. (1980). Willoughby, OH: A-T-O Inc.

Flanagan, T.J., and McLeod, M. (eds.). (1983). *Sourcebook of criminal justice statistics.* Washington, D.C.: U.S. Department of Justice.

Garofalo, J. (1977). *Public opinion about crime.* Washington, D.C.: National Criminal Justice Information and Statistics Service.

Jacob, H. (1971). Black and white perceptions of justice in the city. *Law Soc R* 6:68–89.

Joyner, I. (1977). People and police. In *Black crime: A police view*, ed. H.J. Bryce. Washington, D.C.: Joint Center for Political Studies.

Kansas City, Missouri Police Department (1977). *Response time analysis: Volume II.* Mimeograph.

LEAA (1977). *The police and public opinion.* Washington, D.C.: National Criminal Information and Statistics Service.

——— (1979). *Criminal victimization in the United States 1973-1977.* Washington, D.C.: National Criminal Justice Information and Statistics Service.

League of United Latin American Citizens (1978). *A description of Latin Americans in the United States.* Mimeograph.

Mandel, J. (1979). Hispanics in the criminal justice system—The "non-existent" problem. *Agenda*, May/June, 16–20.

Mirande, A. (1981). The chicano and the law. *Pac Soc R* 1:65–86.

Morales, A. (1972). *A study of Mexican-American perceptions of law enforcement policies and practices in East Los Angeles.* Ph.D. dissertation, University of Southern California.

Munn, J.R., and Renner, K.E. (1978). Perceptions of police work by the police and the public. *Crim Just B* 5:165–80.

Parisi, N. et al. (eds.). (1979). *Sourcebook of criminal justice statistics—1978.* Washington, D.C.: National Criminal Justice Information and Statistics Service.

Parks, R.B. (1976). Victims and police response. *Victimology* 1:314–16.

Peek, C.W.; Alston, P.; and Lowe, G.D. (1978). Comparative evaluation of the local police. *Pub Opinion Q* 37:370–79.

Petersilia, J. (1983). *Racial disparities in the crimi-*

nal justice system. Santa Monica, CA: The Rand Corporation.

President's Commission on Law Enforcement and Administration of Justice. (1967). *Task force report: Police.* Washington, D.C.: U.S. Government Printing Office.

Quintanilla, G. (1983). Cross cultural communication: An ongoing challenge. *FBI Law Enforcement Bulletin*, February, 1–8.

Radelet, L.A. (1980). *The police and the community.* 3d. ed. Encino, CA: Glencoe.

Roberg, R. (1976). *The changing police role.* San Jose, CA: Justice Systems Development.

Scaglion, R., and Condon, R. G. (1980). Determinants of attitudes toward city police. *Criminol* 17:485–94.

Schaefer, R.; Vanderlook, W.; and Wisnoski, E. (1979). Television police shows and attitudes toward the police. *J Police Sci Adm* 7:104–13.

Schuman, H., and Gruenberg, B. (1972). Dissatisfaction with city services: Is race an important factor? In *People and politics in urban society*, ed. H. Hahan. Beverly Hills, CA: Sage.

Sommers, A. (1982). Improving human relations between the Hispanic community and law enforcement. *Police Chief*, March, 32–33.

Staples, R. (1972). White racism, black crime, and American justice. Proceedings of the International Association of Victimology Conference, Caracas, Venezuela.

Teske, R.H.C. et al. (1982). *Public perceptions of the police in Texas.* Huntsville, TX: Criminal Justice Center.

U.S. Commission on Civil Rights (1961). *Justice: Book V.* Washington, D.C.: U.S. Government Printing Office.

——— (1965). *A report on equal protection in the south.* Washington, D.C.: U.S. Government Printing Office.

——— (1967). *A time to listen . . . a time to act.* Washington, D.C.: U.S. Government Printing Office.

——— (1970). *Mexican-Americans and the administration of justice in the southwest.* Washington, D.C.: U.S. Government Printing Office.

——— (1981). *Who is guarding the guardians?* Washington, D.C.: U.S. Government Printing Office.

Walker, D. et al. (1972). Content and support: An empirical assessment of public attitudes toward the police and courts. *N C L Rev* 51:43–79.

Whitaker, G.P. et al. (1982). *Basic issues in police performance.* Washington, D.C.: National Institute of Justice.

White, M. F., and Menke, B.A. (1982). On assessing the mood of the public toward the police: Some conceptual issues. *J Crim Just* 10:211–50.

THE CHICANO AND THE LAW

An Analysis of Community-Police Conflict in an Urban Barrio

ALFREDO MIRANDÉ
University of California, Riverside

A case study of a Southern California barrio with a history of police conflict is used to test several hypotheses concerning fear of crime and of the police in relation to support for increasing or curtailing police power and protecting civil liberties. There was considerable diversity of attitudes toward the police, crime, and civil liberties. The hypothesis that fear of crime leads to increased support for police power was strongly supported by these Chicano respondents. A second hypothesis—that Chicanos who fear the police most are likely to favor the protection of civil liberties— received only limited support in our survey. Finally, there appeared to be strong support for the hypothesis that fear of the police among barrio residents is associated with desire to curtial police power. These findings suggest that even among a group of people such as Chicanos, who have been subjected to systematic police abuse and harassment, increases in the crime rate generally lead to greater support for increasing police power and limiting civil liberties, while fear of the police reduces support for police power and increases support for civil guarantees.

The rising rate of crime and urban unrest in the late 1960s led to an overwhelming concern not only with issues of crime and civil disorders but with official violence and the violation of civil liberties. Of particular interest was whether fear of crime increased support for police power and decreased support for civil liberties. Much of the research that emerged in the aftermath of these urban disorders focused either on the evaluation of the police and police services by black respondents or on racial differences in perceptions of the police and crime (e.g., Smith and

AUTHOR'S NOTE: *This study was partially funded by an Intramural Research Grant from the University of California, Riverside.*

PACIFIC SOCIOLOGICAL REVIEW, Vol. 24 No. 1, January 1981 65-86
© 1981 Pacific Sociological Assn.

65

Hawkins, 1973; Furstenberg and Wellford, 1973; Phillips and Coates, 1971; Chackerian and Barrett, 1973; and Hahn, 1971). Such studies showed that black respondents were consistently more negative in their evaluation of the police (Bayley and Mendelsohn, 1969; Ennis, 1967; Raine, 1970; Hahn, 1971; Furstenberg and Wellford, 1973) and that these negative attitudes were not limited to lower status respondents but might in fact be more intense among persons of higher status[1] (Murphy and Watson, 1970; Raine, 1970). Although these studies provided useful insights into minority-police relations, their almost exclusive focus on blacks resulted in the neglect of perceptions of the police and crime held by other minority group members. There has been, in particular, very little research on Chicano perceptions of the police or relations with them.

The U.S. Commission on Civil Rights, in perhaps the most systematic and far-reaching study of Chicanos and the legal and judicial system, found strong evidence of a pattern of systematic harassment and abuse of Chicanos by the police. The Commission concluded that "Mexican American citizens are subject to unduly harsh treatment by law enforcement officers, that they are often arrested on insufficient grounds, receive physical and verbal abuse, and penalties which are disproportionately severe" (1970: iii). Although patterns of police abuse and mistreatment are common and widespread,[2] the study of Chicano-police relations has been neglected by sociologists. There is a need for research that examines the attitudes of barrio residents toward law enforcement not only during major incidents but in their day-to-day contact with police. This study attempts to add to our understanding of Chicano-police relations by presenting an overview of conflict with police in an urban barrio, testing several hypotheses concerning fear of the police, attitudes toward increasing or curtailing police power, support of civil liberties, and fear of crime. For example, do barrio residents blame the police for major disturbances in the community or are they basically supportive of police? Does support for increasing police power increase as fear of crime increases? Does fear of the police by Chicanos lead to greater support for civil liberties and increase the desire to curtail police power as is the case in other racial-ethnic groups?

THE SETTING

The setting for this case study of Chicano-police conflict is a barrio in a Southern California community of 150,000 inhabitants. This barrio was selected not only because it has been the site of recent civil disorders which have gained national attention, but because it appeared representative of other barrios in the Southwest in being isolated from Anglo society and having a long history of conflict with the police. Like most barrios, it is a distinctive community within the city, extending over an area that is approximately one square mile and includes about 3000 persons within its boundaries.

From its inception as housing quarters for citrus pickers, the community has been segregated from the city. As early as 1874 the City Board of Education created a separate school district to exclude Chicano children from Anglo schools. Since there were not many Chicano residents in the 1880s and 1890s, the area became an Anglo suburb and was the site of several exclusive social clubs, a tennis club, and a polo club. But segregation prevailed, and within 25 years the suburb was transformed into a Chicano barrio surrounded by large, prestigious homes. Problems with the law surfaced early. In 1916 a citizen's committee chaired by the Mayor requested and obtained the hiring of extra policemen for the barrio, and the following year an extra officer was hired to patrol on Saturday nights. In the same year requests were made for as many as eight additional policemen. Since the 1940s killings, shootings, and beatings of Chicanos have been commonplace.

The barrio shares certain important features with urban slums in that the income and educational level of many residents is low and some of the housing is poor or substandard, but it differs from the slum in some important respects. First, although there is poverty in the barrio, not everyone is poor. There is considerable variability in the economic and educational attainment of residents.[3] Second, the barrio has emerged partly as a result of prejudice and segregation, but there is an element of voluntarism in barrio residence, and a strong sense of community identification prevails. Barrios are literally *colonias* (colonies), ethnic enclaves within the territorial boundaries of the United States.

This particular barrio is similarly isolated. Its isolation has been so extensive that until recent years many of the streets in the barrio were unpaved and residents were not afforded normal city services. Today ambulances are still reluctant to enter the community without a police escort.

The confluence of two diverse though mutually reinforcing forces—residential segregation and a positive identification with barrio residence—have worked to produce a remarkably stable pattern of community residence. Not only are most residents of the community Chicano (about 90%), but typically they have lived there all or virtually all of their lives. This does not necessarily mean that most people born and raised in the barrio remain there for the rest of their lives, since a community survey obviously excludes those persons who have moved out. What is significant is not that most people who are born in the barrio stay there but that very few new residents move in. New arrivals, especially if they come from Mexico, are likely to have relatives or friends already living in the community. The stability of the community is further intensified by what appears to be a tendency toward endogamous marriage, so that a strong sense of familism pervades community life. The statement frequently made in jest that "everyone in the barrio is related to everyone else" is not without some factual basis. One person, for example, noted that he had over 260 relatives living in the community.

The stability, cohesiveness, and apparent serenity of the community stand in sharp contrast to the conflict and tension that pervades community-police relations. The police have traditionally been viewed not only as outsiders but as representatives of the dominant oppressive Anglo society. Over the past seven or eight years there has been about one Chicano shot per year. Residents complain of extensive police abuse and harassment. Community-police conflict is especially intense among youth, who are frequently the target of such abuse and harassment.

Community-police conflict culminated in two major incidents in August of 1975. One incident occurred on August 2, as the police broke up a bachelor party, tear-gassed the home where the party was held, and beat up and arrested a large number of the guests. Although 52 persons were arrested, almost all charges were subsequently dropped for insufficient evidence, and the city has since settled a number of civil suits out of court. The second incident was unrelated but served to exacerbate antipolice sentiment. The stabbing of an Anglo male believed to be a police informer, at a park in the community on August thirteenth, provided the impetus for this incident. The police, in pursuit of the assailant(s), surrounded a corn field throughout the evening of August thirteenth and the morning of August fifteenth. Tear gas was dropped from a helicopter, and there was extensive gunfire throughout the night. Sheriff's units from the County and a nearby county were brought in to reinforce city police, as was the SWAT team from San Diego. The result was a police siege. Residents were stopped and questioned by police as they attempted to go to work or carry on normal daily activities. The August thirteenth incident was termed a riot by the police and the media. If it was a "riot," it was more of the "commodity" than the "communal" variety, although there was no looting or destruction of business property. It was more accurately a community-police confrontation, with the police intermittently exchanging gunfire with residents.

HYPOTHESES, METHOD, AND SAMPLE

Our survey of community attitudes toward the police was carried out within two months of these incidents. Its primary objective was to assess attitudes toward the police not only relative to their handling of the August incidents but in general. The interview schedule covered a number of areas including: (1)

general attitudes concerning the police, protection of civil liberties, and fear of crime, (2) specific attitudes toward the police and their handling of the August incidents, and (3) social and demographic characteristics.

Given the putative extensiveness of police abuse and widespread official violence perpetrated against Chicanos, there is need for research that focuses on the conditions under which Chicanos are willing either to increase or to curtail police power and to support or not support civil liberties. Several hypotheses tested by Block (1971) in an NORC study were tested with our barrio respondents. While the hypotheses were originally tested with white and black respondents, they seem especially applicable to Chicanos. One hypothesis proposes that since fear provides a rationale for granting the state power, fear of crime should lead to greater support for increasing police power. A second similarly argues that if fear is the primary basis for delimiting the power of the state, then fear of the police should intensify support for civil liberties. The rationale for these hypotheses is as follows:

> If fear is a foundation of support for the state and the police are the state's instrument to control internal threat, then those people with the greatest fear of crime should be most willing to increase the power of the police. Similarly if fear of the state is the basis for limitation of the power of the state, and the police, as an instrument of the state, are a basis of fear of the state, then those respondents who most fear the police would be most likely to want their power limited through the protection of civil liberties [Block, 1971: 93-94].

In applying these hypotheses to Chicanos we expected that while barrio residents would not generally support increasing police power, those who feared crime most would be most willing to support such increases. Also, since police abuse and brutality entail the violation of civil liberties, we expected widespread support for such safeguards and considerable fear of the police, but support of civil liberties should be especially high among respondents who are most fearful of the police. We hypothesized, finally, that those barrio respondents who were most fearful of the police would want not only to protect civil liberties but to curtail or limit police power.

A random sample of households yielded 170 completed interviews. Though the sample is based on a random selection of households, it is somewhat purposive in the sense that a special effort was made to include youthful respondents, since it is among them that conflict with the police is believed to be most intense. Interviewers were instructed to interview an adult member of the household and a teenaged member, whenever possible. This procedure was facilitated by interviewers normally working as two-person teams. Inclusion of youth was deemed important also because Chicanos as a group are on the average much younger than the overall population.[4] The sample consists of 38% male adults, 35% female adults, 16% male teenagers, and 9% female teenagers. Approximately one out of every four respondents then is a dependent child.

Interviews were conducted by bilingual-bicultural interviewers, trained and sensitive to the nuances of Chicano culture and the prevailing values of the barrio. Comments and suggestions of various political, civic, and community leaders were sought and incorporated into the interview schedule. Interviewers and the principal investigator met with these leaders and were briefed on practices, procedures, dress, and demeanor that were believed would elicit maximum cooperation from the community in carrying out the project. Without the help and endorsement of these community members our task would have been difficult, if not impossible.

Basically the same questions used in the NORC survey were included as measures of the four major test variables in the study. Fear of crime was measured by the question:

> How likely is it that a person walking around here at night might be held up or attacked—very likely, somewhat likely, somewhat unlikely, or very unlikely?

The index of fear of the police was the person's perception of "police respectfulness toward people like himself." Those respondents who rated police respectfulness as "not so good" were assumed to fear the police more than those who rated it as "pretty good" or "very good." In order to assess support for increases in police power respondents were asked:

> Do you favor giving the police more power to question people, do you think they have enough power already, or would you like to see some of their power to question people curtailed?

The last variable, protection of civil liberties, was measured by two questions regarding support for police review boards and for the right of a suspect to an attorney during police interrogations. Respondents who felt that a suspect has a right to a lawyer and who were in favor of establishing a police review board were said to have "full support" of civil liberties.

FINDINGS

ATTITUDES TOWARD POLICE AND
THEIR HANDLING OF THE INCIDENTS

A number of open and closed questions were used to ascertain respondent perception of the August incidents and the police handling of them. In response to an item that asked "What do you see as the major reasons for the August 2 incident?" few respondents blamed the youth at the bachelor party, and most specified police overreaction as the major factor leading to the disturbance. Significantly, 57% felt that the police overreacted a great deal and used force and violence which were not needed. Most respondents felt that the August second incident could have been avoided (59%), 14% felt that it could not, and 26% either did not know for sure or did not answer. Those who felt that it could have been avoided were asked to indicate how it could have been avoided. The most common response was that it could have been avoided had the police used better judgment or not overreacted, at least indirectly blaming the August second incident on the police.

Our barrio residents were similarly critical of the police handling of the August thirteenth incident. In response to an open-ended question on reasons for this disturbance, a large percentage (41) said they did not know, while the majority of those who responded saw poor judgement and overreaction by the police as major reasons for the disturbance. Most persons who responded also felt that the August thirteenth incident could have been avoided if the police had handled the situation better and if they would stop overpatrolling and harassment of residents.

In a broader light, a series of open-ended questions asked respondents to indicate what they saw as the most important reasons for conflict between the community and city police as a whole. Although a variety of reasons were given, by far the most common one given for community-police conflict (35%) was police prejudice, harassment, and overpatrolling. Another open-ended question asked what they saw as the best way to solve the problem of barrio-police conflict. Although 47% did not offer any solution, most who did, specified a need either to improve communication with the police or to reform them, and few blamed the community for the problem.

The final open-ended question asked how the city police department could improve its services "to you, your neighbors, and community" and provided an interesting diversity of results. The responses ranged from those that felt the police were "doing a good job" or "needed to enforce the law more" to those who felt that the "situation was hopeless" or that the police should "leave us alone"; intermediate between these extremes were persons who simply wanted to improve police services. A substantial number called for the police to treat them with "respect" or "like humans" and to have more "understanding" of barrio residents.

While it is clear from the preceding that most respondents were critical of the police handling of the August incidents and saw their mishandling of these incidents as part of a broader pattern of pervasive police harassment and abuse, their negativity was neither all-encompassing nor predictable. In order to obtain a more direct measure of perceptions of community-police conflict, respondents were asked to "rate relations between police and residents of the barrio" on a five point scale ranging from excellent to poor. Only 1% rated relations between the police and community as excellent, and 48% rated them as poor.

Though relations between the police and the community are rated very low, barrio residents are not uniformly critical of the police. When they were asked to give the police department an overall rating, it was rated higher than were relations between the police and the community. Yet more persons rated the department as below average or poor than rated it as good or excellent. Differences between the rating of the police department per se and rating of relations between them and the community suggest considerable sophistication on the part of barrio residents and a keen awareness of differential treatment toward them by police. Chicanos do not tend to see the police as ill-trained or inept as much as they see them as treating them differently and unequally relative to others. A common complaint expressed by barrio residents is not that they want special or unusual treatment, only equal treatment with others.

Fear of Crime and Support for the Police in the Barrio

The preceding description suggests that Chicano dissatisfaction was relatively specific and not generalized to all situations. Not only did Chicano perceptions of the police vary across situations, but there was considerable diversity among them in their perceptions and evaluations of the police. A number of barrio residents were, in fact, supportive of the police and in some instances felt that they should be granted more power to deal with crime and quell disturbances. Let us now examine certain conditions that may be associated with a willingness to increase police power and limit civil liberties. The questions are worded more broadly, so rather than eliciting specific attitudes toward a given police department or actual incidents, they tap more general and abstract attitudes.

The first hypothesis posits that fear of crime among barrio residents is translated into a greater willingness to support increases in police power. It must initially be noted that fear of crime in the barrio appears to be minimal. Only 23% feel that attack in their neighborhood is "very likely," while 28% see it as "very unlikely." As expected, few respondents want to increase police power and many wish either to curtail or to limit police power to its current level. Thirty-two percent wish to curtail police power and only about 14% wish to increase it from its current level.

From Table 1 it is clear that the hypothesis is supported in this sample. Those barrio residents who say street attack is very likely are more likely to favor increases in police power. Eighteen percent of the respondents who believe attack is very likely support increasing police power, whereas only 4% of those who feel it is very unlikely do so. Chicanos who see attack as very unlikely, on the other hand, are much more inclined to want to curtail police power (54%) than those who see attack as very likely (26%).

Table 1 also shows the effect of several important background variables on the relationship between fear of crime and support for the police. Age appears to affect this relationship. That the relationship is strongest among barrio residents under 25 is perhaps not surprising, since it is Chicano youth who more typically have direct experience with both crime and the police.

Two important patterns are evident when length of residence in the community considered. First and most obvious is the great stability of residence among our respondents; only about 13% have lived in the community for less than five years, whereas 29% have lived there from five to fifteen years and 58% for sixteen or more. Second, the relationship between fear of crime and support for the police is not as strong or significant among short-term residents, among whom the relationship is inverse, although not significant. Apparently among short-term residents those who fear crime most are least supportive of the police. Length of residence in the barrio seems to enhance identification with the community and to intensify the relation between fear of crime and support of the police.

A related control variable is whether the resident is satisfied living in the community or is dissatisfied and would like to move. The hypothesis is much more strongly supported among persons who like living in the barrio. It may well be that community

TABLE 1
Support for the Police and Fear of Attack

Support Police	Fear of Attack			
	Very Likely	Somewhat Likely	Somewhat Unlikely	Very Unlikely
More	18%	18%	19%	4%
Enough	55	69	45	41
Curtail	26	12	35	54
Total	100%	100%	100%	100%
N	38	49	31	46

Gamma = .35   Chi square = 22.42, P < .001

Support for the Police by Fear of Attack Controlling for[*]:

	Gamma	Chi square	P <	N
1. Age				
24 or less	.60	5.91	.05	44
25-40	.22	.52	.77	39
41 or more	.31	2.28	.31	43
2. Length of Residence				
Less than 5 years	-.38	.90	.64	21
5-15 years	.55	10.42	.005	46
16 years or more	.58	11.01	.005	93
3. Like Living in Community				
Yes	.58	15.04	.001	114
No	-.12	.19	.91	47
4. Sex				
Male	.71	18.01	.001	89
Female	.06	2.08	.35	75
5. Family Income				
Under $7,000	.58	4.68	.10	39
$7,000-9,999	.21	4.16	.12	30
$10,000 or more	.11	.32	.85	35
6. Education				
8 years or less	.68	8.65	.01	34
Some high school	.19	.82	.66	30
12 years or more	.44	3.94	.14	46

[*]Because of the small N's Fear of Attack was dichotomized into "Likely" and "Unlikely."

identification increases involvement with community issues such as crime and control of the police so that the relationship between these variables is most intense among those who identify with and are committed to the barrio.

The effect of gender on fear of crime and support for the police is clear and predictable. Since males in the barrio typically have more direct contact and exposure to crime and to the police, it may be expected that the relationship between these variables is much stronger among men than among women. The extent to which women in the barrio fear crime is less likely to affect their attitudes toward either increasing or curtailing police power.

The effects of income and education are less clear, but the relationship between fear of crime and support for increasing police power is strongest among respondents with low incomes and little formal education. Chicanos with low incomes and little schooling, like men and youth in the barrio, are more likely to be victims of crime and of police abuse.

Fear of the Police and Support for Civil Liberties in the Barrio

The second major hypothesis concerns the effects of fear of the police on support for civil liberties among barrio residents. My hypothesis is that those Chicanos who are most fearful of police tend to be more supportive of civil guarantees, since such guarantees are designed to limit police abuses. Table 2 shows that the relationship is in the predicted direction but not statistically significant. Approximately 70% of those Chicanos who fear the police most support both measures to protect civil liberties compared to only 50% of those who fear the police least. The lack of statistical significance is undoubtedly due at least in part to the overall level of commitment to civil liberties among the Chicanos in our sample.[5] There was, in fact, little variation in the dependent variable, given that *none* was opposed to both measures and about 82% supported both measures.[6] In view of the level of support for civil liberties among barrio respondents, it may not be considered surprising to find substantial fear of police among them. Approximately 39% rated police respect toward persons

TABLE 2

Support for Civil Liberties and Fear of the Police

Support Civil Liberties	Police Respect		
	Very Good	Pretty Good	Not So Good
Less Support	50%	38%	30%
Full Support	50	62	71
Total	100%	100%	100%
N	34	60	61

Gamma = .27   Chi square = 3.95, P < .14

Support for Civil Liberties and Fear of the Police Controlling for[*]:

	Gamma	Chi square	P <	N
1. Age				
24 or less	.21	.11	.73	43
25-40	.50	1.16	.28	36
41 or more	.03	.09	.76	39
2. Length of Residence				
Less than 5 years	-.41	--	.41[**]	21
5-15 years	.38	.79	.37	44
16 years or more	.35	1.98	.16	88
3. Like Living in Community				
Yes	.27	1.31	.25	111
No	.14	0.00	1.00	42
4. Sex				
Male	.14	.13	.72	87
Female	.09	0.00	1.00	68
5. Family Income				
Under $7,000	.08	.02	.90	38
$7,000-9,999	1.00	--	.04[**]	28
$10,000 or more	0.00	.15	.70	33
6. Education				
8 years or Less	.09	--	.62[**]	30
Some high school	.41	--	.26[**]	30
12 years or more	.20	.10	.75	45

*Because of the small N's the "Very Good" and "Pretty Good" response to Police Respect were combined into a single "Good" category.
**Based on Fisher's Exact Probability test.

like themselves as "not so good," and only 22% rated it as "very good."

The relationship between fear of the police and support for civil liberties appears stronger among Chicanos who are 25-40 years of age than among younger or older ones, and when age is dichotomized it is considerably stronger among those 30 or older than among those under 30. Perhaps the reason for this is that the relationship between fear of the police and support for civil liberties is more indirect and abstract than the relationship between fear of crime and support for increasing police power, thereby manifesting itself more clearly among older or more mature barrio residents.

The hypothesis is more strongly supported among long-term residents of the community. In fact, among short-term residents the relationship is in the opposite direction; those Chicanos who fear the police most are least supportive of civil liberties. Although not statistically significant, there is also slightly more support for the hypothesis among those who like living in the barrio than those who do not, men than women, Chicanos of moderate rather than low or high income, and those with moderate rather than low or high educational attainment.

Fear of the Police and Support for the Police in the Barrio

The preceding hypotheses have been based on the assumption that much of the willingness of barrio residents to increase police power and limit civil guarantees is grounded in fear, fear both of crime and of the police. Fear of crime is likely to lead some residents of the barrio to support increasing the power of the police. Fear of the police, on the other hand, intensifies the support of civil liberties, thereby limiting police abuses. Just as fear of the police should lead to greater support for civil liberties so should it increase the desire to limit the power of police in the barrio, a hypothesis which will now be examined.

From Table 3 it is clear that the relationship between fear of the police and support for the police is strong and significant among our barrio respondents. As predicted, those Chicanos who fear the police most are least likely to support increases in police

TABLE 3
Support for the Police and Fear of the Police

	Police Respect		
Support Police	Very Good	Pretty Good	Not So Good
More	32%	20%	2%
Enough	59	67	35
Curtail	9	13	63
Total	100%	100%	100%
N	34	61	60

Gamma = .72   Chi square = 51.84, P < .001

Support for the Police and Fear of the Police*:

	Gamma	Chi square	P <	N
1. Age				
24 or less	.74	10.06	.01	43
25-40	.94	14.25	.001	36
41 or more	.63	5.19	.07	40
2. Length of Residence				
Less than 5 years	1.00	9.29	.01	20
5-15 years	.98	29.39	.001	45
16 years or more	.73	18.10	.001	88
3. Like Living in Community				
Yes	.84	35.83	.001	111
No	.89	9.88	.01	42
4. Sex				
Male	.95	38.35	.001	88
Female	.65	9.60	.01	67
5. Family Income				
Under $7,000	.91	13.38	.001	39
$7,000-9,999	.95	12.61	.001	28
$10,000 or more	.71	11.15	.005	33
6. Education				
8 years or less	.96	13.71	.001	30
Some high school	.56	3.21	.20	30
12 years or more	.92	11.69	.005	45

*Because of the small N's the "Very Good" and "Pretty Good" responses to Police Respect were combined into a single "Good" category.

power. Of the respondents who fear the police, 63% (i.e., who see police respect toward people like themselves as "not so good") desire to curtail or to limit police power, whereas only 9% of those who do not fear the police desire to curtail it.

From Table 3 it is also clear that the relationship between fear of the police and support for limiting police power remains significant even when background variables are controlled. The relationship cuts across age groups in the barrio, although it appears weaker among older respondents. It is similarly supported among newly arrived and long-term residents, those who like living in the community as well as those who wish to move out of the barrio, men and women, persons of low, moderate, and high income, and across educational groups, although it is not significant among Chicanos with "some high school" education.

SUMMARY AND DISCUSSION

This is a case study of a Southern California barrio that, like many others in the Southwest, has a tradition of conflict with the police. Several hypotheses were tested concerning fear of crime and of the police and support for increasing or curtailing police power and protecting civil liberties.

The hypothesis that fear of crime leads to increases in support for police power, a hypothesis which received only moderate support in the NORC study, was strongly supported by our Chicano respondents. This suggests that the view of Chicanos as uniformly antipolice and supportive of crime should be modified and take into account the diversity of attitudes found among them. There appears to be a significant segment of the barrio who are fearful of crime and seek to increase police power. While it would be wrong to characterize them as a "silent majority," since most barrio residents feel that the police already have enough power and many more wish to curtail than to increase police power, there is a need to acknowledge the existence of this segment of the Chicano community. It is noteworthy that the hypothesis is more strongly supported among those who are more involved with both crime and the police (e.g., men, youth).

The second hypothesis—that Chicanos who fear the police most are most likely to favor the protection of civil liberties received only limited support in our survey, substantial support among whites, and virtually none among blacks in the NORC survey. One reason for the relatively weak support for the hypothesis among Chicanos was their almost universal approval of civil liberties. More than four of five Chicanos supported *both* forms of civil liberties, discussed at the end of the section entitled "Hypotheses, Method, and Sample," compared to six of ten blacks and only three of ten whites in the NORC survey who supported both. The almost universal support of civil liberties among Chicanos suggests a need for discarding prevailing measures of civil liberties in favor of more sophisticated ones capable of discerning possible intragroup differences in such support.

The final relationship examined was fear of the police and support for increased police power. There was very strong support for the hypothesis that fear of the police among barrio residents increases the desire to curtail police power. As significant as the magnitude of the relationship was the fact that it generally held across age groups, long, medium and short-term residents of the barrio, Chicanos who liked living in the community and those who did not, men and women, persons of low, moderate and high income, and those of varying educational levels. The strength of this relationship is perhaps not surprising when one considers the history of conflict between Chicanos and the police. As victims of police harassment and abuse, Chicanos have sought to limit and control police power, and much of the desire to curtail their power is grounded in fear of the police and their excesses.

Differences between our findings and those of the NORC study appear consistent with historical differences among the three racial-ethnic groups in attitudes toward crime, treatment by the police, and their relationship to the legal-judicial system. Anglos obviously receive better treatment from the police and are more supportive of them than are blacks or Chicanos. They also have less reason to be fearful of personal attack, since they are less apt to be victims of violent crime. Predictably then, fear of crime is least among white and greatest among black respondents. It is interesting that though Chicanos fear crime less than blacks, they appear to fear the police more. This fear is not without justification. The history of Chicano-police relations has been one of conflict and tension, as has been noted. The police have traditionally served as tools for maintaining not only the oppressed position of Chicanos in the Southwest but their spatial and cultural isolation as well. The police are viewed by Chicanos as a vehicle for perpetuating the interests of Anglo-American society rather than as a supportive or protective agency.

The findings of this study suggest that even among a group of people such as Chicanos, who have been subjected to systematic police abuse and harassment, increases in the crime rate generally lead to greater support for increasing police power and limiting civil liberties, while fear of the police reduces support for police power and increases support for civil guarantees. Because our study is limited to a single barrio in Southern California, these results must be interpreted with caution. Although the barrio appears typical of many other barrios in the Southwest, we cannot be certain the same patterns would be found in other regions, in rural settings, or among nonbarrio Chicanos. Before our generalizations are accepted as conclusive, research is needed in other settings. Such research will, I hope, provide additional insights into the dynamics of community-police relations among minority groups and in the population as a whole.

NOTES

1. Household surveys, however, tend to exclude those persons who are most critical of the police—lower-class young adult black males. A comparison of black street and household respondents found that "The pattern found in previous surveys, suggesting a negative relationship between social status and attitudes of blacks toward police, as indexed by rating of police service, was not supported when the street population was taken into account" (Boggs and Galliher, 1975: 405).

2. From the signing of the Treaty of Guadalupe-Hildalgo to the present, a dual standard of justice has existed in the Southwest for Anglos on the one hand, and for Chicanos on the other. Not only has the legal and judicial system been used to perpetuate the economic, political, and social oppression of the Mexican-American people, but also the police have served as a domestic military force to quell disturbances and maintain order in the barrio. The relation between the police and barrio residents has been characterized by distrust, resentment, open hostility, and violence. Rather than diminish-

ing, Chicano-police conflict appears to have intensified (MALDEF, 1978). Many of the riots of the 1940s (Adler, 1974; Endore, 1942; Sleepy Lagoon Defense Committee, 1942) were "communal" riots involving direct confrontations between racial-ethnic groups (Janowitz, 1969: 418-424), whereas most so-called Chicanos riots today are "commodity" riots and entail a direct confrontation with the police. There is still considerable hostility and conflict directed at Chicanos, but more and more it is expressed indirectly via the police and the courts. (For documentation of police abuse and mistreatment of Chicanos, see U.S. Commission on Civil Rights, 1970; Hoffman, 1974; McWilliams, 1949, 1968; Acuña, 1972; Castillo and Camarillo, 1973; Goldfinch, 1949; Gómez-Q, 1970; Rosenbaum, 1973; Schlesinger, 1971; Trujillo, 1974; Morales, 1972; Adler, 1974; Paredes, 1958; Sleepy Lagoon Defense Committee, 1942; Webb, 1965, 1975; and MALDEF, 1978a, 1978b).

3. The median income in 1970 of all families residing in the census tract where the barrio is located was $6,520 and more than 21% of the families were below the poverty level. Approximately 30% of the families had incomes below $5000, 47% more than $5000 but less than $10,000, 18% between $10,000 and $24,999, and 4% $25,000 or more. The incomes of our respondents were fairly comparable to the census figures, although a smaller proportion of upper-income families ($25,000 or more) was represented in our sample. About 27% of our respondents had incomes under $5,000, 41% between $5,000 and $9,999, 32% $10,000 to $24,999, and 1% $25,000 or more. The discrepancy in the proportion of high-income families may have resulted from the fact that the census tract in which the barrio is located contains a number of affluent Anglo residences that are on the fringe of the barrio in the prestigious Green Belt area. The educational attainment of barrio residents is also low. The median years of school completed for persons 25 years old and over residing in the Census tract was 8.4 (compared to 11.0 for the city as a whole), and the proportion who had graduated from high school was 18.4 (compared to 42.5 for the city as a whole). The level of educational attainment was higher in our sample because persons under 25 are included and younger Chicanos have higher educational attainment. The proportion of high school graduates was 43.9 in our sample.

4. The median age for persons of Mexican origin living in the United States is 20.3 years, compared to a median age of 28.9 years for the population as a whole (U.S. Bureau of the Census, 1976: 1).

5. It should be noted that the measure of support for civil liberties shown in Table 2 among Chicanos is a conservative estimate of such support, since persons whose response to these questions was "not sure" were treated as though they were not in support of civil liberties. In other words, responses were grouped into those who supported civil liberties and those who definitely did not or were not sure. When "not sure" responses are excluded the hypothesis is more strongly supported but is still not statistically significant.

6. The figure that 82% of the respondents support both measures of civil liberties is obtained when "not sure" responses are excluded. When "not sure" responses are included in the computation, the percentage supporting both measures is 63.

REFERENCES

Acuña, R.
    1972   Occupied America: The Chicano's Struggle Toward Liberation. New York: Harper & Row.

Adler, P. R.
1974   "The 1943 Zoot-Suit Riots: brief episode in a long conflict," pp. 142-158 in
       M. P. Servin (ed.) An Awakened Minority: The Mexican-Americans. Encino,
       CA: Glencoe.
Bayley, D. H. and H. Mendelsohn
1969   Minorities and the Police. New York: Macmillan.
Block, R. L.
1971   "Fear of crime and fear of the police." Social Problems 19 (Summer): 91-101.
Boggs, S. L. and J. F. Galliher
1975   "Evaluating the police: a comparison of black street and household respon-
       dents." Social Problems 22 (February): 393-406.
Castillo, P. and A. Camarillo
1973   Furia y Muerte: Los Bandidos Chicanos. Los Angeles: Aztlán.
Chackerian, R. and R. F. Barrett
1973   "Police professionalism and citizen evaluation." Urban Affairs Q. 6 (March):
       345-349.
Endore, G.
1942   The Sleepy Lagoon Mystery. Los Angeles: Citizens' Committee for the Defense
       of Mexican-American Youth.
Ennis, P. H.
1967   Criminal Victimization in the United States: A Report of a National Survey.
       Washington DC: Government Printing Office.
Furstenberg, F. F., Jr. and C. F. Wellford
1973   "Calling the police: the evaluation of police service." Law and Society Rev.
       (Spring): 393-406.
Goldfinch, C. W.
1949   "Juan N. Cortina, 1824-1892: A re-appraisal." Master's thesis, University of
       Chicago.
Gómez-Q, J.
1970   "Plan De San Diego reviewed." Aztlán: Chicano J. of Social Sciences and
       Arts 1 (Spring): 124-132.
Hahn, H.
1971   "Ghetto assessments of police protection and authority." Law and Society Rev.
       6 (November): 183-194.
Hoffman, A.
1974   Unwanted Mexican-Americans in the Great Depression. Tucson: Univ. of
       Arizona Press.
Janowitz, M.
1969   "Patterns of collective racial violence," pp. 412-444 in H. D. Graham and T.
       R. Gurr (eds.) The History of Violence in America: Historical and Comparative
       Perspectives. New York: Praeger.
McWilliams, C.
1949   "California and the wetback." Common Ground 9 (Summer): 15-20.
1968   North from Mexico. New York: Greenwood.
Mexican-American Legal Defense and Education Fund (MALDEF)
1978a "MALDEF documents official abuse of authority against Mexican-Amer-
       icans in letter to Attorney General Griffin Bell." San Francisco.
1978b "Dallas brutality conference displays Chicano unity." MALDEF 8 (Summer):
       1-8.

Morales, A.
    1972   Ando Sangrando [I Am Bleeding]: A Study of Mexican-American Police
            Conflict. La Puente, CA: Perspective.
Murphy, R. J. and J. W. Watson
    1970   "The structure of discontent: relationship between social structure, grievance,
            and riot support," pp. 140-257 in N. Cohen (ed.) The Los Angeles Riots. New
            York: Praeger.
Paredes, A.
    1958   With His Pistol in His Hand: A Border Ballad and Its Hero. Austin: Univ. of
            Texas Press.
Phillips, J. L. and R. B. Coates
    1971   "Two scales for measuring attitudes toward police." Wisconsin Sociologist 8
            (Spring): 3-19.
Raine, W.
    1970   "The perception of police brutality in South Central Los Angeles," pp. 380-412
            in N. Cohen (ed.) The Los Angeles Riots. New York: Praeger.
Rosenbaum, Robert J.
    1973   "Las Gorras Blancas of San Miguel County, 1889-1890," pp. 128-133 in R.
            Rosaldo et al. (eds.) Chicano: The Evolution of a People. Minneapolis: Winston.
Schlesinger, A. B.
    1971   "Las Gorras Blancas, 1889-1891." J. of Mexican Amer. History 1 (Spring):
            87-143.
Sleepy Lagoon Defense Committee
    1942   The Sleepy Lagoon Case. Los Angeles: Citizens' Committee for the Defense of
            Mexican-American Youth.
Smith, P. E. and R. O. Hawkins
    1973   "Victimization, types of citizen-police contacts, and attitudes toward the po-
            lice." Law and Society Rev. 8 (Fall): 135-152.
Trujillo, L. D.
    1974   "La Evolución del 'Bandido' al 'Pachuco': a critical examination and evaluation
            of criminological literature on Chicanos." Issues in Criminology 9 (Fall): 43-67.
U. S. Bureau of the Census
    1976   "Persons of Spanish origin in the United States: March 1976." Current Popula-
            tion Reports, Series P-20, No. 302. Washington DC: Government Printing
            Office.
U.S. Commission on Civil Rights
    1970   Mexican Americans and the Administration of Justice in the Southwest. Wash-
            ington DC: Government Printing Office.
Webb, W. P.
    1965   The Texas Rangers. Austin: Univ. of Texas Press.
    1975   The Texas Rangers in the Mexican War. Austin: Jenkins Garrett Press.

*Alfredo Mirandé is Associate Professor of Sociology and Chair of Chicano Studies
at the University of California, Riverside. He has recently coauthored a book,* La
Chicana: The Mexican American Woman, *published by the University of Chicago
Press. Professor Mirandé's research and teaching interests include Chicano
sociology, the Chicano family, the Chicano and the law, and deviance and
criminology.*

FEAR OF CRIME AND FEAR OF THE POLICE IN A CHICANO COMMUNI[

Alfredo Mirande**
University of California, Riverside

ABSTRACT

This study compared the attitudes of Chicanos in a southern California barrio toward crime, the police, and civil liberties with the attitudes on these issues of black and white respondents from a previous NORC survey. There was support among the three groups for the hypotheses that fear of crime leads to support for augmenting police power and conversely, that fear of the police increases support for civil liberties. Fear of the police similarly was associated with a desire to curtail police power.

Significant differences among the three racial-ethnic groups were also observed. Anglos reported receiving better treatment from the police and were more supportive of them. They also appeared to be less fearful of crime than Chicanos who, in turn, appeared less fearful than blacks. Though Chicanos seemed to have less fear of crime than blacks, they have had more fear of and were less supportive of the police. Chicanos were also most supportive of civil liberties, and anglos least supportive. The strong fear and distrust of the police, and the intense support for civil liberties was, undoubtedly, a product of the long history of police abuse and harassment of Chicanos.

Over the past decade, fear of crime and crime in the streets have become salient issues in American society, eliciting concern not only among politicians and the mass media but the public at large. Public concern with crime and with the fear of victimization is increasing as evidenced by the fact that many Americans indicate that they are afraid to walk alone at night in their neighborhoods and feel insecure or unsafe in the confines of their own home. Whether these attitudes are a direct result of actual increases in the incidence of crime or a response to media portrayals,[1] fear of crime is an area worthy of sociological study. Why, for example, do people fear crime? What forces intensify or diminish this fear? Is there a relationship between attitudes toward the police and fear of crime? Does fear of crime lead to greater support for increased police power and curtailment of civil liberties? Do white and nonwhite respondents differ in their perceptions of crime and of the police?

Despite the important theoretical and practical implications of these questions, sociologists have shown a remarkable disinterest in them. A notable exception is Richard L. Block's (1971) study "Fear of Crime and Fear of the Police." Using data collected by the National Opinion Research Center (NORC) in the summer of 1966, Block tested a number of suggestive hypotheses. He found that fear of crime was only weakly related to either support for increased police power of protection from them, while fear of the police was strongly related to both of these variables. The study is especially significant because the data were gathered in the midst of urban unrest and black protest, and the findings provide some insights into

*Please do not cite or quote without the author's written permission.
**The preparation of this manuscript was supported by an intramural research grant from the University of California, Riverside.

110

racial differences in the operation of these variables. The hypothesis that fear of the police would be positively related to a demand for increased protection of civil liberties, for example, was supported among white but not among black respondents.

Though several years have passed since its publication and more than a decade has elapsed since the data were collected, there have been, to this writer's knowledge, no attempts to replicate its results. There is research, however, that relates indirectly. A number of surveys have attempted to assess attitudes toward the police and the evaluation of police services (see, for example, Smith and Hawkins, 1973; Furstenberg and Wellford, 1973; Phillips and Coates, 1971; Chackerian and Barrett, 1973; and Hahn, 1971). Such studies show that black respondents are consistently more negative in their evaluation of the police (Bayley and Mendelson, 1969; Ennis, 1967; Raine, 1970; Hahn, 1971; Furstenberg and Wellford, 1973) and that these negative attitudes are not limited to lower status respondents but may, in fact, be more intense among persons of higher status (Murphy and Watson, 1970; Raine, 1970).

From the preceding it is clear that an important outcome of the turbulent 60's was an increased concern among researchers with issues such as police abuse and brutality and black perceptions of the police. Significantly, although urban unrest and police confrontations have been common occurrences in chicano urban barrios since the zootsuit riots of the 40's, there has been little empirical research on chicano/police conflict.[2] Most analyses of "minority" police relations turn, upon closer examination, to be analyses of black-police relations. While the importance of these studies should not be minimized, there is also a need for research that examines the dynamics of community-police relations in Chicano communities. The goals of this study are, therefore, two-fold: (1) to assess attitudes of chicanos toward the police and compare them with the attitudes of white and black respondents in the NORC study, and (2) to test Block's major hypotheses concerning fear of crime, fear of the police, support for increased police power, and support for civil liberties in a chicano community.

The Setting

The setting for this study is a chicano barrio in a southern California community of approximately 150,000 inhabitants. Like most barrios in the southwest, it exists as a distinctive sub-community within the city. The barrio extends over an area that is approximately one square mile and includes about 3,000 persons within its boundaries.

The barrio shares certain important features with urban slums in that the income and educational level of many residents is low and some of the housing is poor or substandard, but it differs from the slum in some important respects. First, although there is poverty in the barrio, everyone is not poor. There is considerable variability in the economic and educational attainment of residents. Second, the barrio has emerged partly as a result of prejudice and segregation, but there is a strong element of voluntarism to barrio residence, and a strong sense of community identification prevails. Barrios are, literally, *colonias* (colonies), ethnic enclaves within the territorial boundaries of the United States. A distinctive feature of barrios, then, is not only their cultural but their geographical isolation. This barrio is similarly isolated.

The confluence of two diverse though mutually reinforcing forces -- residential segregation and a positive identification with barrio residence -- have worked to produce a remarkably stable pattern of community residence. Not only are most residents of the community chicano (about 90 percent), but, typically, they have lived there all, or virtually all, of their lives. This, of course, does not necessarily mean that most people born and raised in the barrio would remain there for the rest of their lives, since a community survey obviously excludes those persons who have moved out. What is significant is not that most people who are born in the barrio stay there but that very few new residents move in. New arrivals moreover, expecially if they come from Mexico are likely to have relatives or friends already living in the community. The stability of the community is further intensified by what appears to be a tendency toward endogamous marriage so that a strong sense of familism pervades community life. The statement frequently made in jest that "everyone in the barrio is related to everyone else" is not without some factual support. It is not uncommon for residents to claim 200 or 300 relatives in the community.

The stability, cohesiveness, and apparent serenity of the community stand in sharp contrast to the conflict and tension that pervades community-police relations. The police have traditionally been viewed not only as outsiders but as representatives of the dominant, oppressive anglo society. Over the past seven or eight years prior to the survey, there had been about one chicano shot per year. Residents complain of extensive police abuse and harassment. Community-police conflict is especially intense among youth, who are the most frequent targets of police abuse and harassment.

Community-police conflict culminated in two major incidents in August of 1975. One incident occurred on August 2, as the police broke up a bachelor party, tear-gassed the home where the party was going on, and beat up and arrested a large number of the guests. Although fifty-two persons were arrested, almost all charges were subsequently dropped for insufficient evidence and the city has since settled a number of civil suits out of court. Though the second incident was unrelated, it served to exacerbate anti-police sentiment. The stabbing of an anglo male, believed to be a police informer at a park in the community on August 13, provided that impetus for this incident. The police, in pursuit of the assailant(s), surrounded a cornfield throughout the evening of August 13 and the morning of August 14. Tear gas was dropped from a helicopter and there was extensive gunfire throughout the night. Sheriff's units from the County and a nearby county were brought in to reinforce city police, as was the SWAT team from a neighboring city. The result was a police siege. Residents were stopped and questioned by police as they attempted to go to work or carry on normal daily activities. Our survey of community attitudes toward the police was carried out within two months of these incidents. Its objective was to assess community attitudes toward the police, especially with respect to their handling of the incidents. Our study, although more focused, is, therefore, similar to the NORC survey which sampled opinions in the aftermath of urban disorders in Harlem, Watts, and other urban centers.

Despite differences in time and place between the NORC survey and our study, they are similar in being fielded following civil disorders and confrontations with police. The Block study differs, however, in that it is based on self-reported victims of crime and includes persons who claimed to have been victims and those who did not. The data were obtained by the National Opinion Research Center (NORC) in the summer of 1966 and cover crimes which were alleged to have taken place during the past year. Another limitation is that Block combines the response of victims and non-victims (1971:92). In addition, to increase comparability, he only considered a sub-sample of 790 residents of major cities outside the south, excluding suburban residents of these cities.

Method and Sample

A random sample of households yielded 170 completed interviews. Though the sample is based on a random selection of households, it is somewhat purposive in that, unlike the NORC survey, a special effort was made to include youthful respondents, since it is among them that conflict with the police is believed to be most intense.[3] Interviewers were instructed to interview an adult member of the household and a teen-aged member, whenever possible. This procedure was facilitated by the fact that interviewers normally worked in two-person teams. Inclusion of youth was also deemed important because chicanos as a group are, on the average, much younger than the overall population.[4] The sample consists of 38 percent male adults, 35 percent female adults, 16 percent male teenagers, and 9 percent female teenagers. Approximately one out of every four respondents, then, are dependent children.

Interviews were conducted by bilingual-bicultural interviewers, trained and sensitive to the nuances of chicano culture and the prevailing values of the barrio. Comments and suggestions of various political, civic, and community leaders were sought and incorporated into the interview schedule. Interviewers and the principal investigator met with these leaders and were briefed on practices, procedures, and dress and demeanor that were believed to elicit maximum cooperation from the community in carrying out the project. Without the help and endorsement of these community members, our task would have been more difficult, if not impossible.

While the interview schedule covered a number of areas, the focus of this paper is on the four major test variables in Block's NORC survey. The two independent variables in the Block study were fear of crime and fear of the police and the two dependent ones were support for increased police power and attitudes toward protection of civil liberties. The same indicators used in the NORC study were used *verbatim* to measure these variables. Fear of crime was measured by the following question taken from Block (1971: 93):

> "How likely is it that a person walking around at night might be held up or attacked" -- very likely, somewhat likely, somewhat unlikely, or very unlikely?

Also, as in the Block study, it was assumed that perceptions of police respectfulness provide a valid inverse indicator of fear of the police. Each person was, therefore, asked to indicate the degree of police respectfulness "toward people like myself," and those who rated police respectfulness as "not so good" were considered to fear the police more than those who rated it as "pretty good" or "very good." Support for increases in police power was assessed by the response to the following question

taken from the NORC study:
"Do you favor giving the police more power to question people, do you think they have enough power already, or would you like to see some of their power to question people curtailed?" (Block, 1971:93)
Finally, support for increased protection of civil liberties was ascertained by the response to two questions regarding support for police review boards and for the right of a suspect to an attorney during police interrogations.

Hypotheses
Two simple hypotheses proposed and tested in the Block study will be tested with our sample of Chicano respondents. The fact that Block tested these hypotheses controlling for race also enables us to make a systematic comparison of white, black, and Chicano responses to these variables. The first hypothesis he proposed is that the more a person feared crime, the greater would be the likelihood that he would support increases in police power. The second is that the greater a person's fear is of the police, the greater should be his support for increased protection of individual civil liberties. The reasoning behind these hypotheses, according to Block, is as follows:

If fear is a foundation of support for the state and the police are the state's instrument to control internal threat, then those people with the greatest fear of crime should be most willing to increase the power of the police. Similarly, if fear of the state is the basis for limitation of the power of the state, and the police as an instrument of the state are a basis of fear of the state, then those respondents who most fear the police would be most likely to want their power limited through the protection of civil liberties (Block, 1971: 94).

A third related hypothesis is also examined, namely that fear of the police and support of the police are inversely related. If fear of crime is the foundation for supporting increasing police power and fear of the state the basis for limiting it, then those respondents who are most fearful of the police should be least willing to increase their power.

Findings
Fear of Crime and Support for the Police. The data used to test the hypothesis that fear of crime is associated with greater support for the police are presented in Table 1. From the Table it is clear that the hypothesis was only moderately supported in the NORC survey of white and black respondents but it was strongly supported in our Chicano sample. Within all three racial groups, those respondents who said street attack was very likely were more likely to favor increases in police power, but the relationship was only statistically significant in the Chicano group ($p < .01$). Specifically, 67 percent of the white respondents who thought attack was very likely supported greater police power, compared to only 53 percent of those who thought attack was very unlikely. A similar pattern was found among black respondents: 42 percent of those who believed attack was very likely and only 24 percent of those who believed it was very unlikely felt the police should be given more power to question or interrogate people. The relationship was even

Table 1

Support for the Police by Fear of Attack by Race of Respondent

White NORC Sample*
Fear of Attack

Support Police	Very Likely	Somewhat Likely	Somewhat Unlikely	Very Unlikely	N
More	67% (42)	57% (100)	50% (114)	53% (82)	(338)
Enough	30 (19)	37 (65)	46 (104)	42 (65)	(253)
Curtail	3 (2)	6 (10)	4 (9)	5 (7)	(28)
Total	100% (63)	100% (175)	100% (227)	100% (154)	(619)

Gamma = .10   Chi-square = 7.54,   df = 6   (p < .30)

Black NORC Sample*
Fear of Attack

Support Police	Very Likely	Somewhat Likely	Somewhat Unlikely	Very Unlikely	N
More	42% (22)	21% (12)	28% (14)	24% (4)	(52)
Enough	41 (21)	65 (37)	58 (29)	53 (9)	(96)
Curtail	17 (9)	14 (8)	14 (7)	23 (4)	(28)
Total	100% (52)	100% (57)	100% (50)	100% (17)	(176)

Gamma = .13   Chi-square = 8.54,   df = 6   (p < .30)

Chicano Sample
Fear of Attack

Support Police	Very Likely	Somewhat Likely	Somewhat Unlikely	Very Unlikely	N
More	18% (7)	18% (9)	19% (6)	4% (2)	(24)
Enough	55 (21)	69 (34)	45 (14)	41 (19)	(88)
Curtail	26 (10)	12 (6)	35 (11)	54 (25)	(52)
Total	100% (38)	100% (49)	100% (31)	100% (46)	(164)

Gamma = .35   Chi-square = 22.42,   df = 6   (p < .01)

*Adapted from Richard L. Block, 1971, "Fear of Crime and Fear of the Police." Social Problems 19 (Summer), p. 95.

Table 2

Support for Protection of Civil Liberties by Fear of the Police
(Police Respectfulness) by Race of Respondent

White NORC Sample*
Police Respectfulness

Support Civil Liberties	Not so Good	N	Pretty Good	N	Very Good	N	N
Both	37%	(13)	39%	(67)	22%	(89)	(169)
One	57	(20)	47	(80)	53	(214)	(314)
None	6	(2)	14	(24)	25	(101)	(127)
Total	100%	(35)	100%	(171)	100%	(404)	(610)

Gamma = .34   Chi-square = 45.54, df = 4 (p < .001)

Black NORC Sample*
Police Respectfulness

Support Civil Liberties	Not so Good	N	Pretty Good	N	Very Good	N	N
Both	71%	(42)	53%	(42)	62%	(22)	(106)
One	26	(15)	47	(38)	36	(12)	(65)
None	3	(2)	--		2	(1)	(3)
Total	100%	(59)	100%	(80)	100%	(35)	(174)

Gamma = .07   Chi-square = 9.33, df = 4 (p < .10)

Chicano
Police Respectfulness

Support Civil Liberties	Not so Good	N	Pretty Good	N	Very Good	N	N
Both	70%	(43)	62%	(37)	50%	(17)	(97)
One	30	(18)	38	(23)	50	(17)	(58)
None	--		--		--		
Total	100%	(61)	100%	(60)	100%	(34)	(155)

Gamma = .27   Chi-square = 3.95, df = 4 (p < .20)

* Adapted from Richard L. Block, 1971, "Fear of Crime and Fear of the Police," Social Problems 19 (Summer), p. 96.

stronger in the Chicano sample. Eighteen percent of the barrio respondents who believed attack was very likely supported greater police power, whereas only 4 percent of those who felt it was very unlikely, did so.

The marginal differences among the three groups are also worth noting. White respondents, as might be expected, were less likely to feel that attack was very likely (10 percent) than were blacks (30 percent) or Chicanos (23 percent). Although the crime rate has increased consistently over the past decade, there was apparently less fear of crime, at least among Chicanos in our sample than among blacks in Block's NORC sample. For example, 28 percent of the chicanos and only 10 percent of the blacks said that attack was very unlikely in their neighborhoods. Not only did Chicanos appear to have less fear of crime than blacks but they also more willing than either blacks or whites in the NORC study to want to curtail police power. Thirty-two percent of Chicanos wanted to curtail police power, compared to 16 percent of black and only 5 percent of white respondents.

Fear of the Police and Support for Civil Liberties. There was considerable support in the NORC study among white respondents but not among black respondents for the hypothesis that persons who feared the police most were most likely to support the protection of civil liberties. Table 2 shows that 37 percent of the white respondents who feared the police most (evaluated police respect as not so good) supported both measures to protect civil liberties, while only 22 percent of those who had little fear of the police (evaluated police respect as very good) supported both measures. Among blacks, however, those respondents who were somewhat afraid of the police were least apt to support civil liberties.[5] Among Chicano respondents, the relationship was in the predicted direction, although it was not statistically significant. Seventy percent of those respondents who feared the police most support both measures to protect civil liberties, compared to only 50 percent of those who fear the police least. Perhaps more significant was the overall level of commitment to civil liberties in the Chicano sample. In fact, there was very little variation in the dependent variable among Chicanos, since none were opposed to both measures of civil liberties and approximately 82 percent favored both measures, compared to only 28 percent of the white and 61 percent of the black respondents.[6]

Support for the Police and Fear of the Police. The relationship between support for the police and fear of the police is found in Table 3. The figures in the Table indicate that fear of the police and support for police power are inversely related. Respondents who feared the police most, in other words, were least likely to support increases in police power. Among white respondents only 36 percent of those who feared the police most supported increasing the power of the police, while 62 percent of those who did not fear the police sought to increase their power. The same pattern was found among blacks and Chicanos, and the relationship was especially strong in the Chicano group. Only two percent of the Chicanos who feared the police most desired to increase police power, whereas 32 percent of those who did not fear the police desired to curtail it, a difference which was highly significant (p=.001). It is also interesting to note that fear of the police appeared most intense among Chicanos and least among whites. Thirty-nine percent of the Chicano respondents expressed fear of the police

Table 3

Support for the Police by Fear of the Police
(Police Respectfulness) by Race of Respondent

White NORC Sample[*]
Police Respectfulness

Support Police	Not so Good	N	Pretty Good	N	Very Good	N	N
More	36%	(11)	44%	(73)	62%	(237)	(321)
Enough	45	(14)	48	(79)	35	(134)	(227)
Curtail	19	(6)	8	(13)	3	(11)	(30)
Total	100%	(31)	100%	(165)	100%	(382)	(578)

Gamma = -.37   Chi-square = 33.39, df = 4 (p < .001)

Black NORC Sample*
Police Respectfulness

Support Police	Not so Good	N	Pretty Good	N	Very Good	N	N
More	15%	(5)	22%	(16)	44%	(24)	(45)
Enough	56	(19)	68	(50)	39	(21)	(90)
Curtail	29	(10)	11	(8)	17	(9)	(27)
Total	100%	(34)	100%	(74)	100%	(54)	(162)

Gamma = -.34   Chi-square = 17.92, df = 4 (p < .01)

Chicano
Police Respectfulness

Support Police	Not so Good	N	Pretty Good	N	Very Good	N	N
More	2%	(1)	20%	(12)	32%	(11)	(24)
Enough	35	(21)	67	(41)	59	(20)	(82)
Curtail	63	(38)	13	(8)	9	(3)	(49)
Total	100%	(60)	100%	(61)	100%	(34)	(155)

Gamma = -.72   Chi-square = 51.84, df = 4 (p < .001)

[*] Adapted from Richard L. Block, 1971, "Fear of Crime and Fear of the Police," Social Problems 19 (Summer), p. 97.

118

(rated police respect toward persons like themselves as not so good) compared to 21 percent of the black and 5 percent of the white respondents.

Summary and Discussion

The rising rate of crime and urban unrest have led to an overwhelming concern with crime and crime in the streets. Of particular interest has been whether fear of crime increases support for police power and decreases support for civil liberties. Much of the research that emerged in the aftermath of urban disorders in the 60's focused either on the evaluation of the police and police services by black respondents or on racial differences in perceptions of the police and crime. Emphasis on black respondents has led to an almost total neglect of perceptions of the police and crime held by other minority group members. Though Chicanos have a long history of conflict with police agencies that dates from the Treaty of Guadalupe-Hidalgo to the present, there has been very little research on Chicano-police relations.

This study has sought to assess attitudes of residents of a southern California barrio toward the police, crime, and civil liberties and to compare these responses with those of black and white respondents in a survey conducted more than a decade ago. Two major hypotheses proposed and tested by Block in the earlier study were also subjected to test with the Chicano sample.

Despite the obvious differences between the Chicano survey and the NORC study, there was support for both hypotheses in each of the surveys. While Block found only moderate support among white and black respondents for the hypothesis that fear of crime leads to increases in support for police power, Chicano respondents very strongly supported it. The second hypothesis that persons who feared the police most would be most likely to favor the protection of civil liberties, received limited support among Chicanos in our survey, substantial support among whites in the NORC survey, and virtually none among blacks in the NORC survey.

One reason for lack of support for the second hypothesis with black respondents may be the unrepresentativeness of the NORC sample, particularly its black component. Block himself acknowledges that

> the survey has been severely criticized for underrepresenting people who are particularly critical of the police. Young male adult males, especially blacks, were frequently excluded, even though they were victims of crime, because they did not happen to tell thier mothers that they were assaulted and their mothers served as household crime enumerators (1971:92).

In our Chicano sample, on the other hand, special efforts were made to insure that youthful respondents were included.

Perhaps another reason for lack of support for the second hypothesis among blacks and its somewhat limited support among Chicanos is the almost universal approval of civil liberties among minority group members. More than four of five Chicanos and six of ten blacks supported *both* forms of civil liberties and virtually none were opposed to both. Only three of ten white respondents, on the other hand, supported both forms of civil liberties. If support for civil liberties continues to increase among ethnic minorities, prevailing measures of support for civil liberties will have to be supplanted by more sophisticated measures capable of discerning intra-racial differences in such support.

The final relationship examined was between fear of the police and support for increased police, power. The findings suggested that among black, white, and Chicano respondents fear of the police was associated with a desire to curtail police power and that the relationship was especially strong in the Chicano sample.

There were also significant differences within the three ethnic groups in attitudes toward crime, perceived treatment by the police, and their relationship to the legal-judicial system. Anglos obviously believed they received better treatment from the police and were more supportive of them than blacks or Chicanos. They also had less reasons to be fearful of personal attack, since they were less apt to be victims of violent crimes. Predictably then, fear of crime was least among white and greatest among black respondents. Interestingly, though Chicanos seemed to fear crime less than blacks, they apparently feared the police more, his fear is not without justification. The history of Chicano-police relations has been one of conflict and tension. The U.S. Civil Rights Commission (1970:88), for example, found "evidence of widespread patterns of police misconduct against Mexican-Americans in the southwest." Police agencies such as the Texas Rangers have traditionally served as tools for maintaining the oppressed position of Chicanos in the southwest. This abuse and mistreatment, not surprisingly, has contributed not only to greater fear and distrust of the police, but to increased support for civil liberties. The police are not typically viewed as supportive and protective agencies but as vehicles for maintaining and protecting the interests of anglo-American society. For Chicanos, justice in the United States has come to mean "just us."

Despite the lack of comparability between our survey and the NORC study, the patterns that emerged have potentially significant implications if supported by subsequent research. That Chicanos appear least fearful of crime and most fearful of the police and supportive of civil liberties is significant for this pattern is contrary to the general movement in the society as a whole. There appears to be a clear trend toward acceptance of a "law and order" stance, increasing support of the police, and tolerance for the abridgment of civil guarantees in the interest of curtailing crime. Many of the landmark Supreme Court decision upholding the rights of suspects came in the early 60's. The NORC study followed on the heels of riots and urban disturbances that served to highlight police abuses and the need for safeguarding civil liberties. The landmark Escobedo decision, guaranteeing a suspect's right to a lawyer during police interrogations, was rendered just one month before the NORC survey was fielded. These events should have intensified support for civil liberties and the desire to curtail police power, especially in black communities where such abuses were undoubtedly most persistent.

Chicanos have not been immune to these trends but confrontations with police, rather than declining, have escalated over the past decade (MALDEF, 1978a, 1978b). As a result, fear of the police and concern with curtailment of police power and with violations of civil liberties are more salient issues in Chicano communities than fear of crime.

Given differences in attitudes toward the police and crime and experiences with them, the comparability of the findings in the two studies appears even more striking. This suggests substantial stability in the operation of these variables over time and across racial-ethnic groups. Thus, though Chicanos and blacks are generally more fearful of the police, less supportive of increased police power, and more supportive of civil liberties than anglos, the interrelationships among these variables are virtually the same in the three groups.

The findings of this study are instructive but they should be interpreted with caution. Differences in time and space between the samples make generalizations beyond these populations hazardous. The NORC survey was conducted more than a decade ago and is, therefore, not directly comparable to the Chicano survey. In addition, the study is limited to a single barrio in southern California and although it appears typical of many other barrios, we cannot be certain the same patterns would be found in other regions or among non-barrio Chicanos. There are also limitations in the NORC study in that the sample, as noted earlier, may have under-represented younger black respondents who are most likely to be victims of crime and critical of the police.

These limitations notwithstanding, the results have important theoretical and practical implications. Among black, white and Chicano respondents, increases in the crime rate generally lead to greater support for increasing police power and limiting civil liberties, while fear of the police seems to lessen support for police power and to increase support for civil guarantees. Despite these similarities, the three racial-ethnic groups differ in their overall support and fear of the police and in fear of crime and advocacy of civil liberties. Before these generalizations are accepted as conclusive, however, research is needed to substantiate them in other settings. Such research will hopefully provide additional insights into the dynamics of community-police relations among minority groups and in the population as a whole.

FOOTNOTES

[1] There is evidence which suggests that public conceptions of crime may be shaped more by media portrayals than by direct exposure, whether as a result of victimization or knowledge of the victimization of others. See, for example, Davis (1952); Bachmuth, Miller, and Rosen (1960); and Quinney (1970: 281-285).

[2] Existing research consists primarily of historical rather than hypothesis-testing empirical studies. See McWilliams (1949), Acuna (1972), Castillo and Camarillo (1973), Trujillo (1974), United States Commission on Civil Rights (1970), and Morales (1972).

[3] While this procedure may appear to "stack the deck," so to speak, it is important to mention that the youth included in the survey probably are less negative than those youth who were excluded. It is generally acknowledged that household surveys tend to exclude persons who are most critical of the police. In a comparison of black street and household respondents, for example, "the pattern found in previous surveys, suggesting a negative relationship between social status and attitudes of blacks toward police, as indexed by rating of police service, was not supported when the street population was taken into account" (Boggs and Galliher, 1975: 405).

[4] In 1976, the median age for persons of Mexican origin living in the United States was 20.3 years, compared to a median age of 28.9 years for the population as a whole (U.S. Bureau of the Census, 1976: 1).

[5] An additional problem is that some of the expected frequencies in the black NORC sample are less than 5. It is generally agreed that Chi-square should not be applied when this occurs. It should also be noted that when $df > 1$, Chi-square is insensitive to the effects of order. The Chi-square test was used to facilitate comparisons between our study and the NORC study.

[6]It should be noted that the measure of support for civil liberties among Chicanos in Table 2 is a conservative estimate of such support, since persons whose response to these questions was "not sure" were treated as though they were not in support of civil liberties. In other words, responses were grouped into those who supported civil liberties and those who definitely did not or were not sure. When "not sure" responses are excluded the hypothesis is more strongly supported but is still not statistically significant. It is not clear from the Block (1971: 93) article, how "not sure" responses were classified. The figure that 82 percent of the Chicano respondents support both measures of civil liberties is obtained when "not sure" responses are excluded. When "not sure" responses are included in the computation the percentage supporting both measures is sixty-three.

REFERENCES

Acuna, Rodolfo
    1972 · Occupied America: The Chicano's Struggle Toward Liberation. San Francisco: Canfield Press.
Bachmuth, Rita, S. M. Miller, and Linda Rosen
    1960 "Juvenile delinquency in the daily press." Alpha Kappa Delta (Spring): 47-51.
Bayley, David H., and Harold Medelsohn
    1971 Minorities and the Police. New York: Free Press.
Block, Richard L.
    1971 "Fear of crime and fear of the police." Social Problems 19 (Summer): 91-101.
Boggs, Sarah L., and John F. Galliher
    1975 "Evaluating the police: a comparison of black street and household respon-dents." Social Problems 22 (February): 393-406.
Campbell, Angus, and H. Schuman
    1968 "Racial Attitudes in Fifteen American Cities." Supplemental Studies for the National Advisory Commission on Civil Disorders." Washington, D.C.: U.S. Government Printing Office.
Castillo, Pedro and Albert Camarillo
    1973 Furia y Muerte: Los Bandidos Chicanos. Los Angeles: Aztlan Publications, Monograph No. 4.
Chakerian, Richard, and Richard F. Barrett
    1973 "Police professionalism and citizen evaluation." Urban Affairs Quarterly 6 (March): 345-349.
Davis, F. James
    1952 "Crime news in Colorado newspapers." American Journal of Sociology 57 (January): 325-330.
Ennis, Philip H.
    1967 Criminal Victimization in the United States: A Report of a National Survey. Washington, D.C.: U.S. Government Printing Offoce.
Furstenberg, Frank F. Jr., and Charles F. Wellford
    1973 "Calling the police: the evaluation of police service." Law and Society Review 7 (Spring): 393-406.
Hahn, Harlan
    1971 "Ghetto assessments of police protection and authority." Law and Society Review 6 (November): 183-194.
Mexican American Legal Defense and Education Fund (MALDEF)
    1978a "MALDEF Documents Official Abuse of Authority Against Mexican-Americans in Letter to Attorney General Griffin Bell." San Francisco.
    1978b "Dallas Brutality Conference Displays Chicano Unity." MALDEF 8 (Summer): 1-8.
Morales, Armando
    1972 Ando Sangrando (I Am Bleeding): A Study of Mexican American-Police Con-flict. La Puente, CA: Perspectiva Publications.
Murphy, Raymond J., and James W. Watson
    1970 "The structure of discontent: relationship between social structure, grievance,

and riot support," pp. 140-257 in Nathan Cohen (ed.), The Los Angeles Riots. New York: Praeger.

McWilliams, Carey
1949   North From Mexico. Philadelphia and New York: J.B. Lippincott.

Phillips, Jerri Linn, and Robert B. Coates
1971   "Two scales for measuring attitudes toward police." Wisconsin Sociologist (Spring): 3-19.

Quinney, Richard
1970   The Social Reality of Crime. Boston: Little, Brown.

Raine, Walter
1970   "The perception of police brutality in south central Los Angeles." Pp. 380-412 in Nathan Cohen (ed.), The Los Angeles Riots. New York: Praeger.

Smith, Paul E., and Richard O. Hawkins
1973   "Victimization, types of citizen-police contacts, and attitudes toward the police." Law and Society Review 8 (Fall): 135-152.

Trujillo, Larry D.
1974   "La evolucion del 'bandido' al 'pachuco': a critical examination and evaluation of criminological literature on Chicanos." Issues in Criminology 9 (Fall): 43-67.

United States Bureau of the Census
1976   "Person of Spanish Origin in the United States: March 1976." Current Population Reports, Series P-20, No. 302. Washington, D.C.: U.S. Government Printing Office.

United States Commission on Civil Rights
1970   Mexican Americans and the Administration of Justice in the Southwest. Washington, D.C.: U.S. Government Printing Office.

ETHNICITY AND JUSTICE IN THE SOUTHWEST: THE SENTENCING OF ANGLO, BLACK, AND MEXICAN ORIGIN DEFENDANTS[1]

Malcolm D. HOLMES, *New Mexico State University*

Howard C. DAUDISTEL, *The University of Texas at El Paso*

This study compares severity of case disposition for Anglo, black and Mexican origin burglary and robbery defendants in two metropolitan jurisdictions in the southwestern United States. Both the additive effects of the race variables and their interactions with other determinants of sentence severity were considered. Substantial evidence of discrimination in both additive and interactive models was obtained for one jurisdiction, but the evidence of discrimination was considerably weaker for the other. Jurisdictional differences which may explain this contrast are discussed.

Majority-minority sentencing differentials have been the subject of extensive social scientific and legal research. As with many studies of race and ethnic relations, the criminological literature reflects a traditional research orientation that focuses on blacks to the veritable exclusion of other minorities. Here we also examine the sentencing of black and white felons, but, more importantly, our analysis emphasizes the legal system's treatment of those of Mexican origin in the southwestern United States.

Many social scientists consider it axiomatic that racial and ethnic minorities receive harsh and unequal treatment in the American criminal justice system (e.g., Quinney, 1970; Chambliss and Seidman, 1971; Blauner, 1972). Certainly evidence of this exists with respect to blacks (National Advisory Commission on Civil Disorders, 1968) and those of Mexican origin (U.S. Commission on Civil Rights, 1970), but the data regarding sen-

[1] The data used in this study were collected under the auspices of Grant 77-NI-99-0049 awarded to H. S. Miller, W. McDonald, J. Cramer, and H. Rossman, Institute of Criminal Law and Procedure, Georgetown University Law Center, by the National Institute of Law Enforcement and Criminal Justice, Law Enforcement Assistance Administration, U.S. Department of Justice. Ronald A. Farrell and Cookie White Stephan provided very helpful comments on an earlier draft of this paper. The referees of *SSQ* also provided useful comments. The authors are solely responsible for the data analysis and points of view presented in this study. Editor's note: Reviewers were Rodolfo de la Garza, Ricardo Romo, and Susan Welch.

tencing are hardly unequivocal. Two recent reviews of the substantial black-white sentencing literature (Hagan, 1974; Kleck, 1981) offer only inconclusive support for the hypothesis that otherwise similar black and white defendants receive unequal sentences. Moreover, Hagan (1974) cautions that even where *statistically* significant differences in the sentences given blacks and whites have been reported, the *substantive* significance or magnitude of the disparities has often been quite marginal (a function of the large samples commonly employed in such research). Kleck (1981) has reached an even stronger conclusion, arguing that, at least in the aggregate, *overt* discrimination in the sentencing of blacks is no longer detectable.

The relatively limited data on the sentencing of Mexican origin defendants also offer little systematic evidence of discrimination (e.g., Lemert and Rosberg, 1948; Baab and Furgeson, 1967; Garza, 1973; Sissons, 1977; Petersilia, 1983; Welch, Gruhl, and Spohn, 1984). As with many studies of black-white sentencing patterns, some of these do not adequately control relevant characteristics of the defendant or crime (Lemert and Rosberg, 1948; Garza, 1973; Sissons, 1977). However, even well-executed studies provide only mixed results (cf. Baab and Furgeson, 1967; Petersilia, 1983; Welch, Gruhl, and Spohn, 1984).

Despite the mixed data and consequent conclusions, concern about equality persists. Since it has been well documented that criminal justice agents at all stages of the system have been granted a significant amount of discretionary freedom (e.g., LaFave, 1965; Blumberg, 1967; Alschuler, 1968; Rosett and Cressey, 1976), the legal system offers relatively few real restraints to decision-makers charged with enforcing the law. Extralegal (i.e., nonstatutory) considerations may informally influence the administration of justice in ways that are formally regarded as illegitimate. Since crimes are acts which are defined as criminal by officials of the legal system who must interpret both the meaning of the law and the behavior of those alleged to have acted criminally, informal notions about the character of defendants may constitute self-fulfilling prophecies. Institutionalized within the legal system are stereotypical conceptions of criminality which affect the treatment of defendants throughout the adjudication process (e.g., Sudnow, 1965; Quinney, 1970; Swigert and Farrell, 1977). Since lower-class, minority males are more likely to fit popular images of criminality, such defendants are especially susceptible to stigmatization and, consequently, differential treatment (Simmons, 1965; Swigert and Farrell, 1977). Indeed, the "subculture of justice" (Rosett and Cressey, 1976) in a particular jurisdiction may consist of several lay theories about human behavior that disadvantage minorities.

A related consideration is whether we can expect *all* minority defendants to be sentenced differently than their majority group counterparts. The answer is unquestionably no. Characteristics of an alleged criminal act certainly affect the perceived character of the defendant. LaFree (1980), for instance, has shown that racial identities within the criminal-victim dyad strongly influence sentencing in rape cases. He concludes that "American society is characterized by a sexual stratification system which imposes more serious sanctions on men from less powerful social groups who are accused of assaulting women from more powerful social groups" (La Free, 1980:852). Thus, how the various attributes of a case affect sentence may vary because special significance can be attached to a particular combination of race and another characteristic. A number of legal (e.g., prior record, use of weapon) and extralegal (e.g., access to bail, jury trial) attributes apparently influence case disposition (e.g., Green, 1961; Ares, Rankin, and Sturz, 1963; Rankin, 1964; Sudnow, 1965; Chiricos, Jackson, and Waldo, 1972; Burke and Turk, 1975; Bernstein, Kelly, and Doyle, 1977; Uhlman and Walker, 1980), but scant attention has been paid to the possible interaction of race-ethnicity with such factors in the sentencing decision. Therefore, the research reported below not only considers whether race-ethnicity per se has an effect on sentence, net of the effects of relevant controls, but whether other predictors of sentence operate differently across subsamples of race or ethnic identity.

Finally, it is reasonable to anticipate that the relative quality of justice varies from jurisdiction to jurisdiction. Kleck (1981) suggests that not all informal notions about race-ethnicity and crime adversely affect minority defendants; rather, some actually operate to their benefit. Moreover, in cities where minorities represent a high proportion of the total population, they may be perceived as more threatening than in areas which are comprised predominantly of majority members (Blalock, 1967), thereby exacerbating the salience of negative criminality stereotypes. Since such issues could be pertinent to the present study, we conducted the analysis separately for the two metropolitan jurisdictions discussed below. The implications of jurisdictional differences are explored in our concluding remarks.

Research Setting and Data

The statistical analysis presented in this study is based on case files for "closed" (no appeal pending) burglary and robbery convictions prosecuted during the period of January 1976–August 1977 in the state district courts of El Paso, Texas, and Tucson, Arizona. Although other felonies and misdemeanors appear in these case files, the vast majority involved burglary or robbery offenses as the primary violation for which defendants were convicted.[2]

Probably one reason for the mixed results reported in sentencing studies is differences in the dependent measures used. Sentence length is commonly utilized (see Kleck, 1981:790–91), but is not without its disadvantages. Sentences of relatively indeterminate length are commonly imposed and, consequently, the actual period of incarceration (or probation) is con-

---

[2] Too few women, native Americans, acquittals, bench trials, and jail terms appear in these data to permit analysis of such cases. After the deletion of these cases, El Paso data only contained primary convictions for burglary or robbery offenses. Over 80 percent of the Tucson sample involved primary convictions on burglary and robbery charges. Other felonies were excluded to avoid infelicitously generalizing on the basis of a few cases (no other felony was represented by more than a handful of cases) and to maintain a high degree of comparability across the city subsamples.

tingent on factors such as inmate behavior and parole board decisions. Therefore, relatively small differences in length of imposed sentence could be essentially meaningless. A more clear-cut indicator of sentencing discrimination is variation in the likelihood of incarceration, a measure which also has been employed in previous studies. This measure corresponds well to the perceived severity of legal penalties (Erickson and Gibbs, 1979), and a great deal of the discretion available to the courts involves the decision to probate or incarcerate (Rosett and Cressey, 1976).

Although the most important distinction is probation versus incarceration, our dependent variable also included an intermediate category comprised of split sentences (e.g., prison with probation). Thus, the dependent variable was coded 0 = probation; 1 = split sentence; 2 = prison. The intermediate category represented the mode for the Tucson data (probation = 30.2%; split = 39.6%; prison = 30.2%), and it was important to separate this sentence type because maximum sentences (in years) were quite short ($\bar{X} = .79$; $SD = 1.15$) compared to prison sentences ($\bar{X} = 9.17$; $SD = 7.78$). Obviously this is an important distinction. In the El Paso data, only a single case was coded as a split sentence (probation = 55.2%; split = 0.6%; prison = 44.2%). Consequently, the El Paso results reported below are virtually identical to those obtained with a dichotomous dependent variable.[3]

Race-ethnicity was incorporated into the multiple regression analyses reported below as a set of dummy variables representing Anglo (non-Mexican origin white), black, and Mexican origin defendants. The use of dummy variables requires the deletion of one category (Anglo here) to avoid linear dependence, which category then serves as the baseline to interpret the regression coefficients estimated for the included categories.

As noted above, sentencing studies have been concerned with a number of other legal and extralegal predictors of sentence. An important criticism of many studies of race-ethnicity and sentencing is that they do not include such variables. Insofar as possible, we have incorporated such variables in this analysis, which helps guard against concluding that disparities in sentencing exist when the observed differences are actually a spurious indication of uncontrolled variation in other variables that may be

---

[3] The regression analyses reported below were also conducted with the split sentence and prison categories combined to create a dichotomous dependent variable. The regression coefficients obtained for Tucson were of the same direction, but were much weaker predictors than those reported here. The El Paso results were essentially identical; except the metric coefficients and their standard errors are approximately twice as large in the results presented here. Metric coefficients for the trichotomous dependent variable were reported because they can be compared directly to those presented for Tucson. Copies of the dichotomous regression results may be obtained from the authors upon request. It should also be noted that dependent variables such as used here technically violate the assumptions of ordinary least squares (OLS) regression, which assumes that the dependent variable is continuous. Normally, however, OLS regression is quite robust in the face of such violations (Bohrnstedt and Carter, 1971). Furthermore, an examination of the frequency distributions of the dependent variables (presented above) indicates that the distributions were not inordinately skewed, which substantially increases our confidence in the OLS regression results reported below.

correlated with race-ethnicity and sentence. Some such variables were not included in this analysis because they possessed negligible variation or too much missing data to be useful. These included factors such as type of counsel, race-ethnicity of victim, harm to victim, employment status, and citizenship.

Among the legally relevant controls is a set of dummy variables for the robbery and burglary felonies included in the data, which control for the length of sentence imposed by statute. The "felony one" category includes those offenses carrying a sentence of 5 to 99 years or life in prison in Texas, and not less than 5 years in Arizona. The felonies included in this category are aggravated robbery and major burglary offenses. The "felony two" felonies represent the necessarily deleted category for this set of dummy variables. The category includes offenses carrying a penalty of 2 to 20 years in Texas, and either 1 to 10 or 1 to 15 years in Arizona. This category is comprised of serious nonaggravated robbery and less serious burglary offenses. The "felony three" category includes crimes with sentences of 2 to 10 years in Texas, and less than 7½ years in Arizona. In the El Paso data, this category includes only burglary of an automobile, while in the Tucson data it includes several statutes concerning relatively petty burglary and robbery offenses.

Needless to say, a great deal of discretion is embodied in the essentially indeterminate sentencing codes of Texas and Arizona, particularly since these are felonies for which probation is often routinely granted. Consequently, a number of other legal factors are considered in our analysis, including prior felony convictions $(0-5+)$, whether the conviction was for multiple charges $(0 = no; 1 = yes)$, and whether a weapon was used in the commission of the crime $(0 = no; 1 = yes)$.

Several extralegal attributes of the defendant or his case disposition were also included as controls. These indicated whether the defendant achieved pretrial release $(0 = no; 1 = yes)$, whether he was convicted by a jury $(0 = no; 1 = yes)$, and number of prior *nonconviction* arrests $(0-5+).$[4]

Analysis and Results

The results of our sentencing analysis appear in Table 1. For reasons mentioned above, the ordinary least squares multiple regression analyses reported here were conducted separately for El Paso and Tucson. If evidence of overt discrimination exists for only one city, combining the city subsamples could easily mitigate or inflate the strength of such evidence.

Additionally, two models were estimated for each subsample. Model 1 presents the additive statistical model that permits us to examine the main

[4] The degree of intercorrelation among the independent variables included in this analysis generally was not substantial, although the correlation of use of a weapon and the felony one dummy variable category was fairly high in Tucson $(r = .67)$. Consequently, multicollinearity does not appear to be a significant problem in this analysis, although the Tucson coefficients for weapon use and felony one cannot be interpreted too literally. A copy of the correlation matrices and other descriptive statistics may be obtained from the authors upon request.

TABLE 1

Metric Coefficients, Standard Errors (in parentheses), and Standardized Coefficients for the OLS Regression of Sentence Severity on Legal and Extralegal Atributes

Independent Variables	El Paso (N = 163) Model 1	Model 2	Tucson (N = 321) Model 1	Model 2
Legal variables				
Felony one	−.058	−.108	.305**	.256*
	(.123)	(.115)	(.149)	(.149)
	−.029	−.053	.151	.127
Felony two[a]	—	—	—	—
Felony three	.277	.324	−.129	−.155*
	(.215)	(.201)	(.095)	(.094)
	.078	.092	−.083	−.099
Prior felony convictions				
(0–5+)	.237***	.238***	.108***	.107***
	(.044)	(.041)	(.018)	(.018)
	.344	.347	.312	.310
Multiple charge conviction (0 = no;				
1 = yes)	.535***	.448***	.044	−.036
	(.186)	(.176)	(.099)	(.115)
	.165	.138	.024	−.020
Use of a weapon				
(0 = no; 1 = yes)	.780***	.817***	.053	.052
	(.136)	(.129)	(.122)	(.122)
	.344	.360	.030	.029
Extralegal variables				
Pretrial release				
(0 = no; 1 = yes)	−.438***	−.523***	−.213**	−.211**
	(.120)	(.116)	(.084)	(.083)
	−.216	−.258	−.136	−.135
Prior nonconviction felony arrests				
(0–5+)	.122***	.108***	.090***	.089***
	(.040)	(.037)	(.028)	(.028)
	.192	.168	.166	.166
Jury trial (0 = no;				
1 = yes)	.136	−.795***	−.034	−.292
	(.149)	(.257)	(.144)	(.194)
	.054	−.315	−.012	−.108
Anglo[a]	—	—	—	—
Black	.870***	.870***	−.064	−.149
	(.218)	(.245)	(.117)	(.127)
	.246	.246	−.030	−.070
Mexican origin	.158	−.013	.013	−.084
	(.133)	(.129)	(.090)	(.100)
	.077	−.006	.008	−.050
Interaction terms				
Black × jury	—	—	—	0.548*
				(0.304)
				0.128
Mexican origin × jury	—	1.302***	—	0.757*
		(0.299)		(0.455)
		0.449		0.094

130

TABLE 1—continued

Independent Variables	El Paso (N = 163)		Tucson (N = 321)	
	Model 1	Model 2	Model 1	Model 2
Black × pretrial release	—	0.788* (0.404) 0.123	—	—
Mexican origin × multiple charge	—	—	—	0.292 (0.208) 0.091
Constant	0.344	0.505	0.840	0.903
R^2	.546	.611	.221	.238
Increment to R^2	—	.065***	—	.017*

a This category in each group of variables was necessarily deleted from the regression model and serves as the benchmark for interpreting this set of dummy variables.

*$p < .10$.

**$p < .05$.

***$p < .01$.

effects of the race-ethnicity variables on sentence after controlling for legal and extralegal attributes of the defendant and the crime for which he was convicted. Here an effort is made to determine if race-ethnicity affects case disposition severity independently of effects such as prior record. Model 2 permits us to assess whether the coefficients estimated in the additive model differ across race-ethnicity categories. For example, do jury trials work to the advantage or disadvantage of minority defendants? What about the use of a weapon or other facts of the case which might be perceived in a different light when the defendant is a minority member? The interaction terms added in model 2 were obtained using a forward stepwise procedure. Coefficients which achieved statistical significance ($p < .10$) were retained.

El Paso. Model 1 indicates that the use of a weapon, conviction on multiple charges, and especially prior felony convictions increased sentence severity. A felony one conviction did not increase a defendant's likelihood of being incarcerated, but those in the felony three category were actually somewhat more likely to be incarcerated than those in the deleted felony two category. We can only speculate about the latter finding, but we suspect that at least some automobile burglary dispositions involved a single offense even though the defendant may have been apprehended with a considerable amount of stolen property. Such adjudications are clearly expeditious from the standpoint of controlling court dockets.

With respect to the extralegal controls, we find that both pretrial release and prior felony arrests were related to dispositional severity. Making bail apparently reduced sentence severity, which is consistent with previous findings (Ares, Rankin, and Sturz, 1963; Rankin, 1964). Nonconviction prior arrests were associated with greater sentence severity. Although legally irrelevant, such arrests may act as a negative index of character. Although model 1 suggests that a jury trial had little effect on sentence severity, this seemingly negligible coefficient masks substantial interactions which will be analyzed with reference to model 2.

Our final observation with respect to model 1 concerns the main effects of the race-ethnicity variables on sentence severity. Here we find that the dummy variable for blacks is one of the best predictors of sentence. The metric coefficient ($b = .870$) represents nearly a full point on the severity scale. Thus, black defendants were virtually assured of incarceration, regardless of the circumstances of their personal biography and the crime for which they were convicted. Although the coefficient for Mexican origin defendants did not quite achieve statistical significance, it was again positive.

Turning to model 2, we find two interaction effects which merit attention. First and most significantly, the Mexican origin × jury interaction appears to be the best predictor of sentence among the variables contained in the regression. The metric coefficient ($b = 1.30$) approaches one-half the range of the severity scale, which attests to the virtual assurance of a prison sentence for Mexican origin defendants whose cases were heard by juries. The small coefficient for the Mexican origin category suggests that this interaction is responsible for the sentencing differential found in model 1.

In Texas, not only do juries determine guilt, they impose sentence. We cannot, however, simply attribute the Mexican origin × jury interaction to discrimination on the part of Anglo jurors. We have no systematic information about jury composition in these data, but it is general knowledge that those of Mexican origin commonly serve on El Paso juries. To the degree that they participated in these apparently discriminatory sentencing decisions, two factors may be involved. First, it has been observed that high-status jurors exert disproportionately high influence on jury decisions, while low-status jurors exert relatively little influence (Strodtbeck, James, and Hawkins, 1957). The high ethnic (and probably occupational) status of Anglo jurors might greatly influence mixed juries, even though their input may well reflect stereotypical conceptions about race-ethnicity and criminality. The other factor involves intragroup cleavages within the Mexican origin community. Some have argued that class differentiation can supersede ethnic similarity among those of Mexican origin (e.g., Stoddard, 1973). Therefore, middle-class Mexican origin jurors may perceive typically lower-class robbery and burglary defendants as threatening, not only relative to their property interests, but to their status within the middle-class community as a whole.

The substantive significance of this finding cannot be overemphasized. Thirteen percent of this subsample were Mexican origin defendants tried by juries, and the size of the interaction reported here is so great that alone it adds nearly 5 percent to the already quite substantial R^2 obtained in model 1.

The second interaction of interest is black × pretrial release. Unlike others, it would appear that blacks were not advantaged by obtaining bail. However, this interaction involved only a few cases; consequently, we must stress that great caution must be attached to any generalization from this finding.

Within the El Paso data it appears that Mexican origin defendants received harsher sentences *only* when tried by juries, while blacks consistently received more severe sentences. The El Paso state district court judges are elected officials, and the majority of El Paso's population is of Mexican origin (U.S. Bureau of the Census, 1983a). Consequently, it is likely that El Paso judges are especially sensitive to the Mexican origin community, since allegation of prejudicial sentencing could be quite damaging. Also, many courthouse actors, especially attorneys and police officers, are of Mexican origin. Blacks, on the other hand, are poorly represented both in the community and the courthouse. Thus, nothing acts to mitigate prejudicial sentencing, at least on the part of judges, who sentenced most blacks in these data.

Tucson. In this city, the legal variables which apparently affected case disposition severity are prior felony convictions and conviction for a felony one category offense. The coefficient for the felony three category was negative, although it did not achieve statistical significance. The remaining variables in the legal block appear not to have influenced the likelihood of incarceration. Use of a weapon was correlated with felony one here, which probably explains its seeming lack of influence.

Among the extralegal variables, again obtaining pretrial release worked to a defendant's advantage, while prior arrests did not. Although there appears to have been no effect of jury trial on sentence, this again is deceptive, as model 2 will demonstrate.

Insofar as race-ethnicity is concerned, the coefficients here indicate virtually no relationship to sentence. A comparison of the metric coefficients obtained here with those obtained for model 1 in El Paso indicates a marked contrast. With respect to the main effects, substantial evidence of discrimination exists in the El Paso data, while no such evidence appears in the Tucson data.

The findings of model 2 for Tucson also are not as striking as for El Paso, but an interesting parallel does exist—jury convictions affected negatively the sentences of both black and Mexican origin defendants. Juries do not sentence in Arizona, but judges appeared to punish inordinately the relatively small number of minority defendants who exercised their right to a jury trial, with 4 percent of the sample being adversely affected. This finding is consistent with evidence that justice is more punitive when defendants incur the time and cost of a jury trial (Uhlman and Walker, 1980).

Also, Mexican origin defendants convicted of multiple charges received more severe dispositions, on the average, than others (this coefficient was not quite statistically significant, but was retained because it was the first interaction entered in the stepwise regression). This is probably due to the severity of the lesser violations, which is not controlled for by the multiple charge variable.

Discussion and Conclusion

Our purpose in this study was to examine the degree to which black and Mexican origin defendants receive harsher sentences than their dominant group counterparts, *ceteris paribus*. In addition to the main effects of minority status on sentence severity, the interactions of race with other variables were considered. Within the two cities under consideration, the greatest disparities in felony sentencing were observed in El Paso. Blacks and those of Mexican origin tried before juries were considerably more likely to receive a severe sentence than otherwise similar Anglo defendants. Similarly, minority defendants in Tucson were more harshly treated when convicted by juries. On the whole, however, sentencing in Tucson appears considerably more uniform.

Perhaps the simplest explanation of this difference is that judges and juries are fairer in some areas than others. Texas, for instance, has an especially unfavorable history of mistreatment of those of Mexican origin (McWilliams, 1948/1968). Thus, our findings conceivably reflect differences in the quality of justice found in each city.

Probably more important, however, are differences in the criminal justice systems of the two cities. In one especially important aspect Tucson and El Paso were quite different during the period in which these data were collected. At that time, El Paso had instituted a policy of stringent case screening while prohibiting plea bargaining. Plea bargains were the rule in Tucson. Furthermore, minimal case screening allowed relatively unsupervised initial charge decisions by assistant prosecutors, who were also allowed a great deal of discretion in negotiating pleas (LaFree, 1983). Barriers against prejudicial charging or plea bargaining were thus quite formidable in El Paso and virtually nonexistent in Tucson. Discrimination in charging and plea negotiations could easily have occurred at an earlier stage in Tucson, with the adverse outcomes masked in the present study by focusing on evaluation at a later point in the adjudication process.

Another important factor is the sociodemographic composition of the two cities. At the end of the decade during which these data were gathered, El Paso's Spanish (primarily Mexican) origin population comprised 62 percent of the city total, while only 21 percent of Tucson's population was so classified (U.S. Bureau of the Census, 1983a, 1983b). Many have hypothesized that the larger the relative size of a minority group, the greater the perceived threat among the dominant group (e.g., Blalock, 1967). Evidence to this effect has recently been reported in the literature of race and the legal system. Jacobs (1979) has demonstrated that particularly after the urban upheaval of the 1960s, the police strength in cities is positively associated with both percent black and degree of economic inequality. Other research has demonstrated that percent black has an initially positive curvilinear relationship to police expenditures on salaries and operations (Jackson and Carroll, 1981). Plausibly, then, sentencing in high-minority areas may be more severe for minority defendants because they are perceived as threatening to the dominant community.

These arguments, while pertinent to the present research setting, are also intended to illustrate the many factors which might operate to the detriment of minority defendants convicted in particular jurisdictions. Well-executed studies also occasionally report evidence suggestive of reverse discrimination (e.g., Bernstein, Kelly, and Doyle, 1977). Kleck (1981) has argued that local conceptions about race and justice can work to the advantage of minority defendants in some jurisdictions. Ironically, the balancing equations of aggregate analyses such as Kleck's effectively ignore the possibility of direct and reverse discrimination at the jurisdiction level, even though he explicitly acknowledges that both forms of discrimination operate in at least some jurisdictions. Certainly, one important area for future research is the systematic evaluation of how community characteristics affect the sentencing of different groups.

The data presented here also emphasize the necessity of examining the interactions of race-ethnicity and other determinants of case disposition severity. If we had ignored such interactions in this study, comparatively little of importance would have appeared with respect to race-ethnicity and sentencing. We suspect that many studies reporting negative findings might have found quite different results had such interactions been considered.

Finally this analysis affirms the significance of research on race-ethnicity and sentencing. Given the paucity of data on the Southwest, the evidence presented about the sentencing of Mexican origin defendants is especially interesting. Scholars and policymakers should not facilely dismiss race as a factor in the judicial process. Increased attention to this problem from both camps is clearly warranted. SSQ

REFERENCES

Alschuler, Albert. 1968. "The Prosecutor's Role in Plea Bargaining," *University of Chicago Law Review*, 36 (Fall):50–112.

Ares, Charles E., Anne Rankin, and Herbert Sturz. 1963. "The Manhattan Bail Project: An Interim Report on the Use of Pre-Trial Parole," *New York University Law Review*, 38 (January):67–95.

Baab, George William, and William Royal Furgeson, Jr. 1967. "Texas Sentencing Patterns: A Statistical Study," *Texas Law Review*, 45 (February):471–503.

Bernstein, Ilene Nagel, William R. Kelly, and Patricia A. Doyle. 1977. "Societal Reaction to Deviants: The Case of Criminal Defendants," *American Sociological Review*, 42 (October):743–55.

Blalock, Hubert M., Jr. 1967. *Toward a Theory of Minority-Group Relations* (New York: Wiley).

Blauner, Robert. 1972. *Racial Oppression in America* (New York: Harper & Row).

Blumberg, Abraham. 1967. *Criminal Justice* (Chicago: Quadrangle).

Bohrnstedt, George W., and T. Michael Carter. 1971. "Robustness in Regression Analysis," in H. L. Costner, ed., *Sociological Methodology 1971* (San Francisco: Jossey-Bass).

Burke, Peter, and Austin Turk. 1975. "Factors Affecting Postarrest Dispositions: A Model for Analysis," *Social Problems*, 22 (February):313–32.

Chambliss, William J., and Robert B. Seidman. 1971. *Law, Order and Power* (Reading, Mass.: Addison-Wesley).

Chiricos, Theodore G., Phillip D. Jackson, and Gordon P. Waldo. 1972. "Inequality in the Imposition of a Criminal Label," *Social Problems*, 19 (Spring):553-72.

Erickson, Maynard L., and Jack P. Gibbs. 1979. "On the Perceived Severity of Legal Penalties," *Journal of Criminal Law and Criminology*, 70 (Spring):102–16.

Garza, Hisauro. 1973. "Administration of Justice: Chicanos in Monterrey County," *Aztlan*, 4 (Spring):137–46.

Green, Edward. 1961. *Judicial Attitudes in Sentencing* (London: Macmillan).

Hagan, John. 1974. "Extra-legal Attributes and Criminal Sentencing: An Assessment of a Sociological Viewpoint," *Law and Society Review*, 8 (Spring):357–83.

Jackson, Pamela Irving, and Leo Carroll. 1981. "Race and the War on Crime: The Sociopolitical Determinants of Municipal Police Expenditures in 90 Non-Southern U.S. Cities," *American Sociological Review*, 46 (June):290–305.

Jacobs, David. 1979. "Inequality and Police Strength: Conflict Theory and Coercive Control in Metropolitan Areas," *American Sociological Review*, 44 (December):913–25.

Kleck, Gary. 1981. "Racial Discrimination in Criminal Sentencing: A Critical Evaluation of the Evidence with Additional Evidence on the Death Penalty," *American Sociological Review*, 46 (December):783–805.

LaFave, Wayne R. 1964. *Arrest: The Decision to Take a Suspect into Custody* (Boston: Little, Brown).

LaFree, Gary D. 1980. "The Effect of Sexual Stratification by Race on Official Reactions to Rape," *American Sociological Review*, 45 (October):842–54.

———. 1983. "Adversarial and Nonadversarial Justice: A Comparison of Guilty Pleas and Trials in the United States." Unpublished manuscript, University of New Mexico, Department of Sociology.

Lemert, Edwin, and Judy Rosberg. 1948. "The Administration of Justice to Minority Groups in Los Angeles County," in R. L. Beals, L. Bloom, and F. Fearings, eds., *University of California Publications in Culture and Society*, vol. 2 (Berkeley: University of California Press).

McWilliams, Carey. 1948. *North from Mexico*. Reprint (New York: Greenwood, 1968).

National Advisory Commission on Civil Disorders. 1968. *Report of the National Advisory Commission on Civil Disorders* (New York: Bantam).

Petersilia, Joan. 1983. *Racial Disparities in the Criminal Justice System* (Santa Monica, Calif.: Rand).

Quinney, Richard. 1970. *The Social Reality of Crime* (Boston: Little, Brown).

Rankin, Anne. 1964. "The Effect of Pretrial Detention," *New York University Law Review*, 39 (June):641–55.

Rosett, Arthur, and Donald R. Cressey. 1976. *Justice by Consent: Plea Bargains in the American Courthouse* (Philadelphia: Lippincott).

Simmons, J. S. 1965. "Public Stereotypes of Deviants," *Social Problems*, 13 (Fall):223–32.

Sissons, Peter. 1977. *The Hispanic Experience of Criminal Justice* (New York: Fordham University, Hispanic Research Center).

Stoddard, Ellwyn R. 1973. *Mexican Americans* (New York: Random House).

Strodtbeck, Fred L., Rita M. James, and Charles Hawkins. 1957. "Social Status in Jury Deliberations," *American Sociological Review*, 22 (December):713–19.

Sudnow, David. 1965. "Normal Crimes: Sociological Features of the Penal Code in a Public Defender Office," *Social Problems*, 12 (Winter):255-76.

Swigert, Victoria Lynn, and Ronald A. Farrell. 1977. "Normal Homicides and the Law," *American Sociological Review*, 42 (February):16–32.

Uhlman, Thomas M., and N. Darlene Walker. 1980. "He Takes Some of My Time; I Take Some of His: An analysis of Judicial Sentencing Patterns in Jury Cases," *Law and Society Review*, 14 (Winter):323–41.

U.S. Bureau of the Census. 1983a. *Census of Population and Housing: 1980*. Census Tracts, PHC80-2-144. El Paso, TX, SMSA (Washington, D.C.: U.S. Government Printing Office).

———— 1983b. *Census of Population and Housing: 1980*. Census Tracts, PHC80-2-355. Tucson, AZ (Washington, D.C.: U.S. Government Printing Office).

U.S. Commission on Civil Rights. 1970. *Mexican Americans and the Administration of Justice in the Southwest* (Washington, D.C.: U.S. Government Printing Office).

Welch, Susan, John Gruhl, and Cassia Spohn. 1984. "Dismissal, Conviction, and Incarceration of Hispanic Defendants: A Comparison with Anglos and Blacks," *Social Science Quarterly*, 65 (June):256–63.

Notes

Bias Crimes: Unconscious Racism in the Prosecution of "Racially Motivated Violence"

Tanya Katerí Hernández

After being attacked by a gang of whites and in turn being blamed by police investigators, Rafael Gonzalez attempted to commit suicide because of his fear of walking the streets where his attackers continued to walk freely and he was blamed for his own victimization. . . . Rafael did not want to live in a world where his pain was not recognized.*

Within the past four years, a perceived surge of "bias crimes" has seized the nation's attention. Bias crimes, physical acts of violence used as an outlet for prejudiced hostilities, are usually street crimes spontaneously committed by casual clusters of "normal people on the street" with very little advanced planning. This Note focuses on the physical injuries to persons that result from bias crimes. Such physical injuries represent cognizable harms that can be redressed through criminal statutes.[1]

Although there are no accurate data on the number of bias crimes committed each year, every national indicator shows that violence against individuals based on their race, ethnicity, and sexual orientation is increas-

---

* Puerto Rican Legal Defense & Education Fund, Testimony Presented to the Committee on International Intergroup Relations and Special Events of the New York City Council 2–3 (Oct. 21, 1987) (unpublished manuscript available from Puerto Rican Legal Defense & Education Fund, N.Y., N.Y.) [hereinafter Testimony].

1. Other forms of violence such as arson, vandalism, and verbal harassment, whose harms are no less serious than physical injuries, are beyond the scope of this Note.

ing.² Three thousand acts of bias-related violence were documented nationwide between 1980 and 1986.³ For example, the Puerto Rican Legal Defense & Education Fund has seen a marked increase in racial violence (hate crimes or bias crimes) against Latinos, to a point where it now receives an average of two calls per week about such incidents.⁴ More than one in five gay men and nearly one in ten lesbians have been physically assaulted because of their sexual orientation.⁵ As such statistics indicate, the term commonly known as "racially motivated violence" is not quite accurate in as much as such bias-related violence extends to discrete groups other than racial minorities.⁶

The pervasive recognition that racially motivated violence is on the rise has led the House of Representatives to direct the Justice Department to begin collecting and publishing statistics on the incidence of these crimes.⁷ Civil rights organizations have lobbied on behalf of bias crime victims for the maintenance of consistent and accurate statistics in order to persuade state prosecutors to treat the increase in bias crimes as a serious problem.

This Note is based on the premise that bias incidents more often than not elude prosecution. The number of prosecutions has not increased at the same rate as reported incidents of bias-related violence. For example, in 1988, in New York, a city with chronic and highly publicized bias crime, only thirty-three bias crimes were prosecuted out of the estimated 800 incidents that were brought to the attention of the New York City Bias Unit.⁸

This Note focuses on the need for carefully drafted state statutes directed against bias crime, and in particular on the need for statutes that encourage prosecutors to prosecute. Part One will show the need for stat-

---

2. *See, e.g.*, CRIM. JUST. NEWSL., June 15, 1988, at 3 (30 state attorneys general note that all national indicators show violence against individuals based on race increasing).

3. States News Service, Jan. 14, 1988 (LEXIS, Nexis library, Omni file) (citing CENTER FOR DEMOCRATIC RENEWAL, THEY ALL DON'T WEAR WHITE SHEETS (1988)).

4. Testimony, *supra* note *, at 1.

5. NATIONAL GAY & LESBIAN TASK FORCE, DEALING WITH VIOLENCE: A GUIDE FOR GAY AND LESBIAN PEOPLE i (1986).

6. Although this Note specifically discusses the problem of racially motivated violence, it uses the term "race" to represent all discrete groups that are subject to threats of physical violence because of a common and particular characteristic that is so much a part of their being that the violence cannot be avoided by simply attempting to negate that characteristic. More specifically, this Note considers violence committed because of ethnic background, sexual orientation, religion, color, ancestry, or language. This Note's analysis selects race as representative because of the well-known and long history of persecution Black people have suffered due to their immutable characteristic. One premise of this Note is that all forms of arbitrary hatred are inextricably connected and that a bias crime against a white gay male is also a bias crime against every member of any discrete and disfavored group. Although violence against white women could also be included in this study, the history of women's oppression is such that it demands a fuller analysis than could be done within the scope of this Note.

7. *See* CRIM. JUST. NEWSL., *supra* note 2.

8. Interview with John Fried, Chief of Trial Division within New York County District Attorney's Office, in New York City (July 20, 1989); Telephone interview with Police Officer Walls, New York City Bias Unit (July 20, 1989) (most incidents are deemed prosecution-worthy cases by the police because in their experience, disfavored group community members do not make frivolous claims about such attacks).

utes specifically addressing bias-related violence at the state level, by pointing out the limitations of the Federal criminal and civil rights statutes. Part Two will discuss current state criminal statutes and their efficacy, and will demonstrate that most of these statutes leave too much discretion to the prosecutor, with the result that such crimes are not likely to be prosecuted. Part Two will then set forth an argument justifying the reduction of prosecutorial discretion in a model statute, by showing how both unconscious racism and the involvement of the police in bias-related incidents make bias crime an area that is uniquely affected by prosecutorial discretion. Part Three will explain the elements of a proposed model state statute and set forth the statute.

I. INADEQUACY OF FEDERAL STATUTES AS CAUSE FOR STATE STATUTES

The current level of bias-related incidents of violence demands that state statutes supplement already existing Federal racial violence statutes. Federal statutes are only equipped to confront conspiracies of extremist group violence, epitomized by the tactics of the Ku Klux Klan or neo-Nazi groups, not the scattered racial violence that suddenly erupts in urban settings. But increasingly, bias crimes are being committed by people with no Klan-like affiliations. This means that it is "average Americans," not organized racist extremists, that are now committing these crimes.[9] These average North Americans must be corrected through the criminal justice system *before* their hatred channels them into paramilitary organizations and the Ku Klux Klan becomes a legitimate political party, and not the aberration society now considers it to be.[10]

An examination of Federal statutes points to significant shortcomings in the legislative scheme. The principal Federal criminal and civil statutes that can be applied to private racially motivated violence are respectively 18 U.S.C. § 241, "conspiracy against rights of citizens," and 42 U.S.C. § 1985, "conspiracy to interfere with civil rights." These statutes state in part that a crime has been committed when "two or more persons conspire to injure, oppress, threaten, or intimidate any citizen in the free exercise or enjoyment of any right or privilege secured to him by the Constitution or laws of the United States";[11] or when:

---

9. Kellner, *The Ku Klux Klan: Our Neighbors to the Radical Right*, 6 PHILADELPHIA SCAN 28, 30 (1988) (people who have never affiliated with KKK starting to express strong support for goals of organization).

10. *See* Comment, *Racially-Motivated Violence and Intimidation: Inadequate State Enforcement and Federal Civil Rights Remedies*, 75 J. CRIM. L. & CRIMINOLOGY 103, 117 nn.108–09 (1984) (Gallup polls show increase over past 10 years in number of persons who approve of Klan activities; increase also evidenced by major party congressional nominations of avowed Klan and Nazi members).

11. 18 U.S.C. § 241 (1982).

two or more persons in any State or Territory conspire or go in disguise on the highway or on the premises of another, for the purpose of depriving, either directly or indirectly, any person or class of persons of the equal protection of the laws, or of equal privileges and immunities under the laws.[12]

In order to apply these Federal statutes, the prosecutor would first have to establish that there was a conspiracy, and then that the conspiracy was motivated by a desire to interfere with rights that are protected by the Constitution or Federal law. The difficulty of fitting arbitrary racial violence into the realm of interferences of constitutional magnitude has led to very selective enforcement of the statutes. This selective enforcement fails to address the pervasiveness of spontaneous violence. Federal criminal statutes help to vindicate the injuries[13] when a victim has been physically harmed at a voting booth, but not necessarily when that same person wants to walk without fear in an all-white neighborhood.[14]

The solution to the problem of bias-related violence lies in state statutes specifically drafted to redress this harm, rather than in the more general conspiracy focused statutes at the federal level. Federal statutes are not tailored to address the spontaneous violence caused by unconscious and conscious racism. Although Federal conspiracy statutes could be an aid to states in prosecuting and attempting to deter bias crimes, such Federal statutes cannot make as strong a statement as state criminal statutes directed specifically at bias violence.

The harm which arises from bias crimes is distinct because an entire disfavored and discrete group of people is assaulted whenever an individual is assaulted as a result of an immutable characteristic. Communal harmony within society in general is totally disrupted by a single act of arbitrary hatred because of the distrust and fear that is ignited. What is needed is public recognition of these distinct and serious harms, to be achieved through separate state criminal statutes that make an official statement that bias crimes will not be tolerated. The next section will show that state statutes, as currently drafted, also fail to address the problem of bias crime.

II. EFFICACY OF STATE STATUTES

Several states have attempted to confront the problem of increased incidence of bias crimes with a variety of statutes. These states include Cali-

---

12. 42 U.S.C. § 1985(3) (1982).

13. *See* Comment, *supra* note 10, at 116 (suggesting that Federal statutes can operate as backup for failure to prosecute racial violence on state level until states make up for deficiencies in enforcement).

14. *See* N.Y. Times, Aug. 30, 1989, at B4, col. 3 (Yusef Hawkins, Black 16-year-old, killed when he walked into predominantly white neighborhood of Bensonhurst, Brooklyn, to look at used car for sale).

fornia, Connecticut, Idaho, Illinois, Massachusetts, New York, North Da-
kota, Oklahoma, Oregon, Pennsylvania, Washington, and West
Virginia.[15] What is most significant about the statutes, in general, is that
they do not consider the greatest obstacle to their enforcement—the power
of unmonitored prosecutorial discretion.[16]

The statutes appear to fall in two general categories,[17] but the distinction is not relevant to the focus of this Note. The first category of statutes[18] contains provisions that emulate federal civil rights legislation that
requires perpetrators to have interfered with a right secured by the Constitution or by law. The Massachusetts statute is representative of the language used in this category of statute:

> No person, whether or not acting under color of law, shall by force
> or threat of force, willfully injure, intimidate or interfere with, or
> attempt to injure, intimidate or interfere with, or oppress or threaten
> any other person in the free exercise or enjoyment of any right or
> privilege *secured to him by the constitution or laws of the Common-
> wealth or by the Constitution or laws of the United States.*[19]

The second category of statutes focuses on physical injury as a method of
intimidation or harassment.[20] Category two statutes have language similar
to that in the Oklahoma statute:

> No person shall maliciously and with the specific intent to intimidate
> or harass another person because of that person's race, color, reli-
> gion, ancestry, national origin or disability . . . [a]ssault or batter
> another person . . . .[21]

Unlike any other state, the California statute[22] covers discrimination based
on sexual orientation. In general, these statutes only enumerate race, religion, and national origin as criteria for inclusion within their provisions.

---

15. The Pennsylvania statute only deals tangentially with the physical injury focus of this Note
because it is a regulation against property destruction. *See infra* notes 18-21 and accompanying text.
16. *See infra* Part II.B. (discussion of prosecutorial discretion).
17. This Note will not discuss the possibility of an action in tort for the intentional infliction of
emotional distress. Civil actions complicate criminal prosecutions because the financial interest in the
outcome of the criminal case creates an avenue of attack on the victim's credibility. Criminal statutes
better address the unconsciously racist prosecutorial presumption that bias crime victims are not credible. Interview with Marlene Besterman, Assistant District Attorney with the New York County District Attorney's Office, in New York City (July 12, 1989).
18. CAL. PENAL CODE § 422.6 (West 1988); CONN. GEN. STAT. ANN. § 46a-58 (West 1986);
MASS. GEN. LAWS ANN. ch. 265, § 37 (West Supp. 1988); N.D. CENT. CODE § 12.1-14-04 (1985);
W. VA. CODE § 61-6-21 (1988).
19. MASS. GEN. LAWS ANN. ch. 265, § 37 (West Supp. 1988) (emphasis added).
20. IDAHO CODE §§ 18-7901 to 7903 (1987); ILL. ANN. STAT. ch. 38, para. 12-7.1 (Smith-Hurd
Supp. 1989); N.Y. PENAL LAW § 240.30 (Consol. 1984); OKLA. STAT. ANN. tit. 21, § 850 (West
Supp. 1988); OR. REV. STAT. § 166.155 (1987); R.I. GEN. LAWS § 11-42-3 (Supp. 1988); WASH.
REV. CODE ANN. § 9A.36.080 (1988).
21. OKLA. STAT. ANN. tit. 21, § 850 (West Supp. 1988).
22. CAL. PENAL CODE § 422.6 (West 1988).

Although bias-crime statutes may call prosecutors' attention to the magnitude of the problem, their mere existence on the books is not enough. Evidence of the inadequacy of the current statutes may be found in the fact that the few cases[23] that have been reported under these state statutes have not involved the sudden and arbitrary physical attacks which are continuously being recorded by various civil rights organizations.[24] Even if the statutes have been enforced by prosecutors more frequently than is shown by the cases which are selected for reporting, the dearth of reported cases is itself an indication of a low bias crime enforcement record. During the years since the current statutes were first enacted, over three-thousand acts of bias-related violence were documented nationwide.[25] None of the thirty-three cases chosen for prosecution in New York City in 1988 were prosecuted under the bias statute.[26]

Clearly, these statutes are not an adequate solution to the problem. Indeed, it is possible that such statutes, when properly drafted, could provide at least a partial solution: "Racial and religious violence persists in part because existing state legislation, and state court systems fail to adequately deter and punish perpetrators of these crimes."[27]

The lack of reported cases, contrasted with the surge in reported incidents, leads to the conclusion that state statutes are not being enforced against bias crimes. The following sections will examine several explanations for this apparent lack of enforcement.

Existing state statutes are deficient because they do not address the real problem with bias crime statutes—the lack of enforcement. There are three possible explanations for this lack of enforcement: the exclusion of disfavored groups other than Black Americans from statutory protection; unmonitored prosecutorial discretion; and the related problem of unconscious prosecutorial racism. Unmonitored discretion, coupled with unconscious racism and lack of explicit inclusion of other disfavored groups in the statute, allows prosecutors to: ignore bias crimes; not consider them serious enough for full enforcement; or refuse to realize that many discrete groups are subject to the same bias attacks as are Blacks.

---

23. See, e.g., Commonwealth v. Stephens, 25 Mass. App. Ct. 117, 515 N.E.2d 606 (1987) (home of Cambodian families in community damaged after verbal harrassment); Commonwealth v. Poor, 18 Mass. App. Ct. 490, 467 N.E.2d 877, review denied, 393 Mass. 1103, 470 N.E.2d 798 (1984) (community members damaged home of Black family in neighborhood); State v. Harrington, 67 Or. App. 608, 680 P.2d 666, review denied, 297 Or. 547, 685 P.2d 998 (1984) (abusive language spoken with intent to harm not exception to State Constitution guarantee of freedom of expression).

24. See supra text accompanying notes 2-5.

25. See States News Service, supra note 3.

26. Interview with John Fried, supra note 8 (most bias cases dealt with anti-gay incidents, and since sexual preference is not covered under protected groups of statute, incidents can only be charged as "violations"—hence decision to charge only regular assault that has misdemeanor or felony sentence possibility).

27. Comment, supra note 10, at 104-05.

A. *Inadequate Coverage*

The current statutes are inadequate because they fail to include members of other discrete groups, such as gay men and lesbian women,[28] who are often targets of bias crimes. The lack of inclusion ignores the dangers of bias crimes for all discrete groups. If bias crimes against all people of color could miraculously be eradicated, the acceptance of bias crimes against people of the Jewish faith would still pose a threat to the safety of people of color; because a bias crime is not only an action of oppression against targeted groups, it is an action based on illegitimate categorizations. The acceptance of expressions of hatred based upon one kind of illegitimate categorization can only encourage further illegitimate categorization.[29]

Such acceptance of illegitimate categorizations engendered by bias crimes is directly analogous to the concept of racialism (racial ways of thinking) considered dangerous in anti-discrimination law.[30] When criminals undervalue a person's life because of racist or sexist ways of thinking, the illegitimate manner of categorizing that person becomes dangerous to all discrete group members, whether they are Black or gay. The statutory omission of many discrete groups whose members are likely to be victims of bias crimes translates into state acquiescence toward bias crimes against those groups' members, which in turn undermines the deterrence value of the statute for all bias crime victim groups.

B. *Prosecutorial Discretion*

Unchecked prosecutorial discretion—completely overlooked in the current statutes—is another explanation for the lack of enforcement of state statutes. The current statutes lack a mechanism for pressuring prosecutors to exercise their discretion carefully, rather than to maintain a policy of non-prosecution for politically unpopular bias crimes. The lack of a pressure mechanism is what accounts for the non-enforcement and undermining of the statutes.

Prosecutorial discretion affects the prosecution of bias crimes to a greater extent than other areas of the criminal law for two major reasons: First, prosecutorial dependence on the police keeps prosecutors from in-

---

28. *See supra* notes 6 & 22 and accompanying text.
29. *See Civil Rights Commission Examines Anti-Asian Activity*, PR Newswire, July 25, 1986 (resentment against economic prosperity of group of newly arrived Asian immigrants motivates attacks upon diversity of Asian ethnic groups already established in the community). Such attacks in part stem from the "they all look alike" syndrome, where a Black or Asian individual is mistaken for another Black or Asian person who looks nothing like her. *See* Lawrence, *The Id, The Ego, and Equal Protection: Reckoning with Unconscious Racism*, 39 STAN. L. REV. 317, 341 n.100 (1987).
30. *See generally* Gewirtz, *Choice in the Transition: School Desegregation and the Corrective Ideal*, 86 COLUM. L. REV. 728 (1986) (underscoring racialism operates to disadvantage of Blacks, such as when concept that separate races should be maintained in society leads to unequal opportunities).

.g the many cases of bias crimes which are raised against police
.s; second, the unconscious racism of the prosecutors themselves af-
.s prosecution.

One factor which accounts for the disparate effect of prosecutorial discretion on bias crimes, as opposed to other crimes, is that many of the
perpetrators of bias crimes are police officers. Local prosecutors are understandably reluctant to prosecute the police officers on whom they depend in order to function.[31] This is not a new problem. Within the context of federal and state police brutality cases, "U.S. attorneys . . . have
consistently opposed . . . prosecution . . . ."[32] But this reluctance to prosecute police is not without effect on the public at large and in particular,
on members of disfavored groups. "[T]he fact that police officers are
rarely tried on civil rights charges has led the public to believe that few
serious charges are ever made, and has reinforced the belief among offend-
ing peace officers that they may treat or mistreat Negroes as their whims
direct them."[33] Prosecutors' reluctance to investigate police officers in general police brutality cases arguably increases when victims are members of
discrete groups and unconscious racism becomes a factor of prosecutorial
inaction.

C. *Unconscious Racism in Prosecution*

The unconscious racism of prosecutors is more of a danger in bias
crime prosecution than in the enforcement of other statutes because the
premise of bias crime statutes is that racial motivation makes a physical
injury more harmful. In order to enforce the statutes, prosecutors must be
willing to recognize illegitimate motivation. Unconscious racism, ingrained
in North American culture, makes it difficult for prosecutors to concede
that racially-motivated violence is indeed a crime.

This Note does not assume that prosecutors typically act in bad faith
when bias crime investigations arise, even though many civil rights attorneys believe that is the case.[34] Even though bad faith prosecutorial inac-

---

31. For an example of such reluctance, see Latino Coalition for Racial Justice, Press Release
(Feb. 29, 1988). *See also* Dixon v. District of Columbia, 394 F.2d 966 (D.C. Cir. 1968) (Black
defendant harassed by two police officers and prosecutor who later offered not to enforce two
trumped-up traffic offenses if defendant promised not to initiate complaint against officer's
misconduct).

32. Note, *Discretion to Prosecute Federal Civil Rights Crimes*, 74 YALE L.J. 1297, 1311 n.64
(1965) (emphasis added) (quoting U.S. COMM'N ON CIVIL RIGHTS, REPORT 64 (1961) (Book 5)).

33. MISSISSIPPI ADVISORY COMM. TO THE U.S. COMM'N ON CIVIL RIGHTS, ADMINISTRATION
OF JUSTICE IN MISSISSIPPI 25 (1963).

34. Telephone interview with Jose L. Morin, Revson Fellow Professor at the City College of
New York Center for Legal Education & Urban Policy (Nov. 28, 1988) (consistent and systematic
cover-up occurs in all cases of bias crime involving white civilians and police officers as defendants;
cover-up is part of criminal justice system's built-in bias against people of color and prosecutors'
desire to maintain cooperation of police force with whom they must work on regular basis).

tion can be a problem, the phenomenon of unconscious racism is more subtle and therfore more dangerous.

Unconscious racism allows many prosecutors not to treat racial violence as a serious crime or consider its victims true victims. One commentator explains: "The social construction of victimhood rests in large measure on the problem that some theorists would call rests in large measure on the problem that some theorists would call 'difference'—here, the inability of the dominant culture to understand as victimhood anything not likely to happen to its members."[35] For example, local prosecutors often dismiss bias crimes as "pranks" and in that manner justify sparse investigation.[36] When prosecutors classify bias crimes as mere "pranks," they are unconsciously taking illegitimate factors (like race) into account—as is done in racialist decision making.[37] Racialism can be defined as the belief that "racial categorizations, even oppressive ones, might be acceptable as long as a case can be made for rational fit between ends and means."[38] Because people of color and gay people are marginalized in society, the thinking goes, the victimization of members of such marginalized groups is not accorded the same level of gravity as the victimization of others. The theory of racialist decision making recognizes that this way of thinking can become part of a person's rational decision making process, and is not always a purposefully discriminatory plan.[39]

The traditionally unreviewable discretion of prosecutors can thus result in systematic, though unintentional, discrimination.[40] Empirical evidence supports this hypothesis. Research on the death penalty has shown that prosecutors are more rigorous in their investigation of cases involving white victims than they are of cases involving Black victims.[41] Attacks on disfavored and oppressed peoples do not have the same effect on the bu-

---

35. Carter, *When Victims Happen to Be Black*, 97 YALE L.J. 420, 421 n.3 (1988).

36. Comment, *supra* note 10, at 116.

37. The term "racialist decisionmaking" is unique to Professor Carter's work. *See* Carter, *supra* note 35. Nonetheless the concept of racialist decisionmaking is one that has developed generally through the body of work on race and the legal system. *See, e.g.*, Johnson, *Unconscious Racism and the Criminal Law*, 73 CORNELL L. REV. 1016, 1019 (1988) ("cognizance of the frequency with which racial stereotypes alter judgment should influence how 'stark' a statistical disparity must be to raise a presumption of a race-based decision, particularly where . . . noninvidious explanations have been exhausted"); Lawrence, *supra* note 29, at 355–58 (proposing new test to trigger judicial recognition of race-based behavior; "Cultural Meaning Test" would interpret unreasonableness of articulated nonracial criteria as evidence of the racial meaning of defendant's action or violence); *Developments in the Law—Race and the Criminal Process*, 101 HARV. L. REV. 1472, 1547 (1988).

38. *See* Carter, *supra* note 35, at 431.

39. *Id.* at 434 ("millions of tiny, individual, racialist decisions are made each day, and are justified, in the minds of most of the decisionmakers, not on the ground that they oppress, but on the ground that they are rational.").

40. *See* Noll, *Controlling a Prosecutor's Screening Discretion Through Fuller Enforcement*, 29 SYRACUSE L. REV. 697, 699 (1978).

41. *Cf.* Radelet & Pierce, *Race and Prosecutorial Discretion in Homicide Cases*, 19 LAW & SOC'Y REV. 587 (1985) (compilation of empirical research demonstrates more thorough investigation of crimes with Black defendants and white victims than of crimes with white defendants and Black victims; these research results were used in the challenge to death penalty as racially discriminatory in McCleskey v. Kemp, 481 U.S. 279 (1987)).

reaucratic and political system as does the attack of a white victim. An attack on a white victim is perceived as more threatening by politically powerful groups that keep prosecutors in office. Even if a prosecutor never explicitly focuses on race, the concern with exerting the most energy on cases that the electorate favors allows racism to enter into the legal system. "[R]egardless of the race of the defendant, prosecutors may consider White victims more credible than [B]lack victims or their troubles more worthy of full prosecution."[42]

There has also been a suggestion that there may be a greater tendency among prosecutors to accept the decisions of minority assault victims to forego prosecution rather than those of white assault victims.[43] Unconscious racism plays such a large role in the perpetuation of bias crimes that the oversight of its effect on prosecutorial discretion completely undermines the enforcement purposes of the statutes.[44] Commentators who blame the lack of enforcement of bias crime statutes on other factors—such as the requirement of proof beyond a reasonable doubt and the ambiguous understanding of what constitutes racial motivation as an element of meeting the burden of proof—miss the point.[45] The problem is not in adjudication; once bias crimes reach the adjudication process, media attention compels prosecutors to handle the cases professionally and to overcome the burden of proof swiftly. The real difficulty lies in compelling prosecutors to bring these cases forward in the first place. Prosecutorial discretion forms an integral part of the criminal system. But

---

42. *Id.* at 616 (emphasis omitted) (quoting Myers & Hagan, *Private and Public Trouble: Prosecutors and the Allocation of Court Resources*, 26 Soc. Probs. 439, 447 (1979)).

43. F. Miller, Prosecution: The Decision to Charge 175-76 (1969).

44. Unregulated prosecutorial discretion has such a strong potential for allowing unconscious racism to enter the legal system that it has been suggested that selective downgrading of crimes with Black victims and White defendants constantly occurs. *See Developments in the Law—Race and the Criminal Process, supra* ntoe 37, at 1547 ("unique potential of unconscious racism imperceptibly to affect prosecutorial decisionmaking justifies a standard more receptive to statistical evidence as proof of discriminatory motive in the context of racial selective prosecution"). This Note will not delve into issues of discriminatory selective prosecution from the perspective of the defendant, because its focus is on compelling prosecution on behalf of victims who are wrongfully neglected. Of course, the same forms of unconscious racism may account for bias crime victims being overlooked and minority criminals receiving harsher sanctions.

45. *See* Note, *Combatting Racial Violence: A Legislative Proposal*, 101 Harv. L. Rev. 1270 (1988). The author recommends that racial motivation be completely removed from state bias crime statutes as an element of the offense by presuming that any physical assault between a white perpetrator and a Black victim is racially motivated. Such a presumption totally weakens the premise that bias crimes are more malicious because of the specific intent involved and therefore more harmful than other crimes which may occur in a racially mixed setting. The presumption makes the statement that everyone in the world is racist. Not only is that an overly broad and harsh assessment of the reality of North-American race relations, it equates prejudice with racism. This Note defines prejudice as the baggage of prejudgments and stereotypes each individual carries when meeting a person of a different background. Racism is the translation of that prejudice into statements or actions which harm those same people of different backgrounds. Placing everyone in the same category is not effective in punishing those individuals who cause the actual physical harm. Although universal prejudice is harmful, a criminal statute which seeks out social deviants to punish is not the most effective way to address the problem of universal prejudice.

when factors underlying prosecutors' discretion lead to an unjustifiable bias toward non-enforcement, such tendencies should be corrected.

III. POLICY PROPOSAL FOR MODEL STATE STATUTE

The inadequacy of state bias crime statutes—especially their failure to address the very real problem of prosecutorial discretion—demands a new approach to dealing with bias crimes that takes into account the entire judicial process. Given that the greatest obstacle to bias crime prosecution is the unconscious racism that causes prosecutorial inaction, the most efficient means of checking the abuse of prosecutorial discretion is to create a statutory regime in which prosecutors are monitored, victims are given standing to challenge inaction, and judges are permitted to review cases of biased prosecutorial methods. The most important elements of such a model statute are discussed below.

A. *Bias Reporting Agency*

A model bias crime statute should establish an independent Bias Reporting Agency (BRA) to aid in regulating prosecutorial discretion. Unlike several bias divisions which are connected to police departments or state's attorney offices,[46] the BRA would be a separate administrative agency with investigatory powers, and its chair would be appointed by the Governor. The Governor would also appoint a board of ten directors from among the community's active civil rights leaders and attorneys.

The BRA would report to, and be directly responsible to, the Governor. The BRA board would in turn hire attorneys to staff the agency based upon merit and commitment to civil rights issues. As an administrative agency funded by the state government, the BRA would have access to the state's central computer database containing all reports of bias crimes. As soon as the police entered reports of bias crimes into the computer, those same reports would be available to the BRA. Such a centralized computer system would aid the BRA in performing its role as a watchdog agency and advocate of victims' rights. In addition, victims would be able to report attacks directly to the BRA. These reports would allow the BRA to investigate bias crimes committed by police officers.

The BRA would thus overcome the problem of prosecutorial reluctance to act. First, the BRA's attorneys would avoid the close working relationship with police officers that prevents prosecutors from acknowledging

---

46. In order to function, bias-reporting agencies must be independent of state and municipal police forces or prosecutors' offices. A lack of independence can lead to corruption. In New York State, for example, police officers make up a major part of the Bias Unit and the Civilian Complaint Review Board that investigate police brutality allegations. Telephone Interview with Jose L. Morin, *supra* note 34 (lack of independent source of investigation makes cover-up of bias crimes internally systematic; cover-up also transferred from corrupt units to prosecutors' offices due to lack of independence).

them as bias crime perpetrators. Second, focusing solely on bias crimes would help the BRA attorneys ferret out any of their own prejudices against victims; daily contact with victims and committed members of the staff cannot help but influence and educate the ignorance that informs bias. Third, staffing the BRA with civil rights attorneys who have a special commitment to the bias crime area would counterbalance any institutionally inherent reluctance to act.

1. Justification of Prosecution Decisions

To accomplish its purpose, the statute should institute a mandatory justification process for plea bargaining or failure to prosecute in bias crimes cases. The BRA would accordingly require and review written justifications for failures to prosecute, and thereby encourage prosecutors to enforce the statutes more vigorously. The articulation of legitimate reasons for decisions not to prosecute would also help to create public confidence in the prosecutor's performance of her duties.[47] In addition, this process might produce greater consistency in charging decisions by encouraging prosecutors to consider cases carefully. Public accountability would be enhanced, and those aggrieved by decisions not to prosecute would have an easier time mounting a challenge. The burden of preparing a written justification for a plea bargain or failure to prosecute would be insignificant compared to the benefits of increased prosecutorial accountability.

2. Helping Victims Seek Judicial Review

The BRA would aid victims who want to challenge a decision not to prosecute.[48] Israel administers a similar challenge process. There, prose-

---

47. See Ashworth, The "Public Interest" Element in Prosecutions, 1987 CRIM. L. REV. 595, 605.
48. Traditionally, courts base their refusal to compel prosecutors to file charges on standing grounds. See Gifford, Equal Protection and the Prosecutor's Charging Decision: Enforcing An Ideal, 49 GEO. WASH. L. REV. 659, 710–11 (1981). In suits to compel prosecution, as in other litigation, a party has standing if she has "such a personal stake in the outcome of the controversy as to assure that concrete adverseness which sharpens the presentation of issues upon which the court so largely depends for illumination of difficult . . . questions." Baker v. Carr, 369 U.S. 186, 204 (1962). But as victims have become more alienated from the criminal justice system, fewer people tend to report crimes and fewer still find any advantage in cooperating with prosecutors. To address these problems, the Federal government instituted the Victim and Witness Protection Act of 1982, Pub. L. No. 97-291, 96 Stat. 1248 (codified at 18 U.S.C. §§ 1512-1515 (1988)). The Act establishes a greater role for victims in the criminal justice system. Prosecutors are required to consult victims during various phases of the prosecution, including plea bargaining sessions. Most important, the prosecutor submits a "victim impact" statement to the court. This consists of a written statement by the victim informing the court how the crime affected her and how she views the terms of a negotiated plea agreement. Legislation like the Federal Victim and Witness Protection Act is evidence that the victims' rights movement has had such an impact that state courts will now be more receptive to a bias crime victim's challenge to nonprosecution.
Currently, there are a few states in which a victim has a clear right to bring a criminal action in minor offenses. Gittler, Expanding the Role of the Victim in a Criminal Action: An Overview of Issues and Problems, 11 PEPPERDINE L. REV. 117, 151 & n.112 (1984). Commentators recognize that victims should play a greater role in prosecutions. The main reason for giving victims standing to challenge nonprosecution is that, especially in the bias crime context, they have a unique knowledge of

cutors must notify the complaining party in writing of their reasons for not prosecuting. The complaining party may then seek review of the decision with the Attorney General, an official comparable to the U.S. Solicitor General.[49]

This Note proposes a variation on the Israeli system. With a written justification in hand, the victim could ask the BRA to undertake an additional investigation into her case. After investigating the facts, the BRA would *advise* the victim whether it would be prudent for her to seek judicial review of the prosecutor's decision.

Although the BRA would play an instrumental role in aiding the victim, only the victim or a proxy victim[50] may actually activate the challenge process. Because victims of bias crimes on the whole are disproportionately poor and without bargaining power,[51] merely giving them the right to challenge prosecutorial inaction would be meaningless without also providing the means to exercise that right.[52] One of the BRA's functions is to serve as the means by which victims can exercise the statutory right to challenge prosecutorial decisionmaking and pressure prosecutors into action.

---

the facts and an interest in diligent prosecution. *See* Note, *Private Prosecution: A Remedy for District Attorneys' Unwarranted Inaction*, 65 YALE L.J. 209, 225 (1955). In addition, private citizens should have input into determining what the public interest actually is: "[W]hat is in the 'public interest' is both a complex judgment and an important one . . . . Its importance indicates a need for accountability and consistency. The case for accountability is particularly strong because of the profound effect and even the finality of some prosecution decisions . . . ." Ashworth, *supra* note 47, at 605. With the risk of unconscious racism entering into decisions of non-prosecution in the bias crime context, it is especially important that victims as representatives of the general population have an input into what constitutes the public interest. Granting victims standing could be regarded as a check on the worst excesses of prosecutorial discretion—specifically, the use of "administrative convenience" as a pretext for selective indifference to the victims of bias crimes. Thus, given the devastating effects of bias crimes, as discussed in Part One, and given that Federal victims' rights legislation has laid the groundwork for states to adopt similar legislation, courts should grant standing to victims of bias crime.

49.   *See* Abrams, *Internal Policy: Guiding the Exercise of Prosecutorial Discretion*, 19 UCLA L. REV. 1, 48-49 (1971).

50.   *See* Goldstein, *Defining the Role of the Victim in Criminal Prosecution*, 52 MISS. L.J. 515, 559 (1982) (where provided for by statute, public interest groups may assume role of proxy victim for purpose of "attending to the criminal law enacted out of concern for their constituents"). In order for victim-initiation of prosecution to be an efficient check on prosecutorial discretion, civil rights organizations should be able to serve as proxy victims. Proxy victims attend to the criminal law out of concern for their constituents. This claim to intervention on the part of civil rights organizations is especially powerful when one considers both the widespread impact of a single bias crime on an entire community and the harmful impact on other members of the disfavored group. *See also* Diamond v. Charles, 476 U.S. 54, 65 n.17 (1986) (dictum) ("The Illinois Legislature, of course, has the power to create new interests, the invasion of which may confer standing. In such a case, the [standing] requirements of Art. III may be met.").

51.   Telephone Interview with Jose L. Morin, *supra* note 34 (bias crime victims are typically very vulnerable population that would not benefit from private prosecution option requiring disposable income).

52.   For those victims who are already socially disadvantaged, the BRA may appear to be an overly burdensome bureaucracy. But it should be kept in mind that the purpose of the BRA is to empower disfavored groups with dignity, within the framework of the existing criminal justice system. Although a more transformative vision of the criminal justice system may be even more empowering, its full development is beyond the scope of this Note.

If the victim decides she wants to challenge the prosecutor's decision, the BRA would aid the victim by preparing a report of its investigatory findings and a victim impact statement for submission to the reviewing judge.[53] The victim impact statement would not only include a description of the physical and psychological harms that the bias crime has caused the individual victim, but would also describe the harmful effects such crimes generally tend to have upon the discrete group of which the individual victim was a symbol to the perpetrator. Based on the BRA's report, the judge can decide whether there was probable cause such that the prosecutor should have prosecuted the case. During this hearing the prosecutor may present the reasons she decided not to prosecute. Because the victim impact statement will have advised the judge of the danger of unconscious racism, courts will be likely to closely scrutinize the prosecutor's testimony and the written justification that the prosecutor gave the victim. The impact statements will also alert the judge to her own unconscious racism, with the hope of ensuring a fair appraisal of the victim's harms.

3. Declaratory Judgments

If the judge finds that there was probable cause for a prosecution and that the prosecution would have furthered the public interest, the judge could issue a declaratory judgment that the prosecutor abused his discretion.[54] For example, in *Aetna Life Insurance Co. v. Haworth*,[55] a Federal

---

53. As dictated by the Victims' and Witness Protection Act of 1982, Pub. L. No. 97-291, § 3, 96 Stat. 1248, 1249 (1982), victim impact statements are written statements informing the court of the impact the crime has had upon the victim.

54. A declaratory judgment is a "binding adjudication of the rights and status of litigants even though no consequential relief is awarded," BLACK'S LAW DICTIONARY 368 (5th ed. 1979). The historical attitude of the courts has been one of hostility to the notion of review of prosecutorial inaction, as demonstrated in United States v. Cox, 342 F.2d 167 (5th Cir.), *cert. denied sub nom.* Cox v. Hauberg, 381 U.S. 935 (1965), and Powell v. Katzenbach, 359 F.2d 234 (D.C. Cir. 1965), *cert. denied*, 384 U.S. 906 (1966), yet at least one commentator has suggested that the courts' hostility appears to be poorly reasoned, *see* Noll, *supra* note 40, at 730-37. The major objection to judicial review is that it would violate separation of powers by usurping the executive duties of the prosecutor. But this argument does not take into account the fact that through unsupervised screening the prosecutor assumes a judicial function. Whenever the prosecutor declines to charge because of doubt as to the accused's guilt or as to the admissibility of evidence, he is in effect acting as a judge. *See id.* at 714-15. Thus, given that the prosecutor's job commingles executive and judicial functions, it follows that there ought to be less concern with judicial involvement in prosecutorial decisionmaking. Indeed, "[w]hile the Constitution diffuses power the better to secure liberty, it also contemplates that practice will integrate the dispersed powers into a workable government. It enjoins upon its branches separateness but interdependence, autonomy but reciprocity." Youngstown Sheet & Tube Co. v. Sawyer, 343 U.S. 579, 635 (1952) (Jackson, J., concurring). Moreover, even the case law cited for the proposition that judicial review of prosecutorial decisions violates the separation of powers doctrine suggests that judicial review might be permissible if provided for by statute: "We will assume, without deciding, that where Congress has withdrawn all discretion from the prosecutor by special legislation, a court might be empowered to force prosecutions in some circumstances." *Powell*, 359 F.2d at 235. In addition, the constitutional grant of the executive's prosecutorial power in the take care clause, U.S. CONST. art. II, § 3, indicates that a statutory grant of judicial review would be constitutionally permissible at least for the limited purpose of granting the victim declaratory relief. The take care clause is a positive grant of power to act, not a power to refrain from acting. Because it is legally defined and not an absolute license, prosecutorial discretion is judicially reviewable. For example, the Administra-

dispute adjudicated under the Declaratory Judgment Act of 1934,[56] the Court held that a controversy did exist and that the admittance of a party's legal rights by declaratory judgment did not require an "award of process or the payment of damages."[57] Because a declaratory judgment declares legal rights arising out of a real case or controversy, a declaratory judgment is not an advisory opinion. Nor would the judge be compelling the prosecutor to act. The declaratory judgment would merely suggest that prosecution is called for, with the BRA's results from the investigation attached to the judgment. In other words, such a declaratory judgment would serve as a *signal* to a prosecutor that she ought to re-evaluate the victim's case because the judiciary has considered the case worthy enough to be deemed a legal controversy. "Having issued a declaratory judgment that a prosecutor has abused his discretion in declining to prosecute, a court would have good reason to 'assume' that the prosecutor subsequently might change his mind and satisfy his obligations under the take care clause."[58] The prosecutor would review the BRA's results and could change his mind about prosecuting. If the prosecutor still remained unpersuaded, the judge could appoint a special prosecutor.

4. *Special Prosecutor*

A special prosecutor could be utilized in a number of circumstances. When the BRA receives complaints of bias crimes perpetrated by police officers[59] and it deems the local prosecutors' close working relationship with the police force a hindrance to effective enforcement of the statute, a special prosecutor would be available. The request for a special prosecutor would be only a measure of last resort because it is assumed that the BRA would exercise reasonable judgment and not advocate prosecution of every reported case. Those cases about which the BRA feels so strongly that it would make a formal request for a special prosecutor will logically be

---

tive Procedure Act's statutory grant allows courts frequently to review the executive's exercise of discretion. *See* Noll, *supra* note 40, at 732 n.152. To accommodate whatever constitutional objections still exist, the model statute provides for a very limited judicial review of prosecutorial discretion. The use of the declaratory judgment allows the prosecutor to make the final decision on whether to prosecute. Thus, the proposed declaratory judgment infringes less on prosecutorial autonomy than does ordinary judicial review. *See* Note, *Private Challenges to Prosecutorial Inaction: A Model Declaratory Judgment Statute*, 97 YALE L.J. 488, 504–06 (1988). In this way, the model statute uses narrowly tailored means to achieve a desirable result: "[T]he most effective and reliable way to protect unpopular minorities against majoritarian abuse is through the courts, not through a reliance on a [putatively] politically sensitive prosecutor." Noll, *supra* note 40, at 728.

55. 300 U.S. 227 (1937).

56. 48 Stat. 955 (1934) (current version at 28 U.S.C.A. §§ 2201–2202 (West 1982 & Supp. 1989)).

57. *Aetna Life Ins. Co.*, 300 U.S. at 241.

58. Note, *supra* note 54, at 504 (footnotes omitted).

59. Local prosecutors are often accused of covering-up such police conduct and refusing to prosecute the assaults. *See, e.g.*, Latino Coalition for Racial Justice, Press Release (Feb. 10, 1988).

such strong cases that the local prosecutor will be publicly embarrassed if the special prosecutor secures a conviction.

The abuse of such an option, or even the appointment of a permanent special prosecutor, defeats the BRA's purpose of persuading all local prosecutors to investigate bias crimes on a routine basis, just as they do all other types of crimes. If a special prosecutor office were instituted, it would also likely be insufficiently staffed to handle all the bias crimes in a state. There is a greater potential for deterring bias crimes if the large number of routine public prosecutors in a jurisdiction were prompted to enforce the bias statutes on a regular basis. Moreover, a permanent special prosecutor would always permit local prosecutors to avoid the difficulties of enforcing bias crime statutes.

5. Nonfeasance Suits

As a watchdog agency, the BRA would keep track of how often the special prosecutor option was used. If individual prosecutors display a pattern of refusing to prosecute all bias crimes, the BRA could organize a class action on behalf of all those victims that were denied vindication because of the prosecutor's policy, and accuse the prosecutor of nonfeasance. A compilation of all written justifications would be a part of the BRA's investigation into nonfeasance.

Although suits for nonfeasance are a seldom used remedy for abuse of prosecutorial discretion, some statutes have provided for the removal of prosecutors from office in egregious cases.[60] Like the special prosecutor option, suits of nonfeasance will be a measure of last resort.

B. Inclusiveness of Statute

The proposed model statute would extend coverage to habitually disfavored or marginalized groups such as gay men and lesbian women,[61] in addition to racial minorities, because of the commonality regarding motivations of irrational hatred. The coverage would be extended with the understanding that those who are members of such groups would qualify if there has been a history of violence against the discrete group, there are pervasive and well-known stereotypes about the group, or there is a resentment against the group based on a perception of economic clashes of

---

60. See F. MILLER, supra note 43, at 298–306 (1969); State v. Winne, 12 N.J. 152, 96 A.2d 63 (1953) (leading case upholding validity of indictment charging prosecutor with criminal nonfeasance in office).

61. Even though gay men and lesbian women are not considered a suspect class under the Federal Constitution, see Bowers v. Hardwick, 478 U.S. 186 (1986), states can and should go much further in protecting individual rights. See Keynote Address by Attorney Elaine Jones, Conference on Women of Color in the Law (audio tapes on file with Rutgers University Law School) (Apr. 14, 1988) (given Federal government's current reticence to advance cause of civil rights, state governments and courts must protect individual rights).

interest. The statute will also cover attacks on individuals who are perceived by their attackers to be members of a disfavored group. Even though such individuals are not actually members of disfavored groups, the harm to the disfavored group under attack is the same.[62]

Although the model statutory definition of bias crime will not be confined solely to assaults of minority persons by white people, the statutes are written with the understanding that assaults which are motivated by arbitrary hatred are most often directed against disfavored groups for the purpose of oppression.[63] Not every cognizable group finds itself in such a condition of disfavor. Therefore, even though the statute is generally written to encompass any perpetrator, the BRA will more closely scrutinize bias crime allegations against a member of a disfavored group in case the prosecutor is using the statute for the purpose of further oppression. But the statute on its face would apply to a Black person's bias attack on a white person. Given this understanding, if BRA records reveal that specific prosecutors are using the statutes to *persecute* members of the disfavored groups rather than to deter racial violence, the BRA then would have standing to bring charges of malfeasance against those prosecutors. It may be that certain white victims may feel threatened by criminals who happen to be people of color, but that is a concern to be distinguished from the fear of bias motivated attacks which contributes to the oppression of disfavored groups.

BIAS CRIME MODEL STATE STATUTE

A person is guilty of a bias crime when—with the intent to harass, annoy, threaten, intimidate, or alarm another person—he: strikes, shoves, kicks, or otherwise subjects another person to physical contact, or attempts or threatens to do the same, because of some immutable characteristic which the victim possesses or is perceived to possess as a member of a disfavored group.

(1) Definition—As used in this section a victim will be considered a member of a "disfavored group" if she is a member of a distinct group, if there has been a history of violence against such group, and if there are pervasive and well-known stereotypes about such group. Among the characteristics that define a "disfavored group" are: race, color, religion, ances-

---

62. Interview with Marlene Besterman, *supra* note 17 (bias statute in New York, N.Y. PENAL LAW § 240.30 (Consol. 1984), has been inadequate in prosecution of bias crimes, because in cases where victim is abused because of attacker's perception of victim's sexual orientation, victim's lack of membership in disfavored group only allows such attacks to be charged as "violations" rather than more serious misdemeanor or felony charges).

63. Oppression is a term used to designate conditions and experiences of subordination and injustice. Oppression involves " 'a system of interrelated barriers and forces which reduce, immobilize and mold people who belong to a certain group, and effect their subordination to another group (individually to individuals of the other group, and as a group' to that group.)" A FEMINIST DICTIONARY 314-15 (1985).

try, national origin, and sexual orientation. A group characteristic will be considered immutable if it is so much a part of each group members' being that physical violence cannot and should not be avoided by denying possession of the trait to the attacker.

(2) Duty of the Prosecutor—When prosecutors receive cases from the police or victims, they must either prosecute the case as a bias crime or formulate a written justification for not prosecuting the case.

Copies of the written justification must be given to the victim and kept on file with the prosecutor's office and the Bias Reporting Agency instituted under provision (3) of this statute.

If prosecutors receive cases from the police or victims that *have not been classified as bias crimes*, but involve an act of violence either between distinct members of the oppressed groups detailed in provision (1) of this statute or between members of a disfavored group and white heterosexual persons, prosecutors *must* thoroughly investigate the case for the circumstances enumerated below which each individually raise the inference that the act is a bias crime:

 i. uttering of racial slur(s) or statement(s) concerning the victim's membership within a disfavored group, by the perpetrator anytime before, during, or after the act of violence;

 ii. relevant history of the relations between the victim and the perpetrator (i.e., whether victim is a complete stranger to perpetrator, and/or a recent arrival in residential area where attack occurred, or whether victim and perpetrator have had a long history of hostility caused by other factors).

(3) Bias Reporting Agency—The state shall establish and fund a Bias Reporting Agency (BRA)

 i. which shall collect any information, records and statistics regarding bias crimes in the state;

 ii. which will receive copies of all the written justifications prosecutors are required to give victims when a decision is made not to prosecute;

 iii. part of whose staff shall include a pathologist/forensic scientist for autopsy purposes;[64]

 iv. which shall investigate cases free of cost for victims and proxy victims when those victims are given standing to challenge a nonprosecution decision by seeking declaratory judgments stating that 1) the

---

64. The BRA pathologist will be able to evaluate the accuracy of the state medical examiner's report and be able to conduct a new autopsy when necessary. This investigatory power will be helpful in cases of police brutality where state medical examiners have been known to falsify autopsy reports which advantage the police. For general information about such a coverup, see N.Y. Times, Apr. 11, 1986, at B4, col. 6; N.Y. Times, Oct. 30, 1985, at B4, col. 4 (when 18-year-old graffiti artist Michael Stewart was taken into custody by New York Transit Police, he sustained lethal injuries before he finally died; New York medical examiner intially issued death ceritificate listing ambiguous term "cardiac arrest" as cause of death; after allegations of corruption, death certificate changed to reflect choking that was actual cause of death).

prosecutor has abused her discretion not to prosecute; and/or 2) the victim has a legitimate case that should be prosecuted even though the prosecutor is not compelled to do so;

v. which shall maintain a file of all declaratory judgments the judiciary confers upon individual prosecutors.

(4) Judicial Standard for According Declaratory Judgment

i. Victim(s) may be declared to *have a right* to have their attacker(s) prosecuted if the facts presented in the BRA investigatory report establish adequate probable cause for prosecution.

ii. The prosecutor may be declared to have abused her discretion not to prosecute if her investigation of the case appears insufficient as compared with the fact finding of the BRA's investigation; or if her written justification for not prosecuting contain subtle indication(s) that unconscious racism[65] may have accounted for the decision not to prosecute.

Unconscious racism may be inferred from prosecutorial descriptions of the case as being unworthy of prosecution because the act was a mere prank and not an actual bias crime; or if the victim is characterized as not being credible; or if the prosecutor stated that prosecution of bias crime is not an effective use of the criminal justice system.

(5) Special Prosecutor—In the event that a prosecutor disagrees with the rationale of a declaratory judgment, the judiciary is empowered to appoint a special prosecutor. [Special prosecutor may also be appointed in whatever manner certain states may have already instituted.]

(6) Penalties—Bias crimes shall be punishable by either imprisonment not to exceed two years or a fine not to exceed one thousand dollars for threatened bodily injury, and ten years imprisonment or ten thousand dollars for actual bodily injury.[66] When used in conjunction with other criminal statutes, sentences may be applied consecutively.

IV. CONCLUSION

In its analysis of bias crimes, this Note has identified a number of problems which account for the nonenforcement of bias crimes. The problems include: the exclusion of disfavored groups; prosecutorial discretion; and unconscious racism. The proposed model statute attempts to ad-

---

65. *See* Lawrence, *supra* note 29, at 355–58 (1987) (proposing cultural meaning test that asks courts to interpret meaning of human behavior when judging whether something is racially discriminatory act rather than requiring proof of concrete discriminatory purpose). "[H]uman behavior must be examined in context, as it may well derive its meaning from the specific historical and cultural milieu in which it takes place." *Id.* at 369–70. *See* ANTI-DEFAMATION LEAGUE OF B'NAI B'RITH LAW REPORT, HATE CRIMES STATUTES: A RESPONSE TO ANTI-SEMITISM, VANDALISM AND VIOLENT BIGOTRY app. A (1988) (draft of model legislation providing for penalty enhancement of various crimes which are motivated by bias). Unlike the model statute proposed in this Note, the ADL model statute focuses upon the state's duty to collect data regarding bias crimes rather than problems which arise with prosecution of bias crimes.

66. This penalty provision is the standard sentencing structure currently employed in the existing statutes described in Part Two of this Note. States should revise the sentencing options as they see fit.

dress those problems by monitoring prosecutorial discretion and empowering victims.

The myriad of problems associated with arbitrary hatred will not disappear overnight, nor will they be solved by any single innovative legal process. The creation of state criminal statutes in combination with a special Bias Reporting Agency must be used in addition to Federal remedies to be most effective. Although some commentators might criticize a statutorily-created Bias Reporting Agency because it represents too drastic a measure, it should be noted that existing prosecutorial structures have been deficient in handling bias crime prosecution. Slight modifications of existing arrangements would be futile in changing the status quo perception that bias crimes are isolated incidents that do not require widespread prosecution. As difficult as instituting a new administrative agency might be, the only way that crimes of arbitrary hatred can be opposed is by waging a full scale attack. Anything less than a comprehensive optimistic approach is a poor attempt to confront the social dilemma of bias crimes.

OFFICIAL REACTIONS TO HISPANIC DEFENDANTS IN THE SOUTHWEST

GARY D. LaFREE

Despite a long-term interest in the treatment of minorities by the legal system, few criminologists have specifically considered the case of Hispanics. The purpose of this study was to determine whether and to what extent criminal justice outcomes and their determinants differ for Hispanics and non-Hispanics in two southwestern jurisdictions. An analysis of 755 defendants whose most serious charge was robbery or burglary showed major differences between the two jurisdictions. There was no evidence of unfavorable Hispanic treatment in Tucson. Being Hispanic had no effect on the type of adjudication received, verdicts, or sentence severity. Tucson Hispanics received more favorable pretrial release decisions than whites. In contrast, Hispanic defendants in El Paso received less favorable pretrial release outcomes than white defendants, were more likely to be convicted in jury trials, and received more severe sentences when they were found guilty by trial. Interviews suggested that treatment differences in Tucson and El Paso may be due to differences between established Hispanic citizens and less well-established Mexican-American citizens and Mexican nationals, different mechanisms for providing attorneys to indigent defendants, and differential language difficulties in the two jurisdictions.

Politicians and criminologists have long been concerned with the extent to which the defendant's race[1] affects processing decisions in criminal cases. Most U.S. examinations of this question have compared the treatment of black defendants and white defendants. In contrast,

This project was supported by Grant Number 82-IJ-LX-0039, awarded by the National Institute of Justice, U.S. Department of Justice, under the Justice System Improvement Act of 1979. Points of view or opinions stated in this article are mine and do not necessarily represent the official position or policies or the Department of Justice. I would like to thank Carol Lujan for her in collecting these data and the criminal justice systems of Pima and El Paso Counties for their cooperation and support. The research was partially supported by the Research Allocation Committee, The University of New Mexico.

JOURNAL OF RESEARCH IN CRIME AND DELINQUENCY, Vol. 22 No. 3, August 1985 213-237
© 1985 Sage Publications, Inc.

213

little research has been done on the treatment of Hispanics[2] by the legal system.[3] This neglect is difficult to justify given that Hispanics constitute the nation's second largest minority, are one of the fastest growing minorities (Jaffe et al., 1980), and are now the largest single minority group in several states. I address this oversight here by comparing criminal justice reactions to Hispanic, white, and black defendants in two southwestern jurisdictions.

PRIOR RESEARCH

Early research on Hispanics typically assumed that they had higher crime rates than the general population, and then offered explanations. For example, researchers attempted to link Hispanic crime to culture (Handman, 1931; Tuck, 1946), family patterns (Warnhuis, 1931), intelligence (Young, 1922), illiteracy (Warnhuis, 1931), and unemployment (Bogardus, 1943). Besides methodological limitations (e.g., small sample sizes, nonrandom samples, no control variables), these early studies usually examined causes of Hispanic criminal behavior but ignored the possibility of different Hispanic/non-Hispanic treatment.

These early studies began to give way to a different view of Hispanics in the legal system, evident as early as 1931 in the report of the National Commission on Law Observance and Enforcement (the Wickersham Report). According to this report, Hispanics face heavier police deployment and, compared to other citizens, are more likely to face illegal police practices, language barriers, overt racism, and discrimination in the administration of the law. Other recent sources (Acuna, 1972; Morales, 1972; Rivera, 1974) reach similar conclusions. Unfortunately, although these studies have been useful for drawing attention to potential problems faced by Hispanics in their dealings with the legal system, many of them have been based on little or no empirical research. For example, the 1970 Commission on Civil Rights collected data by interviewing law enforcement personnel and private citizens, and by holding hearings in several southwestern cities. Yet their published report is primarily a description of several individual cases of official misbehavior.[4]

Several recent studies that explicitly examine official reactions to Hispanic defendants through empirical research are exceptions to the general trend and are thus particularly important. Unnever (1982) studied 313 convicted male drug offenders in Miami, Flordia, and found evidence of different treatment of Hispanics in sentencing: Controlling for prior record, seriousness of offense, and number of counts, Hispanics received longer sentences than whites (but shorter sentences than blacks). However, Unnever's study is limited to one offense and location.

In a more comprehensive study, Petersilia (1983) examined data from official California criminal justice records and from a survey of 1,400 male prison inmates in California, Michigan, and Texas. She found that white suspects were less likely than blacks or Hispanics to be released after arrest. However, minority offenders convicted of felonies were more likely than whites to go to prison and received longer prison sentences than whites. Unfortunately, many of Petersilia's conclusions are based on descriptive statistics that do not control for variables such as type of offense and prior criminal record.

Recent studies by Zatz (1984) and Holmes and Daudistel (1984) use multivariate analyses that control for case differences. Controlling for offense and disposition type, evidence, prior record, and defendants' attributes, Zatz found no main effects of race on sentences for 4,729 Chicano, white, and black defendants. However, she did find inter-actions between race and several important determinants of sentence length. In particular, Chicanos with prior criminal records received especially harsh sentences. Holmes and Daudistel compared sentence severity for white, black, and Hispanic defendants in two metropolitan jurisdictions in the American Southwest. Controlling for offense seriousness, prior felony convictions, use of a weapon, and several previous processing outcomes, they found that Hispanics received harsher sentences in one of the two cities. Moreover, like Zatz, they found that the variables that affected sentence length operated different-ly for Hispanics and non-Hispanics. Most notably, Hispanics convicted by jury trial in one of the two jurisdictions received particularly severe sentences. The major limitation of the Zatz and Holmes and Daudistel studies is that they only examine sentencing outcomes.

Because there are few criminological studies of Hispanics, generali-zations are difficult. However, the extensive research literature on official reactions to black defendants provides insights that may generalize to Hispanics. First, conclusions of discrimination aganist blacks by the legal system (Cameron, 1964; Partington, 1965; Southern Regional Council, 1969) have gradually given way to results that imply that different treatment of blacks and whites depends on specific circumstances, including the year in which the case was processed (Thomson and Zingraff, 1981), the sentencing judge (Gibson, 1978), the radical composition of the victim-defendant dyad (Farrell and Swigert, 1978; LaFree, 1980), the type of offense (Unnever, 1982; Peterson and Hagan, 1984), and the region of the country in which data were collected (Hagan, 1974; Kleck, 1981). Assuming that Hispanics are treated no worse by the criminal justice system than blacks (which is consistent with prior research, e.g., Petersilia, 1983; Zatz, 1984), we might expect evidence of discrimination against Hispanics to be no more obvious than it has been in studies of black defendants.

Second, the criminal justice system operates like a sieve in which police process the largest number of suspects, the prosecution fewer, and the courts fewer still. Thus, by examining only one decision in isolation, we may reach misleading conclusions about the system as a whole. The implications of this are apparent in the Petersilia (1983) study. Petersilia reports no evidence of racial differences in the probability of arrest, the type of charge filed, or the probability of conviction. By contrast, she finds significant differences in the type and length of sentence imposed. These findings suggest that studies that examine only one or two processing outcomes may not accurately reflect the effect of processing as a whole. Thus, the greater the number of decisions examined, the more confident we can be about the conclusions reached.

Finally, reviews (Bernstein et al., 1977; Kleck, 1981; Garber et al., 1982; Petersilia, 1983: 17; Hagan and Bumiller, 1983) consistently show that measures of offense seriousness, evidence, and defendant's prior criminal record affect criminal processing outcomes regardless of defendant's race.

The present research aims to improve our understanding of the legal system's treatment of Hispanics by comparing official processing decisions made for Hispanic, black, and white defendants in two southwestern criminal justice systems. My specific purpose is to determine whether and to what extent legal outcomes and their determinants vary by the defendant's race.

CRIMINAL PROCESSING OF
SOUTHWESTERN DEFENDANTS

Data for this study are from official records and interviews with legal agents in Pima County (Tuscon), Arizona, and El Paso County, Texas.[5]

I examine case processing information for 755 male defendants whose most serious offense was robbery or burglary.[6] The data were originally collected by the Institute of Criminal Law and Procedure, Georgetown University Law Center, under a grant from the National Institute of Justice (Miller et al., 1978; Miller, 1980), and include defendants prosecuted during 1976-1977. Prosecution and court records provide data on the defendant's characteristics and prior criminal record, the characteristics of the offense, and the final disposition. In addition, I interviewed 60 police officers, deputy prosecutors, defense attorneys, public defenders, judges, and probation officers in Tucson and El Paso in December 1982 and January 1983. The interviews, which lasted from 45 to 90 minutes, provide qualitative data on the social organization of both systems and how it changed from the mid-1970s.

VARIABLES AND METHODS

Table 1 shows the variables and their coding (see Appendix for correlations). Race is coded as two dummy variables with "white" being the excluded category. Because the major question in the analysis is whether Hispanic defendants received different treatment than whites or blacks, controlling for offense seriousness and characteristics, I include four measures of defendants' prior criminal record and behavior. The most important of these is a weighted index of prior convictions. Record of drug or alcohol abuse is coded positively if either type of behavior was alleged in official records. Probation, parole, or pretrial release is coded positively if the defendant was classified in any of these categories at the time of the offense.[7]

The analysis includes four measures of offense seriousness. Statutory seriousness measures the mean number of years prescribed by law in each state for the most serious charge against the defendant at the arraignment. Number of counts measures all charges against the defendant at the arraignment. Because the importance of each additional charge is probably less than the importance of the charge that preceded it, I used a log transformation of the number of counts in the analysis. "Type of crime" is a dummy variable, coded positively if the case involved robbery. "Weapon" is coded positively if any mention of a weapon was made in the case file.[8]

The last four variables in Table 1 are the dependent variables. Adjudication type measures whether the defendant went to trial or pled

TABLE 1:   Variables, Coding, and Frequencies

Variable	Coding	Distribution[a] N	%
Race/Ethnicity[b]	Hispanic	283	37.5
	Black	115	15.2
	White	357	47.3
Defendant age	Interval Scale (18-65)	Mean = 26.16	
Weighted index of prior convictions[c]	0-40	Mean = 4.50	
Record of drug abuse	0 No	572	75.9
	1 Yes	182	24.1
Record of alcohol abuse	0 No	663	87.8
	1 Yes	92	12.2
Probation, parole or pretrial release at time of offense	0 No	555	73.5
	1 Yes	200	26.5
Statutory Seriousness (in years)	Interval (0-40)	Mean = 13.59	
Number of counts	Log transformation (0-3.55)	Mean = 1.03	
Type of crime	0 Burglary	288	38.2
	1 Robbery	466	61.8
Weapon	0 Not mentioned	539	71.4
	1 Mentioned	216	28.6
Employment status (Tucson only)	0 Unemployed or other	355	74.7
	1 Employed	120	25.3
Pretrial release status	0 Released on own recognizance or conditional release	230	31.9
	1 Cash bond and released	128	17.8
	2 Bail denied, or cash bond but not released	363	50.3
Adjudication type	0 Guilty plea	637	84.4
	1 Trial	118	15.6
Verdict (jury or bench trials)	0 Not guilty	32	27.1
	1 Guilty	86	72.9
Sentence severity	0 Suspended sentence	51	6.8
	1 Probation 1-12 months	44	5.9
	2 Probation 13-24 months	42	5.6
	3 Probation 25-36 months	102	13.6
	4 Incarcerated in jail or prison 1-6 months or probation 37 months or more	115	15.3
	5 Incarcerated in jail or prison 1-6 months and probation for unspecified period	159	21.2

164

TABLE 1   (Continued)

Variable	Coding	Distribution[a] N	%
6	Incarcerated in jail or prison 7-12 months	9	1.2
7	Incarcerated in jail or prison 7-12 months and probation for unspecified period	1	0.1
8	Incarcerated in jail or prison 13-24 months	26	3.5
9	Incarcerated in jail or prison 13-24 months and probation for unspecified period	1	0.1
10	Incarcerated in jail or prison 25-36 months	45	6.0
11	Incarcerated in jail or prison 37-48 months	26	3.5
12	Incarcerated in jail or prison 49-60 months	15	2.0
14	Incarcerated in jail or prison 61-84 months	37	4.9
17	Incarcerated in jail or prison 85-120 months	39	5.2
21	Incarcerated in jail or prison 121-168 months	19	2.5
30	Incarcerated in jail or prison 169 months or more	19	2.5

Mean = 6.71

a. Variation in total number of cases is due to missing data.
b. Dummy-coded as two vectors with "white" being the excluded category.
c. Prior felony convictions were assigned three points, misdemeanor convictions two points, after Bernstein et al. (1977).

guilty. Pretrial release status is a three-point scale with 2 being the least favorable and 0 the most favorable release status (see Bernstein et al., 1977: 749). For those defendants who were tried, "verdict" measures the outcome. The coding of the sentence severity measure derives from recent efforts (Tiffany et al., 1957; Hagan et al., 1980; LaFree, forthcoming) to devise an approximate interval scale of the severity of sentencing options.[9]

Table 2 shows the percentage of Hispanic, black, and white defendants in the criminal justice system for six criminal justice outcomes.[10] If the criminal justice system discriminates against Hispanics, we should find a higher proportion of Hispanics in the criminal justice system in later than earlier processing stages—a consequence of their being differentially selected for the imposition of official sanctions. In general, Table 2 does not support this interpretation. Hispanics constitute 62.9% of the El Paso felony sample, 61% of those who receive prison terms, and 60% of those offenders receiving sentences of more than five years. Hispanics make up 26.2% of the Tucson felony sample; 26.7% of the offenders who receive prison sentences, and 23.3% of convicted offenders who receive sentences of more than five years.[11] The biggest Hispanic/non-Hispanic differences in Table 2 are for guilty verdicts. Hispanics make up 62.9% of the El Paso sample, but 70.4% of defendants found guilty at trial. In contrast, Hispanics constitute 26.2% of the Tucson sample, but only 14.3% of those found guilty at trial. Thus Hispanics are overrepresented in El Paso guilty verdicts and under-represented in Tucson guilty verdicts.

To summarize, although there are differences between Hispanics and non-Hispanics in Table 2—most notably a greater probability of guilty verdicts in El Paso and a lesser probability of guilty verdicts in Tucson—there is little evidence of systematically more severe outcomes for Hispanics compared to non-Hispanics. In El Paso, the proportion of defendants receiving prison sentences who were Hispanic was within two percentage points of the proportion of Hispanics in the sample; in Tucson, it was within one percentage point. In both El Paso and Tucson, the proportion of defendants receiving sentences of five or more years who were Hispanic was 2.9 percentage points less than the proportion of Hispanics in the sample. Of course, bivariate comparisons may be misleading. Hence I turn now to the multivariate anlaysis.

Pretrial Release

Pretrial release decisions have both immediate and longer-term implications for the defendant. An immediate implication is the inherent punishment of jail. In the longer-term, failure to make bail may reduce defendants' ability to defend themselves by eliminating the income they would ordinarily receive during the period of detention if they were free, by reducing their ability to aid their attorneys in their own defense, and by predisposing legal agents to recommend more serious sentences (Rankin, 1964; Wald, 1964; Skolnick, 1967). My specific aim in this part of the analysis was to determine whether compared to other defendants, Hispanics received less favorable pretrial release outcomes.

TABLE 2: Percentages of Hispanic, Black, and White Defendants in El Paso and Tucson for Six Processing Outcomes

	Filed as Felonies	Guilty Pleas	Guilty Verdicts[a]	Total Convictions	Prison Sentences	Five-Year or Greater Sentences
El Paso						
Hispanics	62.9	63.1	70.4	64.6	61.0	60.0
Blacks	8.2	6.1	13.6	7.6	14.0	12.0
Whites	28.9	30.7	15.9	27.8	25.0	28.0
N	232	179	44	223	100	75
Tucson						
Hispanics	26.2	27.9	14.3	26.8	26.7	23.3
Blacks	18.4	16.6	28.6	17.6	20.4	22.2
Whites	55.4	55.4	57.1	55.6	52.9	54.4
N	523	458	42	500	329	90
Sample Total						
Hispanics	37.5	38.0	43.0	38.4	34.7	40.0
Blacks	15.2	13.7	20.9	14.5	18.9	17.6
Whites	47.3	48.5	36.0	47.0	46.4	42.4
N	755	637	86	723	429	165

a. Includes both bench and jury trials.

TABLE 3: Regression of Pretrial Release Status on Independent Variables for Tucson and El Paso Defendants

	Tucson (N = 497)				El Paso (N = 224)			
	r	b	B	S	r	B	B	S
Hispanic	−.09	−.18	−.08	.074	.13	.26	.23	.002
Black	.03	−.09	−.04	NS	.09	.26	.14	.056
Age	.11	.01	.10	.037	.22	.01	.12	NS
Prior convictions	.13	.01	.08	.096	.22	.01	.11	NS
Drug abuse	.11	.13	.06	NS	.00	−.05	−.05	NS
Alcohol abuse	−.03	−.24	−.08	.092	−.04	−.09	−.07	NS
Probation, parole, pretrial release	.17	.34	.17	.000	.20	.30	.17	.013
Statutory seriousness	.25	.02	.23	.001	.15	.01	.10	NS
Number of counts	.15	.12	.06	NS	.09	.21	.08	NS
Type of crime	.12	.08	.04	NS	.11	.05	.05	NS
Weapon	.23	.08	.04	NS	.10	.11	.10	NS
Employment status	−.17	−.37	−.17	.000				
Intercept		.125				.745		
R^2		.173				.167		

NOTE: Variation in number of cases is due to missing data.

Table 3 shows the results of regressing pretrial release status on the independent variables. Contrary to the expectation of discrimination against Hispanics, Hispanic defendants in Tucson received more favorable pretrial release than other defendants (although the effect is relatively small).[12] Being black had no effect on pretrial release outcomes in Tucson. In contrast, both Hispanic and black defendants received less favorable pretrial release outcomes in El Paso. Moreover, the effect of race on pretrial release was stronger in El Paso than Tucson. The standardized regression coefficients in Table 3 show that being Hispanic was the single best predictor of an unfavorable pretrial release decision in El Paso—more important than prior criminal record or seriousness of the offense.

Tucson defendants who were on probation, parole, or pretrial release at the time of the offense, who had more serious charges against them, who had prior criminal records, and who were older received less favorable pretrial release outcomes. Consistent with prior literature (e.g., McIntyre, 1967), employed defendants received more favorable pretrial release dispositions.

In El Paso, only one variable besides being Hispanic or black affected pretrial release status: Defendants who were on probation, parole, or pretrial release at the time of the offense received less favorable outcomes.

Adjudication Type

Unnever (1982) and others (e.g., Alschuler, 1975) have argued that differential access to plea agreements may consitute a form of "organizational discrimination." For example, if minority defendants are less likely to have access to favorable plea agreements, different treatment of Hispanics may be mediated by type of adjudication. This is the conclusion reached by Petersilia (1983: 26), who found that only 7% of white defendants were tried by bench or jury, compared to 12% of blacks, and 11% of Hispanics.

In El Paso, 32% of blacks, 21% of Hispanics, and 10% of whites were tried by judge or jury. By comparison, in Tucson, 12.5% of blacks, 8.3% of whites, and 4.4% of Hispanic defendants were tried. The larger proportion of defendants tried in El Paso is explained by the policy of the chief prosecutor, who prohibited his assistants from plea bargaining once his office had filed felony charges (Miller, 1980; Daudistel, 1980). Consistent with Petersilia's findings, both blacks and Hispanics in El Paso were more likely than whites to go to trial. In contrast, Tucson Hispanics were less likely than whites to go to trial. Instead, blacks were most likely to go to trial, Hispanics were least likely to go to trial, and whites were midway between the two in terms of trial likelihood.

To determine whether Hispanic, black, and white defendants differed significantly with respect to adjudication type controlling for the other independent variables, I performed a multiple discriminant analysis of the adjudication outcome (Cooley and Lohnes, 1971; Hair et al., 1979).

Table 4 (panels 1 and 2) shows the discriminant analysis results for defendants who pled guilty or were tried in Tucson or El Paso. The standardized discriminant function coefficients measure the relative contribution of each variable to each function.[13] Independent variables with large discriminatory power generally have large weights and those with little discriminatory power have small weights. The direction of the relationship is shown by the group centroids. For example, according to Table 4, black defendants in Tucson had a coefficient of .513. This means that black defendants were more likely to go to trial than plead guilty. To assess the relative importance of each variable for classifying cases as adjudicated by trial or guilty plea, I include Rao's V (1952: 257), a generalized distance measure of dispersion.[14]

TABLE 4:   Discriminant Function Coefficients, Group Centroids, and Canonical
Correlations for Type of Adjudication and Verdicts[a]

	Adjudication Type		Verdict	
Variable	Tucson (N = 444)	El Paso (N = 209)	Tucson (N = 45)	El Paso (N = 40)
Hispanic	−.231	.222	−.260	.353*
Black	.513*	.423*	−.033	−.044
Age	.030	.033	−.461	.430
Prior convictions	.398*	.354*	.294	−.234
Drug abuse	−.043	.373*	−.390	−.010
Alcohol abuse	.384*	.140	.544*	.187
Probation, parole, pretrial release	−.142	.036	−.469	.676
Statutory seriousness	−.213	.257	−.386	−.567*
Number of counts	−.375*	−.342*	.455	.236
Type of crime—robbery	.224	.207	.514	−.589
Weapon	.456*	.279*	.159	−.093
Employed	−.045	—	−.263*	—
Unfavorable pretrial release	.024	.372*	.896*	−.436
Group centroids:				
Guilty pleas/Not Guilty verdicts	−.087	−.231	−1.187	−1.430
Trials/Guilty verdicts	.591	.776	.432	.358
Canonical correlation	.222	.392	.591	.592

NOTE: Variation in number of cases is due to missing data.
a. For Tucson and El Paso defendants.
*Rao's V ≤ .10.

Table 4 shows that controlling for other variables, Hispanic defendants were no more likely than other defendants to go to trial in either Tucson or El Paso. In contrast, black defendants were more likely to go to trial in both jurisdictions. In Tucson, defendants with more serious criminal records, defendants with alcohol problems, and defendants who allegedly used a weapon were also more likely to go to trial. Cases involving more charges were less likely to go to trial. In El Paso, defendants with more serious criminal records, defendants alleged to be drug abusers, defendants who used a weapon to commit the offense, and defendants who had less favorable pretrial release decisions were more likely to go to trial. As in Tucson, cases involving more charges were less likely to be tried.

These results provide no evidence of differential treatment of Hispanics. However, the results do show that blacks in both jurisdictions were more likely to be tried. In fact, being black is the single best predictor of adjudication type in both jurisdictions.

Jury Trials

Of the 755 cases filed as felonies in these data, 118 (15.6%) were adjudicated by jury or bench trial. Because verdicts are categorical outcomes (i.e., guilty/not guilty), I again use discriminant analysis. The variables included are the same as those used in the analysis of adjudication type. Judges adjudicated 13 (20%) of the 65 Tucson trials and 9 (17%) of the 53 El Paso trials. Because different variables may influence jury and bench trials, I limited the analysis of verdicts to jury trials.[15] The results are shown in Table 4 (panels 3 and 4).

Being Hispanic or black had no effect on verdicts in Tucson. Tucson defendants with alleged alcohol abuse problems, unemployed defendants,[16] and defendants who received less favorable pretrial release outcomes were more likely to be found quilty.

In contrast, being Hispanic was a significant predictor of guilty verdicts in El Paso.[17] The other determinant of El Paso verdicts was offense seriousness: Statutorily serious cases were less likely to result in conviction. This counterintuitive finding may reflect hesitancy on the part of jurors to convict in cases where the probable severity of sanctions for defendants is greater.

Sentence Severity

The analysis of sentencing included the same variables as described above with the exception that three earlier decisions, pretrial release status, adjudication type (i.e., guilty plea or trial), and type of trial (i.e., bench or jury) are also included. To determine whether the effect of the independent variables was different for Hispanic defendants, I included product terms (independent variables by race of offender; Hispanics equal 1, others equal 0). I analyzed all independent variables and their corresponding product terms for both Tucson and El Paso defendants. Table 5 shows regressions of sentence severity on the significant independent variables and their corresponding product terms. None of the race by independent variable product terms were significant ($p < 0.10$) in Tucson. Thus there was no evidence that being Hispanic affected sentencing in Tucson through statistical interaction with the other variables.

TABLE 5:   Regression of Sentence Severity on Independent Variables for Convicted Tucson and El Paso Defendants (p ⩽ .10)

Variables	Sentences—Tucson (N = 475)				Sentences—El Paso (N = 223)			
	r	b	SE	B	r	b	SE	B
Hispanic					(−.07	−.30	.716	−.02)
Prior convictions	.19	.15	.034	.17	.47	.94	.153	.92
Drug abuse	.22	2.55	.619	.16				
Alcohol abuse	.08	−2.20	.833	−.10				
Probation, parole, pretrial release	.18	1.73	.558	.13				
Statutory seriousness	.39	.29	.031	.37	.21	.09	.045	.10
Number of counts	.26	1.82	.599	.12	.27	4.17	1.394	.16
Weapon					.30	2.90	.698	.23
Unfavorable pretrial release	.31	.93	.280	.13	.34	2.01	.561	.19
Adjudication by trial					(.27	−1.96	1.393	−.14)
Bench trial					.02	−3.58	1.673	−.12
Product terms (Independent variables by defendant race—Hispanic)								
Prior convictions					.36	−.59	.164	−.56
Adjudication by trial					.26	5.79	1.658	.36
Intercept		−1.35				−2.63		
R²		.324				.490		

NOTE: Parentheses indicate effects that are statistically insignificant. Variation in number of cases is due to missing data.

Table 5 shows that Hispanics and blacks in Tucson did not receive more severe sentences than whites. The best predictor of sentence severity in Tucson was statutory seriousness—more serious charges resulted in more serious sanctions. Defendants with a more extensive criminal record, who had more charges against them, who had records of drug abuse, or who were on probation, parole, or pretrial release at the time of the offense received more severe sentences. Defendants with alleged alcohol abuse problems received less severe sentences. Consistent with prior research (Landes, 1974; Unnever, 1982; Garber et al., 1982), Tucson defendants who received less favorable pretrial release decisions also received more severe sentences. However, we have already seen (Table 3) that Tucson Hispanics did not receive less favorable pretrial release decisions.

For El Paso, I found significant race by adjudication type and race by defendant's criminal record interactions. To allow an interpretation of the product terms I retained the nonsignificant variables with significant product terms. The product term for adjudication type indicates that for Hispanics only, guilty verdicts result in more severe sentences than guilty pleas $(-.14 + (.36) = .22)$. The product term for criminal record shows that defendants with serious criminal records received more severe sentences, regardless of race, but this effect was less important for Hispanics than other defendants $(.92 = (-.56) = .36)$.[18]

El Paso sentences were also more severe when charges were more serious, there were multiple counts, the case involved a weapon, and the defendant had an unfavorable pretrial release status. Sentences were less severe for bench than jury trials.

DISCUSSION AND CONCLUSIONS

The results were consistent with recent research on discrimination against black defendants in the application of the law; that is, I found evidence of different treatment, but it was limited to particular processing decisions and one of two jurisdictions. In Tucson, Hispanics received more favorable pretrial release outcomes than other defendants, and being Hispanic had no effect on adjudication type, verdict, or sentence severity. The only evidence of different treatment by race in Tucson was for black defendants, who were more likely to go to trial than plead guilty. And even the importance of this effect is moot because adjudication type was not a significant determinant of final verdict in Tucson.

In contrast, El Paso Hispanics received less favorable pretrial release outcomes than other defendants, were more likely to be convicted in jury trials, and received more severe sentences when they were found guilty by trial. Moreover, the fact that El Paso Hispanics had less favorable pretrial release outcomes also meant that they were more likely to go to trial and that they received more severe sentences when they were tried. Despite the small number of cases, the most convincing evidence of differential Hispanic treatment was for the analysis of El Paso juries, which showed that being Hispanic was one of two predictors of guilty verdicts. At the same time, El Paso Hispanics were not more likely to go to trial, did not receive more severe sentences controlling for case characteristics, and the results showed that Hispanic defendants with more serious criminal records received less severe sentences than whites with serious criminal records.

The differences between the two cities is of particular interest. Officially, Hispanics make up over 61% of the citizenry of El Paso, and because of El Paso's proximity to the Mexican border, unofficial estimates place the actual figure much higher. Thus, in El Paso, Hispanics are not a numeric minority. By contrast, Hispanics officially make up only about 21% of the Tucson population. Thus we might expect Hispanics to face greater injustices in Tucson than El Paso. Interviews with legal agents in the two cities suggest several reasons why they did not. First, El Paso is a "border town." An El Paso assistant district attorney explained:

> We're sitting here on a border. Across the river from us, which is nothing more than an oversized mud puddle, is the city of Juarez, with over a million and a quarter residents. . . . Our police force is geared to the size of this city and what it can afford. El Paso does not have a large economic base to support the city itself. In other words, we perceive El Paso as the city north of the Rio Grande, but bullshit, we're talking about another million and a quarter people that go back and forth like a tide.

The fact that El Paso is located on a semipermeable national border has direct implications for all the outcomes examined. Obviously, Mexican nationals make poor bail and probation risks. Moreover, closeness to the border means that the El Paso Hispanic community is likely to be more highly stratified than is the case for Tucson. As defined by official records, Hispanics in El Paso include everyone from prominent Hispanic families, who may go back many generations in the Southwest, to recently migrated, unemployed or underemployed Mexican nationals. A likely possibility is that El Paso jurors (which include many upper- and middle-class Hispanics), are harsher than Tucson jurors on lower-class Hispanic defendants. This interpretation was generally supported by our interviews with legal agents in El Paso. For example, one assistant district attorney in El Paso told us, "The older Mexican-Americans tend to be pretty conservative, they will nail you [i.e., defendants]." An El Paso defense attorney offered a similar opinion: "I've had middle-class Mexican-Americans on my jury, and boy they just rammed it at the defendant." We heard no similar comments from Tucson officials.

A second difference between the two jurisdictions that might help explain the results relates to the type of defense provided indigent defendants in the two cities. Indigent Tucson defendants are assigned a public defender. Our interviews with Tucson legal agents indicated that the Public Defender's Office generally pursued an aggressive, adversarial stance toward the prosecution. For example, in response to a question about how the Tucson and Phoenix Offices differed, a Tucson public defender told us:

> It's my impression that our defender's office here is more adversarial—has a more adversarial relationship with the prosecutors. I think that the public defenders in Phoenix are much more prone to quickly plead a case out than we are. I think that's the basic difference.

Another Tucson public defender said simply, "It's more of a combat mentality here."

In contrast, Texas does not have a public defender system. Instead, judges maintain lists of private attorneys who handle criminal cases. Attorneys are randomly assigned to defendants who cannot afford their own counsel from these lists. Thus the type of defense indigent defendants receive in El Paso is likely to be more variable with regard to trial experience and overall quality than is the case in Tucson.

Finally, another important difference between the cities is their relative ability to provide adequate language assistance for Spanish-speaking defendants. Language difficulties were cited by the 1970 Commission on Civil Rights (pp. 66-74) as a major block to equal legal treatment for southwestern Hispanics. Criminal justice agents in both El Paso and Tucson stressed that the legal system was making serious efforts to provide Spanish-speaking defendants with translators. Indeed, evidence of these efforts was obvious in our observations of both systems. However, because the proportion of Spanish-speaking defendants is much higher in El Paso than in Tucson, the magnitude of the language problem is correspondingly greater. Moreover, providing translators undoubtedly increases legal costs, and compared to Tucson, El Paso is a much poorer jurisdiction.[19] Thus it is probable that language difficulties remain a more serious problem in El Paso than in Tucson.

In a recent comparison of the sentencing of white and nonwhite drug offenders, Peterson and Hagan (1984: 56) argue that "meaning of race must be understood in historical, contextual terms." This observation seems particularly relevant to Hispanics. The term "Hispanic" itself encompasses a wide variety of groups with distinctive cultures and histories, including Mexicans, Puerto Ricans, Cubans, Central and South Americans, and Hispanos. Although this study concentrated on two southwestern jurisdications, even here, the rubric Hispanic included large numbers of individuals from several distinct groups: Spanish ancestry, Mexican-American, Mexican nationals, and various mixes between these groups and the other people of the Southwest. Future research on race must begin to consider such differences more directly.

Much of the recent literature on the criminal processing of Hispanic defendants has assumed discriminatory treatment, often without empirical evidence. Although such literature may be useful for drawing attention to the problems faced by Hispanics in the legal system, it can also encourage complacency: By blaming everyone we hold no one responsible. The results presented here suggest a more complex picture. I found major differences between and within these two legal systems with regard to the treatment of Hispanics. Armed with such specific information about differential treatment, it may ultimately be easier to increase justice for all defendants.

APPENDIX: Zero-Order Correlations for All Independent and Dependent Variables in Analyses[a]

Variables	(1)	(2)	(3)	(4)	(5)	(6)	(7)	(8)	(9)	(10)	(11)	(12)	(13)	(14)	(15)
(1) Def. hispanic	—	-.39	.01	.07	-.03	-.03	-.06	-.01	-.21	-.08	-.31	—	.13	-.01	-.04
(2) Def. Black	-.28	—	.08	.05	.01	-.01	.05	-.01	.08	.07	.15	—	.09	.14	.10
(3) Def. age	-.10	.02	—	.63	.11	.04	.09	.13	.01	-.01	-.03	—	.22	.15	.38
(4) Prior convictions	.02	.01	.34	—	.21	.11	.16	.08	-.04	.02	-.09	—	.22	.20	.45
(5) Drug abuse	.10	-.07	.07	.07	—	.29	.19	-.12	.07	.12	.08	—	.00	.15	.16
(6) Alcohol abuse	.00	-.11	.26	.13	.16	—	.14	-.05	-.05	.09	.06	—	-.04	.08	.12
(7) Probl., par. ptr.	.06	.07	.04	.19	.16	-.01	—	-.03	.02	.20	.15	—	.20	.12	.31
(8) Stat. seriousness	-.12	.05	-.00	-.09	.02	-.02	-.14	—	.12	-.00	.12	—	.15	.08	.18
(9) Counts	-.02	-.01	-.01	.07	.19	-.08	.20	.13	—	.15	.27	—	.09	-.06	.27
(10) Type crime	.03	.03	-.08	.02	.16	-.10	-.01	.27	.07	—	.36	—	.11	.12	.17
(11) Weapon	-.14	.08	.03	-.02	.04	-.02	-.09	.76	.14	.26	—	—	.10	.15	.24
(12) Employment	-.10	.01	.05	-.01	-.07	-.08	-.05	.02	.01	-.01	-.05	—	—	.21	—
(13) Pretrial status	-.08	.02	.10	.14	.11	-.03	.18	.25	.14	.13	.24	-.17	—	—	.31
(14) Trial	-.09	.09	.01	.11	.01	.11	-.02	.01	.03	.03	.07	-.03	.04	—	.17
(15) Sentence	.00	.03	.11	.19	.22	-.08	.18	.39	.26	.21	.32	-.01	.31	.08	—

NOTE: N = 496 for Tucson; N = 231 for El Paso. Full variable descriptions are given in Table 1.
a. El Paso cases are above diagonal; Tucson cases are below diagonal.

231

177

NOTES

1. Although race and ethnicity are often used interchangeably in research on discrimination, "race" refers to physical characteristics such as skin color whereas "ethnicity" refers to cultural factors such as language and customs (Barrera, 1979: 4). In reality, "black" and "Hispanic" designations in the United States are often based both on racial and ethnic distinctions. For simplicity, I refer to "racial" differences throughout.

2. The term "Hispanic" applies to a large and diverse group. The 1970 U.S. Census permitted people to classify themselves in one of five "Spanish heritage" categories: Mexican, Puerto Rican, Cuban, Central and South American, and Hispano. This research focuses on Hispanics in the American Southwest. The majority of persons of Spanish heritage in this region identify themselves as Mexican-American (or Chicano), or Hispano.

3. A review by Savitz (1973) reports over 500 research articles on the treatment of blacks by the legal system (see also, Kleck, 1981; Hagan and Bumiller, 1983). In contrast, a comprehensive review by Trujillo (1974) reports only eighteen studies dealing with Hispanics and crime, and Carter (1983: 226) reports only seven articles on the experiences of Hispanics in the criminal justice system.

4. Except for an appendix on the percentage of grand jurors with Spanish surnames in selected California counties, the Report includes only six data tables: two show the distribution of Spanish surname citizens in five states; one compares the median levels of education for Spanish surname and other persons; and three compare ethnicity of criminal justice agents in several jurisdictions.

5. For convenience, I refer to "Tucson" and "El Paso" although both jurisdictions actually include the entire county in which each city is located. Jaffe et al. (1980: 123) report that in 1970, five southwestern states (Arizona, California, Colorado, New Mexico, and Texas) contained 90% of all Mexican/Americans. While California and Texas have the highest absolute number of Hispanics, Arizona, New Mexico, and Texas have the hightest proportion (U.S. Department of Commerce, 1977). And within these states, Tucson, Albuquerque, and El Paso are the three cities with populations over 250,000 that have the highest proportion of Hispanics. The legal system of Albuquerque is currently being examined in a related project (Tyler, 1983).

6. Robbery and burglary are general terms representing behaviors defined somewhat differently in the two states. Regardless of definition, only felonies are included here. In both Tucson and El Paso, robbery refers to the illegal taking of property from the person of another by using force or threat of force. Burglary refers to breaking and entering the house of another person with the intention of committing theft.

7. Like other empirical research on official reactions to Hispanic defendants (e.g., Zatz, 1984; Holmes and Daudistel, 1984) the El Paso data did not include a measure of economic status. However, the Tucson data included both whether the defendant was employed and the type of defense counsel. Because these data involve only robbery and burglary defendants, there may be less variation in economic status than there would be for some other crimes (e.g., drug offenses; see Unnever, 1982). In fact, because only 2.8% of the Tucson defendants had private attorneys, I had to exclude this variable from the analysis. To permit comparisons between Tucson and El Paso I ran separate analyses that either include or exclude the employment variable for the Tucson models.

8. The criminal code for each state was used to determine legally what constituted a weapon.

9. For offenders who received indeterminate sentences, I assigned the mean of the maximum and minimum sentence received before converting the sentence to the severity measure. I experimented with other measures of sentence severity before choosing this one. The most common alternative to the type of measure used here is simply final sentence if convicted (Eisenstein and Jacob, 1977; Nardulli, 1978). The major disadvantage of using length of final sentence as a measure of sentence severity is that it disregards defendants who receive only probation, or prison and probation.

10. Because the data included an insufficient number of Native Americans (N = 10) to allow meaningful comparisons, I excluded these cases from the analysis.

11. I note in passing that the proportion of Hispanics in the felony sample was similar to their official proportion in both cities. Hispanics officially constitute 61.9% of the total El Paso population (U.S. Department of Commerce, 1982), compared to 62.9% of the felony cases in the sample. In contrast, blacks are greatly overrepresented in both samples of felony cases. Officially, blacks constitute 3.8% of the El Paso population but make up 8.2% of the felony cases in the sample. Blacks constitute only 2.8% of the Tucson population but 18.4% of the felony cases in the sample.

12. In a separate analysis of Tucson pretrial release decisions I excluded employment status to determine whether the effect of race on the pretrial release decision was being suppressed by the effect of employment status. The results (available upon request) were identical to those obtained with employment status in the model: Hispanics received slightly more favorable pretrial release outcomes.

13. The interpretation of the standardized discriminant function coefficient is analogous to the interpretation of "beta weights" in multiple regression.

14. Rao's V evaluates each variable in terms of whether it increases discriminatory power. A variable that contains a large amount of information already included in previously selected variables may reduce discriminatory power by bringing the groups closer together. The change in V has a chi-square distribution with one degree of freedom.

15. However, a separate analysis that included bench trials showed similar results with regard to the effect of defendant's race on verdicts.

16. As with the analysis of pretrial release, I considered the possibility that the effect of race on verdicts in Tucson was being suppressed by the effect of employment status. But in separate analyses (available on request) that excluded the employment variable, being Hispanic still had no effect on Tucson verdicts. Thus it appears that Hispanics were no more likely to be convicted than whites in Tucson and that this fact is not explained by different employment statuses.

17. Rao's V estimates are done in a stepwise fashion so that the best single variable in terms of discriminating between two or more groups is selected first, the best two-variable combination is selected next, and so on. An analysis using Rao's V showed that being Hispanic was the single best determinant of a guilty verdict in El Paso.

18. The two product terms in Table 5 were both highly correlated with their corresponding independent variables (for criminal record and its product term r = .92; for adjudication type and its product term r = .81). The collinearity between these variables probably accounts for the positive zero-order correlation and the negative standardized regression coefficient for defendant's criminal record. In order to help determine whether these effects were artifacts of collinearity between the independent variables, I estimated

separate models of sentence severity for Hispanics and whites. These models included the same independent variables, but no product terms. The results (available upon request) confirmed the interpretations from the model with product terms. The standardized cofficients for adjudication type showed that Hispanic defendants found guilty at trial received more severe sentences (B = .20) than Hispanic defendants who pled guilty. Standardized regression coefficients for defendant's criminal record estimated separately for Hispanics and whites also supported the interpretation that criminal record had a greater effect on sentence severity for whites than Hispanics (for whites, B = .54; for Hispanics, B = .28).

19. Mean personal income per capita for Pima County in 1981 was $9,818 compared to a mean per capita income of $7,360 for El Paso County residents (U.S. Department of Commerce, 1983: 39, 529).

REFERENCES

Acuna, R.
1972   Occupied America: The Chicano's Struggle Toward Liberation. Caulfield.
Alschuler, A.
1975   "The defense attorney's role in plea bargaining." Yale Law J. 84: 1179-1313.
Barrera, M.
1979   Race and Class in the Southwest: A Theory of Racial Inequality. Notre Dame, IN: Univ. of Notre Dame Press.
Bernstein, I. N., W. R. Kelly, and P. A. Doyle
1977   "Societal reaction to deviants: the case of criminal defendants." Amer. Soc. Rev. 42: 743-755.
Bogardus, E.
1943   "Gangs of Mexican-American youth." Sociology and Social Research (September).
Cameron, M. O.
1964   The Booster and the Snitch. New York: Free Press.
Carter, D. L.
1983   "Hispanic interaction with the criminal justice system in Texas: experiences, attitudes, and perceptions." J. of Criminal Justice 2: 213-227.
Cooley, W. W. and P. R. Lohnes
1971   Multivariate Data Analysis. New York: Wiley.
Daudistel, H. C.
1980   "On the elimination of plea bargaining: the El Paso experiment," pp. 57-75 in W. F. McDonald and J. A. Cramer (eds.) Plea Bargaining. Lexington, MA: Lexington Books.
Eisenstein, J. and H. Jacob
1977   Felony Justice: An Organizational Analysis of Criminal Courts. Boston: Little, Brown.
Farrell, R. A. and V. L. Swigert
1978   "Prior offense as a self-fulfilling prophecy." Law and Society Rev. 12: 437-453.

Garber, S., S. Klepper, and D. Nagin
   1982   The Role of Extralegal Factors in Determining Criminal Case Dispositions:
           Toward More Reliable Statistical Inference. Pittsburgh: Carnegie-Mellen
           Univ. Press.
Gibson, J. L.
   1978   "Race as a determinant of criminal sentences: a methodological critique and a
           case study." Law and Society Rev. 12: 455-478.
Hagan, J.
   1974   "Extra-legal attributes and criminal sentencing." Law and Society Rev. 8:
           357-384.
Hagan, J. and K. Bumiller
   1983   "Making sense of sentencing: a review and critique of sentencing research," pp.
           1-54 in A. Blumstein et al. (eds.) Research in Sentencing: The Search for
           Reform, Volume 2. Washington, DC: National Academy Press.
Hagan, J., I. B. Nagel (Berstein), and C. Albonetti
   1980   "The differential sentencing of white-collar offenders in ten federal district
           courts." Amer. Soc. Rev. 45: 802-820.
Hair, J. F., P. E. Anderson, R. L. Tatham, and B. J. Grablowsky
   1979   Multivariate Data Analysis. Tulsa, OK: Petroleum Publishing.
Handman, M.
   1931   "Preliminary report on nationality and delinquency: the Mexican in Texas."
           Special report on Crime and the Foreign Born, Vol. II, National Commission
           on Law Observance and Enforcement.
Holmes, M. D., and H. C. Daudistel
   1984   "Race and justice in the Southwest: the sentencing of Anglo, Black and
           Hispanic defendants." Social Science Q. 65: 265-277.
Jaffe, A. J., R. M. Cullen, and T. D. Boswell
   1980   The Changing Demography of Spanish Americans. New York: Academic.
Kleck, G.
   1981   "Racial discrimination in criminal sentencing." Amer. Soc. Rev. 46: 783-804.
LaFree, G. D.
   1980   "The effect of sexual stratification by race on official reactions to rape." Amer.
           Soc. Rev. 45: 842-854.
   forth- "Adversarial and nonadversarial justice: a comparison of guilty pleas and
   coming trials." Criminology.
Landes, W. M.
   1974   "Legality and reality: some evidence of criminal procedure." J. of Legal Studies
           3: 287-337.
McIntyre, D. M.
   1967   Law Enforcement in the Metropolis. Washington, DC: American Bar Asso-
           ciation.
Miller, H. S.
   1980   Plea Bargaining in the United States. Volume I. Institute fo Criminal Law and
           Criminal Procedure, Georgetown University Law Center. (unpublished)

Miller, H. S., W. F. McDonald, and J. A. Cramer
    1978 Plea Bargaining in the United States. Washington, DC: National Institute of
          Law Enforcement and Criminal Justice.
Morales, A.
    1972 Ando Sangrando (I am Bleeding): A Study of Mexican-American Police
          Conflict.Portland, OR: International Scholarly Books.
Nardulli, P. F.
    1978 The Courtroom Elite: An Organizational Perspective on Criminal Justice.
          Cambridge, MA: Ballinger,
Partington, D.
    1965 "The incidence of the death penalty for rape in Virginia." Washington and Lee
          Law Rev. 22: 43-75.
Petersilia, J.
    1983 Racial Disparities in the Criminal Justice System. Santa Monica, CA: Rand.
Peterson, R. D. and J. Hagan
    1984 "Changing conceptions of race: towards an account of anomalous findings of
          sentencing research." Amer. Soc. Rev. 49: 56-70.
Rankin, A.
    1964 "The effect of pretrial detention." New York University Law Rev. 39: 641-655.
Rao, C. R.
    1952 Advanced Statistical Methods in Biometric Research. New York: Wiley.
Rivera, J.
    1974 "Justice, deprivation and the Chicano." Aztlan 4: 123-136.
Savitz, L.
    1973 "Black crime," pp. 467-516 in K. S. Miller (ed.) Comparative Studies of Blacks
          and Whites in the United States. New York: Seminar.
Skolnick, J. H.
    1967 "Social control in the adversary system." J. of Conflict Resolution 11: 51-70.
Southern Regional Council
    1969 Race Makes the Difference. Atlanta, GA: Southern Regional Council.
Thomson, R. J. and M. T. Zingraff
    1981 "Detecting sentencing disparity: some problems of evidence." Amer. J. of
          Sociology 86: 869-880.
Tiffany, L. P., Y. Avichai, and G. W. Peters
    1975 "A statistical analysis of sentencing in federal court: defendants convicted after
          trial, 1967-1968." J. of Legal Studies 4: 369-390.
Trujillo, L. D.
    1974 "La evolucion de 'Bandido' al 'Pachuco': A critical examination and evaluation
          of criminological literature on Chicanos." Issues in Criminology 9: 43-67.
Tuck, R.
    1946 Not With Fist. New York: Harcourt Brace Jovanovich.
Tyler, S. L.
    1983 The Disposition of Felony Arrests for Hispanic and Anglo Defendants. Ph.D.
          disseration, University of New Mexico.
Unnever, J. D.
    1982 "Direct and organizational discrimination in the sentencing of drug offenders."
          Social Problems 30: 212-225.

U.S. Commission on Civil Rights
    1970   Mexican-Americans and the Administration of Justice in the Southwest. Washington, DC: Government Printing Office.
U.S. Department of Commerce, Bureau of the Census
    1977   County and City Data Book. Washington, DC: Government Printing Office.
    1982   General Population Characteristics: 1980. Washington, DC: Government Printing Office.
    1983   County and City Data Book. Washington, DC: Government Printing Office.
Wald, P.
    1964   "Pretrial detention and ultimate freedom: a statistical study." New York University Law Rev. 39: 631-640.
Warnhuis, P.
    1931   "Crime and criminal justice among Mexicans in Illinois." Special report on Crime and the Foreign Born. Volume II. National Commission on Law Observance and Enforcement.
Young, K.
    1922   "Mental differences in certain migrant groups." University of Oregon Publications 1, 11.
Zatz, M. S.
    1984   "Race, ethnicity, and determinate sentencing: a new dimension to an old controversy." Criminology 22: 147-171.

3

SPANISH-SPEAKING PEOPLE
AND THE NORTH AMERICAN
CRIMINAL JUSTICE SYSTEM

Bonnie J. Bondavalli

Illinois State University

Bruno Bondavalli

University of Illinois

INTRODUCTION

The number of Spanish-speaking persons residing in the United States is growning rapidly. Spanish-origin individuals numbered approximately 9.1 million according to the 1970 census, accounting for 4.4% of the total population (U.S. Department of Commerce, *Subject Reports*, 1973). Spanish was the second most common mother tongue of those included in the census (U.S. Department of Commerce, *Detailed Characteristics*, 1973). These figures probably underestimate the number of Hispanics in the United States. The Census Bureau has had difficulty conceptually defining the Hispanic population, for example, Spanish language, Spanish heritage, Spanish surname, or self-identification as Hispanic (U.S. Commission on Civil Rights, 1974; Hernandez et al., 1973). Moreover, a considerable number of individuals fitting the census definitions may not have been counted as the census is believed to have ignored large numbers of urban poor. Also not included were an estimated 7.4 million illegal aliens. The 1978 census estimates approximately 12 million Hispanic Americans, but many continue to believe that Spanish-origin individuals are seriously undercounted and that the total number is closer to 19 million (It's Your Turn in the Sun," 1978).

49

Whatever the exact number of Spanish-heritage residents in the United States, the figure is large and is increasing at a dramatic pace. The issue of crime in the Spanish-speaking community is just beginning to receive the attention it warrants. Given the characteristics of many of the Spanish-speaking individuals, it would appear that they constitute a "population at risk" in terms of crime. According to the census reports, while the median age of the total U.S. population is 28.5, the median age of persons of Puerto Rican origin is 19.8; and the median age of those of Mexican origin is 18.9. The median income of Spanish-origin men with incomes is about $2,000 less than the median income of all men with incomes. The unemployment rate among Spanish-speaking persons is higher than the unemployment rate for the total population by 2.8%. About 1 in 5 Spanish-speaking adults (compared to 1 in 20 men and 1 in 25 women in the nation as a whole) has completed less than five years of school; and 83% of the Spanish-speaking families in the United States live in metropolitan areas (U.S. Department of Commerce, 1975). Although more recent reports show that the incomes and educational levels of Hispanics are rising, they remain low relative to most other groups (U.S. Commission on Civil Rights, *Social Indicators*, 1978).

Further, some researchers have noted emotional as well as socioeconomic factors which could conceivably contribute to crime in the Spanish-speaking community. Henggler and Tavormina's study of children of Mexican-American migrant workers, for example, indicated that the children showed a pattern of vulnerability on emotional, as well as verbal weaknesses on intellectual, indices (1978: 103-104). Indeed, living and working in an alien society can itself involve "a profound challenge . . . to one's problem-solving abilities and to one's ability to maintain emotional composure" (Guthrie, 1975: 96).

DETERMINING THE SCOPE OF THE PROBLEM

Arrest Reports

At present, it is difficult to assess the extent of the crime problem among Spanish-speaking individuals. The Federal Bureau of Investigation which assembles the Uniform Crime Reports does not at present distinguish Hispanic persons in their arrest data. If state crime-reporting agencies choose to gather such information, they can, but it appears that few do. (Table 1 shows the type of information which can be assembled from the Illinois crime reports.)

Among the few states which collect relevant data, definitions of the relevant population and reporting practices vary. In Illinois, for example, "Mexican" and "Puerto Rican" are listed as racial categories; but each police department is left to determine who should be placed in these categories (Towner, 1978). Also, reporting procedures in Chicago reduce the validity of the data still further (Statistical Analysis Center, N.D.: 34-42).

Court Statistics

Relevant court statistics are even more difficult to locate. Several years ago, the Law Enforcement Assistance Administration (LEAA) began providing funds for the development of a computerized information system for the courts. The Prosecution Management Information System (PROMIS) is now in differing stages of development in the various jurisdictions. It permits classification of clients by race and, if desired, by ethnicity. Only Los Angeles County, San Diego County, Tallahassee, and Manhattan list Hispanic ethnicity in the PROMIS data, however (Mandel, 1979: 17).

Prison Statistics

Prisoner data are more readily available. The Bureau of the Census reports on persons of Spanish-origin in correctional institutions. Tables 2 and 3 were produced by combining data on persons in institutions with other census data.

Although the quality of the data varies considerably, some individual prison systems also collect data. Perhaps, however, surveys in state correctional facilities and local jails conducted for LEAA between 1972 and 1978 contain the most reliable information on Hispanic prisoners. Race and ethnicity were included in the questionnaires. As Mandel notes, the raw data produced in these studies are excellent; the problem is that

TABLE 1   Arrests by Ethnicity in Illnois, 1975-1976

	White		Black		Mexican and Puerto Rican		Total	
	1975	1977	1975	1977	1975	1977	1975	1977
Crime index arrests	58,896	53,347	60,203	53,346	1,302	944	126,311	113,403
Crimes against persons	3,021	6,838	14,819	8,893	272	219	24,501	18,042
Crimes against property	50,875	46,509	45,384	43,503	1,030	725	101,801	95,361
Murder and voluntary manslaughter	267	256	1,094	809	19	1	1,512	1,253
Forcible rape	333	322	858	700	11	19	1,263	1,124
Aggravated assault, battery and attempted murder	5,310	4,371	4,524	2,067	199	154	10,561	6,712
Robbery	2,111	1,889	8,343	6,317	43	45	11,165	8,953
Burglary	12,139	10,348	9,939	8,273	229	137	23,622	20,065
Theft	35,904	33,193	32,563	32,159	769	535	72,036	68,584
Criminal damage	21,967	11,713	4,247	4,044	221	150	26,516	16,927

SOURCE: Department of Law Enforcement. *Crime in Illinois, 1976* and *Crime in Illinois, 1977*, Crime Statistics Section, Bureau of Identification, Springfield, Illinois.

52

TABLE 2 Percent Hispanic in Correctional Institutions in States with the Largest Spanish-Origin Populations, 1970

	Percent Hispanic in Federal and State Prisons	Percent Hispanic In Jails and Workhouses	Percent Hispanic in Training schools and Detention Homes	Percent of State's Population Hispanic
California	19.0	15.9	19.4	11.9
Texas	16.0	12.0	18.4	16.4
New York	18.1	14.4	11.3	7.4
Florida	3.6	2.0	1.0	6.0
Illinois	3.8	.5	11.2	3.5
New Mexico	25.8	34.8	55.3	30.3
New Jersey	5.3	2.6	10.7	4.0
Arizona	20.3	17.5	20.7	14.9

SOURCES: U.S. Department of Commerce, *Subject Reports: Persons in Institutions and Other Group Living Quarters*, 1973; U.S. Department of Commerce, *Subject Reports: Persons of Spanish Origin*, 1973; U.S. Department of Commerce, *Characteristics of the Population*, 1973.

53

TABLE 3   Distribution of Inmates in the United States, by
Ethnic Group, 1970

	White	Black	Spanish-Origin	Total
Prisons and Reformatories	114,608	80,742	13,596	198,831
Jails and Workhouses	72,591	52,800	8,209	129,189
Training Schools	39,757	24,099	5,287	66,457
Public	33,428	21,894	5,066	57,691
Private	6,329	2,205	281	8,766
Detention Homes	6,754	3,329	765	10,272

SOURCE: U.S. Department of Commerce, *Subject Reports: Persons in Institutions and Other Group Living Quarters,* 1973.

published summaries do not include Hispanic background. Mandel did acquire Hispanic data from the 1974 state prisoner survey, however, some of which is included in Table 4 (Mandel, 1979: 17).

More statistical data on arrests, offense and offender characteristics, police and court dispositions, and correctional outcomes are necessary before any conclusions can safely be drawn from the data. The limited available data, however, suggest several areas of inquiry, such as the following. Is crime among Spanish-speaking individuals, like crime among Blacks, more likely to be person-directed and less likely to be property-directed than crime among whites (cf. Tables 1 and 4)? Do Spanish-speakers with different national backgrounds tend to have different crime patterns, for example, Mexicans in the Southwest, Puerto Ricans in New York, and Cubans in Florida (cf. Table 2)? Are Spanish-speaking juveniles discriminated against in placement, a smaller percentage being placed in private and larger percentage in public institutions than for whites or Blacks (cf. Table 3)? Are Hispanics more prone to drug abuse than other ethnic groups (cf. Table 4)? Additional official data would also be useful in determining the reliability of conclusions reached in earlier studies. Is there support for the conclusion of a 1948 study based on dispositional figures that police are more likely to make unsupportable arrests of Chicanos than whites (Lemert and Rosberg, 1948)? Do the offenses of Spanish-heritage individuals become more like those of the general population the more acculturated they become (Rudoff, 1971)? There are any

TABLE 4   Sentenced Inmates by Offense and Hispanic Origin
1974 LEAA State Prisoner Survey

	Hispanics		Non-Hispanics	
	Number	Percent	Number	Percent
Violent Offenses	3,368	6.2	51,220	93.8
Property Offenses*	4,681	5.1	86,611	94.9
"Other" property offenses	353	3.2	10,624	96.8
Drug or Public Order	3,456	12.3	24,609	87.7
TOTAL	11,858	6.4	173,064	93.6

* Robbery is included in Property Offenses, along with burglary, larceny, and auto theft.

SOURCE: Jerry Mandel, "Hispanics in the Criminal Justice System – The Non-existent Problem," Agenda, 1979 (9): 19.

number of issues to be raised, but without reliable data, many of the conclusions must be based on opinion or research in limited areas, often using small samples. Efforts to improve the quantity and quality of data are certainly warranted.

INTERACTION WITH THE POLICE

In addition to improvement of statistical data, attention can profitably be directed toward interaction between Spanish-speaking individuals and law enforcement, court, and correctional officials.

In 1931, the National Commission on Law Observance and Enforcement indicated that Mexican-Americans, both aliens and citizens, "are frequently subjected to severe and unequal treatment by those who administer the laws" (National Commission on Law Observance and Enforcement, 1931: 243). In 1970, the Civil Rights Commission observed much the same kind of treatment. In the five southwestern states which were the subject of the commission's study, allegations that law enforcement officers discriminated against Mexican-Americans were common:

Such discrimination includes more frequent use of force against Mexican-Americans than against Anglos, discriminatory treatment of juveniles, and harassment and discourteous treatment toward Mexican-Americans in general. Complaints also were heard that police protection in Mexican-American neighborhoods was less adequate than in other areas. The Commission investigations showed that belief in law enforcement prejudice is wide-spread and is indicative of a serious problem of police-community relations between the police and Mexican-Americans in the Southwest [U.S. Commission on Civil Rights, 1970: 13].

A significant part of the friction in relations is probably related to language. Chevigny suggests that "policemen often take the speaking of a foreign language to be a form of defiance" (1969: 69) and many problems arise simply from law enforcement officers' inability to communicate with Spanish-speakers and resulting misunderstandings. Also, Spanish-speakers are underrepresented among law enforcement personnel (U.S. Commission on Civil Rights, 1970: 83).

Overall, the commission's report painted a "bleak picture" of relationships between Mexican-Americans and criminal justice officials. The commission concluded:

> The attitude of Mexican-Americans toward the institutions responsible for the adminstration of justice . . . is distrustful, fearful, and hostile. Police departments, courts, the law itself are viewed as Anglo institutions in which Mexican-Americans have no stake and from which they do not expect fair treatment.
>
> The Commission found that the attitudes of Mexican-Americans are based, at least in part, on the actual experience of injustice . . . There is evidence of police misconduct against Mexican-Americans. In the Southwest, as throughout the nation, remedies for police misconduct are inadequate.
>
> Acts of police misconduct result in mounting suspicion and incite incidents of resistence to officers. These are followed by police retaliation, which results in escalating hostilities [1970: 87].

Similar abuses and misunderstandings have been noted in other areas with heavy concentrations of Spanish-speakers, such as New York City (Chevigny, 1969: 3-29; 69-70) and Chicago (Safford, 1977: 18).

Suggestions are being proposed for improving relationships between police officers and Hispanics. Police officers are encouraged to be aware of cultural traits which might have an affect on interaction. Abad has suggested that if police are aware of the concept of machismo, for example, they can avoid a great deal of difficulty when dealing with young Puerto Ricans who feel they "have to resist authority when approached in a harsh, domineering way" (1974: 587).

Many proposals for improving relationships focus on communication problems. Surveying staff to determine what languages they speak, encouraging bilinguals to apply for positions, and seeking help from community organizations and language departments of colleges and universities are among the recommendations (Nagle and Mata, 1977: 7). The objective is to have someone who speaks the suspect's language readily available.

SPANISH-SPEAKERS IN THE COURTS

The issue of need for an interpreter becomes increasingly critical as the non-English-speaking defendant moves into the courts. It is the non-English speaker's difficulties at this stage which have received more attention from legislative bodies and appellate courts.

Thus far there has been no Supreme Court decision to insure the rights of non-English-speaking defendants in criminal court, in spite of the fact that there are some obvious problem areas in dealing with a non-English-speaking defendant. First, an accused should be notified of the charges against him/her. If that notification is in English, the accused may not understand the nature and consequences of the charge (El Derecho de aviso, 1973). The sixth amendment guarantees the right to counsel. That right may not, however, be meaningful if the accused is unable to communicate with counsel. Further, the sixth amendment guarantees the accused the right to confront and cross-examine witnesses. If those witnesses testify in English which is not translated for the defendant, and particularly if the defendant is unable to adequately consult with counsel, he/she is not in a position to effectively confront and cross-examine. The waiver of rights is also a matter of concern when dealing with a non-English-speaking defendant. Does the defendant who pleads guilty, who waives the right to counsel, or to trial by jury really comprehend the consequences of his/her action? Indeed, there is some question of whether the non-English-or limited-English-speaking defendant can receive a fundamentally fair trial as guaranteed by the due process clause of the fourteenth amendment without the services of an interpreter.

It has largely been left to the judge to evaluate the specific needs, if any, of non-English-speaking defendants, particularly their need for court-appointed interpreters. The only case dealing with this issue reviewed by the Supreme Court held that the decision to appoint an interpreter rests entirely on the discretion of the judge, *Perovich v U.S.* 205 U.S. 86 (1907). Moreover, appellate courts have been reluctant to question the decision of the trial court judges. Trial transcripts do not provide the kind of information necessary to evaluate the defendant's understanding of the proceedings or the adequacy of any translations which may have occurred (Chang and Araujo, 1975: 803).

Nevertheless, some state appellate courts and federal district courts have ruled on cases involving non-English-speaking defendants, and some significant cases can be cited. In New York, an indigent defendant named Rogelio Nieves Negron who did not speak English was assigned counsel who did not speak Spanish. Testimony of witnesses who spoke Spanish was translated; testimony of English-speaking witnesses was not. The defendant, Negron, received only brief periodic summaries of portions of the testimony. Negron was convicted of murder in the second degree. He filed an application for a writ of habeas corpus with the federal court. Judge Bartels granted the writ and indicated that defendants must be informed of the right to a court-appointed interpreter. The second Circuit Court of Appeals affirmed the grant of the writ of habeas corpus, indicating that indigent defendants who are unable to understand English are entitled under the due process clause to assistance of a competent translator throughout the trial, *U.S. ex rel. Negron v. New York*, 434 F.2d 386 (1970).

This decision, however, involved the case of a defendant who spoke no English. Negron's inability to communicate in English was "obvious, not just a possibility" (434 F.2d at 390). In 1973, the First Circuit Court in *United States v. Carrion*, recognized that protection of a defendant's rights may require an interpreter, even if the defendant has some ability to understand and communicate in English, 488 F.2d 12 (1st Cir. 1973). It continued to leave the decision about need for an interpreter in the hands of the judge, but suggested that "precisely because the trial court is entrusted with discretion, it should make unmistakably clear to the defendant who may have a language difficulty that he has the right to a court-appointed interpreter if the court determines one is needed, and, whenever put on notice that there may be some significant language difficulty, the court should make a determination of need" (448 F.2d at 14-15).

The *Carrion* and *Negron* decisions, of course, are legally binding only on courts in the First and Second Circuits. Other federal courts have not clearly supported the right to a court-appointed interpreter. The Tenth Circuit Court of Appeals, in a 1965 decision, indicated that "there is no consitutional right, as such, requiring the assistance of a court-appointed interpreter to supplement the right to counsel. Nor is there a duty to an accused to furnish counsel who can communicate freely with the accused in his native tongue" (*Cervantes v. Cox*, 350 F.2d 855 10th Cir. 1965). Similarly, the Ninth Circuit Court in a case where an interpreter was not requested, and the defendant did communicate in English, held that "it was not abuse of discretion to fail to advise the defendant of availability of interpreter," *U.S. v. Barrios*, 457 F.2d 680 (1972). This court, like courts in the Seventh, *U.S. v Sosa*, 379 F.2d 525 (1967), and Fourth Circuits, *U.S. v. Rodrigues*, 424 F.2d 205 (1970), emphasized the discretion of the trial court.

There are some state courts which have recognized the need for court-appointed interpreters. For example, in *State v. Vasquez*, the Supreme Court of Utah held that the trial court's refusal to provide an interpreter constituted a reversable error, 101 Utah 444, 121 F.2d 903 (1942); and in *Garcia v. State*, the court reversed the conviction because the defendant could not understand evidence presented by the prosecution, 151 Tex. Crim. 593, 201 S.W.2d 574 (1948). Also, some state appellate court decisions indicate that waiving of rights by non-English-or limited-English-speaking defendants is not done knowingly and intelligently, for example, *Parra v. Paige*, 430 P.2d 834 (Okl. Crim. 1967); *Landeros v. State*, P.2d 273 (Okl. Crim. 1971); and *In re* Muraviov, 92 Cal. App. 2d 604, 13 Cal. Rptr. 466 (1961).

In addition, there have been some attempts at the legislative level to insure the rights of non-English-or limited-English-speaking defendants. Thirty-five states have some statutory provision for appointment of interpreters (Safford, 1967: 15). For example, the Illinois law reads:

> Wherever any person accused of commiting a felony or misdemeanor is to be tried in any court of this State, the court shall upon its own motion of that of defense or prosection, determine whether the accused is capable of understanding the English language so as to be understood directly by counsel, court or jury. If the court finds the accused incapable of so understanding or so expressing himself, the court shall appoint an interpreter for the accused whom he can understand and who can understand him [Ill. Crim. L. and P. Ch. 38, Sec. 165-11 (1978)].

The California constitution grants "a person unable to understand English who is charged with a crime a right to an interpreter throughout the proceedings" (Cal. Const. Art. 1, Sec. 14, cited in Chang and Araujo, 1975: 820). However, only two states, California and New Mexico, provide for a right to an interpreter in their state constitutions (Chang and Araujo, 1975: 820; Cronheim and Schwartz, 1976: 298).

At the federal level, the Court Interpreters Act (P.L. 95-539) was signed by President Carter on October 29, 1978. This law establishes the right to a certified court interpreter for any party in any civil or criminal action if the court determines that the individual speaks only or primarily a language other than English. Although this law applies only in the federal court system, it serves as a model for state legislation. Thus far, however, it has received little attention and, in fact, the Administrative Office of the United States Courts which is responsible for administration and implementation of P.L. 95-539 is still in the process of estimating the cost of implementing the law (Barcelo, 1979: 25).

The court decisions and state and federal statutes which do exist generally fail to clarify some critical questions with respect to defendants who do not adequately understand English. How is the accused's ability to communicate in and understand English to be evaluated? If an interpreter is to be provided, at what point in the process should he/she be introduced? Does failure to assert the right to an interpreter constitute a waiver of that right? What qualifications must an interpreter possess?

No determination has been made as to the minimum ability of the accused to communicate in English. The appellate courts have repeatedly stated that evaluation of the defendant's ability to communicate and the need for an interpreter is to be left to the trial court judge. The First Circuit Court in the *Carrion* case did indicate that a right to an interpreter exists when the defendant has "obvious difficulty with the language" and further suggested that the complexity of the issues for trial should be considered in making the decision to appoint an interpreter (488 F.2d at 14,15).

Almost nowhere in the statutes or in the court decisions is provision of an interpreter at early stages of the criminal process (arrest, bail setting, preliminary hearing) required. In Illinois, for example, the earliest stage in the criminal process where the law recognizes that there might be a need for an interpreter is at the arraignment (Safford, 1977: 16, 19).

With regard to the non-English-speaking defendant's waiving of rights, particularly the right to an interpreter, Cronheim and Schwartz speak of a "waiver by silence" (1976: 300), indicating that the burden of notifying the court of any language difficulty is often placed on the defendant and his counsel. The Second Circuit Court implied disapproval of this "waiver by silence," pointing out that the standard for a constitutional waiver is that it be "an intentional relinquishment or abandonment of a known right." In the *Negron* case, the defendant had not waived his right to an interpreter, said the court, by his failure to request those services (434 F.2d at 387, 390). Again, however, the scope of the Second Circuits decision is limited.

The language interpreter statutes and court decisions say very little about qualifications of interpreters. California does provide that judges may use examinations to insure the competency of interpreters. In most states this is not done, however, In Illinois, for example, the courts have found interpreters incompetent in only a few cases, and those involved translation of testimony of witnesses where confusion caused by the interpreter's incompetence was obvious (Safford, 1977: 26,27). Convictions have resulted in cases where the interpreter was a law enforcement officer involved in the investigation and arrest, the complainant, a witness, an employee of the prosecutor's office, and illiterate codefendant (Cronheim and Schwartz, 1976: 307; Safford, 1977: 25, 26). The Court Interpreters Act requires the Director of the Administrative Office of the United States Courts to establish a program to certify individuals who may serve as interpreters in Federal District Court. A certification process has not yet been established, however (Barcelo, 1979: 25).

The similarity between the situation of the person who is "incompetent" to stand trial because of language difficulties and the person who is incompetent for "mental" reasons has been noted by several observers. The Second Circuit Court pointed out that Negron's language problem was "as debilitating to his ability to participate in the trial as a mental disease or defect. But it was more readily 'curable' than any mental disorder" (434 F.2d at 390). The Supreme Court has indicated, in discussing mental incompetence, that due process requires that the defendant have "sufficient present ability to consult with his lawyer with a resonable degree of rational understanding," *U.S. v. Dusky*, 362 U.S. 402 (1960). The Supreme Court has further held that when there is an indication that the defendant is mentally incompetent, the trial court must stop the proceedings and conduct a hearing to make such a determination, *Pate v. Robinson*, 383, U.S. 375 (1966). While the relevance of these cases to the non-English speakers. The Ninth Circuit Court had held that school districts are under no obligation to provide compensatory language instruction and that there is no right to a bilingual education. The Supreme Court, however, held that forcing non-English-speaking children to attend classes taught only in English denies them a meaningful opportunity to participate in the public education program and violates the Civil Rights Act of 1964, which prohibits discrimination in programs receiving federal financial assistance, *Lau v. Nichols*, 414 U.S. 563 (1974). Likewise, Chang and Araujo suggest that requiring court proceedings be in English without provision of an interpreter constitutes discrimination. "When a non-English speaking defendant is denied an interpreter it would seem undeniable that discriminatory state action exists" (1975: 805, 808).

CORRECTIONAL PROGRAMMING FOR SPANISH SPEAKERS

In the area of corrections, the literature has several relevant references to class and cultural differences between the change-agent and the client which hamper communication and effective treatment. "Beyond some recognition of some ethnic 'differences,'" however, "little is done in corrections to assess the effect of the traditional incarceration process and resocialization techniques" on Hispanics (Rudoff, 1971: 224). "Corrections itself appears to have gone on the assumption that all offenders are alike and has made little differentiation among them. Any variations in treatment have centered mainly around psychological rather than cultural differences" (Sanfilippo and Wallach, 1967: 65).

Working with Spanish-heritage individuals is often particularly troublesome for the therapist. "The intimacies necessary in therapy are traditionally avoided" by Hispanics. "One simply does not discuss one's mother . . . or one's father with other people. Problems . . . are also avoided. The therapist represents an authority figure and is viewed with suspicion and distrust . . . Finally, there is fear of acculturation itself . . . , the fear that therapy will pull him away from his . . . identity and that he might lose the acceptance of his people." The Anglo, by contrast, more readily learns and accepts "the role of the client" (Rudoff, 1971: 236). Group therapy is an especially sensitive issue. Not only do Hispanics often resent attempts to force them to reveal their "inner selves" in front of others, many reportedly experience embarrassment regarding their inability to speak English well (Bullington, 1977: 133, 134).

Perhaps language problems combined with problems resulting from cultural traits explain, at least in part, why there is an observed tendency for Hispanics involved in psychotherapy to receive intensive verbally oriented treatment less often and drug-oriented intervention more often then Anglo clients (Henggler and Tavormina, 1978: 98).

Corrections officials might be well-advised to concentrate their efforts on behalf of Spanish-speaking offenders in the area of education. New techniques for bilingual instruction are being developed which can probably be incorporated into correctional programs. Since 1970, the Spanish Curricula Development Center has been developing and producing instructional materials needed in bilingual programs (Hartner, 1977). In 1976, the Office of Education contracted for a study of the state of bilingual material development which was recently released, and nine materials development centers have been created (National Advisory Council on Bilingual Education, 1976: 31). Thus, while the U.S. Commission on Civil Rights concluded that minorities, including Hispanics, "do not obtain the benefits of public education at a rate equal to that of their Anglo classmates" (1971: 41), significant advances have been made in bilingual/ bicultural education, especially since the *Lau v. Nichols* decision.

Emphasis on educational programs for Spanish-speakers would also be in keeping with current trends in the field of corrections. A considerable amount of money is spent each year on correctional programs. The total amount spent on corrections education by both federal and nonfederal institutions is approximately $546 million. Focus on correctional education has increased in recent years. Relative to other "rehabilitation" programs, education has become a high priority. Also, education has come to include social education as well as academic and vocational education. "Social education programs is on helping (offenders) understand themselves, providing insight, developing realistic self-concepts, gaining appropriate skills and inter-personal relationships, and coping with problems they must face . . . as consumers, family members, employees and responsible citizens" (U.S. Department of Health, Education and Welfare, 1977: 46).

Some corrections education programs aimed at Spanish-speaking offenders do exist. For example, there is a correctional institution which includes a program for Spanish-speaking juveniles funded under the Elementary and Secondary Education Act., Title 1, at Rikers Island in New York (Griggs, 1975); the Texas State Department of Corrections has an Adult Bilingual Laboratory and Learning Center at Huntsville (Texas State Department of Corrections, 1973); and the Illinois Department of Corrections has a bilingual/bicultural program at Stateville (Campos, 1978.) These programs, however, seem to be developing largely independent of one another and based more on general recognition of need on awareness of the existence, experience, and effectiveness of other bilingual corrections education programs.

Corrections officials concerned with the plight of Spanish-speaking, and other non-English-speaking, offenders must be kept abreast of relevant developments in correctional education and in bilingual/bicultural education in particular. The number of Spanish-speakers in corrections programs is increasing, and educational theorists have concluded that non-English speakers learn better in a bilingual/bicultural setting because of the positive effect the setting has on the cognitive and affective domain (National Advisory Council on Bilingual Education, 1976: 18).

Further, corrections personnel working with Spanish-speakers should be given the oppurtunity to learn the language, something about the history and values of their clients (e.g., Mexican, Puerto Rican), and the "problems faced by migrants who relocate physically and culturally" (Knowlton, 1967: 26; Monserrat, 1967: 57). They "should be aware of the traditional patterns of etiquette followed by this group of people" and even of "differences between and within the various groups of Spanish-heritage persons" (Chaves, 1976: 219; 30-31).

The "Seminar on the Implications of Cultural Differences" for Corrections indicated:

That an understanding of social and cultural characteristics of minority group members will lead correctional agencies and the educational institutions which are training personnel for corrections to develop more effective curriculum content, training methods, and utilization and recruitment of personnel . . . Planning and development which take account of cultural differences can help greatly in bringing about the rehabilitation of offenders who come from minority groups in our society [Sanfilippo and Wallach, 1967: 68].

If corrections programs ignore the existence of language and cultural differences, "people will continue not to respond to the treatment, to the rehabilitation, or to whatever program we're trying to give them" (Montez, 1967: 12).

SUMMARY

Spanish-speaking residents of the United States are frequently faced with socioeconomic and emotional pressures often associated with crime. Their income and educational levels are below average and residing in an unfamiliar culture deprives them of "familiar cues and controls." The subtle, unspoken, conventions that one has learned from childhood are changed and familiar gestures take on new meanings; many of the old experiences from which one derived satisfaction and support are no longer there" (Guthrie, 1975: 98).

The actual amount of crime in the Spanish-speaking community, however, has not been accurately determined. Statistical data is limited. More data must be collected if significant questions regarding the nature and extent of crime in the Spanish-speaking community are to be answered.

Information presently available suggests that there is need for considerable improvement in the handling of Spanish-speaking offenders. Spanish-heritage individuals are often distrustful of law enforcement officials, and law enforcement officials often misunderstand and sometimes mistreat Hispanic suspects. Recommendations for improving police-Hispanic-community relations should be given serious attention.

The rights of the Spanish-speaking, and other non-English-speaking, defendants in court have been considered by some appellate courts and legislative bodies. The non-English-speaking defendant's right to counsel, to confront and cross-examine witnesses, and to a fundamentally fair trial, some have concluded, require the presence of an interpreter. The Supreme Court, however, has not ruled on the rights of non-English-speaking defendants; and several critical areas remain unclear.

Spanish-speaking defendants who are found guilty present a special problem to correctional officials. If their situations are to be "corrected," programs must be designed to meet their needs. Traditional therapy is often difficult to apply to Spanish-heritage individuals. There have, however, been some significant developments in bilingual/bicultural education which might profitably be applied in correctional programs. Also, correctional personnel must be made sensitive to cultural differences.

It would appear that in years to come the criminal justice system (police, courts, and corrections) will be forced to seriously consider the unique perspectives and needs of Spanish-speaking individuals. Their numbers are growing rapidly. Attention to their rights seems to be increasing. Hispanics are becoming more politically aware and aggressive; they have formed several organizations, including La Raza Unida, the Political Association of Spanish Organizations, and the Mexican-American Political Association (U.S. Commission on Civil Rights, 1970: xiii; "It's Your Turn in the Sun," 1978). Hopefully, the sooner the issues involved are confronted, the sooner they can be resolved.

CASES

BARRIOS v. U.S., 457 F2d 680 (9th Cir. 1972)
CARRION v. U.S., 488 F.2d 12 (1st Cir. 1973)
CERVANTES v. COX, F.2d (10th Cir. 1965)
DUSKY v. U.S., 362 U.S. 402 (1960)
GARCIA v. STATE, 151 Tex. Crim. 593, 501 S.W.2d 574 (1948)
LANDEROS v. STATE, P.2d 273 (Okl. Crim. 1971)
LAU v. NICHOLS, 414 U.S. 563 (1974)
MARAVIOV, *In Re* 192 Cal. App. 2a 604, 13 Cal. Rptr. 466 (1961)
NEGRON, U.S., *ex rel.* v. NEW YORK, 434 F.2d 386 (1970)
PARRA v. PAIGE, 430 P.2d 834 (Okl. Crim. 1967)
PATE v. ROBINSON, 383 U.S. 375 (1966)
PEROVICH v. U.S., 205 U.S. 86 (2nd Cir. 1907)
RODRIGUES v. U.S., 424 F.2d 205 (4th Cir. 1970)
SOSA v. U.S., 379 F.2d 525 (7th Cir. 1967)
VASQUEZ v. STATE, 101 Utah 444, 121 P.2d 903 (1942)

REFERENCES

Abad, V., J. Ramos, and E. Boyce, (1974) "A model for delivery of mental health services to Spanish-speaking minorities." *American Journal of Orthopsychiatry*, 44: 584-595.

Barcelo, C. (1979) "The Court Interpreters Act—A step towards equal justice." *Agenda* 9: 21-25; 33.

Bullington, B. (1977) *Heroin Use in the Barrio*. Lexington, MA: D.C. Heath.

Campos, L. (1978) Personal interview.

Chang, W.B.C. and M.V. Araugo, (1975) "Interpreters for the defense: Due process for the non-speaking defendant." *California Law Review*, 68; 801-823.

Chaves, F. J. (1976) "Counseling offenders of Spanish heritage." *Federal Probation*, 40: 29-33.

Chevigny, P. (1969) *Police Power: Police Abuses in New York City*. New York: Pantheon.

Cronheim, A. J. and A. H. Schwartz (1976) "Non-English-speaking persons in the criminal justice system: Current state of the law." *Cornell Law Review*, 61: 289-311.

Department of Law Enforcement (1977) *Crime in Illinois 1977*. Springfield, IL: Crime Statistics Section, Bureau of Identification.

——— (1976) *Crime in Illinois 1976*. Springfield, IL: Crime Statistics Section, Bureau of Identification.

"El derecho de aviso: Due process and bilingual notice." (1973) *Yale Law Journal*, 83: 385-400.

Griggs, S. (1975) *Program for Adolescents in Corrective Institutions—Rikers Island*. Brooklyn: New York City Board of Education. (ERIC Document Reproduction Service No. ED 138 681)

Guthrie, G. M. (1975) "A behavioral analysis of cultural learning." In R. W. Brislin et al. (eds.) *Cross-Cultural Perspectives on Learning*. New York: Wiley.

Hartner, E. (1977) "How we develop bilingual instructional materials—Spanish Curricula Development Center." *Educational Leadership*, 35: 42-46.

Henggeler, S. W. and J. B. Tavormina (1978) "The children of Mexican-American migrant workers: A population at risk?" *Journal of Abnormal Child Psychology*, 6: 97-106.

Hernandez, J., L. Estrada, and D. Alvirez (1973) "Census data and the problem of conceptually defining the Mexican-American population." *Social Science Quarterly*, 53: 671-687.

Illinois State (1979) *Illinois Criminal Law and Procedure for 1978*. St. Paul, MN: West.

"It's your turn in the sun." (1978) *Time* (October 16): 48-52; 55; 58; 61.

Knowlton, C. S. (1967) "Spanish-speaking people of the southwest." In R. K. McNickle (ed.) *Differences that Make a Difference: Papers Presented at a Seminar on the Implications of Cultural Differences for Corrections*. Washington, DC: Joint Commission on Correctional Manpower Training.

Lemert, E. M. and J. Rosberg (1948) "The administration of justice to minority groups Los Angeles County." In R.L. Beals et al. (eds.) *University of California Publications in Culture and Society, II.* Berkeley and Los Angeles: University of California Press.

Mandel, J. (1979) "Hispanics in the criminal justice system—the "non-existant" problem. *Agenda* 9: 16-20.

Monserrat, J. (1967) "Puerto Ricans." In R. K. McNickle (ed.) *Differences that Make a Difference: Paper Presented at a Seminar on the Implications of Cultural Differences for Corrections.* Washington DC: Joint Commission on Correctional Manpower and Training.

Nagle, B. and J. Mata (1977) "Improving police contact with non-English speaking peoples." *Law Enforcement News* (December 20): 1.

National Advisory Council on Bilingual Education (1976) *Second Annual Report* Washington, DC: Interamerica.

National Commission on Law Observance and Enforcement (1974) "Report on crime and the foreign born: 1931." In C. E. Cortes (advisory ed.) *The Mexican American and the Law.* New York: Arno Press.

Rudoff, A. (1971) "The incarcerated Mexican-American delinquent." *Journal of Criminal Law, Criminology, and the Police Science*, 62: 224-238.

Safford, J. B. (1977) "No comprendo: The non-English-speaking defendant and the criminal process." *Journal of Criminal Law*, 68: 15-30.

Sanfilippo, R. and J. Wallach (1967) "Cultural differences: Implications for corrections." In R. K. McNickle (ed.) *Differences that Make a Difference: Papers Presented at a Seminar on the Implications of Cultural Differences for Corrections.* Washington, DC: Joint Commission on Correctional Manpower and Training.

Statistical Analysis Center (n.d.) *IUCR User's Guide and Codebooks.* Springfield: Illinois Law Enforcement Commission.

Texas Department of Corrections (1973) *Adult Reading.* Huntsville, TX: Bilingual Laboratories and Learning Center.

Towner, P. (1978) Personal Interview.

U.S. Commission on Civil Rights (1978) *Social Indicators of Equality for Minorities and Women.* Washington, DC: Government Printing Office.

——— (1974) *Counting the Forgotten: The 1970 Census Count of Persons of Spanish Speaking Background in the United States: A Report.* Washington, DC: Government Printing Office.

——— (1971) *The Unfinished Education.* Washington DC: Government Printing Office.

——— (1970) *Mexican Americans and the Administration of Justice in the Southwest.* Washington DC: Government Printing Office.

U.S. Department of Commerce, Bureau of the Census (1975) *Persons of Spanish Origin in the United States: Current Reports, 1975.* Washington, DC: Government Printing Office.

——— (1973a) *Detailed Characteristics: United States Summary, 1973.* Washington, DC: Government Printing Office.

――― (1973b) *Subject Reports: Persons in Institutions and Other Group Living Quarters, 1973*. Washington, DC: Government Printing Office.

――― (1973c) *Subject Reports: Persons of Spanish Origin, 1973*. Washington, DC: Government Printing Office.

U.S. Department of Health, Education, and Welfare (1977) *A Review of Corrections Education Policy*. Washington, DC: MetaMetrics (ERIC Document Reproduction Service No. ED 141 585)

ESTRANGEMENT, MACHISMO AND GANG VIOLENCE[1]

HOWARD S. ERLANGER
University of Wisconsin, Madison

THE SUBCULTURE OF VIOLENCE THESIS SEES VALUES RELATING TO VIOlence as playing an important causal role in the generation of violent behavior. Subcultural values, it is argued, define certain circumstances and stimuli that appropriately evoke physical aggression, especially on the part of young black and Hispanic males. Within the subculture, failure to respond violently to physical or verbal challenge may well lead to negative sanctions, while violent response to such challenges is said to be supported, encouraged and at times directly required (Wolfgang and Ferracuti, 1967).

By and large, the literature relating to the subculture of violence thesis has concentrated on two questions. The first of these is an empirical question: Can the hypothesized value differences be demonstrated? What little evidence exists on the issue is mixed; several studies (e.g., Ball-Rokeach, 1973; Erlanger, 1974) suggest that the differences do not exist, while others suggest that they do (e.g., Ferracuti et al., 1970; Ferracuti and Wolfgang, 1973). The second question is more theoretical: Assuming that the value differences do exist, should they be regarded as the product of a semiautonomous subculture (as implied, although not unequivocally, in the work of Wolfgang and Ferracuti [1967]), or should they be regarded as an adaptation to situational exigencies induced by social structure (a position explicitly taken by Cloward and Ohlin [1960] in their discussion of the "conflict subculture" and by Curtis [1975] in his elaboration of Wolfgang's model)? This paper attempts to advance discussion on both of these questions, in the specific context of the Chicano barrios of East Los Angeles. It concludes that, while subcultural values of the barrio may be different from those of Anglo society and may exist independently of Anglo society, they do not directly require or condone violence. Rather, behavior is a product of the way in which structural conditions limit the expression of these values.

[1] This research was supported in part by funds granted by the National Institute of Mental Health, and in part by funds granted to the Institute for Research on Poverty, University of Wisconsin pursuant to the provisions of the Economic Opportunity Act of 1964. Work on this project and preparation of this paper would not have been possible without the advice and assistance of Fred Persily. Of the many other persons who contributed to this project I would especially like to thank Monte Perez and Steve Sanora for their comments and support, and Marilyn Zeitlin and Nick Danigelis for their work on earlier phases of the research.

Social Science Quarterly, Vol. 60, No. 2, September 1979
© 1979 by the University of Texas Press   0038–4941/79/020235–14$01.25

In the study of Chicano life, a major theme has been that of manliness, or machismo. Many popular accounts of machismo portray it as encompassing a strong emphasis on sex-role differentiation, with a concomitant emphasis on physical aggressiveness. The materials reported on here suggest, however, that a machismo orientation, if it does exist, is not nearly as narrow in content as portrayed in the literature. Rather, the subcultural trait understood as machismo seems to be one that can contribute to physical aggression, but one that does so only indirectly and under certain structural conditions.

One set of these structural conditions appears to be political conditions in the community. The usual state of political affairs in East Los Angeles is one in which Chicano youth experiences a feeling of estrangement. This estrangement fosters a strong identity with the peer group in the immediate neighborhood (barrio) because the peer group is the most readily available source of identity. The consequence is a strong consciousness of turf, which in turn greatly increases the potential for conflict and thus for violence. However, these structural conditions can change, as they did in roughly the period from late 1967 to early 1972, when a strong, locally based political movement succeeded in greatly reducing the level of estrangement. For this period there is evidence of a change in group identity, the opening of different avenues for the expression of machismo and a reduction in the incidence of gang violence. Then, as the movement subsided, gang violence increased.

METHOD

The interpretations presented in this paper are based on more than 35 open-ended interviews. About two-thirds of the respondents were Chicano males aged 15 to 30 who lived in one of the barrios of East Los Angeles and who were participating or had participated extensively in gang activity. This age range allows an assessment of both the contemporary situation and that of the middle and late 1960s. These respondents came from many different gangs, including those generally considered to be the toughest in East Los Angeles. The remaining respondents were persons with a comprehensive knowledge of the community and the events discussed in this paper. These included police and probation officials, community program directors and political figures.

As a case study with a small, nonrandom sample, this study is of necessity exploratory and its findings tentative. It does not purport to be an empirical test of the subculture of violence thesis, but rather is an attempt to develop an explanation that, while compatible with the thesis' stress on values, offers a different understanding of the role of values in determining outcomes. Its object then, is to urge a broadening of the range of future inquiries into the subculture of violence.

In East Los Angeles the number of persons of Mexican heritage, numbering one million or more, is comparable to the population of Guadalajara or Monterey and is substantially exceeded only by Mexico City. Governmental authority is divided among several jurisdictions, but many of the Chicano residents (especially in the barrios near the central city, where a very high percentage of the residents in the barrios are Chicano) view East Los Angeles as a single community. The sections nearest the central city are the oldest and also the poorest, and in these areas the income per capita and the mean educational level are among the lowest in the Los Angeles area, as low or lower than in the black ghettos of Watts and surrounding areas.

East Los Angeles is divided into numerous subcommunities; contrary to common Anglo usage, Chicanos use the term *barrio* to refer to these subcommunities or neighborhoods rather than to the community as a whole. In the barrios nearest the central city, most male youth belong to the barrio gang, which bonds together all those who wish to be part of the group. In the more affluent barrios, gang membership is somewhat less common. There are subdivisions (some formal, some informal) of each gang, and a member spends virtually all his free time associating with this subgroup.

THE MEANING OF MACHISMO

Studies of Chicanos and Latin Americans have placed great emphasis on machismo, or manliness, which is reputed to be a cultural trait predisposing men to an exaggerated sense of honor, hypersensitivity, intransigence, sexual promiscuity, callousness and cruelty toward women, physical aggression and lack of respect for human life (see, e.g., Aramoni, 1971; Burma, 1970). There is a substantial literature attacking many of the negative stereotypes of Chicanos (see especially Hernandez, 1970; Romano, 1968) and some that deals with the machismo stereotype (see, e.g., Alvarez, 1973; Montiel, 1971). However, the relationship of machismo to physical aggressiveness has not been studied directly.

For all the Chicanos interviewed, machismo meant having courage, not backing down or being ready to fight. Without further inquiry, these phrases would most likely be taken as connoting physical aggression. However, to those interviewed, violence in itself was not directly a macho trait. For example, each respondent was asked whether César Chavez— a Chicano who eschews all forms of physical aggression, goes on hunger fasts, allows himself to be arrested, etc.—had machismo. Almost all respondents knew of Chavez, and all of these strongly felt that Chavez did have a good deal of machismo. It is particularly noteworthy that most of the respondents stressed that Chavez did indeed fight, and rejected a presentation of him as a man who wouldn't fight. Thus, fighting, being strong and having machismo can be much broader than simply physical aggression. The following response is representative:

> I don't know [Chavez] personally, but from what I hear about him and what I've read about him, I don't think he'd [pause]. If somebody came up to him and slapped him, I think he'd try [pause]. He wouldn't fight back you know, but he'd fight back in words, not with fists.

Several of the older respondents resented the use of the word *machismo* and complained that it was being misused by Anglos. One of the more articulate respondents stated.

> We get [machismo] slapped on us all the time by the *gabachos* [whites]. They use it more than we do—"He's a macho dude." We've been stereotyped to death on that.

The interviews thus suggest that the core values of the subculture are not directly concerned with violence, but rather with defense of self in a much more abstract sense. Although it is true that defense of personal dignity can be a justification for physical fighting, it is also true that Chavez, one of the heroes of the subculture, refuses to engage in physical aggression. In this subculture, it appears that violence results not from the definition of certain situations as appropriate for or demanding a violent response, but rather from the blocking of alternative avenues to the maintenance of dignity, a broader value. This interrelationship between subcultural values and the structural conditions under which they are expressed is elaborated in the following section.

ESTRANGEMENT AND INTERPERSONAL VIOLENCE IN THE GANG CONTEXT

The Emergence of Estrangement. From the time of the American conquest of the northern territories of Mexico in 1848, persons of Mexican heritage living within the United States have been subject to economic and cultural domination by Anglos. Moore (1970), for example, has suggested that the model of internal colonialism is especially appropriate for the analysis of the Chicano experience. The historical experience of the Chicano in the United States has been well documented and need not be reviewed here.

The record of discrimination against Chicanos in East Los Angeles is also well documented, and the educational situation faced by Chicanos has been particularly unsatisfactory. All those interviewed attended schools—both public and parochial—in which Chicanos were punished for speaking Spanish, even among themselves in the schoolyard. Many reported that their first confrontation with Anglo authorities was over language. For example:

They asked, "What's his name?" and someone said, "His name is Juan," so right then my name changed to John. "Well, now he'll be called John because that's his American name."

Many respondents reported a general atmosphere in school in which Chicano students were not respected or seen as having much potential. The general validity of these observations was corroborated by a Chicano teacher who grew up in an East Los Angeles barrio, went to college and then taught elementary school in the same barrio. He reported that he was quite successful in school and college and that through that period of his life he questioned why other young Chicanos could not do for themselves what he felt he had done for himself. However, once he became a teacher and got a view of the school system from the inside, he fundamentally changed his evaluation of the process. After a year of teaching, he wondered how he had ever made it.

I heard teachers saying out in the field, "You goddamn Mexican" to another teacher who was umpiring. . . . I heard teachers reprimand kids who were speaking Spanish in the hallways . . . and this was supposed to be a time when they were teaching Spanish in school already. I heard teachers saying, "What do you expect of these kids? We can only give them so much."

The school is just one place where the young Chicano is confronted with negative images of his culture. From an early age the Chicano is bombarded with the message that his language, culture, food and habits are inferior and should be changed to conform to those of the Anglo. This is not to say that every Chicano has the same experience but rather that this has been the most common experience over the years. The domination of Chicanos has resulted in their feelings that they are living in an environment controlled by an Anglo structure that they cannot affect. Political action to change these circumstances is difficult because of gerrymandering and because of widespread feelings that there is little prospect that meaningful change will come about. These feelings of powerlessness, exclusion and absence of control over the conditions of one's existence can be summed up as estrangement.

The Result of Estrangement. A major consequence of the estrangement just described is the emergence of a strong identification with the immediate environment—the peer group and the barrio. Adolescent youth particularly are faced with the need to expand identity beyond the family. In the estranged environment the peer group in the barrio, who share the same feelings and experiences, are the most readily available source of identity.

The interviews indicate that this identification is equal to that with the family and is much more intense than that with religion, with political entities (Los Angeles, California, United States) or, except under certain circumstances discussed below, with the Chicano people as a whole. The following exchange with a 21-year-old probationer, talking about the period just before he was incarcerated, illustrates how deep the attachment to the barrio is:

> Q. What I'm trying to figure out is which was more important? What would you consider more serious—an insult to you or an insult to the barrio you were a part of at that time?
> A. Probably the barrio—the neighborhood.
> Q. The barrio was more important?
> A. Yeah, there's people I've seen who have given up their lives for the neighborhood. I've seen people die. . . .
> Q. Literally die?
> A. Yeah, yelling out, like "¡Qué vivas!" [Long live the neighborhood!]

In the estranged setting, the gang member who shouts the name of his barrio with his last breath has, from the point of view of the gang, shown his courage and dignity in one of the few ways open to him. Youth in the barrio are rejected by Anglo society, and that society is rejected in turn, for it demands that they surrender their cultural identity in order to gain positive recognition. Thus most young Chicanos come to rely on the peer group for this recognition. The respondents reported that it is critical that status in the gang be based on attributes that can be reached by anyone—for example, the machismo qualities of courage, dignity and readiness to fight. Since other outlets for demonstration of these attributes are blocked in the barrio, the pursuit of them is often in the context of physical confrontation. But many respondents reported that even in such confrontations the important personal quality is the willingness to fight, more than physical prowess per se:

> I went to this other school when I moved. The first day I went in and right away I started pinpointing who's who—you know, the pecking-order type thing. And the second day that I was there, there was a [gang] already there—little kids, you know, you run around together. So I was jammed: "Where you from?" and all that kind of stuff. And he says, "Well, you're going to have to fight one of us. No, not one of us, you're going to have to fight this dude." I was scared as hell, but I had to go along with the program. But luckily I didn't have to fight. . . . I didn't have to fight with them, but because I wanted to fight with them I was accepted by that clique.

There are many scenarios that push the willingness to fight over the brink into actual fighting. The most frequent and important instigators of gang fights are violations of barrio turf, either physically or symbolically. The gang establishes control over the physical territory that constitutes the barrio, and defends it against all intrusions. A teen-age male may be challenged to identify his barrio at any time. If he responds, and identifies his barrio as one that is on unfriendly terms with that of the challenger(s), physical conflict will usually ensue, and the fight can escalate to involve large numbers of young men from the two barrios. Gang members also do not tolerate outsiders—especially from a rival gang—dating a woman from their barrio, even if she is unattached and even if they meet on another turf. Horowitz and Schwartz (1974) present a useful microsociological account of the processes through which the concern with turf and with honor can lead to violent clashes. The reports of the respondents were similar:

> You know, when a kid is down and if you attack the only things that he has going for him—namely, his manliness, his machismo; his home boys, his barrio—that's all he has. When you attack that you're attacking him to the quick—what else does he have?

This interpretation of the nature of Chicano gang activity differs from that of Suttles, whose study of the Addams area of Chicago included Chicano barrios there. Suttles (1968) sees "named street corner groups," or gangs, as growing out of a distrust of strangers. No resident can possibly know all the others, and street corner groups provide "one of the ways in which the residents can be grouped together to reduce [the] problem of indeterminacy" (p. 170). These groups may act to control their area, protecting outsiders in such a way that conflict may ensue (pp. 142–43). In East Los Angeles, it does not appear that barrio-based gangs result from the simple lack of information about others. Rather, they emerge from the absence of other avenues to achieve identity and power. Control over the physical space of the barrio seems to be sought less for the purpose of reducing uncertainty than for the sense of power it conveys. This can be most clearly seen when (as discussed in the following section) structural circumstances change and these needs are fulfilled through other means.

POLITICAL ACTION AND THE DECLINE OF ESTRANGEMENT

Much can be learned about normal patterns and the basis for them when these patterns are disrupted. Such a situation existed in East Los Angeles in the late 1960s and early 1970s, when there was a broadly based political movement in the community.

The Movement. Contrary to the impression of many writers, Chicanos have been involved in political activity directed at changing their life circumstances for over a century (Guzman, 1968). However, the period from late 1967 to early 1972 marked a particularly intense period of political activity in East Los Angeles, a period that will be referred to as the movement period. The issues in East Los Angeles were similar to those in other minority communities across the country—for example, Chicano control of the schools and of the social and law enforcement agencies operating in the community, greater recognition of Chicano needs by the Catholic church, and development of economic independence through governmental assistance and through the development of an independent local economic base. Basic to these issues was Chicano pride and a quest for unity and power.

Key events during the movement in East Los Angeles included walkouts from the city schools, a moratorium protesting the disproportionate Chicano fatalities in the Vietnam War, protest of allocation of Catholic church funds to construction of churches in West Los Angeles rather than to social programs in the barrios, protests against police treatment of Chicanos, and a protest at a state educational conference. These events involved thousands of people, and some culminated in violent clashes between police and Chicano demonstrators and bystanders.

The Effect of the Movement on Estrangement. From its inception the movement involved large numbers of Chicano youth. Walkouts were held at almost every high school and several of the junior high schools in the community, with large numbers of students participating. The interviews indicate that gang members were not immediately involved in the movement, but many of the gang youth felt that they were receiving repercussions from the police for movement activities and as a consequence decided to become directly involved. One of the better known movement leaders reported that as the movement progressed, not only were gang members involved, but the relationship between them and others, especially college youth, was fundamentally changed:

> It put a whole positive connotation into being [a gang member], the thing is that the movement said everybody is a worker in the movement, no matter who they are. And that gave them less social alienation, so they could go to meetings with college students, whereas before they couldn't, because they felt that definite alienation. They could go to meetings with anybody, 'cause the movement says, "We need you too. Because you're a Chicano too, and you're not some weirdo."

Besides generating unity among youth in the barrios, the movement generated pride and a feeling of power The heightened sense of pride and Chicano identity was perhaps expressed best by a respondent who was released from prison on a pass for El diez y seis de septiembre, Mexican Independence Day:

> A. When I come out, the Chicano convict organization calls me, sticks a button on me, says, you're with us, brother, blah, blah, . . . They have a parade every year and we'll bring up the ranks. As far as I could look back, all I could see was Chicanos. . . . I'm on a pass from Soledad. I still had to go back to prison. I was just out on a pass.
> Q. That day?
> A. Ya. You know what, a pride went over me, I don't think I've had it since.

The sense of power is shown in an incident that occurred early in the movement, during the school walkouts:

> That was the first time I saw students dealing with the principal on an equal level. And they were telling him, "Hey, . . ." because they were coming from a sense of power, 'cause the students were out there, and these [leaders] were the ones that could tell the students to come back.

And the principal knew that, and he sat there and we dealt with the issues on a negotiating basis. So that gave us a whole sense of power that we didn't have before.

Change in Gang Violence During the Movement Period. The validity problems of official statistics are well known and need not be repeated here. The validity of data for gang-related violence is even more questionable because there is usually no complainant, and for a variety of reasons police officers are aware of a large number of assaults among gang members for which they do not make arrests. According to law enforcement officials in Los Angeles, records of gang-related violence prior to 1973 are particularly inaccurate. Hence, in order to determine the rate of violence before, during and after the period of intense movement activity, the qualitative impressions of more than a dozen law enforcement officials knowledgeable about the trend of gang violence in East Los Angeles were sought. These included representatives of the Gang Squad of the Los Angeles Police Department, Youth Authority officers and supervisors in East Los Angeles, and probation officials. All of these law enforcement officials recalled a marked decline in the amount of fighting between gangs and between individuals within the gangs during the movement period. In addition, older gang members were virtually unanimous in reporting a sharp drop in violence during the period. Gang members whose lives were essentially unaffected by the movement were the exception, not the rule.

Processes Through Which the Movement Affected Gang Violence. The movement affected the level of gang-related violence primarily by changing the ideas of those youths affiliated with it, and by changing the environment experienced by those who were not affiliated with it.

For gang members personally involved in the movement (in varying degrees, from serving as leaders to being just loosely affiliated), reduction of fighting came from the heightened sense of efficacy and from a commitment to the principle that all Chicanos are brothers and should not fight each other. For those youths, the focus was on *carnalismo* (brotherhood), which to our respondents connoted the feeling of pride and unity:

A. *Carnalismo* to me would be having people unite, being brothers to each other, so they can relate to each other, know what's happening, and to more or less carry each other.
Q. Is that affected by the *movimiento*?
A. To me it is because, once you're *carnal* to someone else in the *movimiento*, you've got someone to go with to push that movement. The *carnalismo* is like sticking together. You're united, you're united! That's your *carnalismo* right there.

The feeling of *carnalismo* existed prior to the intense period of the movement, but it was only expressed on the barrio level, and could not be effectively used to defuse a confrontation. Chicano gangs from different barrios did not cooperate except in confrontation with a non-Chicano group, for example, the police. During the movement, *carnalismo* took on

special significance. Because courage and dignity were achieved in other
ways through the movement, barrio youth were less likely to take affront
at the actions of others. In the following exchange, the respondent was
asked about the effects of the movement:

A. We'd go to parties during the movement, like fundraisers at a certain
   house. All the gangs would be there. If there was an argument between
   one guy and another from another barrio the first thing anyone would
   say would be, "Hey man, don't go hitting your brother," and the fight
   would cease right there and then. And they'd go, "Forget the barrio
   and being from Hazard [a particular rough barrio] and all that bull-
   shit."
Q. Was there a different kind of identification then? They didn't really
   forget the barrio did they?
A. No. But they tried not to use the barrio against one another. "I'll respect your barrio and you respect mine."

In expanding their identity from the barrio to the broader Chicano
community, several hundred gang members joined groups that maintained some of the characteristics of the gang but that were community
rather than barrio based. The members of these groups became soldiers
of the movement rather than soldiers of the barrio. This was a way of
maintaining courage and dignity while transcending interbarrio conflicts.
Probably the best-known example of an organization of this type was the
Brown Berets.

For gang members not directly affiliated with the movement, the effects were more indirect. These youths often found that, although their
ideas and feelings did not change, other barrio youth, both in their gang
and in others, were much less interested in fighting. The experience of
one respondent well illustrates this situation. Now in his twenties and
still a member of one of the toughest barrio gangs, he was never a part
of the movement, does not have a clear idea of what the issues were or
why the events took place, and does not feel that the movement affected
his sense of being Chicano. But although his ideas and self-concept were
unchanged by the movement, his life style was profoundly affected. He
remembered the movement period as one in which the types of actions
that would otherwise be provocative did not evoke a combative response.
For example, he reported that during the movement period he dated a
girl whose brother was a member of a gang with which his gang has had
an intense rivalry for over 30 thirty years, but that he suffered no repercussions. Although he would have been willing to fight if challenged for
this action, the challenge did not occur, and in general he reported that
a high degree of freedom of movement between the two barrios existed.
This is because those youths who were affiliated with the movement were
playing by the new rules of carnalismo, and did not support their com-
rades who played by the old rules.

Alternative Explanations. The foregoing indicates that there was a
decrease in interpersonal violence during the intense period of activism

in the barrio, and that the key elements of the movement that led to this effect were the increase in political consciousness and the feeling that Chicanos were going to change their life conditions for the better. This section considers whether the effect on violence can properly be attributed to the new sense of power. Possible alternative explanations for the reported reduction in fighting can be divided into those stressing factors that were external to the movement and those stressing nonpolitical consequences of the movement.

The most likely factor outside of the movement that could account for the observed relationship would be a major change in employment opportunities. If the movement were to coincide with very favorable economic conditions for Chicanos, then it could well be that material benefits, rather than ideological change, led to reduced levels of interpersonal violence through reducing the amount of idle time, getting people a bigger stake in the system or whatever. Although the late 1960s was a period of relative prosperity, the economic situation of the Chicano in the barrio, especially that of gang youths (including those interviewed), was not significantly affected.

This is not to deny that the economic conditions of the 1960s may have substantially contributed to the milieu in which the movement developed. But these conditions themselves could not alone be responsible because there have been similar periods of relative prosperity since World War II in which gang violence did not notably change. For example, one respondent, who had extensive experience working with gang youth and who himself belonged to a gang when he was younger, reported that the only fluctuations he was aware of were seasonal, with periods of intense violence followed by lulls. Having worked with gang youth for a long time, he could "almost gauge when it's going to happen." Except for the extended period at the height of the movement, he knew of no other period of more than a few months in which there was a sharp decrease in gang fighting in East Los Angeles.

There are several plausible nonpolitical consequences of the movement that could be considered as contributing to the decline in gang violence. One might argue that the activities of the movement provided sufficient excitement so that violent interpersonal action was not necessary. But if it were simply the excitement of the movement that was having the effect, then nonparticipants would not be affected, and there would not have been any reason for appeals to *carnalismo* to stop a fight that was about to start. Similarly, it might be argued that the political movement simply kept people busy, without regard to the content of what they were doing, and thus they simply had less time to fight. Again, the contrary evidence is that the movement was not that time-consuming, except for the relatively few leaders, and that this alternative explanation would not explain the effect on nonparticipants.

It may well be true that when people are busy they are less likely to fight, and many barrio programs have been based on this premise. Gang workers have promoted car clubs, mural programs to paint over barrio *placas* (graffiti including the gang name and the name of the person who drew it) and a wide variety of recreational projects. However, at best these programs work only during the actual period of activity, and they do not affect people who are not directly involved. They are different from the movement in that they do not change the relationship of the individual to the outer world or fundamentally change the milieu of a community.

CONCLUSION

Chicano culture places a strong emphasis on values such as courage and dignity for males, but how these values are manifested in behavior depends heavily on the broader context in which people function. In an estranged setting, these values can lead to a high incidence of physical confrontation, but in a nonestranged setting, the evidence from this case study suggests that they do not. Virtually the only time within the memory of those interviewed in which there was a viable opportunity for the expression of courage and dignity outside of the gang setting for the masses of Chicano youth was during the movement period of late 1967 through early 1972. During this period identity with the broader community became primary and a sense of power to influence the institutions affecting the community emerged. As a result, gang-related violence decreased markedly.

In subsequent years the intensity of the movement lessened. The last movement events attracting thousands of people occurred in late 1971, and ended in violent confrontations with the police. Remnants of the movement live on, but the sense of power has lessened considerably, and with it the community identity transcending that of the individual barrios. As one of the movement leaders observed in an interview:

> We thought the limits of the struggle were just getting Chicanos together and then everything else would follow. Now we have greater information to work behind and we realize that that's not the case. We can still effect change, but it's going to come through different directions. . . . Now we still have potential power, but I think we're more realistic.

A sense of estrangement has returned, and even though appeals to *carnalismo* can sometimes be effective, gang violence has been on the upswing. In recent years the degree of violence has been greater than in the early 1960s, in part due to the greatly increased availability of weapons.

To the extent that the interpretations presented here are generalizable, they suggest that discussion of the relationship between violence and values needs to be broadened to include the possibility that violence may not flow from values that directly encourage it, but may instead occur when structural circumstances prevent achievement of related values. And, if correct, they also speak to the need for linking theories of deviance to theories of power and its distribution, a need that has been articulated in the conflict approach to criminological theory and in political interpretations of collective action, but that has received only recent attention in the explanation of the behavior of juvenile delinquents. In considering whether the theory developed here can be generalized, the focus of attention must be on the relationship between estrangement and gang behavior. Thus, if the political consciousness and involvement of gang members were unaffected by local or national social movements, their level of estrangement would remain high, and fundamental changes in gang life would not ensue. (See, for example, the discussion of black gangs in Chicago in Short [1974].) If, on the other hand, reduction in estrangement occurred from any source, political or not, we would expect concomitant changes in the day-to-day life of the estranged.

REFERENCES

Alvarez, Rodolfo. 1973. "The Psycho-Historical and Socioeconomic Development of the Chicano Community in the United States," *Social Science Quarterly*, 53 (March): 920–42.

Aramoni, Aniceto. 1971. "The Machismo Solution," in Bernard Landis and Edward S. Tauber, eds., *In the Name of Life: Essays in Honor of Erich Fromm* (New York: Holt, Rinehart and Winston): 100–7.

Ball-Rokeach, Sandra. 1973. "Values and Violence: A Test of the Subculture of Violence Thesis," *American Sociological Review*, 38: 736–50.

Burma, John H. 1970. "A Comparison of the Mexican American Subculture with the Oscar Lewis Culture of Poverty Model," in John H. Burma, ed., *Mexican Americans in the United States: A Reader* (Cambridge, Mass.: Schenkman): 17–28.

Cloward, Richard A. and Lloyd E. Ohlin 1960. *Delinquency and Opportunity: A Theory of Delinquent Gangs* (New York: Free Press).

Curtis, Lynn. 1975. *Violence, Race, and Culture* (Lexington, Massachusetts: Lexington Books).

Erlanger, Howard S. 1974. "The Empirical Status of the Subculture of Violence Thesis," *Social Problems*, 22 (December): 280–92.

Ferracuti, Franco, Renato Lazzari and Marvin E. Wolfgang, eds. 1970. *Violence in Sardinia* (Rome: Bulzoni).

Ferracuti, Franco and Marvin E. Wolfgang. 1973. *Psychological Testing of the Subculture of Violence* (Rome: Bulzoni).

Guzman, Ralph. 1968. "Politics and Policies of the Mexican American Community," in Eugene P. Dvorin and Arthur J. Misner, eds., *California Politics and Policies* (Palo Alto, Calif.: Addison Wesley).

Hernandez, Deluvina. 1970. *Mexican American Challenge to a Sacred Cow* (Los Angeles: University of California, Chicano Studies Center).

Horowitz, Ruth and Gary Schwartz. 1974. "Honor, Normative Ambiguity, and Gang Violence," *American Sociological Review*, 39 (April): 238–51.

Montiel, Miguel. 1971. "The Social Science Myth of the Mexican American Family," *Voices*: 41–47.

Moore, Joan W. 1970. "Colonialism: The Case of the Mexican Americans," *Social Problems*, 17 (Spring): 463–72.

Romano, Octavio Ignacio V. 1968. "The Anthropology and Sociology of the Mexican-Americans: The Distortion of Mexican-American History," *El Grito*, 2 (Fall): 13–26.

Short, James F., Jr. 1974. "Youth, Gangs and Society: Micro- and Macrosociological Processes," *Sociological Quarterly*, 15 (Winter): 3–19.

Suttles, Gerald D. 1968. *The Social Order of the Slum: Ethnicity and Territory in the Inner City* (Chicago: University of Chicago Press).

Wolfgang, Marvin E. and Franco Ferracuti. 1967. *The Subculture of Violence: Toward an Integrated Theory in Criminology* (London: Social Science Paperbacks).

Race and Juvenile Justice Processing in Court and Police Agencies[1]

Dale Dannefer
University of Rochester

Russell K. Schutt
University of Massachusetts—Boston

Studies of race bias in the juvenile justice system have yielded contradictory and inconclusive findings. The diversity of findings, though
due in part to inadequacies in the methods used in previous studies,
is also attributable in part to the differential possibilities for bias in
different settings. This paper develops and tests hypotheses that
specify two conditions which affect the likelihood of bias: the characteristics and procedural constraints of processing agencies and the
characteristics of their social environments. Log-linear analysis is
used, to allow simultaneous control for the influence of prior record,
type of allegation, family type, sex, race, and county in analyzing
data from police and court records in a populous eastern state. Consistent with the hypotheses, the findings indicate that racial bias is
more apparent in police dispositions than in judicial decisions. In the
more urban of the two social settings studied, minorities constitute
a relatively high proportion of the population; police bias is especially pronounced there. In the same setting, however, this bias may
be compensated for, to some extent, by the courts.

The issue of racial and other forms of bias in the processing of juvenile
offenders continues to be a controversial question that is of significance to
both practitioners and students of the criminal justice system (Chambliss
1973; Quinney 1970; Chesney-Lind 1977). The body of published research on the question of bias has grown steadily over the past decade,

[1] The data for this study were collected under the auspices of the Department of Institutions and Agencies, State of New Jersey, with funds provided by that agency and
by the Law Enforcement Assistance Administration. The paper was prepared while the
authors were supported by an NIMH grant at Yale University, through the Sociology
of Social Control Training Program, Albert J. Reiss, Jr., director. We wish to thank
Virginia Lepori, Bernice Pescosolido, and Diane Steelman for their research assistance.
We are grateful to Joseph DeJames, Jackson Toby, and two anonymous reviewers for
their helpful comments. Any remaining shortcomings are our responsibility. Our names
are listed in alphabetical order. Requests for reprints should be sent to Dale Dannefer,
Graduate School of Education and Human Development, University of Rochester,
Rochester, New York 14627.

but the findings are contradictory and inconclusive. For example, Cohen and Kluegel (1978) and Chused (1973) found no evidence of bias in juvenile court processing, but Arnold (1971) did. Carter and Clelland (1979) found evidence of racial bias in court processing, but only for "moral" or victimless offenses. Terry (1967) found no bias in dispositions by either police or court agencies in a midwestern city of 100,000, while Thornberry (1973) concluded that bias operated in both kinds of agencies in the city of Philadelphia. Weiner and Willie (1971) found no evidence of bias in police processing in Syracuse, New York. Wilson (1968) compared two police departments, a traditional one and a modern "professionalized" one, and found bias in the former but not the latter. Ferdinand and Luchterhand (1970) found evidence of bias in processing by police, but not by the juvenile court, in an eastern city of 150,000.

Methodological problems may account for some of these conflicting findings. With the exception of Cohen and Kluegel (1978), all previous studies have relied on tabular analysis or statistical techniques that permit only one or two control variables at a time. In addition, Arnold's work has been criticized for relying on arbitrarily constructed quantitative indices, and Thornberry's conclusions have been called into question because of his reliance on percentage differences rather than measures of association (Wellford 1975).

Given the complexity of the decision-making processes and the diversity of the practice of juvenile justice across jurisdictions and from agency to agency within a given geographical area, it seems unwarranted to assume that all the differences in findings are due to such methodological problems. It seems unlikely that bias is present or absent uniformly over a wide range of social settings. This paper develops and tests hypotheses that attempt to specify some of the conditions under which bias may be expected. We suggest that the presence or extent of bias will vary with (1) characteristics of the social environment and (2) the type of agency studied.

THE SOCIAL ENVIRONMENT

If the application of the law by the police or the courts reflects the influence of social, nonlegal factors, outcomes should vary with the social features of environments. To our knowledge, only three empirical comparisons of juvenile justice processing across jurisdictions have been reported, however, and with varying results. Wilson's (1968) study found that the degree of race bias varies inversely with the professionalization of police, while neither Cohen and Kluegel's (1978) study of dispositions by courts with differing ideologies nor Chused's (1973) study of three New Jersey

1114

counties found evidence of race bias in any setting. None of these studies directly measures or discusses variations in the social environments of the agencies which might operate to produce biased outcomes.

One feature of the social environment that is associated with the quality of race relations and with a number of indicators of bias is the proportion of the population that belongs to minority groups. As that proportion increases, majority group members' fears of economic competition and threats to their power are likely to increase, producing "motivation for discrimination" (Blalock 1967, p. 29; see also Allport 1954, pp. 227–29).[2] The results appear to include higher levels of discrimination (Cutright 1965; Parcel 1979; Spilerman and Miller 1976) and of racial hostility (Morgan and Clark 1973; Spilerman 1976). In addition, Vines's (1964) study of civil rights cases in southern courts found that as the proportion of blacks in a county's population increased the likelihood of favorable outcomes for members of minorities decreased.

Although it has not been tested directly, the expectation of a positive relation between bias in police decisions and a high percentage of minority residents is consistent with Groves and Rossi's (1971, p. 17) finding that white officers who patrolled black communities tended to view them as hostile, or, at best, indifferent. This tendency appeared to result from projection by police of their own fears of blacks "getting out of their place" (also see National Advisory Commission 1972, p. 141) as well as from a lack of knowledge of black residents. We would expect to find similar perceptions of blacks among white officers who patrol white communities adjacent to black ones. However, in communities with a low proportion of black residents, the bases for such perceptions, and hence their potential as sources of bias, would be reduced.

In a study of a national sample that focused on citizen attitudes, Feagin (1971) found systematic variation in attitudes toward the police that is consistent with our expectations. Although he did not characterize communities in terms of percentage black, he used a closely related variable, community size. For whites, Feagin (1971, p. 105) reported, willingness to rely on police for defense of their homes rose with community size, while among blacks, reliance on police was greatest in communities with populations between 2,500 and 100,000 (the size of communities in our setting with a low percentage of blacks). Among blacks in cities of more than 100,000 inhabitants (the size of the large city in our county with a high percentage of blacks), reliance on the police was much less common (Feagin 1971, p. 105).

[2] As Allport states (1954, p. 229), proportion minority is not in itself sufficient as an explanation of differential treatment. Lack of knowledge, prejudice, or other factors must contribute to or intervene in the causal path from ecological characteristics to individual behavior.

1115

As applied to juvenile justice processing, Blalock's (1967) theory and the findings of the studies reviewed suggest the following hypothesis: The larger the proportion of minority group members in a population, the greater the likelihood of discrimination by official agencies against juvenile justice offenders who belong to minorities.

This hypothesis receives initial support in that it appears largely consistent with findings of the studies reported above. Discrimination was found in Philadelphia (Thornberry 1973), in Arnold's (1971) study of a southern city, and for some offenses in Carter and Clelland's study of a "metropolitan area in the southeastern U.S." On the other hand, no discrimination was found in Syracuse, New York (Weiner and Willie 1971); in Denver (Cohen and Kluegel 1978); in Montgomery County, Pennsylvania (Cohen 1975); or in Terry's (1967) midwesten city of 100,000.[3] The only clear contradiction to this hypothesis in previous work is Cohen and Kluegel's (1978) finding of no evidence of discrimination in the Memphis–Shelby County, Tennessee, court.[4]

AGENCY DIFFERENCES IN THE OPPORTUNITY FOR BIAS

Another important kind of variability exists between agencies in the same geographical space. After juveniles are arrested, they may or may not be referred by the police to the juvenile court. The action of officials of the juvenile court is thus dependent on the decisions made by the police—both the arresting patrolman and the juvenile officer who ultimately decides whether the accused juvenile should be referred to court. Most studies (Cohen and Kluegel 1978; Arnold 1971; Chused 1973; Weiner and Willie 1971; Wilson 1968) have examined processing only at one stage or the other, not at both simultaneously. It is clear, however, that bias at earlier stages of processing would affect outcomes at later stages, even if no bias occurs at the later stages (Farrell and Swigert 1978).

There are strong theoretical reasons for suspecting that bias (in any direction) is more likely to occur at the police stage of processing than at the juvenile court. First of all, a relatively large amount of discretion is endemic to police work, and action must often be taken without ade-

---

[3] According to U.S. census data, Philadelphia's population was 26.4% black in 1970. The juvenile population of Arnold's study is said to have been 12%–13% black, above the national average. We assume that Carter and Clelland's southeastern metropolitan area also has a substantial black population. In contrast, the percentage black in settings where no discrimination was found is as follows: Denver 9.1 in 1970; Syracuse 10.8 in 1970; Montgomery County, Pa., 3.6 in 1970. Presumably Terry's midwestern city of 100,000 was also well below the national average.

[4] While our discussion of bias in the treatment of minority groups relies largely on studies that have compared blacks and whites, we assume that our expectations for bias against blacks will apply also to Hispanics.

1116

quate knowledge of the relevant facts. Reiss states that "unlike the lawyer or judge, who may take a long time gathering information to make a diagnosis or reviewing the decisions that lead up to a fate decision, a line officer must often make a quick fate decision. This creates, in many ways, a paradoxical situation for the police. To be professional about the decision often means that more information and more time is required. However, to protect the interests of the client and the public, and to satisfy the interests of operating efficiency, a quick decision is required" (1971, p. 130).

Thus, the police officer must often rely on his or her own judgment in making the decision to arrest and then the decision to refer a case to court. When essential pieces of information about an alleged deviant act are missing, the officer must "fill them in" by constructing an informed conjecture based on experience and general background knowledge. Inevitably, such a process must rely on the perceptual and evaluative constraints of the officer's own biography, including typifications of some juveniles as more likely than others to be probably in need of control or assistance by the juvenile court. In contrast to the speed with which the officer must reach a "verdict," the nature of court decision making both permits and requires more careful deliberation before adjudicating and disposing of a case. Although the decision to refer a case to court can be made with more deliberation than the street arrest, each involves a relatively quick decision based on limited information. In contrast, the court can and must await information that should provide more objective criteria for decision making.

A second factor distinguishing police and court practice is the extent of formalization and bureaucratization of procedures. Especially since certain Supreme Court decisions of the past 15 years,[5] which have had the effect of replacing the traditional *parens patriae* concept with formal due-process proceedings for accused juveniles, the court's discretion relative to that of police has been reduced. The court is now required by law to consider such factors as the establishment of guilt beyond a reasonable doubt and the presence of defense counsel. In addition, in a number of states the range of permissible dispositions for many offenses has been narrowed, and probable-cause hearings may be required. Some observers (e.g., Packer 1966) have suggested that one consequence of these reductions in judicial discretion would be the reduction of the possibility of bias in juvenile court processing. While standardization and formalization of police procedures has also been a policy issue, no comparable legal restrictions have been imposed on police processing, and some changes in procedures have been relatively minor and jurisdictionally confined. Indeed, as noted above, re-

[5] The decisions referred to are as follows: *in re Gault*, 387 U.S. 1967; Kent v. United States, 383 U.S. 541, 1966; and *in re Winship*, 397 U.S. 538, 1970.

1117

moval of a comparable amount of discretion from police decision making is largely precluded by the nature of the work itself.

Finally, and related to the degree of formalization of procedures, police decisions are less visible than court decisions (Reiss 1971, pp. 185–206; Goldstein 1960, pp. 543–94). Many police-citizen encounters that involve a police decision go unrecorded. This is often true in the station house as well as on the street. The police disposition is made without opportunity of appeal or formal adversarial representation. By definition, these are functions of the judicial stage of processing.

In sum, the police are legally and bureaucratically permitted, and functionally required, to exercise a wide range of discretion for which there is relatively little review or accountability, or opportunity for appeal on the part of the accused party. Responses obtained during semistructured interviews with police officers, police juvenile bureau directors, court intake officers, judges, and probation officers in each setting studied suggest that these characteristics are true of the sampled jurisdictions. Thus, our second hypothesis is that racial bias is more likely to occur in police than in juvenile court processing. This hypothesis is consistent with the findings of Ferdinand and Luchterhand (1970) that race had a stronger effect than demeanor in determining the outcome of police encounters but made no difference in court dispositions. Two other studies (Terry 1967; Thornberry 1973) also examined police and court processing jointly but found no differences in bias between them. In addition to the methodological limitations of the studies reviewed earlier, it should be noted that all three of the studies just mentioned utilized data from the early 1960s, before the impact of the Supreme Court decisions noted above. Although it compares only police departments, Wilson's (1968) study provides a comparison of discretion levels that supports our hypothesis: he reports that bias existed in a traditional department but not in a professionalized one that involved a higher level of bureaucratization and formalization.

THE DATA

The Setting

Data for the analysis of dispositions of cases by the police are drawn from two New Jersey counties: River County, one of the most populous and heavily urban counties in the state, and Woodlawn County, a nearby, largely suburban county. (The names of both counties are fictitious.) River County is dominated by a blighted older city of about 300,000 which is surrounded by smaller cities and large suburban towns, increasing in affluence as distance from the center city increases. Its population is 30% black and 9% Hispanic. The extent to which the county is burdened

1118

with urban problems is reflected in high rates of school dropouts and unemployment and by the proportions of unskilled blue-collar workers and families below the poverty line. River County has a high crime rate and a high volume of juvenile complaints. Minority population is concentrated in the center city.

Woodlawn County is largely suburban, with the county seat located in an old city of about 40,000, now outsized by sprawling suburban municipalities and outlying older towns. Only 5% of Woodlawn's population is black, and 5% is Hispanic. In contrast to River County, Woodlawn County has far fewer of the social problems mentioned above; when all counties for the state are ranked, it occupies an intermediate position.

Three police juvenile bureaus were selected from each county: one from the county seat, one from a large town, and one from a small town. Location in the same state and county meant a helpful degree of standardization and consistency in record keeping and procedures. Because of the importance previous work has attributed to the race of the police, we checked the racial composition and policies of the police agencies studied. We found that in each municipality, blacks and Hispanics were substantially underrepresented in the force in comparison with the proportion of blacks residing in the municipality. In the smaller towns, no members of minorities were on the force. Police sources in municipalities having black officers report that no attempts are made to match race of the officers to the racial composition of neighborhoods to which they are assigned.

While demographic characteristics of these two counties differed greatly, the operation of their juvenile courts was quite similar. Some similarities are structural and procedural, as both were required by the state to use some of the same forms and procedures. Beyond this, interviews with judges and other personnel indicated that the philosophy of the head judges and other staff was quite similar in the two courts. Both judges had several years of experience in juvenile court and tended to emphasize the parental model of the court's role, although they endorsed and claimed respect for the recent emphasis on due process. The most frequently noted difference was the repeated claim by other juvenile justice and social service professionals that the Woodlawn judge was consistently overly permissive.

In our log-linear analysis of court dispositions, we include data from the juvenile courts of four additional counties: one additional urban county with a relatively high percentage of minority residents (adjacent to River County) and three nonurban counties with a low percentage of black residents. Tabular analysis of data from each of these counties taken separately produced findings similar to those for River and Woodlawn Counties (see table 2)—in no county was the bivariate relation between race and disposition substantively significant. Inclusion of these additional cases enables us

1119

to perform a higher-order multivariate analysis by increasing the cell sizes in the n-way cross-tabulations.

Sampling

Delinquency cases processed in the first eight months of 1973 and 1975 were selected randomly from official records of individual cases in the county courts and in each of the six municipalities.[6] In the two small towns, data were recorded for all cases processed. The resultant samples consist of 1,271 police juvenile bureau cases, 519 juvenile court cases from River and Woodlawn Counties, and a total of 1,553 juvenile court cases from all six counties. The samples were stratified by sex to insure adequate numbers of females for multivariate analysis; about a third of the cases in each sample are girls.

Measurement and Analysis Procedures

Case data were coded from official police and juvenile court records. At the juvenile court, some pertinent information was found in other documents in the case files, such as reports from schools and welfare workers, and psychiatric and investigative reports. Table 1 lists the variables included in the present analysis. In most cases, coding is straightforward. The legal variables of offense type and prior record, and the extralegal variables of race, sex, and family configuration are employed in both samples. The dependent variables are specific to the police and court samples.

The "release" category of police disposition includes "conditional release," which involves the imposition of certain conditions such as making restitution or compensation, or participating in some kind of "voluntary" social service program. Since there are relatively few such cases, since there appears to be little subsequent checking up on enforcement of the sanctions imposed, and since the young persons are in fact released, it seems most reasonable to collapse these cases into the release category. For court disposition, dismissal includes "adjourned" cases, since they stand as dismissed unless the juveniles are returned to court on subsequent allegations. The intermediate category consists mainly of probation cases but also includes suspended sentences and those few cases waived to adult court.[7] The severe

[6] Two distinct time periods were used because the study was also designed to measure the impact of legal change. Processing patterns in the two years manifest only random variation, however, and therefore they are collapsed in this analysis. For a detailed analysis comparing findings from the two years, see Dannefer and DeJames (1979).

[7] It could be argued that waiver to adult court is a severe disposition. However, incarceration is only one of a number of outcomes of waiver to adult court. More-

1120

category contains only those juveniles actually placed in a correctional facility.

Log-linear analysis is used to test the effects of variables on dispositions. This form of analysis allows assessment of effects of categorical variables on other categorical variables and is thus suited to our data (see Burke and Turk 1975; Cohen and Kluegel 1978). Since a causal structure is assumed for the analysis (i.e., disposition is considered as dependent on the other variables), a "modified multiple-regression" approach (Goodman 1972*b*) is used to develop a model. In this approach, a term representing all interactions of the independent variables with each other is included in each

TABLE 1

INVENTORY OF VARIABLES FOR THE ANALYSIS

Variables	Categories
Dependent:	
Police disposition.........	1. Release (including conditional release) 2. Court: forward case to juvenile court
Juvenile court disposition..	1. Dismissed: includes adjournment (dismissed contingent on good behavior) and placement under care of human service agency 2. Probation or other sanction: consists mainly of cases placed on probation, but also includes those given suspended sentences or waived to adult courts 3. Incarceration: placement in postdispositional correctional facility
Legal:	
Offense type............	1. Violent offenses: murder, manslaughter, forcible rape, atrocious assault and battery, kidnapping, assault and battery 2. Property offenses: breaking and entering, larceny, auto theft, stolen property offenses 3. Drug offenses: possession or usage of marijuana, narcotics, or controlled dangerous substances 4. Minor offenses: vandalism, failure to give good account, disorderly conduct, trespassing, intoxication, loitering, escape, miscellaneous
Prior record............	Number of prior offenses: coded as none or as one or more according to the evidence contained in the file
Extralegal:	
Race...................	1. Black 2. Hispanic 3. White
Family configuration......	1. Two parents 2. One parent, other
Sex...................	1. Male 2. Female
County................	1. River (and one adjacent county in the court data) 2. Woodlawn (and three similar counties in the court data)

over, the law provides that the case may be waived to adult court at the request of the accused juvenile. Since we did not know the eventual outcome for these few ($N = 9$) cases, we chose to place them in the intermediate category.

1121

model. In consequence, only the log of the odds of cell frequencies that vary on the dependent variable are subject to "explanation." Therefore, the model is actually equivalent to a logit equation.[8]

Our model-testing procedure begins with an equation involving all main effects. We also test for all effects due to the interaction of two independent variables. We use a combination of forward selection and backward elimination to determine which interaction terms to include in our final models (Goodman 1971). In evaluating models, we rely on χ^2 tests and the coefficients of partial determination. The latter are suggested by Goodman (1972a, pp. 1056–58) for measuring the magnitude of the contribution of variables in a log-linear equation.

FINDINGS

The cross-tabulations in table 2 provide a preliminary view of the association between race and disposition, prior to controlling for the legal variables in the analysis. In River County, there was a very strong association at the zero-order level between race and disposition by the police. While fewer than half of the black and Hispanic juveniles were released, 79% of the whites were released. In Woodlawn County, however, the association was weaker. While almost the same percentage of blacks were released as in

TABLE 2

POLICE AND COURT DISPOSITIONS BY RACE AND COUNTY

	RIVER COUNTY			WOODLAWN COUNTY		
DISPOSITION	Black	Hispanic	White	Black	Hispanic	White
	By Police (%)					
Released.........	40	50	79	34	62	54
Referred to court...	59	50	21	66	38	46
Total..........	99 (404)	100 (32)	100 (212)	100 (202)	100 (89)	100 (286)
	$\chi^2 = 80.35$, df = 2, $P \leq .001$			$\chi^2 = 25.62$, df = 2, $P \leq .001$		
	By Court (%)					
Dismissed.........	57	71	55	64	47	57
Probation.........	29	11	31	23	47	36
Institutionalized....	14	18	14	13	5	6
Total..........	100 (231)	100 (28)	100 (64)	100 (31)	99 (19)	99 (110)
	$\chi^2 = 4.54$, df = 4, N.S.			$\chi^2 = 4.38$, df = 4, N.S.		

NOTE.—Some percentages do not add to 100 owing to rounding error. N's shown in parentheses.

[8] See Garrison (1979) for a similar use of log-linear techniques.

1122

River County, only 54% of whites were released. Hispanics in Woodlawn County were released somewhat more frequently than whites.

In contrast to its impact on police dispositions, race was only weakly associated with court disposition. Patterns for blacks and whites were almost identical in River County; Hispanic juveniles were dismissed somewhat more often. In Woodlawn County, the blacks were slightly more likely to have their cases dismissed than whites, who were, in turn, more likely to have their cases dismissed than Hispanics. Blacks were slightly more likely to be institutionalized than whites or Hispanics. In neither county were the associations significant.

This table provides preliminary support for the two hypotheses. Race has a strong effect on police dispositions, but not on court dispositions. Social environment is also related to disposition in the predicted pattern for police dispositions: the racial difference in dispositions is greater in River County than in Woodlawn County. However, black and white juveniles are treated similarly by the courts in both River and Woodlawn Counties. Moreover, Hispanic juveniles are treated more severely than blacks and whites in Woodlawn, and less severely in River County. If this pattern of effects for court dispositions is maintained in our final model, it will suggest a need to specify our social context argument.

Log-linear analyses of the main effects of race and the other variables on dispositions by the police and the courts are presented in table 3. Race is the most important predictor of police dispositions, as indicated by its coefficient of partial determination (.27). The two legal variables, allegation and prior record, also have strong effects. The effects of these three variables are all significant at the .001 level. County and family configu-

TABLE 3

LIKELIHOOD RATIO χ^2 AND COEFFICIENT OF PARTIAL DETERMINATION (CPD) FOR MAIN EFFECTS[a] ON POLICE AND COURT DISPOSITIONS

	POLICE			COURT		
VARIABLE	χ^2	df	CPD	χ^2	df	CPD
Race............	59.91	2***	.270	13.85	4**	.065
Sex.............	.34	1	.002	.84	2	.004
Family configuration..	4.65	1*	.028	3.41	2	.017
Allegation.......	34.90	3***	.177	14.31	6*	.067
Prior offense.....	27.78	1***	.146	66.80	2***	.252
County.........	9.68	1**	.056	.15	2	.001
Model..........	162.28	182	...	198.46	364	...

[a] All models in this table and succeeding tables include term representing interaction of all independent variables.

* $P \leq .05$.
** $P \leq .01$.
*** $P \leq .001$.

1123

ration both have much weaker effects on police dispositions, but sex is the only variable which has no significant impact. Court dispositions are influenced by fewer of the variables studied, and the effect of race on court dispositions is much weaker than its effect on police dispositions. Neither sex, family configuration, nor county has a main effect on court dispositions.

Construction of final models is based on the evaluation of two-way interactions in tables 4 and 6. The effects of all two-way interaction terms were tested, and only those which added significantly to the model of all main effects were eligible for inclusion in the final model. There are three such interaction effects on police disposition, as reported in table 4: race by allegation, race by county, and family configuration by county. Since these interaction effects involved terms in common, it is possible to achieve a

TABLE 4

LIKELIHOOD RATIO χ^2 FOR TWO-WAY INTERACTION EFFECTS OF RACE (R), SEX (S), FAMILY CONFIGURATION (F), ALLEGATION (A), PRIOR OFFENSE (P), COUNTY (C) ON POLICE DISPOSITIONS

Reduction of χ^2 from All-Main-Effects Model for:	χ^2	df	P
By Forward Selection			
RS.........	5.35	2	<.10
RA.........	20.11	6	<.01
RP.........	4.00	2	<.20
RF.........	1.51	2	>.20
RC.........	15.60	2	<.001
SA.........	6.24	3	<.20
SP.........	3.12	1	<.10
SF.........	1.44	1	>.20
SC.........	.61	1	>.30
AP.........	3.19	3	>.30
AF.........	.17	3	>.5
AC.........	3.26	3	>.5
PF.........	.18	1	>.5
PC.........	3.68	1	<.10
FC.........	5.20	1	<.05
By Backward Elimination: Addition to χ^2 due to Dropping RA, RC, or FC from Model Containing All Three and Main Effects			
RA.........	22.07	6	<.01
RC.........	15.18	2	<.001
FC.........	2.27	1	<.20
By Backward Elimination: Reduction of χ^2 due to Dropping RA from Model with Main Effects and RC			
....	4.51	4	>.20

1124

more parsimonious model by removing those effects which do not make a significant independent contribution. As indicated in the bottom portion of table 4, neither the interaction of family type and county nor that of race and allegation adds significantly to the explanatory power of the model when the interaction of race and county is included. Only the interaction of race and county is, therefore, left in the final model.[9]

The final model of police dispositions includes all variables in the original specification except sex, and also the interaction of race and county. In table 5, λ coefficients are presented to show the pattern of effects, together with the χ^2 tests which show the significance of these effects. The interaction of race and county adds significantly to the main-effects model presented in table 3, while the removal of sex has no effect.

TABLE 5

EFFECT PARAMETERS (λ) AND SIGNIFICANCE LEVELS
(Likelihood Ratio χ^2) FOR THE FINAL MODEL
OF POLICE DISPOSITIONS

	λ BY POLICE DISPOSITION	
VARIABLE	Release	Court
Race ($P < .001$):		
Black...................	$-.278$	.278
Hispanic................	.044	$-.044$
White..................	.233	$-.233$
Family configuration ($P < .05$):		
Two parents...........	.069	$-.069$
Allegation ($P < .001$):		
Violent................	.006	$-.006$
Property...............	$-.067$	.067
Drug..................	$-.201$	.201
Minor.................	.262	$-.262$
Prior offense ($P < .001$):		
None..................	.167	$-.167$
County ($P < .01$):		
Urban.................	.054	$-.054$
Race by county, urban ($P < .001$):		
Black.................	$-.023$	.023
Hispanic..............	$-.155$	.155
White................	.179	$-.179$

NOTE.—Model: $\chi^2 = 147.14$, df $= 181$, $P > .5$.

[9] In their study of a juvenile court, Carter and Clelland (1979) provide evidence to support the general hypothesis that bias would be more likely in cases involving minor ("victimless/status") offenses than in cases involving "crimes against persons and property." Although our data are not directly comparable since we do not include status offenders, the direction of the RA (race-allegation) interaction was, as indicated by the λ coefficients (data not shown), consistent with their hypothesis. In the court data, however, the race by allegation interaction effect was not significant, even when it was the only interaction term included in the model (see table 6).

1125

The pattern of effects of race is consistent with the corresponding percentages in table 2. Blacks were less likely to be released than whites; Hispanics occupied an intermediate position. The coefficients for the interaction of race and county show that this differential treatment was particularly strong in River County, where Hispanics were especially disadvantaged. Property and drug crimes were treated more harshly than minor crimes. (The relatively lenient treatment of cases involving violence may reflect the nature of the many juvenile cases which involve fights and other conflicts between peers.) Juveniles without a prior record were much more likely to be released than those with a record, and cases in River County were treated somewhat more leniently by the police than those in Woodlawn County.

Two-way interaction effects on court dispositions are evaluated in table 6. Four two-way interactions are significant: race by county, family by prior offense, family type by county, and allegation by county. As with the analysis of effects on police dispositions, all terms which do not add significantly to the predictive power of the model when other terms are included are deleted in constructing the final model. The combination of forward inclusion and backward elimination of effects yields a final specification that includes the interaction of allegation and county and of family type and county.

The final log-linear model of court dispositions is presented in table 7. Sex, which again has no significant main or interactive effects, has not been included in this model. The main effects of family type and county were included in the specification but are not presented because their significant effects were limited to their role in interactions. The pattern of effects of race on disposition indicates that white juveniles were somewhat more likely to have their cases dismissed by the courts and were less likely to be institutionalized than black or Hispanic juveniles. The group that was treated most harshly, however, is Hispanics. Both black and white juveniles had their cases dismissed more often and were institutionalized less frequently than Hispanics. As has been consistently found in research on juvenile justice, juveniles with no prior offenses had a substantial advantage in court.

Because of the importance for our theory of the race-by-county interaction term, we have also examined the λ coefficients of that term when included in the model of court dispositions in table 3, even though its effect is not significant independent of the other terms in the final model (see table 8). These coefficients reveal an unexpected pattern. In comparison with their treatment in Woodlawn, black juveniles in River County are more likely to be dismissed and less likely to be institutionalized than are white juveniles. Hispanics occupy an intermediate position in this interaction effect.

1126

DISCUSSION

The two hypotheses proposed are largely supported by this analysis of police and court dispositions. The race of a suspect is much more important in police than in court dispositions. For police dispositions, the effect of race is much stronger in River County, with its high percentage of black residents, than in Woodlawn County. Our findings also provide some evidence of better treatment of white than black juveniles in court. As our hypothesis

TABLE 6

LIKELIHOOD RATIO χ^2 FOR TWO-WAY INTERACTION
EFFECTS OF RACE (R), SEX (S), FAMILY CONFIGURATION
(F), ALLEGATION (A), PRIOR OFFENSE (P), COUNTY (C)
ON COURT DISPOSITIONS

Reduction of χ^2 from All-Main-Effects Model for:	χ^2	df	P
By Forward Selection			
RS..........	3.55	4	$> .5$
RA..........	7.66	12	$> .5$
RP..........	8.83	4	$< .10$
RF..........	5.35	4	$> .20$
RC..........	9.55	4	$< .05$
SA..........	10.02	6	$< .20$
SP..........	.72	2	$> .5$
SF..........	.02	2	$> .5$
SC..........	.26	2	$> .5$
AP..........	7.86	6	$> .20$
AF..........	7.40	6	$> .20$
AC..........	16.43	6	$< .02$
PF..........	6.52	2	$< .05$
PC..........	1.26	2	$> .20$
FC..........	7.98	2	$< .02$
By Backward Elimination: Addition to χ^2 due to Dropping RC, AC, PF, FC from Model Containing All Four and Main Effects			
RC..........	5.99	4	$< .20$
AC..........	15.25	6	$< .02$
PF..........	4.00	2	$< .20$
FC..........	4.68	2	$< .10$
By Forward Selection: Reduction of χ^2 from All-Main-Effects Model + AC for			
RC..........	7.92	4	$< .10$
PF..........	6.73	2	$< .05$
FC..........	8.13	2	$< .02$
By Forward Selection: Reduction of χ^2 from Adding PF to All-Main-Effects Model + AC + FC			
PF..........	4.39	2	$< .20$

1127

suggested, the difference is not large. Hispanics, a group combined with blacks by Cohen and Kluegel (1978), are treated more harshly by the courts than are white or black juveniles. Contrary to our initial hypothesis, the courts in River County dispose of the cases of black juveniles with less severity than do the courts in Woodlawn County. While this interaction effect is weak, its direction suggests an important specification of the relation between minority percentage and likelihood of bias—an issue we address below. Consistent with other studies, legal variables of allegation and

TABLE 7

EFFECT PARAMETERS (λ) AND SIGNIFICANCE LEVELS (Likelihood Ratio χ^2) FOR THE FINAL MODEL OF COURT DISPOSITIONS

VARIABLE	λ BY COURT DISPOSITION		
	Dismiss	Probation	Institutionalize
Race ($P < .01$):			
Black	.050	−.072	.022
Hispanic	−.141	−.104	.245
White	.091	.176	−.267
Allegation ($P < .05$):			
Violent	.020	−.052	.032
Property	−.073	.148	−.074
Drug	−.164	−.014	.178
Minor	.217	−.082	−.135
Prior offense ($P < .001$):			
None	.336	−.066	−.271
Allegation by county, urban ($P < .05$):			
Violent	.178	−.059	−.119
Property	.002	.098	−.100
Drug	−.180	−.188	.368
Minor	.001	.148	−.149
Family configuration by county ($P < .05$):			
Urban	−.115	.042	.073

NOTE.—Model: $\chi^2 = 174.70$, df = 358, $P > .5$.

TABLE 8

EFFECT PARAMETERS (λ) FOR TWO-WAY INTERACTION EFFECT OF RACE AND COUNTY, IN MAIN-EFFECTS MODEL

RACE BY URBAN COUNTY	COURT DISPOSITION		
	Dismiss	Probation	Institutionalize
Black	.096	.048	−.144
Hispanic	.060	−.066	.006
White	−.156	.018	.138

NOTE.—This model also includes the two-way interaction term for race and allegation. This term does not have a significant effect. The coefficients for the main effect of race on disposition for this model are very close to those reported in table 7.

1128

prior record are very important in dispositions at both levels of the juvenile justice system studied. Although female juvenile cases have been neglected in many previous studies, our results indicate that their inclusion did not alter the race-disposition relationship that would have obtained for males only.

CONCLUSIONS

Our basic hypothesis was that bias in official decision making varies with social-structural factors. As specified in terms of (1) ecological and (2) organizational variables, it has received strong support in this analysis. Moreover, the social-structural dynamics suggested by our findings provide some basis for ordering the conflicting findings of previous research. While there was evidence of substantial bias in the likelihood of the police sending juveniles to court, there was much less evidence of bias in court decisions. The degree of such bias apparent in police dispositions varied greatly across the two social contexts studied, as suggested by our theory. Thus the findings suggest that the importance of social context in producing differences in findings between studies should be given more systematic attention.

Although we found less evidence of bias in the juvenile court than among the police, court decision making is not independent of police decisions. If there is bias at the point of police dispositions, it will ultimately translate into differences in prior record—a variable which had a stronger effect on court dispositions than any other variable studied. The effect of prior record may, in other words, include a component due to police bias. This general problem of "bias amplification," which has been more fully discussed by Farrell and Swigert (1978) and by Liska and Tausig (1979), cannot be resolved in studies of bias without more detailed information on cases which are followed from initial contact with the police to final disposition in court. However, our evidence of more favorable dispositions of cases of back juveniles than of whites in River County, compared with Woodlawn, suggests another connection between police and judicial decisions: judges may actually compensate for differential treatment by the police, to some extent, rather than simply reinforce it.[10] The greater formalization of the decision-making process, and perhaps the greater insulation of judges from direct community contact, may account for this complex interaction between environment and degree of bias in the police data.

Our finding of more severe court dispositions for Hispanic than for black juveniles also has relevance for a social-structural approach to the explana-

[10] This possibility suggests a process whereby decisions made at later stages in the system correct for bias exercised at earlier stages, and thus contrasts with the "bias amplification" findings of Farrel and Swigert (1978). However, it is clear that both processes may occur simultaneously; our findings *do* indicate some bias in the juvenile court, but less in jurisdictions where bias had been more pronounced in earlier stages.

1129

tion of bias in decision making. The differences in the social situations of Hispanics, blacks, and other minority groups should be assessed in future studies before making an a priori decision to use only a minority-non-minority classification.

We do not have the measures of complainant preference and of offender behavior which have been found to have an impact on police dispositions in other settings (Black and Reiss 1970; Piliavin and Briar 1964). Inclusion of these variables might have altered the findings obtained. We did run separate analyses for models of police dispositions which substituted age for sex and a core/periphery variable (within counties) for sex. Neither age nor the core/periphery variable changed the effect of race on police dispositions.

Our findings clearly indicate the importance of attention to social environment. Nonetheless, although the sampled counties differed on a key dimension (percentage minority), the limitation of our samples to one state means that we did not compare maximally different social environments. While our test for bias by the police in the two environments is therefore a relatively stringent test of the potential for environmental effects, our hypotheses need to be tested again in other settings.

On the basis of our findings, we suggest that future research in this area should concentrate on comparative studies in which social environments are sampled and on direct measures of characteristics of social environments. The theoretically important question which research should address is not whether there is bias in the juvenile justice system but, rather, under what conditions it is more likely or less likely to occur. An answer to this question has been suggested in this study in terms of basic features of the social environment, of the criminal justice process itself, and of an interaction between the two.

REFERENCES

Allport, Gordon W. 1954. *The Nature of Prejudice.* Cambridge, Mass.: Addison-Wesley.
Arnold, William R. 1971. "Race and Ethnicity Relative to Other Factors in Juvenile Court Dispositions." *American Journal of Sociology* 77 (September): 211–27.
Black, Donald J., and Albert J. Reiss, Jr. 1970. "Police Control of Juveniles." *American Sociological Review* 35 (February): 63–77.
Blalock, Hubert M., Jr. 1967. *Toward a Theory of Minority-Group Relations.* New York: Wiley.
Burke, Peter J., and Austin T. Turk. 1975. "Factors Affecting Postarrest Disposition: A Model for Analysis." *Social Problems* 22:313–21.
Carter, Timothy J., and Donald Clelland. 1979. "A Neo-Marxian Critique, Formulation and Test of Juvenile Dispositions as a Function of Social Class." *Social Problems* 27 (October): 96–108.
Chambliss, William J. 1973. "Functional and Conflict Theories of Crime." Module 17: 1–23. New York: MSS Modular Publications.

Chesney-Lind, Meda. 1977. "Judicial Paternalism and the Female Status Offender." *Crime and Delinquency* 23 (April): 121–30.

Chused, Richard H. 1973. "The Juvenile Court Process: A Study of Three New Jersey Counties." *Rutgers Law Review* 26:488–539.

Cohen, Lawrence E. 1975. "Delinquency Dispositions: An Empirical Analysis of Processing Decisions in Three Juvenile Courts." U.S. Department of Justice, National Criminal Justice Information and Statistics Service, no. SD-AR-9. Washington, D.C.: Government Printing Office.

Cohen, Lawrence E., and James R. Kluegel. 1978. "Determinants of Juvenile Court Dispositions: Ascriptive and Achieved Factors in Two Metropolitan Courts." *American Sociological Review* 43 (April): 162–76.

Cutright, Phillip. 1965. "Negro Subordination and White Gains." *American Sociological Review* 30:110–12.

Dannefer, Dale, and Joseph DeJames. 1979. *Juvenile Justice in New Jersey: An Assessment of the New Juvenile Code.* Trenton, N.J.: State of New Jersey.

Farrell, Ronald, and Victoria Lynn Swigert. 1978. "Prior Offense as a Self-fulfilling Prophecy." *Law and Society Review* 12:437–53.

Feagin, Joe R. 1971. "Home-Defense and the Police." Pp. 101–18 in *Police in Urban Society,* edited by Harlan Hahn. Beverly Hills, Calif.: Sage.

Ferdinand, Theodore N., and Elmer G. Luchterhand. 1970. "Inner-City Youth, the Police, the Juvenile Court, and Justice." *Social Problems* 17 (Spring): 510–27.

Garrison, Howard H. 1979. "Gender Differences in Career Aspirations of Recent Cohorts of High School Seniors." *Social Problems* 27, no. 2 (December): 170–85.

Goldstein, Joseph. 1960. "Police Discretion Not to Invoke the Criminal Process: Low Visibility Decisions in the Administration of Justice." *Yale Law Journal* 69:543–94.

Goodman, Leo A. 1971. "The Analysis of Multidimensional Contingency Tables: Stepwise Procedures and Direct Estimation Methods for Building Models for Multiple Classifications." *Technometrics* 13:33–61.

———. 1972a. "A General Model for the Analysis of Surveys." *American Journal of Sociology* 77 (May): 1035–86.

———. 1972b. "A Modified Multiple Regression Approach to the Analysis of Dichotomous Variables." *American Sociological Review* 37 (February): 28–46.

Groves, W. Eugene, and Peter H. Rossi. 1971. "Police Perceptions of a Hostile Ghetto." Pp. 175–91 in *Police in Urban Society,* edited by Harlan Hahn. Beverly Hills, Calif.: Sage.

Liska, Allen E., and Mark Tausig. 1979. "Theoretical Interpretations of Social Class and Racial Differences in Legal Decision-making for Juveniles." *Sociological Quarterly* 20 (Spring): 197–207.

Morgan, William R., and Terry N. Clark. 1973. "The Causes of Racial Disorders: A Grievance-Level Explanation." *American Sociological Review* 38:611–24.

National Advisory Commission on Civil Disorders. 1972. "The Police and the Community." Pp. 133–43 in *Police-Community Relationships,* edited by William J. Bopp. Springfield, Ill.: Thomas.

Packer, Herbert L. 1966. "The Courts, the Police, and the Rest of Us." *Journal of Criminal Law, Criminology and Police Science* 57:238–43.

Parcel, Toby L. 1979. "Race, Regional Labor Markets and Earnings." *American Sociological Review* 44 (April): 262–79.

Piliavin, Irving, and Scott Briar. 1964. "Police Encounters with Juveniles." *American Journal of Sociology* 70 (September): 206–14.

Quinney, Richard. 1970. *The Social Reality of Crime.* Boston: Little, Brown.

Reiss, Albert J., Jr. 1971. *The Police and the Public.* New Haven, Conn.: Yale University Press.

Spilerman, Seymour. 1976. "Structural Characteristics of Cities and the Severity of Racial Disorders." *American Sociological Review* 41:771–93.

Spilerman, Seymour, and R. E. Miller. 1976. "Community and Industry Determinants of the Occupational Status of Black Males." Discussion Paper no. 330, University of Wisconsin—Madison, Institute for Research on Poverty.

1131

239

Terry, Robert M. 1967. "The Screening of Juvenile Offenders." *Journal of Criminal Law, Criminology and Police Science* 58:173–81.

Thornberry, Terrence P. 1973. "Race, Socioeconomic Status and Sentencing in the Juvenile Justice System." *Journal of Criminal Law and Criminology* 64:90–98.

Vines, Kenneth W. 1964. "Federal District Judges and Race Relations Cases in the South." *Journal of Politics* 26 (May): 337–57.

Weiner, Norman L., and Charles V. Willie. 1971. "Decisions by Juvenile Officers." *American Journal of Sociology* 77 (September): 199–210.

Wellford, Charles. 1975. "Labeling Theory and Criminology: An Assessment." *Social Problems* 22:332–45.

Wilson, James Q. 1968. "The Police and the Delinquent in Two Cities." Pp. 9–30 in *Controlling Delinquents,* edited by Stanton Wheeler. New York: Wiley.

THE JOURNAL OF CRIMINAL LAW & CRIMINOLOGY
Copyright © 1977 by Northwestern University School of Law

Vol. 68, No. 1
Printed in U.S.A.

NO COMPRENDO: THE NON-ENGLISH-SPEAKING DEFENDANT AND THE CRIMINAL PROCESS

JOAN BAINBRIDGE SAFFORD*

The non-English-speaking defendant in a criminal proceeding poses increasing problems for the administration of criminal justice. Minorities for whom English is not the principal language or who speak such unusual dialects of English as to cloud understanding and communication make up a discouraging proportion of offenders.[1] In areas of large ethnic enclaves where English is not the dominant tongue, officials have estimated that between thirty and forty per cent of criminal defendants require the aid of an interpreter fully to understand the proceedings against them.[2]

Thirty-five states make some statutory provision for appointment of interpreters in specified cases.[3] The Illinois statute is typical of one group:

> Whenever any person accused of committing a felony or misdemeanor is to be tried in any court of this State, the court shall upon its own motion or that of the defense or prosecution determine whether the accused is capable of expressing himself in the English language so as to be understood directly by counsel, court or jury. If the court finds the accused incapable of so understanding or so expressing himself, the court shall appoint an interpreter for the accused whom he can understand and who can understand him.[4]

---

* J. D., Northwestern University School of Law, Office of Illinois Attorney General, Criminal Justice Division.

[1] NATIONAL ADVISORY COMMISSION ON CRIMINAL JUSTICE, STANDARDS AND GOALS, COMMUNITY CRIME PREVENTION 151 (1973).

[2] Testimony before the U.S. Commission on Civil Rights 118, in Los Angeles (Aug. 17, 1968).

[3] States not providing for language interpreters are: Alabama, Colorado, Maine, Missouri, Montana, Nebraska, New Hampshire, Oklahoma, Pennsylvania, Rhode Island, South Carolina, Tennessee, Vermont, Washington and West Virginia. Louisiana makes provision for interpreters only in trials of stat military personnel. LA. REV. STAT. ANN. § 29:12 (West 1975). Pennsylvania makes provision for ap pointment of interpreters to aid the court in th Court of Common Pleas only. PA. STAT. ANN. tit. 17 § 1875 (Purdon 162).

A number of states make generous provisions for deaf persons in criminal cases, but do not make any of the same provisions for those with language difficulty. E.g., W. VA. CODE § 57-5-7 (1974 Supp.); CONN. GEN. STAT. ANN § 17-137 k (West 1975): "(a) In any criminal or civil action involving a deaf person, the court shall appoint a qualified interpreter to assist such person throughout such proceeding." The only other relevant Connecticut statute relates to compensation of interpreters. Nebraska expressly recognizes that appointment of an interpreter for the deaf is necessary to protect the constitutional right of the defendant to participate in the preparation and trial of his case, yet the constitutional rights of the non-English speaking defendant are not considered. NEB. REV. STAT. § 25-2401 to § 25-2406 (1975). Compare ARIZ. REV. STAT. § 12-242 A-D (1974), providing for compulsory appointment of qualified interpreters for the deaf, with ARIZ. REV. STAT. § 12-241 and § 11-601 (5), providing for discretionary appointment of language interpreters with no reference to standards.

[4] ILL. REV. STAT. ch. 38, § 165-11 (1975). The Illinois statute is similar to section 752, chapter 4 of the California Evidence Code which provides for interpreters for witnesses. See CAL. EVID. CODE § 752(a) (West 1966). More common and the form Illinois used until 1973 are statutes patterned after rule 28 of the Federal Rules of Criminal Procedure:

> The court may appoint an interpreter of its own selection and may fix the reasonable compensation of such interpreter. Such compensation shall be paid out of funds provided by law or by the goverment, as the court may direct.

FED. R. CRIM. P. 28. E.g., ARIZ. REV. STAT. § 12-241 (1956); DEL. CT. C.P.R. 28; HAW. REV. STAT. § 606.9 (1969); IND. R. TR 43 (F); MISS. CODE ANN. § 99-17-7 (1972); OHIO REV. CODE ANN. § 2301.12 (Supp. 1974).

Most protective of the non-English-speaking defendant are statutes similar to Michigan's:

> If any person is accused of any crime or misdemeanor and is about to be examined or tried before any justice of the peace, magistrate or judge or a court of record and it appears to the magistrate or judge that such person is incapable of adequately understanding the charge or presenting his defense thereto because of a lack of ability to understand or speak the English language or inability adequately to communicate by reason of being deaf and/or mute, or that such person suffers from a speech defect or other physical defect which handicaps such person in maintaining his rights in such cause, the justice of the peace, magistrate or judge shall appoint a qualified person to act as an interpreter. . . .

MICH. STAT. ANN. § 28.1256 (1) (1971).

See also ARK. STAT. ANN. § 5-715 (1976); IOWA

241

Standards for interpretation are almost non-existent. Illinois requires the interpreter to swear "to truly interpret or translate all questions propounded or answers given as directed by the court."[5] But if the interpreter is translating off-the-record for the benefit of the defendant, there is no check on the accuracy of the translation.

Almost nowhere is statutory provision made for interpreters at early stages after arrest.[6] In almost every jurisdiction, once criminal charges are lodged the judge is given broad latitude to decide whether to appoint an interpreter, while no regular procedures are prescribed for determining need.[7] Reviewing courts rarely question the trial judge's decision if there is any evidence at all of the defendant's ability to understand or speak some English, or if any translation has been provided. When an appeal is made on the basis of a constitutional claim that the defendant did not understand the proceedings or that they were inadequately translated to him, there is no record of what the defendant heard and understood to settle the very question raised for review.

This article examines the problems inherent in arresting, setting bail for, arraigning, accepting a plea from and trying a defendant whose ability to understand and express himself in

English is minimal or non-existent. A critical examination of the Illinois statutes on interpreters and Illinois decisions on the constitutional questions raised by failure to provide an interpreter suggests that Illinois is far behind the federal courts and the courts of some other states in protecting the interests of linguistically handicapped criminal defendants. Yet in those courts in Cook County where a professional interpreter is regularly available, there is developing a judicial practice of calling upon the interpreter when there is any indication of need, even at an early stage in the proceedings. This is far more than is required by Illinois decisions and even beyond that practice suggested by various circuits of the United States Court of Appeals. Although concentrating particularly on the problems of the Spanish-speaking defendant, a member of the largest linguistic minority in Cook County, this article makes criticisms and recommendations that apply equally as well to the handling of the case of any non-English-speaking defendant.

SCOPE OF THE PROBLEM

The 1970 decennial census revealed that more than thirty-three million residents of the United States reported that their "mother tongue" was a language other than English.[8] More than twenty-two million residents were either first generation or second generation immigrants of foreign-speaking parentage.[9] Puerto Ricans, who are considered "native," are not included in this figure. As the 1970 census is known to have ignored large numbers of urban poor,[10] and as the foreign-speaking are largely concentrated in the metropolitan areas of the country, the number for whom English is not the primary language could be much higher. Some scholars have estimated the number as high as twenty-six million.[11]

CODE Ann. § 622 A.1-1-6 (Supp. 1970); KAN. STAT. ANN. § 75-4351 to § 75-4355 (Supp. 1975); MD. ANN. CODE art. 27, § 623 (a) (1968).

The New Mexico Constitution provides: "In all criminal prosecutions, the accused shall have the right . . . to have the charge and testimony interpreted to him in a language he understands." N. M. CONST. art. 2, § 14.

Certain West Texas border counties make provision for conducting the proceedings in Spanish with English interpreters. TEX. STAT. ANN. art. 3737 d-1 (Supp. 1976).

[5] ILL. REV. STAT. ch. 38, § 165-12 (1976).

[6] Kansas is unique in prohibiting interrogation without an interpreter if the defendant's "primary language is one other than English. . . . " KAN. STAT. ANN. § 75-4351 to § 75-4355 (Supp. 1975).

[7] MISS. CODE ANN. § 99-17-7 (1972) is typical:

Interpreters.
In criminal cases, the court may appoint an interpreter when necessary, sworn truly to interpret, and allow him a reasonable compensation, not exceeding five dollars per day, payable out of the county treasury.

For a discussion of problems of trying a non-English-speaking defendant *see* Comment, *Right to an Interpreter*, 25 RUTGERS LAW REVIEW 145 (1970); Comment, *Constitutional Law: Translators: Mandatory for Due Process*, 2 CONN. L. REV. 163 (1969).

[8] "Mother tongue" means language spoken during childhood. UNITED STATES DEPARTMENT OF COMMERCE, BUREAU OF THE CENSUS, 1970 CENSUS OF POPULATION, COUNTRY OF ORIGIN, MOTHER TONGUE, AND CITIZENSHIP OF THE UNITED STATES 1 (Supp. 1974) [Publications from the 1970 census are hereinafter cited as 1970 CENSUS OF POPULATION together with the title of the special publication].

[9] *Id.* at 3, Table 193.

[10] N.Y. Times, Nov. 30, 1975, § 4, at 7, col. 1. Estimates of the number of urban poor not counted in the 1970 census range as high as nine million persons.

[11] 2 T. ANDERSON & M. BOYER, ₤ BILINGUAL SCHOOLING IN THE UNITED STATES 25 (1970).

Although significant portions of this population probably have little or no language difficulty with English, those who have grown up in large and expanding ethnic neighborhoods, those who have migrated back and forth to the United States from Mexico or Puerto Rico, or those whose work groups them with others of the same language, have not had the same push to linguistic assimilation which other generations have experienced.[12]

More than nine million people identified by the 1970 census considered Spanish their first language or came from a household in which the father or mother was reported to have Spanish as a mother tongue.[13] This figure is undoubtedly low. In 1974, the Immigration and Naturalization Service estimated that there were between four and five million illegal aliens in the United States. In December, 1975, the estimate was eight million, the vast bulk of them Spanish-speaking.[14]

Sheer numbers have led to an infrastructure within the Spanish-speaking community which protects but also isolates the Spanish speaker from the English-speaking community.[15] In San Antonio, sixty-two per cent of those low-income Mexican-Americans living in census tracts with more than 400 Spanish-speaking people could speak little or no English. A similar survey in census tracts in Los Angeles with high concentrations of low-income Mexican-Americans revealed that fifty-one per cent of the residents could not speak any English.[16] Another study of Puerto Ricans in New York found more than seventeen per cent of the children and presumably almost twice that number of adults spoke little or no English.[17] A

study of Spanish-speaking people in the southwest revealed that they averaged little more than eight years of education. When students left school, nearly three-fourths of them were below grade level.[18] Inadequately equipped by education and disabled by language from taking jobs outside of the Spanish-speaking community, they lost much of the English which they had learned, and became further isolated.[19]

The large number of Spanish-speaking residents in Chicago and their high concentration in certain areas of that city suggest the same experience of linguistic isolation. The 1970 census counted 247,343 Spanish-speaking residents in the city of Chicago;[20] some estimate that there may be at least another 100,000.[21] Fifty-three census tracts in the city were reported to have 400 or more Spanish-speaking residents.[22] Income and education levels among this group are low.[23] But even rising income, the usual route out of ethnic isolation, has affected Spanish-speaking residents less than earlier groups. Among white Spanish-speaking residents in Chicago above the poverty line, more than

[12] L. GREBLER, J. MOORE AND R. GUZMAN, THE MEXICAN-AMERICAN PEOPLE at 87–94, 424–427 (1970) [hereinafter cited as GREBLER]. See generally, LANGUAGE LOYALTY IN THE UNITED STATES (J. Fishman ed. 1966).

[13] 1970 CENSUS OF POPULATION, PERSONS OF SPANISH ANCESTRY, PERSONS OF SPANISH LANGUAGE BY REGIONS, DIVISIONS AND STATES 9, Table 3 (Supp. 1973).

[14] Hearings Before the Subcomm. on Immigration of the Comm. on the Judiciary, 93d Cong., 2d Sess. 37 (Apr. 3 and June 25, 1974); Leonard F. Chapman, Comm'r, Immigration & Naturalization Service, quoted in N.Y. Times, Dec. 21, 1975, § 1, at 27, col. 1.

[15] Comment, "Citado a Comparacer": Language Barriers and Due Process—Is Mailed Notice in English Constitutionally Sufficient?, 61 CAL. L. REV. 1394, 1400 (1973).

[16] GREBLER, supra note 12, at 424, Table 18-1.

[17] U.S. PUERTO RICO COMM'N ON THE STATUS OF

PUERTO RICO, STATUS DE PUERTO RICO 152 (1966) [herinafter cited as STATUS OF PUERTO RICO]. Only 58 per cent of Puerto Rican children in the New York schools were rated fluent in English.

[18] U.S. CIVIL RIGHTS COMM'N, THE UNFINISHED EDUCATION (1971). Among those who remain in school, 63 per cent are below grade level and 40 per cent have severe reading retardation (two or more years below grade level). Id. at 25–26.

[19] GREBLER, supra note 12, at chs. 5, 7, 18.

[20] 1970 CENSUS OF POPULATION, SOCIAL CHARACTERISTICS OF THE POPULATION. CHICAGO, ILL. 119, Table P-2. Almost one million residents of Chicago were of foreign or mixed parentage, or foreign-born. Id. The 1960 CENSUS did not count Spanish-language residents, 1960 CENSUS OF POPULATION, CENSUS TRACTS, CHICAGO, ILL. 19, Table P-1, but the Puerto-Rican population in Chicago had increased from 32,371 to 78,826 in 1970, the Mexican from 44,600 to 107,925. 1970 CENSUS OF POPULATION, PERSONS OF SPANISH ORIGIN 165, Table 14.

[21] Telephone interview, U.S. Immigration & Naturalization Service, Inspectors Division, (Nov. 4, 1975).

[22] 1970 CENSUS OF POPULATION, ECONOMIC CHARACTERISTICS OF PERSONS OF SPANISH LANGUAGE 559–568, Table P-8.

[23] Median income for a Spanish-language family of median size, 4.63 persons, was $8,983; median years of school, 9.2. The figures are markedly lower for Puerto Rican heads of households of whom only 15.9% completed high school. 1970 CENSUS OF POPULATION, PERSONS OF SPANISH ORIGIN, FAMILY INCOME, POVERTY STATUS 180 (Table 16, income), 112 (Table 9, education).

twenty–seven per cent continue to live in Spanish-speaking, low-income areas.[24]

The inability to cope in any but the most cursory way with the demands of the dominant culture affects the non-English-speaking resident in a host of areas,[25] but it is in confrontations with the law that the risks of incomprehension are highest. A study of the genesis of New York policemen's abuses of power revealed that many officers interpreted the Spanish-speaking resident's failure to answer their questions as a form of defiance.[26] One policeman told New York Civil Liberties Union lawyers that when a young Puerto Rican had answered an officer's questions in Spanish prompting laughter among his companions, the officer had slapped the boy to "maintain his authority."[27]

This same phenomenon was reported by the California State Advisory Committee to the United States Commission on Civil Rights.[28] In a series of cases where Spanish-speaking persons failed to comprehend what was said, the policemen were enraged by the lack of response to orders.[29] In Chicago, a Mexican-American, arriving at school late in the afternoon to see about his brother's truancy, asked directions to the principal's office and was ordered out of the school by an off-duty policeman serving as a school guard. He apparently misunderstood

and pushed past toward the principal's office, leading to a fight and an assault charge.[30]

The Civil Rights Commission concluded after a series of hearings that the source of the trouble is often that the English-speaking policeman cannot comprehend the Spanish-speaker's intent from his speech.[31] The regular rise and fall of the Spanish intonation pattern, when accentuated by excitement, may be interpreted as a harangue. Thus, during a riot in East Los Angeles when police overheard a young Mexican attempting to quiet the crowd, they assumed that he was agitating it and arrested him.[32] Finally, misinterpretation of words similar to those in English can lead to miscomprehension and tragic consequences. When a mother complained to the police that her husband had drunkenly struck their daughter, the police took this to mean that the father was sexually molesting the child and arrested him. Understanding almost no English, the father did not object to the charge. The father remained in jail two months unable to make bail.[33] In Chicago, with a Spanish-speaking population of at least 9.4 per cent and a police force with fewer than 200 Spanish-speaking officers,[34] the potential for these misunderstandings is enormous.

More often, of course, arrest results not from misunderstanding but from probable cause. Once an arrest has been made, an interpreter may be necessary to warn the defendant of the right to counsel and the right to remain silent, and for effective questioning if those rights are waived. If the defendant speaks some English, it is almost impossible to show later that the warning was not understood or the waiver unknowing. Only Kansas requires appointment of

---

[24] 1970 CENSUS OF POPULATION, LOW INCOME NEIGHBORHOODS IN LARGE CITIES, CHICAGO ii (Supp. 1974). Only 16 per cent of non-Spanish-language whites who were below the poverty level lived in such neighborhoods. *Id.* In the low income neighborhood with the highest proportion of Spanish-language residents, Neighborhood 3 (41%), more than 60 per cent of the Spanish-language whites were above the poverty level. *Id.* at 1, Table A-1. More Mexicans live in Chicago than anywhere outside the Southwest. Only New York City has more Puerto Ricans. ILL. STATE ADVISORY COMM. TO THE U.S. COMM'N ON CIVIL RIGHTS, BILINGUAL/BICULTURAL EDUCATION 4 (1974).

[25] Liebowitz, *English Literacy: Legal Sanction for Discrimination,* 45 NOTRE DAME LAW. 7, 51-67 (1969) (catalogues state statutes and regulations requiring knowledge of English).

[26] P. CHEVIGNY, POLICE POWER 69 (1969).

[27] *Id.* at 70. A similar incident happened when Haitian youths spoke Creole when approached by police.

[28] U.S. CIVIL RIGHTS COMM'N, MEXICAN AMERICANS AND THE ADMINISTRATION OF JUSTICE IN THE SOUTHWEST 66 (1970) [hereinafter cited as MEXICAN AMERICANS AND THE ADMINISTRATION OF JUSTICE].

[29] *Id.* at 67.

[30] Case of Carlos R., Nw. U. Legal Assistance Clinic (April 14, 1974).

[31] MEXICAN AMERICANS AND THE ADMINISTRATION OF JUSTICE, *supra* note 28, at 68.

[32] *Id.*

[33] *Id.* at 70.

[34] Telephone interview with Richard Phelan, Ass't Corp. Counsel, City of Chicago (Dec. 5, 1975). As of 1974, only one per cent of Chicago's police force was "Hispanic." During 1971-73, only twenty-three Hispanic officers were added to the police force. United States v. City of Chicago, 385 F. Supp. 543, 548–49 (N.D. Ill. 1974). At the City of Chicago Police Department, 14th District, located in a Latino neighborhood, there were only two Spanish-language officers as of June, 1974. Interview with Police Officer Durr, (July 9, 1974).

an interpreter at this time.[35] Arizona requires that upon the arrest of a deaf-mute, no interrogation of any kind shall take place prior to appointment of an interpreter and that there be a formal determination of the interpreter's competence.[36] But Arizona does not require comparable protection for the non-English-speaking defendant. No case in Illinois has held that the Illinois statute requires appointment of a language interpreter at the time bail is set for the defendant, although it could be argued that the determination of whether bail is excessive, in violation of the eighth amendment, cannot be made if the court is unable to communicate with the defendant.[37]

In *People v. Macias*,[38] the defendant, who spoke no English, and her companions, were charged with aggravated assault and carrying a concealed weapon. Taken before the magistrate at 2:00 A.M., the defendant was unable to explain that she had no arrest record, had been regularly employed for four years, had lived at the same address for three years, and was the mother of a three-year-old child whom she had left with a babysitter when she went to work that evening. All these were factors which the Bail Reform Act of 1966[39] suggested would be proper ones to weigh when considering whether to grant bail and which might have affected the judgment of the court that night as to the bond required. But until May, 1975, no interpreter was available in any Illinois court at this stage of the proceedings.[40]

It also appears that no right to an interpreter at the preliminary hearing is recognized by the Illinois foreign language interpreters statute.[41] This statute provides for appointment of an interpreter when a person accused of committing a felony or misdemeanor "is to be tried in any court of this State."[42] Arguably the prerequisite for implementation of the interpreters statute is not established until *after* the preliminary hearing. Therefore, the earliest stage in the criminal process when Illinois law recognizes that there may be a need for an interpreter for non-English-speaking defendants is at arraignment. On the other hand, Illinois law does require that both at the bond and preliminary hearings a qualified interpreter must be appointed by the court to interpret the proceedings to a deaf person.[43] No challenge has been made to the statute on equal protection grounds as applied to this stage of the criminal process, but it is hard to justify a distinction between the deaf person and the linguistically crippled.

Furthermore, the thrust of the two statutes is markedly different, as is their potential for protecting the defendant's constitutional rights. The statute providing for an interpreter for the deaf makes appointment obligatory, makes clear that the proceedings are to be interpreted to the defendant, and requires a "qualified interpreter of the deaf sign language."[44] The statute for language interpreters in criminal trials provides that the court shall determine upon its own motion or that of counsel whether the accused cannot understand the English language or make himself understood by court, counsel or jury.[45] The focus is on the court's ability to take testimony, not the accused's ability to understand the proceedings. The statute

---

[35] KAN. Stat. ANN. § 75-4351 (Supp. 1975):
  A qualified interpreter shall be appointed in the following cases for persons whose primary language is one other than English, or who are deaf or mute or both:
  (e) . . . . When such person is arrested for an alleged violation of a criminal law of the state or any city ordinance. Such appointment shall be made prior to any attempt to interrogate or take a statement from such persons.
[36] ARIZ. REV. STAT. ANN. 12-242 B (Supp. 1976).
[37] In Stack v. Boyle, 342 U.S. 1 (1951), the Supreme Court held that bail set at an amount which is reasonably necessary to assure the defendant's appearance at trial is excessive.
[38] No. 74-01764 (Cook County Criminal Court, 1974). Macias remained in the Cook County House of Correction, Division 3, for more than three weeks without being provided an interpreter. Information obtained from the Nw. U. Legal Assistance Clinic (June, 1974).
[39] 18 U.S.C. § 3146(b) (1970).
[40] In May, 1975, at the urging of the Cook County

Circuit Court Judge Wayne W. Olson, and through the action of Judge Eugene Wachowski, a full-time interpreter of Spanish was appointed to the Cook County Criminal Court Building in Chicago at an annual salary of $11,800 and an interpreter of French, Spanish and Italian was appointed to cover the Cook County Branch courts. These two interpreters were originally responsible for all other branches of the Cook County Criminal Court. Interview with Judge Wayne Olson, Cook County Criminal Court, Branch 44 (Dec. 2, 1975).
[41] ILL. REV. STAT. ch. 38, § 165-11 (1975).
[42] Id.
[43] ILL. REV. STAT. ch. 51, § 48.01 (1975).
[44] Id.
[45] ILL. REV. STAT. ch. 38, § 165-11 (1970).

contains no requirements of competence beyond those implied by the interpreter's oath,[46] which does not apply to testimony not offered to the court. Furthermore, there is no explicit requirement that the proceedings be interpreted to the defendant.

Because the procedures for determining need and for determining an interpreter's competence are not spelled out in the foreign language interpreters statute, the trial court has much greater latitude for the exercise of discretion than does the court in applying the interpreters-for-the-deaf statute. As a result, a reviewing court is less likely to find an abuse of discretion.

This deference to the trial court's implied conclusion that the defendant can "speak and understand English" is not unreasonable. Understandably, the reviewing court is hesitant to find error in a meagre record if there is *some* evidence to support the trial court. The written record is inadequate on the very question raised. Often the reviewing court has only a few isolated words by which to judge, particularly if the defendant has pleaded guilty or has not testified in his own defense. The principle of deference was articulated by the appellate court in *People v. Tripp*:[47]

> When the witnesses labor under the handicap of language difficulties, an appellate court, which sees only the written record, should pay more than ordinary deference to the conclusions drawn by the trial judge, who observed demeanor and gestures of the witnesses and heard possibly important variables of inflection and emphasis.[48]

That the court is able to make some sense of what the person said is not determinative of whether the defendant "speaks English" sufficiently well to manage without an interpreter. The question is whether the person understands the question addressed to him and can give an answer which conveys what he means to the court.[49] Whether the defendant's English is

sufficient will depend also on the complexity of the issues for trial.

Undoubtedly, determination of the sufficiency of the defendant's English should be made by the trial court, but it should be done expressly. The First Circuit in *United States v. Carrion*[50] endorsed the vesting of broad discretion in the trial court, stressing, however, the consequent obligations on the trial court: (1) to inform the defendant of the right to an interpreter, (2) to appoint an interpreter if the defendant is indigent, and (3) to be alert for such language difficulty during the trial as would require a new determination of need. The First Circuit appeared to require a formal hearing on the question of need or, at least, clear evidence on the record demonstrating the trial court's continuing attention to the defendant's possible need.[51]

The Illinois courts have not met this standard. If the reviewing courts in Illinois are to continue to defer to the trial court, justice requires that even without a request from counsel, when the trial court has notice of language difficulty it should make some more formal determination of the defendant's ability to speak English before concluding that the statute is satisfied. Without such a formal determi-

whom spoke virtually no English, attempted to testify that they had seen the defendant asleep in the living room of his father's apartment at the time of the assault. A review of the abstract of the record reveals a long series of unresponsive or confused answers.
Q: Isn't it a fact, Mr. Ortiz, that your son wasn't living at your house?
A: Yes.
Q: At that time?
A: He living in the house for that time, right.
Q: Mr. Ortiz, isn't it a fact he was living with May?
A: No.
Q: On that date?
A: No, he was not married.
Q: Do you remember the day he was arrested?
A: Oh, that time he got two children . . .
Q: . . . when Salvatore got arrested for this charge, was he living at home?
A: Yes, with me yes . . . with May then.
Abstract of Record 32. The judge however claimed that he understood the testimony and concluded "he brought four people up here to testified [sic] falsely. All four of them contradicted each other." Record of Proceedings at 120.

[46] ILL. REV. STAT. ch. 38, § 165-12 (1970).
[47] 19 Ill. App. 3d 200, 311 N.E.2d 168 (1974).
[48] *Id.* at 203, 311 N.E.2d at 170.
[49] This distinction is illustrated by People v. Ortiz, 22 Ill. App.3d 788, 317 N.E. 2d 763 (1974), in which the defendant claimed the witnesses needed the services of an interpreter. The victim of the assault had had little opportunity to observe and had made an error in identification. Four alibi witnesses, two of
[50] 488 F.2d 12 (1st Cir. 1973).
[51] *Id.* at 14-15. The U.S. District Court for the Northern District of Illinois has not routinized such inquiries, although individual judges consider it wise. Interview with U.S. District Court Judge Prentice Marshall, (N.D. Ill.) (Nov. 15, 1976).

nation, the Illinois statute, despite its obligatory language, provides an inadequate and uncertain shield for a defendant's constitutional rights.

CONSTITUTIONAL ISSUES

The Illinois courts have been slow to recognize the constitutional questions inherent in trial of the non-English-speaking defendant. Even if he speaks some English, the constitutional requirement of a fair trial, that he understand the proceedings and be able to participate in his own defense, may not be met.[52] The courts seem to conclude that the trial court's finding that under the interpreters law the defendant speaks and understands enough English not to require an interpreter means that he must have understood the proceedings against him. The reviewing courts have therefore shown deference to the trial courts even when a constitutional claim is raised.[53] They have not required that there be a greater showing from the record when the question is whether the waivers were understandingly given or whether the defendant understood the testimony of adverse witnesses.

In a series of cases the Supreme Court has made clear that there must be a clear trial record to support a finding that constitutional rights have been knowingly waived. As the Court stated in *Johnson v. Zerbst*,[54] "'[C]ourts indulge every reasonable presumption against waiver' of fundamental constitutional rights and . . . we 'do not presume acquiescence in the loss of fundamental rights.'"[55]

The requirement for a record was well demonstrated in *Boykin v. Alabama*,[56] in which the Supreme Court reversed the conviction on a plea of guilty to armed robbery and remanded for trial despite the overwhelming evidence against the accused. The record was entirely barren on the question of whether the guilty plea was understandingly and voluntarily given. "So far as the record shows, the judge asked no questions of petitioner concerning his plea, and petitioner did not address the court."[57]

Even a record of express waiver may be insufficient and require further inquiry: "The determination of whether there has been an intelligent waiver . . . must depend, in each case, upon the particular facts and circumstances surrounding that case, including the background, experience and conduct of the accused."[58]

The Illinois Supreme Court fully discussed the duty to assure that waiver of constitutional rights are understandingly and expressly made in *People v. Fisher*,[59] a jury waiver case. In *People v. Rambo*,[60] the Illinois appellate court recognized that in some cases, even a clear record that the defendant has been informed of his right to a jury trial and has signed the jury waiver form may require reversal. The court in that case reversed the conviction of a sixteen-year-old boy, stating that the youth of the boy and seriousness of the crime imposed an extra duty of care on the court to assure that the waiver was made with full knowledge of the consequences.[61] The court would not rely on the defense attorney's assent to the waiver of the jury to satisfy the requirement of the Constitution and its implementing statute[62] for an express, knowing waiver.

The Illinois courts have not provided the same protection of the right by jury to the linguistically infirm. Just as youth places special obligations on the judge to assure that the plea of guilty or jury waiver are understandingly made, so, too, should language disability. Yet in *People v. Melero*[63] the reviewing court upheld the bench trial conviction when the attorney alone assented to the jury waiver and the trial began:

> The Court: Could he go to trial without an interpreter?
> Mr. Gilbert: He will try to do it. He speaks Spanish.

---

[52] *See* U.S. v. Dusky, 362 U.S. 402 (1960) discussing mental incompetency: Due process requires that the defendant have a "present ability to consult with his lawyer with a reasonable degree of rational understanding—and . . . a rational as well as factual understanding of the proceedings against him." *Id.* at 402.

[53] *See* People v. Rivera, 13 Ill. App. 3d 264, 300 N.E.2d 869 (1973); People v. Melero, 99 Ill. App. 2d 208, 240 N.E.2d 756 (1968); People v. Ayala, 8 Ill. App. 2d 393, 233 N.E.2d 80 (1967).

[54] 304 U.S. 458 (1938).

[55] *Id.* at 464.

[56] 395 U.S. 238 (1969).

[57] *Id.* at 239.

[58] Johnson v. Zerbst, 304 U.S. at 464.

[59] 340 Ill. 250, 265, 172 N.E. 722, 728 (1930).

[60] 123 Ill. App. 2d 299, 260 N.E.2d 119 (1970).

[61] *Id.* at 305, 260 N.E.2d at 122.

[62] ILL. REV. STAT. ch. 38, § 103-6 (1975).

[63] 99 Ill. App. 2d 208, 240 N.E.2d 756 (1968).

The Court: Do you want me to hear the case or do you want a jury trial?

Mr. Gilbert: Waive the jury, Your Honor.

The Court: State ready?

Mr. Hackett: The State is ready.[64]

Turning the *Rambo* decision on its head, the Illinois appellate court considered this record and concluded: "If the jury waiver here was not understandingly made, this record does not show it."[65] The defendant was presumed to have assented to his attorney's waiver of a jury trial by not objecting. Yet the error raised on appeal was that the defendant was incompetent to know or understand what right was being waived.[66] Without a full exploration by the court of the defendant's ability to comprehend the proceedings, not merely to answer rehearsed questions in English, the conclusion that the waiver was understandingly made was improper.

Other appellate courts have refused to uphold the trial court in similar circumstances, even when the record reveals that the defendant speaks and understands some English. The requirements of due process have been used to narrow the scope of judicial discretion as to appointment of an interpreter. In *In re Muraviov*,[67] the California Court of Appeals, acting on a writ of habeas corpus, reversed and remanded a criminal conviction for wilful failure to support a minor child. The court found that the defendant had not knowingly waived his right to counsel. The trial court had asked Muraviov four perfunctory questions, all of which could be answered by "yes" or "no". The responses had provided the basis for the Appellate Department of the Superior Court to find a sufficient ability in English to sustain the trial judge's action in proceeding without an interpreter. After conducting its own hearing on the accused's ability to speak English, the appeals court concluded:

[I]t should be obvious that if petitioner was unable to understand or speak English, his monosyllabic "yes" and "no" answers had no meaning.[68]

In a similar case, the Oklahoma Supreme Court in *Landeros v. State*[69] reviewed denial of a motion to withdraw a guilty plea. The court examined the record of an illiterate Mexican-American who had pleaded guilty to murder after having his constitutional rights, including his right to a jury trial, explained to him in English. Although the defendant spoke and understood some English, his use of English was so limited that the court concluded he could not have understandingly waived his constitutional rights. Citing an earlier Oklahoma case,[70] the court recommended appointment of an interpreter when language ability is limited as a "wholesome precautionary measure; and to assure that all of the defendant's waivers were knowingly and intelligently entered."[71]

Both cases reached the reviewing court with an addition to the bare record of the trial. In *Muraviov* the habeas proceeding made clear to the court that the defendant could not speak English. In *Landeros* the record of the hearing on the motion to withdraw the plea of guilty provided similar evidence. These California and Oklahoma cases suggest the constitutional insufficiency of the Illinois courts' position. Illinois courts should require a substantial record demonstrating the defendant's ability to speak and understand English before finding that a waiver is knowing.

---

[64] *Id.* at 211, 240 N.E.2d at 757.

[65] *Id.* An example of an Illinois trial judge more conscientiously fulfilling his responsibility is illustrated by People v. Castillon, 132 Ill. App. 2d 581, 270 N.E.2d 268 (1970), in which Judge Collins rejected the defense attorney's estimate of his client's ability to understand English and the jury waiver:

THE COURT: I am sure you have done everything in your power to properly defend this man, however, I am not satisfied that we can proceed to trial without an interpreter. I want someone to tell this man in his own language what is transpiring and we are beginning right at the beginning with a waiver of a very basic constitutional right, the waiver of jury trial, and I am not satisfied that this record shows he understands that.

Id. at 583, 270 N.E.2d at 270.

[66] The theory is that the defendant knows and understands what his agent, that is, the attorney, understands. But surely this theory of agency must break down if the defendant and attorney cannot communicate. *Cf.* Dusky v. United States, 362 U.S. 402 (1962), where in discussing mental incompetency, the Court said due process requires an ability to consult with one's lawyer. *See also* People v. Hernandez, 8 N.Y.2d 345, 207 N.Y.S.2d 668, 170 N.E.2d 673, *cert. denied*, 366 U.S. 976 (1960).

[67] 192 Cal. App. 2d 604, 13 Cal. Rptr. 466 (1961).

[68] *Id.* at 606, 13 Cal. Rptr. at 467.

[69] 480 P.2d 273 (Okla. Crim. 1971).

[70] Parra v. Paige, 430 P.2d 834 (Okla. Crim. 1967).

[71] 480 P.2d at 275 (Okla. Crim. 1971).

Right of Confrontation and Cross-examination of Witnesses

The courts have long recognized that the sixth amendment right to confront witnesses "really means the right of the accused to hear the witnesses testify against him and to cross-examine them."[72] In a 1970 case, *United States ex rel. Negron v. New York*,[73] the Court of Appeals for the Second Circuit held that the right to an interpreter for the indigent non-English-speaking defendant was a necessary adjunct to protection of the defendant's constitutional right to confront the witnesses against him. The Second Circuit affirmed a district court decision sustaining a petition for writ of habeas corpus for an illiterate Puerto Rican migrant worker who had been convicted of murder. Although an interpreter was provided for the convenience of the court when Negron and two other witnesses testified and during a brief conference with Negron's lawyer, twelve English-speaking witnesses had testified without any translation for Negron nor communication between Negron and his attorney. The court found that Negron was linguistically incompetent to stand trial without an interpreter to aid him. "To Negron, most of the trial must have been a babble of voices."[74] Because Negron was indigent, the trial court was obliged to provide the interpreter.[75] The Second Circuit concluded that in no sense did Negron's silence constitute a waiver of his fundamental right to confront the witnesses against him through an interpreter, for his silence did not satisfy the constitutional standard for waiver: "an intentional relinquishment or abandonment of a known right."[76] Nor would Negron's attorney be found

to have waived Negron's right when the right was previously so ill-defined.[77]

The Second Circuit recognized the precedential value of its decision for the defendant who speaks no English. But the decision did little for the defendant who, unlike Negron, speaks *some* English. The court suggested the parallel of the linguistically incompetent to the mentally incompetent.[78] But it did not explicitly hold, as the Supreme Court had held with respect to mental incompetence in *Pate v. Robinson*,[79] that when linguistic incompetence is a possibility, the court should hold a hearing *sua sponte* to determine competence.[80] Negron's linguistic incompetence was "obvious, not just a possibility."[81] By neglecting to suggest procedures for determining whether the defendant had a "severe language difficulty,"[82] the Second Circuit left intact the practice by which a reviewing court would examine the record for hints of the defendant's linguistic competence as a basis for upholding the trial judge's discretionary decision. It was because Negron came to the court on a writ of habeas corpus that the court looked beyond the record. Furthermore, the right to court appointment of an interpreter remained limited to indigent defendants. As the right to an interpreter is now clearly established, the court may presume a waiver of the right if the private attorney does not claim it.

Some of the deficiencies of *Negron* were overcome in *United States v. Carrion*[83] where the First Circuit recognized that protection of a defendant's constitutional rights to a fair trial and to confront witnesses may require an interpreter, even if the defendant has "some ability to understand and communicate" in English:

---

[72] United States v. Barricota, 45 F. Supp. 38 (S.D. N.Y. 1942).

[73] 434 F.2d 386 (1970).

[74] *Id.* at 388.

[75] The Second Circuit had earlier suggested that due process and the right to confront witnesses might require appointment of an interpreter. In United States v. Desist, 384 F.2d 889 (2d Cir. 1967), *aff'd on other grounds*, 394 U.S. 244 (1968), a Frenchman, charged with dealing in heroin, clearly had the resources to pay for an interpreter but disassociated himself from the interpreter when he learned he must pay for the service. Negron satisfied the implied requirement of indigency suggested in *Desist*. 434 F.2d at 389.

[76] 434 F.2d at 390, *citing* Johnson v. Zerbst, 304 U.S. 458 (1938).

[77] 434 F.2d at 390. The court seemed to recognize the danger that an attorney might not assert the right and yet try to carry it on appeal. The obvious cure is for the court on its own motion to hold a hearing on the need.

[78] *Id. citing* Pate v. Robinson, 383 U.S. 375 (1966).

[79] 383 U.S. 375 (1966).

[80] Of course, the Second Circuit decision was not legally binding on any courts except those of the Second Circuit. In People v. Rivera, 13 Ill. App. 3d 264, 267, 300 N.E.2d 869, 871 (1973) the court acknowledged that there might be such an obligation but that it was satisfied by asking the illiterate co-defendant to act as interpreter. *See* text accompanying notes 103 to 106 *infra*.

[81] 434 F.2d at 390.

[82] *Id.* at 391.

[83] 488 F.2d 12 (1st Cir. 1973).

The right to an interpreter rests most fundamentally . . . on the notion that no defendant should face the Kafkaesque spectre of an incomprehensible ritual which may terminate in punishment.

Yet how high must the language barrier rise before a defendant has a right to an interpreter? . . . Because the determination is likely to hinge upon various factors . . . considerations of judicial economy would dictate that the trial court, coming into direct contact with the defendant, be granted wide discretion in determining whether an interpreter is necessary. . . . But precisely because the trial court is entrusted with discretion, it should make unmistakably clear to the defendant who may have a language difficulty that he has the right to a court-appointed interpreter if the court determines one is needed, and, whenever put on notice that there may be some significant language difficulty, the court should make such a determination of need.[84]

The First Circuit suggested that the trial court must weigh the defendant's ability in English together with the complexity of the issues for trial.[85] In the exercise of its discretion, the trial court has an obligation to hold a formal hearing or to follow other procedures[86] to assure that the interpreter will be appointed if needed at any point during the trial.

The First Circuit did not suggest that the court's duty to determine *need* was lessened if the attorney did not ask for an interpreter or the defendant was not indigent. The initiative remained with the court. Even after counsel in *Carrion* stated that no interpreter was necessary, the trial court had continued to be aware of its responsibility to ensure the defendant understood the testimony.

As early as 1957, the Illinois Supreme Court recognized that if the defendant cannot understand the testimony of the witnesses against him because of a language barrier, the defendant has been deprived of his constitutional right to confront adverse witnesses. In *People v. Shok*,[87] the Illinois Supreme Court found an abuse of

[84] *Id.* at 14-15.
[85] *Id.* This court is unique in recognizing the strain of following testimony in another language even if one has some ability to speak it.
[86] *Id.* at 15.
[87] 12 Ill. 2d 93, 145 N.E.2d 86 (1957). The fact that the court might glean what the witness meant from the witness's tone of voice and emotions could not compensate for an extensive record revealing the witness's difficulty in expressing herself.

discretion in failure to appoint an interpreter for a prosecuting witness who spoke almost no English. The cross-examination had been severely limited by the witness's disability. The record was replete with evidence of the need for a competent interpreter.[88]

In *People v. Starling*,[89] it was again the prosecuting witness, and not the defendant who spoke no English. The appointed interpreter's translation was so inadequate that neither the court, counsel nor the defendant could follow the testimony. The interpreter was repeatedly chastised for carrying on an independent colloquy with the defendant. And the abortive cross-examination by defense counsel had to be reshaped to make any sense at all. In *Starling*, the Illinois appellate court recognized for the first time that:

[T]he due process rights of persons charged with crimes cannot be short-cut by avoiding the ritual of translating each question and answer as required in section 2 of the Act relating to interpreters.[90]

The reviewing court again had an adequate record from which it could conclude that there had been an abuse of discretion.[91]

[88] One could also argue that when a prosecuting witness is so hampered in his or her use of English that there is no way to make the testimony precise, definite and sure, and the testimony is critical to the conviction, then, as a matter of law, the defendant has not been proved guilty beyond a reasonable doubt.
[89] 21 Ill. App. 3d 217, 315 N.E.2d 163 (1974).
[90] *Id.* at 222, 315 N.E.2d at 168.
[91] In People v. Ortiz, 22 Ill. App. 3d 788, 317 N.E.2d 763 (1974), the defendant argued that his alibi witnesses needed an interpreter. Without one, their answers were "unresponsive and/or contradictory and therefore unconvincing to the court." He was therefore deprived of his right to present his defense. Brief for Appellant at 50-51. Here, despite the clear record of confusion, the appellate court barely acknowledged the argument since the trial court had "understood" the testimony. The issue in testing a witness's testimony should not be whether the witness's answers are decipherable, but whether the witness understood the question and gave responsive answers. The trial court's lack of recognition of the possibility of linguistic isolation during a long period of residency in the United States is revealed by the judge's impatience with the defendant's contention. At the trial the judge commented: "he brought four people up here to testified [*sic*] falsely. All four of them contradicted each other." Record at 120. At the post conviction hearing the judge said:
They are long term residents of this area. And it

But the Illinois courts have not yet held that there was an abuse of discretion in any case where the defendant claimed that he had not been afforded his right to confront witnesses because he did not have an interpreter for his own use or because the interpretation granted was deficient.[92] The record does not provide any support for his claim that he has not "heard" the testimony, and the Illinois courts appear loath to find an abuse of discretion absent a record of miscomprehension.

This is not to suggest the reviewing court need conclude from every incongruous question and answer or from a record containing only monosyllabic responses that there was error in not providing an interpreter. But where the record is inadequate to make *any* decision on the issue, and the question does not come to the reviewing court in a form where it can determine the defendant's competency through its own hearing, the case should be remanded for an explicit finding.[93]

Such a procedure would also prevent manipulation of the record by the defendant who claims he does not speak adequate English and then does not testify in order to preserve his language disability as grounds for later appeal or a writ of habeas corpus.[94] In *State v. Aguelara*,[95] the Missouri trial court in an *ex parte* hearing weighed the testimony that the defendant spoke Spanish at home and his own claims that he "couldn't get" the questions addressed to him and only knew a few English words sufficient for his job, together with testimony by a friend that she spoke no Spanish but had no difficulty communicating with the defendant. The court concluded that no interpreter was necessary. In upholding the trial court, the Missouri Supreme Court stated that in each instance where inability to understand the proceedings was claimed or apparent there must be an *express* determination of whether an interpreter was necessary before the court will support the decision not to provide an interpreter as a sound exercise of discretion.[96]

Quality of Interpretation

The court in *People v. Starling*[97] recognized that the quality of interpretation may determine whether the defendant has understood the testimony against him sufficiently to satisfy the constitutional requirement. Similarly, the quality of interpretation may affect whether the defendant has understood and knowingly waived his rights.

The interpreter-for-the-deaf statute provides more assurance that the defendant's constitutional rights will be protected than does the language-interpreter statute. The previous deaf-mute statute explicitly required a "qualified" interpreter;[98] the amended statute requires that the interpreter be a "qualified interpreter of the deaf sign language."[99] The Illinois appellate court in *Hudson v. Augustine's, Inc.*[100] found that an interpreter who was not formally trained to interpret for the deaf, but instead only knew what the deaf mute had taught him, did not satisfy the statutory requirement of competency. The interpreter had only been able to testify to what he understood the deaf mute to have said, a translation which the court did not find sufficiently "unequivocal and positive and definite in character."[101]

The language interpreters statute says nothing about qualifications. Policemen, state employees, and co-defendants are not disqualified solely on the ground that they may be interested parties.[102] The court, in the exercise of its

---

is like many times these people, once they didn't get what they want, then they didn't understand what happened. Record at 191.

[92] People v. Rivera, 13 Ill. App. 3d 264, 300 N.E.2d 869 (1973); People v. Martinez, 7 Ill. App. 3d 1075, 289 N.E.2d 76 (1972).

[93] Since the obligation rests on the court as well as the defendant's counsel, the failure of the defendant's counsel to request an interpreter should not be taken as a waiver if there is an indication of need. *But see* People v. Melero, 99 Ill. App. 2d 208, 240 N.E.2d 756 (1968).

[94] This was the obvious concern of the court in People v. Rivera, 13 Ill. App. 3d 264, 300 N.E.2d 869 (1973) and People v. Ayala, 89 Ill. App. 2d 393, 233 N.E. 2d 80 (1967).

[95] 33 S.W.2d 901 (Mo. 1930).

[96] *Id.* at 904.

[97] 21 Ill. App. 3d 217, 315 N.E.2d 163 (1974).

[98] Ill. Rev. Stat. ch. 51, § 48.01 (1963) (current version at Ill. Rev. Stat. ch. 51, § 48.01 (1975)).

[99] Ill. Rev. Stat. ch. 51, § 48.01 (1975).

[100] 72 Ill. App. 2d 225, 218 N.E.2d 510 (1966).

[101] *Id.* at 237, 218 N.E.2d at 516.

[102] Interview with Christina Ruiz, Cook County criminal court interpreter (Dec. 5, 1975). *See* People v. Murphy, 276 Ill. 304, 114 N.E. 609 (1916); People v. Torres, 18 Ill. App. 3d 921, 310 N.E.2d 780 (1974) (police officer); People v. Rivera, 13 Ill. App. 3d 264, 300 N.E.2d 869 (1973) (co-defendant); People v. Delgado, 10 Ill. App. 3d 33, 294 N.E.2d 84 (1973) (unsworn bailiff).

discretion, has used and continues to use relatives and friends or to press court clerical personnel into service.[103] Only one case reviewed revealed an inquiry by the court into the credentials of the interpreter; the burden is on the defendant to show lack of qualification.[104] In only a few cases have the Illinois courts found the interpreter incompetent; those involved translation of witnesses' testimony, where the confusion of court and counsel because of the interpreter's incompetence was clear on the record.[105]

Any subsequent challenge to the competence of the interpreter when the translation has been made for the benefit of the defendant and not the court suffers from the same disability as that presented when no interpreter is provided. *There is no record of the foreign language interpretation.* Yet behind the questions of competency of the interpreter and the quality of the interpretation lies the question of what the defendant heard and agreed to.

In *People v. Rivera,*[106] the Illinois appellate court found that appointment of a co-defendant as interpreter at the suggestion of the public defender satisfied the requirements of the statute. Any objection to the appointment had been waived by counsel's tender of the inter-

preter. The court looked at the careful instructions on jury waiver which the trial court had given to the defendants followed by the question, "He understand that?" and the defendant's answer, "Yes." Despite the absence of any record that the co-defendant had translated the court's words, the reviewing court refused to draw the negative inference that an inadequate translation had taken place.[107] Nor did the court find evidence of incompetence in the co-defendant translator's confession to the court that he did not know how to read, but would "tell" the defendant what the jury waiver form said.[108] This is similar to the Illinois court's practice in accepting interpretations which are not literal translations but merely substantially the same as the testimony.[109] Finally, the court did not question how the co-defendant could provide adequate interpretation once the preliminary proceedings were over and the trial of both defendants was under way.

In *People v. Martinez,*[110] there was no question about the competency of the defense attorney to speak and understand Spanish, but the adequacy of the interpretation which he gave to the defendant was at issue.[111] The defendant, a

---

[103] People v. Rardin, 255 Ill. 9, 99 N.E. 59 (1912). In July, 1974, the author, attending a preliminary hearing for a case handled by the Northwestern University Legal Assistance Clinic, was pressed into service as interpreter for two other cases at the Cook County Criminal Court Building. The same ad hoc procedure was observed during visits to Cook County Court, Municipal Division, Boy's, Gun, and Auto Theft branches, Nov., 1975.

The N.Y. Times, Nov. 7, 1976, § 1, at 48, col. 3, reports that at a pretrial hearing to determine whether a prosecutor-obtained interpreter had served as a prosecution informant, a member of the audience was drafted to interpret the proceedings for the Croatian defendant.

Judge Wayne W. Olson complains that without a professional interpreter it is almost impossible to obtain a translation which would make a record of the defendant's comprehension of the proceedings, since the interpreter is inclined to explain rather than translate, when the defendant doesn't understand. Interview with Judge Wayne W. Olson, Cook County Court, Branch 44 (Dec. 1, 1975).

[104] People v. Martinez, 7 Ill. App. 3d 1075, 289 N.E.2d 76 (1972).

[105] *E.g.*, People v. Starling, 21 Ill. App. 3d 217, 315 N.E.2d 163 (1974). In People v. Allen, 22 Ill. App. 3d 800, 317 N.E.2d 633 (1974), the interpreter, a friend of the complaining witness, was found disqualified as an interested party.

[106] 13 Ill. App. 3d 264, 300 N.E.2d 869 (1973).

[107] [T]he record . . . does not show that any interpretation in fact occurred. Defendant wishes us to indulge in the negative inference that therefore no interpretation did in fact occur; . . .

Such a negative inference is too slender a reed on which to predicate reversible error.
Id. at 268, 300 N.E.2d at 872.

[108] Abstract of Record at 5

[109] People v. Murphy, 276 Ill. 304, 114 N.E. 609 (1916). In *Murphy* the witness referred to the assailants in Greek as "*megalos*" [the big man] and "*mikros*" [the little man]; the interpreter substituted the names of the defendants for those references. *Id.* at 320-21, 114 N.E. at 615.

The insufficiency of summary translations was commented on by the court in United States *ex rel.* Negron v. New York, 434 F. 2d 386 (1970):

However astute [the] summaries may have been, they could not do service as a means by which Negron could understand the precise nature of the testimony against him during that period of the trial's progress when the state chose to bring it forth. Negron's incapacity to respond to specific testimony would inevitably hamper the capacity of his counsel to conduct effective cross-examination. . . . [A]s a matter of simple humaneness, Negron deserved more than to sit in total incomprehension as the trial proceeded.
Id. at 389-90.

[110] 7 Ill. App. 3d 1075, 289 N.E.2d 76 (1972).

[111] Although the fact that an attorney speaks the language of the accused has led courts to hold that no

Puerto Rican who neither spoke nor understood English, pleaded guilty to murder and two charges of attempted murder. On appeal he argued that his attorney had tricked him at the trial, taking the time allowed by the judge for translation of the judge's admonitions to tell him that if he did not plead guilty he would get 100–199 years. The defendant claimed that he believed he was pleading guilty to manslaughter. The court acknowledged that the record carried no indication of the defendant's knowing waiver of his right to a jury trial, but presumed that the attorney, whose ability to translate was established by the trial court, had properly translated the admonitions. Again, because of the absence of any record of the Spanish spoken to the defendant, the record necessary to determine the merits of the appeal was unavailable to the reviewing court. No English-speaking defendant suffers this disability when he asks the court to review the record for evidence of an involuntary plea.

The first solution would be to provide foreign language transcriptions of the interpreter's translation of the proceedings. The transcription could be checked against the English-language proceedings to determine whether sufficient translation was provided so that the defendant could understand the proceedings. One attorney has argued without success that foreign language transcriptions are required by chapter 37, section 163(F)(1) of the Illinois Revised Statutes, which calls for full stenographic notes of the proceedings.[112] The Illinois courts have, however, rejected the contention that the proceedings must be immediately and fully translated to the defendant.[113] An inexpensive and uncomplicated method of preserving the record would be to tape the interpretation for later transcription if necessary, should the competency of the translation be

challenged. But there is no precedent in Illinois for even this modest method of assuring that the *substance* of the proceedings is communicated.

It is no real solution to be able to determine after the trial that the translation was insufficient. Despite the silence of the statute, the trial court is obliged to make an express determination of need if it has notice of language difficulty and to appoint competent interpreters. Neither obligation is relieved by the defense counsel's waiver of an interpreter, tender of an incompetent one, or failure to object to the quality of interpretation. The court should independently determine the competency of the interpreter, unless a professional one is provided by the state. California is almost unique in providing that judges may use examinations or "other suitable means" to assure the competency of interpreters.[114] The Illinois Supreme Court or Illinois legislature should implement similar measures.

Employment of a Professional Interpreter

The right to an interpreter to aid the non-English-speaking defendant in protection of his constitutional rights has been more effectively recognized in the federal courts and some other states than in Illinois. The federal courts have moved toward requiring regular procedures to determine need or substantive evidence that the trial judge has in fact made a determination of need whenever language difficulty has developed during a trial. Despite the fact that no standards for interpreters have been promulgated by the United States Supreme Court and no Supreme Court rule makes appointment obligatory, the various district courts of the Second, Fifth, Seventh and Ninth Circuits and of Puerto Rico now employ professional interpreters. Verbatim interpretation is therefore available for the convenience of the court in taking testimony and to translate the proceedings for the indigent defendant.

In the Fifth and Ninth Circuits and in Puerto

---

interpreter is necessary, it should be clear that the attorney cannot translate the substance of testimony and properly carry out his functions. *But see* People v. Martinez, *id.*, 289 N.E.2d 76; *cf.* People v. Pelgri, 39 Ill. 2d 568, 237 N.E.2d 453 (1968).

[112] Brief for Appellant at 14, People v. Martinez, 7 Ill. App. 3d 1075, 209 N.E.2d 76 (1972). The court reporter at any arraignment must take full stenographic notes of the proceedings, including the plea by the accused, the receipt and entry by the court, and the admonishment by the court. ILL. REV. STAT. ch. 37, § 661 (1975).

[113] People v. Torres, 18 Ill. App. 3d 921, 926, 310 N.E.2d 780, 784 (1974), *citing* Tapia Corona v. United States, 369 F.2d 388 (9th Cir. 1966).

[114] *See* CAL. CIV. PROC. CODE § 264 (West Supp. 1971). Kansas specifically disqualifies relatives of the first or second degree and provides that before appointment, the appointing authority shall make:

a preliminary determination that the interpreter is able to readily communicate with the person whose primary language is one other than English . . . and is able to accurately repeat and translate the statement of said person.

KAN. STAT. ANN. § 75-4353(b) (Supp. 1975).

Rico, the interpreters are always available without regard to indigency.[115] In the United States District Court for the Northern District of Illinois the *right* to an interpreter at government expense is limited to the indigent defendant, although some district court judges will arrange for the interpreter and determine the source of compensation later.[116] Non-English speaking defendants who retain their own attorneys are often inadequately protected.[117] The federal interpreter may be called to appear at the bond hearing after the narcotics agent has informed the United States Attorney that the accused does not speak English, or the Federal Defender's office may call before arraignment. But if the defendant subsequently secures a private attorney, the federal interpreter may no

longer be employed for the defendant's use. The defendant may then enlist a member of his family or a friend who is not trained to translate verbatim.

The Illinois decisions do not match those of the federal courts in protecting the non-English-speaking defendant, but the practice which is developing at the Cook County Criminal Court Building may provide even greater advantages than does the federal system. Until May, 1975, the branch courts located at the Cook County Criminal Court Building depended almost entirely on drafting ad hoc interpreters, relatives, clerical and court personnel, when the need arose. A list of interpreters was maintained for more drawn-out procedures, but quality of translation of the proceedings varied.[118]

The degree to which the need went unrecognized is indicated by the startling increase in the number of cases in which an interpreter has been employed since the judges became aware that the court had hired its first full-time salaried interpreter, skilled in verbatim translation. During the first month, the interpreter was utilized in twenty-four courtroom proceedings. The number of calls for courtroom work increased steadily, so that in the fifth month she made ninety-four courtroom appearances.[119]

While the Illinois language interpreters statute does not provide for an interpreter at the early stages of the criminal process, the practice at the Criminal Court Building exceeds the requirements of the law. The interpreter arrives at 8:30 A.M. and immediately consults with interviewers to determine which prisoners being held for bond hearings do not speak English. Each morning there are five to eight people in this category. "Before we even get

---

[115] MEXICAN AMERICANS AND THE ADMINISTRATION OF JUSTICE, *supra* note 28, at 72; 1966 JUD. CONF. REP. 59. All proceedings in U.S. District Court in Puerto Rico are required to be in English, 48 U.S.C. § 864 (1974). Since only 37.7% of the adult population speaks English, STATUS OF PUERTO RICO 152, *supra* note 17, the need for a full-time interpreter is manifest.

[116] Interview with U.S. District Court Judge Prentice Marshall (N.D. Ill.) (Nov. 15, 1976).

[117] Interview with U.S. District Court (N.D. Ill.) interpreter Alicia Haas, Dec. 3, 1975. Because Mrs. Haas is not salaried, the district court's position had been that she could not be made available to the defendant at government's expense without a showing of indigency; however, the district court is considering a proposal to provide regular court appointed interpreters. Interview with U.S. District Court Judge Prentice Marshall, Nov. 15, 1976. Mrs. Haas expressed dismay that the court had limited the right to court appointed interpreters to indigents based on the precedent of a case in which the defendant was a rich French narcotics dealer. U.S. v. Desist, 384 F.2d 889 (2d Cir. 1967), *aff'd on other grounds*, 394 U.S. 244 (1968). The usual case, she said, is a basically poor defendant who scrapes together money to pay the private attorney in advance. The private attorney is then often not interested in paying the $40-a-day rate. More recently, the district court judges have increasingly used Mrs. Haas' services without regard to defendant indigency. Rule 28 Federal Rules of Criminal Procedure makes provision for appointment.

Mrs. Haas reports that when an interpreter is present at the instigation of prosecutors rather than as an employee of the court, defendants and their attorneys may distrust the interpreter. Interview with Mrs. Haas, Nov. 10, 1976. The problem in using an interpreter obtained by prosecutors is illustrated in the recent case of Croatian nationalists charged with hijacking a jet. The prosecutions may be jeopardized because the interpreter is charged with also serving as a prosecution informant. N.Y. Times, Nov. 7, 1975, at 48, col. 3.

[118] Interview with Judge Wayne W. Olson, Dec. 2, 1975.

[119] Day book of Cook County Criminal Court interpreter, Christina Ruiz, May-Nov. 1975. Increasingly, the judges at the Cook County Criminal Court Building take precautionary measures when there is some doubt of the ability of the defendant to comprehend. One judge who formerly had been quick to conclude no interpreter was necessary now accounts for a substantial portion of the interpreter's caseload. Interview with Christina Ruiz, Dec. 2, 1975. Another judge stated that there was no doubt that the court, knowing that the interpreter is available, can now explore more carefully with the defendant his understanding of the pleading, waivers, and testimony. Interview with Judge Wayne W. Olson, Dec. 2, 1975.

started in the morning [the interpreter] has spotted the cases where she will be needed,"[120] one judge told an interviewer. The interpreter, appearing at the bond hearings, is able to have her schedule considered when later proceedings are being scheduled. When there are delays or continuances, the defendant does not find himself without an interpreter. If the need is not immediately apparent but becomes clear during the trial, the interpreter can be present after only a brief recess.[121]

Once the need for an interpreter is established, interpreter's services are provided at state expense. The availability of a professional interpreter means that the judges at the Cook County Criminal Court Building can recommend her services even when the defendant retains a private attorney. Although private counsel do not yet take proper advantage of the availability of a free interpreter, some judges regularly offer conference time for the private attorney to consult with his client through the interpreter.[122]

In the past there have been almost no standards for interpretation of courtroom proceedings to the non-English-speaking defendant unless and until he testifies. Even then the standards have varied widely. But with the introduction of a professional interpreter translating verbatim, the quality of the defendant's understanding becomes a part of the record. When there is confusion, when the defendant has not understood the court's admonitions, there is no longer a colloquy of explanation in the foreign language between the defendant and the interpreter. The defendant's questions are translated to the court and the court's further explanation provided to the defendant through the interpreter.[123]

Furthermore, when English-speaking witnesses, counsel or the court speak, the court can be confident that the proceedings are being translated. The interpreter has the powers of intense concentration necessary for interpretation and no other duties to distract from that obligation. A professional interpreter also can master the subtleties of dialect[124] and the specialized language of such fields as medical pathology. Moreover, the interpretation is not obtrusive.

For the defendant whose bond hearing is held elsewhere in Cook County or whose alleged criminal act carries him into some other courtroom in the state, the need for interpretation of the proceedings to the defendant continues to be ignored or inadequately met except when provided by conscientious counsel. Even at the Cook County Criminal Court Building, needs in languages other than Spanish are met in a more makeshift manner. And some judges still prefer to avoid using an interpreter's services unless the need is glaring.[125] Thus, protection of the defendant's rights is still somewhat arbitrary.

CONCLUSION

While recognizing that failure to provide an interpreter might violate a defendant's constitutional rights to a jury trial or confrontation of witnesses, the Illinois appellate court continues to give such deference to the trial court's discretion in cases where the defendant speaks little English that appeal is discouraging. The court's failure to insist on an adequate record of the defendant's comprehension of the proceedings to support the trial court's decision not to

---

[120] Interview with Judge Wayne W. Olson, Dec. 2, 1975.

[121] Personal observations of the author during a half day spent with Criminal Court interpreter, Christina Ruiz, Cook County Criminal Court, Dec. 2, 1975. In the first year of the program, the single interpreter was also on call to all branch courts, but she could not meet these demands and also meet the mass need at the central criminal court. A second interpreter now serves the southern branch courts. Interview with Judge Wayne W. Olson, Nov. 12, 1976.

[122] Public defenders also have a greater opportunity to prepare their cases involving non-English-speaking defendants. Common practice in interviews had been to use other Spanish-speaking prisoners. Conversation with Public Defender Thomas Moore, Cook County Criminal Court, Dec. 2, 1975.

[123] See People v. Starling, 21 Ill. App. 3d 217, 221 N.E.2d 163 (1974). Judge Olson reported that this was one of the most recurring and frustrating problems in that he could not know if the explanation contained the substance of the court's words. Interview with Judge Wayne W. Olson, Dec. 2, 1975.

[124] In People v. Starling, 21 Ill. App. 3d 217, 221 N.E.2d 163 the question whether the Spanish-speaking witness had been in a bar was misunderstood when the bailiff–interpreter apparently translated the word as "bara," a Caribbean usage. The witness denied being in the "bara." In Mexico the word is "cantina." Brief for Appellant at 15.

[125] Interview with Criminal Court interpreter Chritina Ruiz, Dec. 2, 1975. One judge has not used the interpreter at all.

provide an interpreter means that appointment of any interpreter is often a matter of chance. Furthermore, even in those cases where an interpreter is used, since no provision is made for appointment of professional interpreters or for transcribing or recording the interpretation given, the trial record often reveals almost nothing of what an interpreter has in fact communicated to the defendant or whether the defendant has understood.

A hearing on a motion to withdraw a guilty plea, if appropriate and timely, or a petition on a writ of habeas corpus may be the only ways that such a defendant can create an independent record of his disability. It may even be more difficult to establish the incompetence of an interpreter who has translated nothing for the record.[126] Until the Supreme Court of Illinois or the Illinois legislature establishes clear procedures and standards to determine need and quality of interpretation, the non-English-speaking defendant's rights to trial by jury, to effective counsel, to confront adverse witnesses and to a fundamentally fair trial are not assured.

[126] *E.g.*, People v. Rivera, 13 Ill. App. 3d 264, 300 N.E. 2d 869 (1972).

Socialization of Chicano Judges and Attorneys

Fernando V. Padilla

Virtually nothing is known about Chicano judges *qua* Chicano judges. Less than 250 words have been written about them and only for the purpose of tallying their number by state and level of court.[1] It is highly probable that not even an accurate list of Chicanos involved in the legal system, i.e., attorneys, prosecutors and judges, is available.

This paper traces the socialization patterns among the Chicano bar and judiciary. The factors of family background, ethnicity, religion, education, age and occupation were traced. The manner in which these factors were defined may differ somewhat from traditional practice but only in a few instances. For example, in what manner, it may be asked, would ethnicity be an important factor in the study of Chicano judges? Geographically, the scope of this paper was limited to the Southwestern states of Arizona, California, Colorado, Nuevo México and Texas, where over eighty percent of all Chicanos living in the United States reside. The specific case of the Chicano bar of Nuevo México is detailed and examined.

Theoretical Setting and Review of Literature

Norms and customs in a society have the function of regulating behavior in order that the individual members as well as the society may survive.[2] Normative behavior develops from two entirely different centers, one cognitive and the other emotive.

The function of cognitive socialization processes is to teach the individual the symbolic structures of society, especially those of familial, religious, political, and economic institutions. Furthermore, the same symbol may have different meanings within different social or institutional settings of the same society. For example, black may become a symbol for Negro, financial profit, or racial pride; red may become a symbol for Indian, communist, or anger; and republican may become a symbol for a political party, an anti-monarch, or one who opposes "pure" democracy.

The function of emotive socialization is to teach the individual what to generally expect in the actions and feelings of the other members of society as well as to channel emotional development within socially acceptable parameters. Part of this emotional development deals with attaching value in concrete situations to abstractions such as status, prestige, influence, power and authority within a society and also setting individual emotional goals for attaining those things one values commensurate with ambition and ability. For example, there is little social value in being a Communist in the United States but there is a great deal of status, prestige, influence, power, and perhaps authority in being a Communist in the Soviet Union.

In summary, there are two aspects to socialization. The cognitive element teaches the symbols and the various distinctions among similar symbols of a given society. The emotive element teaches the values society places on those symbols as well as the actions and feelings of members of society toward those symbols.

Socialization is a lifelong process. It is not limited to school. It is a process an individual learns in all social settings. One function of *political* socialization is to teach common political values, common political norms and acceptable political behavior. Another function of political socialization is to help the individual adjust to the political culture by teaching him to accept the political norms, values and behavior of society. The third function of political socialization is to transmit the political culture from generation to generation. Thus, Gabriel Almond and Sidney Verba believe that the formulation of political values is a lifelong process with different periods having different types of influences. In general, they describe socialization as follows:

> The sources of political attitudes appear to be many. They include early socialization experiences and late socialization experiences during adolescence, as well as post socialization experiences as an adult. They include both political and non-political experiences, experiences that are intended by others to have an affect on political attitudes as well as those that are unintended. Clearly many types of experiences can effect basic political

attitudes, and these experiences can come at a variety of times.[3]

Almond and Verba are unclear about what they mean by *post-socialization* experiences. Adults are also socialized often in much more specific and more direct manners.

In summary, political socialization is a lifelong process which may be said to include a complex of sub-processes ". . .by which acceptable, agreed political values, norms, and behavior patterns are transmitted from generation to generation and by which individuals are adjusted to the [political] culture."[4]

Political socialization is a dynamic process. As society changes so do some of the political norms, values and/or behavior. Thus for different times, different constituencies and different political offices there arise requirements for varying skills and personalities. The concern in this paper is not with general socialization or with general political socialization but with the political and professional socialization of a specific segment of the political community, Chicano members of the legal system, especially judges. Quoting Almond in part, Joel B. Grossman pinpoints the political socialization of those who are recruited to become political leaders:

> "All members of societies go through common socialization experiences." But these experiences do not prepare them for the specialized roles that every society must have, including the roles of political leadership. *It is the recruitment function to draw members of a society out of particular subcultures and "induct them into the specialized roles of the political system, train them in the appropriate skills, provide them with political cognitive maps, values, expectations, and affects."* Recruitment thus consists of special role socializations built on the foundation of general socializations.[5]

Gordon S. Black, although referring only to elected politicians, takes a similar view of professional socializaton:

> Professionalization . . . refers to the assimilation of the standards and values prevalent in a given profession. Every profession, including politics, tends to have some set or sets of values that are widely held and which define what it means to be a "professional" within that field. These values are important because they affect the likelihood that the individual will achieve success in his profession. If the values are widely held, those that deviate from them are likely to be sanctioned by their colleagues, and people who fail to maintain the minimal standards of their profession are not likely to obtain professional advancement.[6]

The problem with most studies of ethnic groups and ethnic politicians is most authors accept the premise and the social value that assimilation and integration should be the goal of all ethnic groups as if there existed a mystical "culture" all were attempting to reach. The existence of a core culture in the United States is plausible, though questionable. The acceptance of this premise has led Leo

Grebler, Joan W. Moore, and Ralph C. Guzmán to find a great deal of assimilation of the Chicano occurring as reflected in *The Mexican American People.* They state in their concluding chapter:

> Only a generation ago the most crucial hypothesis about Mexican Americans postulated that they would never assimilate. Scholarly studies tended to support this notion by focusing on people living in urban ghettos or remote rural areas. Yet, we have observed . . . Mexican Americans are showing a growing potential for participation in the larger society.[7]

However, the evidence on which this assumption is made is contradictory. The authors cite as proof of their assertion the fact that forty-eight Chicano state legislators, four Chicano United States Representatives, and one Chicano United States Senator have been elected in the Southwest. Yet the fact also remains quite clear that many of these individuals were elected from districts which have heavy concentrations of Chicano voters. Could it be that the Chicano politician in most districts in which he has won election has required strong ethnic identification rather than assimilative and integrative characteristics?

Such an explanation is in line wtih Edgar Litt's notion that the ethnic politician must be able to bridge the gap between the "dominant culture" and the "ethnic subculture."[8] He makes a distinction between acculturation and assimilation and places total assimilation, i.e., disappearing into the dominant society, outside the range of all but an infinitesimal number of "ethnic individuals." By acculturation Litt means the acquiring of the norms, values and attitudes of the dominant sector of society. He places ethnic members on a continuum ranging from unacculturated to acculturated. For Litt, the successful ethnic politician is one who is acculturated yet maintains sufficient contact with his ethnic group to maintain their loyalty. Thus, the ethnic politician can be neither too ethnic nor too acculturated; he represents a bridge.

In one sense, both Grebler, et. al. and Litt can be criticized for the same reason. Only the terms change. Acculturation and assimilation become substitutes for assimilation and integration. Yet in another sense, Litt is a significant advance over Grebler. Litt at the very least recognizes the limits of assimilation. In addition, he recognizes a positive value in ethnic identification. Lastly, he realizes that not all members of an ethnic subculture can or desire to acquire all the norms, values and attitudes of the dominant sector of society.

There is scant literature on the general socialization of the Chicano. Even then, most of the literature is in either sociology or anthropology. It is only this year that the first book or dissertation was produced on the general political socialization of the Chicano.[9] Nothing exists on the political socialization of formal political leadership, (elected Chicanos). What little general literature exists usually contains long-standing stereotypes or generalizations based on studies of tiny rural communities.[10] Not surprising is that political science among the social sciences has least studied the Chicano, but as a body of literature it has the greatest myths. For example, the late V. O. Key, Jr., concluded ". . .there occurs among the Mexican-American a high incidence of political indifference, ignorance, timidity, and sometimes venality."[11] Edward Banfield's opinion of the Chicano is that "the people who might be expected to want the most from an active city government . . . are apathetic and politically ineffective."[12] Conclusions such as these are interspersed throughout social science literature compelling Octavio Ignacio Romano to suggest that the common social science stereotype of Chicanos is that they are ". . . virtually all alike, resigned to their lot, basically lazy, irrational, lax in their habits, have no initiative, less ambition, and, as such, are criminally prone."[13] The general values of a society largely determine the political values. Precisely how those values are transmitted and inculcated is at best a most difficult task to trace. Because of the great differences in the political history of the three sub-regions of the Southwest, (1) California, (2) Texas, and (3) Arizona, Colorado, and Nuevo México, plus the lack of an adequate body of literature, it is exceedingly difficult to pinpoint the general or political values of Chicanos. For example, Chicanos as Chicanos lost all political power in nearly all areas of California by 1885. Everywhere they were overwhelmed by an Anglo majority. Texas Chicanos on the other hand, have historically been limited to power and influence in parts of South Texas, totally dominating some counties. In 1968 there was one Chicano in the California Legislature and there were ten in the Texas Legislature — all from South Texas. Southern Colorado and Northern Nuevo México have traditionally been Chicano strongholds, particularly the latter. There was not even an Anglo majority in Nuevo México until the Twentieth Century. Chicanos in this state have at one time or another held virtually every position including the Governorship and the Chief Justiceship of the State Supreme Court. Moreover, a Chicano has been elected to the U.S. Senate continuously since 1929 and in the U.S. House of Representatives since 1943.

These regional patterns of political impotence, sub-state regional political potence, and state political potence must have obviously affected the political sub-cultures and the characteristics of Chicano political leaders in each of these regions. Yet the literature does not reflect these critical differences. What are the characteristics of Chicano leadership? Part of the problem in answering this question is that almost everything written about Chicano leadership is primarily or exclusively dealing with informal patterns of community leadership or discussing why Chicanos are powerless.

A succinct summary of two studies will enable us to focus on this problem. Ruth Tuck in *Not With the First* describes Chicano leadership in the city of San Bernardino, California, as essentially conservative, working within the system to accommodate the desires of the Anglo majority, and tending to be drawn from the more "respectable" elements of the Chicano community.[14] Sister Frances Woods describes Chicano leadership in San Antonio, Texas, as generally tending to be between 45 and 55 years of age, traditionally lawyers, although businessmen are becoming increasingly important, and they are generally from respectable backgrounds.[15] Few leaders are young and few come from a lower-class background. In summary, individuals selected as Chicano leaders tend to be conservative, accommodating, middle-aged, middle-class, and members of "respected" families.

The Chicano Judiciary

Virtually nothing is known about Chicano judges. There is yet to be developed a comprehensive and accurate list of Chicano judges, or a consensus reached on what type of judges should be included on the list. An even more fundamental problem emerges — what is a "Chicano" judge?

According to the United States Commission on Civil Rights there are twelve Federal District Court districts in the Southwest sitting 59 Federal District Court judges.[16] Two of the 59 Federal District Court judges have Spanish-surnames, Judge Real of California and Judge Reynaldo De La Garza of Texas. Judge Real is Portuguese, not Chicano.

The same study found that at the state court level there are 961 judges serving in the region. Only 32, or three percent, are Spanish-surnamed. Among the 32 Supreme Court justices in the five states only one, David Chávez, Jr., Chief Justice of the Nuevo México Supreme Court, is Chicano. Eugene D. Luján is a retired Nuevo México Supreme Court Justice. At the intermediate or appellate level there are 183 judges of which five are Chicano; three in Nuevo México, one in Colorado and one in Texas. As of this writing, Roberto L. Armijo of Nuevo México and Carlos Cadenas of Texas have been identified as Chicano appellate court judges. Lastly, there are 26 Chicano judges out of 746 state trial court judges; none in Arizona, seven in California, three in Colorado, fourteen in Nuevo México, and two in Texas. In summary, the Chicano judiciary appear insignificant in all the states except Nuevo México where eighteen Chicano judges constitute 31.58 percent of that state's total judiciary.

Table 1
Table 1
Chicano Judiciary in the State Courts of the Southwest

		Chicano	Other	Total
Arizona[1]		0	61	61
California[2]		7	430	437
Colorado[3]		4	166	170
Nuevo México[4]		18	39	57
Texas[5]		3	233	236
	Total	32	929	961

[1]Includes Supreme, Appellate, and Superior Courts.
[2]Ibid.
[3]Includes Supreme, District, County Courts, and Probate Courts.
[4]Ibid.
[5]Includes Supreme, Civil and Criminal Appellate, and District Courts.

Source: U.S. Commission on Civil Rights, *Mexican Americans and the Administration of Justice in the Southwest* (Washington, 1970) p. 84.

The accuracy of the Commission's study is questionable as is the methodology established to determine which judges would be included. There are supposedly seven Superior Court judges in California since none exist at the intermediate appellate or Supreme Court level. Yet according to the State of California there are only four: Arthur L. Alarcón, Leopoldo Sánchez, Carlos Teran and Francis M. Estudillo.[17] There is no certainty as to whether Mexican-born Jewish judge, Philip Neuman, is included *or ought to be included* among the seven Superior Court judges. On the other hand, there appears to be a glaring omission of California Municipal Court judges including nine who are Chicano. These nine are Benjamin Vega, Carlos Velarde, Antonio Chávez, John A. Arguelles, William Fernández, Alfonso Hermo, James O. Perez, Earl J. Cantú and Elmer Machado. Judge Hermo is included in the list although he is a Spaniard. Excluding Judges Hermo and Neuman there nevertheless still remain eleven Municipal and Superior Court judges. Excluding Judges Velarde, Chávez, and Fernández because they were either appointed or elected to the bench in 1968 and 1969 would still leave a total of eight Municipal and Superior Court judges. It may be that Municipal Court Judges Fernández of Sunnyvale and Elmer Machado of Monterey are Spaniards, Portuguese, Dutch, or Latin Americans but not Chicano. The total number of Municipal and Superior Court judges is now seven but anyone reading this account would surely suggest that the evidence was being stretched to fit the "facts."

It is rather surprising to find that Municipal Court judges have not been included in the total number of California judges. It would appear they were considered equivalent to justices of the peace which were also excluded. Yet what justification is there to include probate courts in Nuevo México but exclude municipal courts in Arizona, California, and Texas? The problem of defining what is meant by a "Chicano" judge arises most acutely in California. A Chicano is defined, for the purpose of this paper, to be an individual of Mexican descent who does not acknowledge another country or ethnic group as his primary bloodline. Thus, Judge Neuman is not a Chicano, although he is Mexican-born, because he considers himself to be Jewish. Likewise, Federal Judge Real and Municipal Court Judge Hermo are not Chicanos because they consider themselves Portuguese and Spaniards respectively.

The same pattern of questionable accuracy is also evident in Texas and Nuevo México. According to the U.S. Commission on Civil Rights there are only three Chicano judges in Texas. Research, contrary to the U.S. Commission on Civil Rights, indicates that there are seven Chicano judges in the State.[18] Municipal Court Judge Mike M. Machado, District Court Judges R. F. Luna, E. D. Salinas, Fidencio M. Guerra, George Rodríguez, and John G. Benavides. Judge Carlos Cadena is an appellate court justice. In addition, the only Chicano Federal District Court Judge in the nation is Judge De La Garza of Corpus Cristi, Texas.

The Commission's study also indicates no Chicano judges in Arizona. There are at least two Chicano Municipal Court judges in the State, Judge Cota-Robles and former Judge Castro, the latter was the Democratic Party candidate for governor in 1970.

The least data available was on the Chicano judiciary of Nuevo México. The Commission lists one Supreme Court justice, three appellate court justices, and fourteen district court judges in the state. Research identified only eight judges. They include Chief Justice David Chávez, Jr., Retired Supreme Court Justice Eugene D. Luján, Appellate Court Justice Roberto L. Armijo, and District Court Judges Joe Angel, Santiago E. Campos, Paul F. Larrazolo, J. V. Gallegos, and Samuel Z. Montoya. Unlike the Study's undercounting of Chicano judges in the other States, in the case of Nuevo México it overcounted.

There are significant differences among Chicano judges from the various states. (See Table 2 and 3). Most California judges are Republican as a result of Governor Ronald Reagan's deliberate campagin to woo Chicano leaders into the Republican Party. Most of these appointments took place in 1968 and 1969. Nothing is known about the political affiliation of judges in other states. A guess would be that most but not all Nuevo México judges are Democrats representing the shift from the Republican to Democratic Party that took place among

Chicanos during the Depression. It is highly probable that all Chicano judges are Democrats in Texas since the state is not known to have a history of important Republican participation.

Table 2

Age, Political Affiliation and Level of Chicano Judges In California, Nuevo México and Texas

	California	Nuevo México	Texas
Average Age (in years)	48.27 years	61.25	59.6
Party of Majority of Chicano Judges	Republican	Democratic	Democratic
Level of Judiciary	4 Superior 7 Municipal Court	2 Supreme Court 1 Appellate Court 5 District Court	1 Federal District Court 1 Appellate Court 5 District Court 1 Municipal Court

Table 3

Schooling of Chicano Judiciary

	California		Nuevo México		Texas	
Schooling of Judges	Public	Private	Public	Private	Public	Private
Law School	2	9	1	7	3	2
Undergraduate	4	6	6	1	3	2
Night Law School		3		none		1
Favorite Law School	University of So. California		Georgetown University		University of Texas	

Another difference is the degree of penetration throughout the state judiciaries by Chicano judges. It is immediately clear that in Nuevo México where Chicanos have historically played an important political role, that Chicanos are amply distributed throughout the entire judiciary. In Texas, where Chicanos have always been a regional power, they appear, albeit in small numbers, at all but the State

Supreme Court level. In California, where Chicanos have been politically insignificant for the last hundred years, Chicano judges are found only at the bottom levels of the judiciary and then only recently.

There are geographical differences in the distribution of judges within each state. In California, twelve of the fourteen Chicano judges are from Southern California, nine from Los Angeles County, and one each from San Diego County, Orange County and Riverside County. There is also a geographical concentration of Chicano judges in South Texas with District Court Judge John G. Benavides of Bexar County (San Antonio), Texas, representing the Northernmost district court judgeship held by a Chicano in the state. Nuevo México judges are represented throughout the state but there are more in the northern part where the majority of the Chicano population is located than in the southern portion of the state.

In addition, there are significant differences in the average ages of the various Chicano state judiciaries. In California, where there were no Chicanos on the bench until 1957 when Governor Brown appointed Carlos M. Teran to the Los Angeles County Municipal Court, the average age of Chicano judges is 48.27 years. In Nuevo México and Texas, where Chicanos have always been on the bench, the average is 61.25 and 59.6 years respectively.

The great majority of judges are strongly tied to their districts by birth, residence, training and experience. The same is generally true for Chicano state judges. With the exception of a few California judges, all the judges were born and raised in the state where they practiced law and in which they became members of the judiciary.

Finally, there are significant differences in the patterns of undergraduate and law school education. Each of the three states has its own distinct pattern, its own Chicano elite schools one might say. California judges favor the University of Southern California and Southwestern University Law Schools, Nuevo México judges favor Georgetown University and the University of New Mexico Law Schools, and Texas judges split between the University of Texas Law School and St. Mary's University Law School (San Antonio, Texas). Among California judges, three had attended strictly night law schools, one might have attended a night law school in Texas but none is known to have attended one in Nuevo México.

There is another difference in the educational patterns among the various states. One study of lower Federal court appointments during the Eisenhower and Kennedy administrations indicated that approximately a third of the judges had attended public law schools and the rest had attended private law schools.[19] Nuevo México particularly stands out in this regard since only one out of every eight judges is a graduate of a public law school. In Texas, on the other hand, the majority of judges attended state supported law schools. Nearly all the Chicano judges have attended undergraduate colleges and universities in their home states.

The importance of schooling in the socialization of the Chicano judiciary cannot be underestimated. The function of undergraduate education is to selectively draw out Chicanos and introduce "them into the specialized roles of the political system, train them in the appropriate skills, provide them with political cognitive maps, values, expectations and affects."[20] The socialization function of the law school is a little more specific. Kenneth Vines writes:

> While there is a common core of values and practices in legal training wherever it is taught in the United States, state and regional law schools and particularly state universities have strong ties with the state political system. Lawyers who practice in one state meet only the political values of that state, contact only local politicians, and gain practice only in the political process of that state. On the other hand, lawyers who have gone to law school outside the state or region of their association, receive training in other political symbols and meet a different set of political values.[21]

In California and Texas, Chicano judges attended law schools within their respective states whether public or private law schools. In Nuevo México there are no private law schools. One might ask, then, what particular value lies in attending Georgetown University Law School as opposed to the University of Texas, St. Mary's University or the University of Colorado? The chief value is, in all probability, a political value. By attending Georgetown University they develop a perspective on national political cognitive maps, values, expectations and affects.[22]

In summary, Chicano state judges are born and raised in the state where they are judges. Local judges commonly sit in localities where they were born. They nearly all attended undergraduate colleges and universities in their home state and most attended law schools in their state except for Nuevo México judges.

The Chicano Legal Profession of Nuevo México

There were approximately 650 Chicano attorneys in the Southwest in 1968.[23] In order to study more intensely the socialization of the judiciary let us focus attention on the legal profession of one state. The reasons for choosing Nuevo México are: (1) there is a relatively small legal profession; (2) the research material is relatively readily available; (3) there is a source available for verifying some of the material; (4) the material available is presented in the same identicial format in all Southwestern states; (5) Chicano judges are found at every level within the State's judiciary; (6) Chicanos are found throughout the legal profession, especially important in terms of future judges; they are found among district attorneys and assistant district attorneys in reasonable numbers; and (7) Chicanos are found throughout all levels of law enforcement agencies. For example, the Chief of the State Police and the Chief of Police of Santa Fe are both Chicanos. Primary focus is on the indices of socialization, e.g., education, age, family background, and political and/or judicial background. Only brief mention will be made of religion, sex, and ethnicity.

Eighty-two Chicano attorneys were identified in the *Martindale-Hubbell Law Directory* for the years 1969-1970.[24] Twenty were identified as being in public practice.[25] Public practice is here defined to include any attorney on public payroll such as judges, district attorneys, assistant district attorneys, United States Attorneys, United States Commissioners, members of the State Legislature, and any attorney employed by an Executive Branch public agency. The term "public attorney" will henceforth be used interchangeable with "attorney in public practice." Another sixty-two attorneys were found to be engaged in private practice, i.e., attorneys not on a public payroll.

Education is an important indicator of socialization. The schooling pattern of the Chicano bar in Nuevo México indicates preference is given to private law schools over public, state-supported law schools, private Catholic law schools over non-Catholic private law schools, and Georgetown University Law School over other Catholic Law Schools. (see Tables 4, 7, and 10). Georgetown ranks high among public as opposed to private attorneys. An undergraduate education in a Nuevo México university is also important. A deviation from this pattern since 1949 is that the University of New Mexico law school graduates are becoming an increasingly large factor among private attorneys.

There are sixty-two known Chicano attorneys engaged in private practice in Nuevo México. Twenty-six graduated from public law schools, twenty from the University of New Mexico. Thirty-three graduated from private law schools; nineteen from Catholic law schools and of these, thirteen graduated from Georgetown

Chicano attorneys have clearly favored private law schools. (See Table 5). Of the twenty-two Chicano attorneys (26.82 percent of all attorneys) who have graduated from Georgetown University, nine (47.35 percent) are attorneys engaged in public law. One is led to the conclusion that Georgetown University plays an exceptionally important role for those who desire to go into public practice, particularly for those who may desire to become judges or prosecutors; five of twelve judges and prosecutors are Georgetown graduates. In addition, thir-

Table 4

Schooling of Chicano Attorneys by Private and Public Practice (N=82)

	Public Law School			Private Law School			Unknown
	Total	In-State	Out-of-State	Total	Catholic	Non-Catholic	
Private Practice	26	20	6	33	19	14	3
Public Practice	4	3	1	15	10	5	1
Total	30			48			4

teen (15.8 percent) of all private attorneys have attended Georgetown. Since a high percentage of Chicano attorneys engage in public practice it appears likely that Georgetown alumni in private practice will continue to exert considerable influence in the public sector.

Table 5
Private Law School Graduates

Law School From Which Graduated	Attorneys Public	Private	Total
Georgetown University	9	13	22
University of Denver	2	3	5
George Washington University	2	1	3
Harvard University	1	1	2
St. Louis University	1	1	2
Notre Dame University		2	2
Creighton University		2	2
Other*	1	9	10

*One each for DePaul University, Stanford University, Northwestern University, University of Chicago, Tulane University, American University, Columbia University, Vanderbilt University, Washington and Lee University, and Kent College of Law (Chicago).

Thirty-four of the private attorneys as well as twelve of the twenty public attorneys went to school as undergraduates in Nuevo México. Twelve attended private undergraduate and law schools. Only three of those who attended public law school also attended private undergraduate schools. Furthermore, seventeen went to Nuevo México universities then matriculated at private law schools.

In the late 1940's several opportunities for legal education were opened. Forty-seven of the sixty-two attorneys in private practice were admitted to the bar in 1949 and after. Moreover, none were admitted to the bar in 1945, 1946, 1947, and 1948 leading to the implication that both World War II and the G.I. Bill played an important role in expanding opportunity for the legal education of Chicanos. For example, twenty-three Chicanos were admitted to the bar during the first ten years immediately after World War II and only twenty-four have been admitted in the last fifteen years. Another reason for an expanded opportunity to obtain a legal education was that the University of New Mexico opened its Law School in 1946. Among the public law schools, the University of New Mexico is far and away the dominant choice. Three of the public attorneys are graduates of the University of New Mexico Law School as are twenty of those in private practice.

Undergraduate education is another important indicant of socialization. It provides an opportunity for establishing local contacts as well as introducing the individual to state and national political and legal norms and values. Information is available on the undergraduate education of fifty-five private attorneys and nineteen public attorneys. For both groups an undergraduate education at a Nuevo México university appears to be important. Thirty-four private attorneys as well as 12 public attorneys are graduates of Nuevo México universities. Twelve attended both private undergraduate and law schools while only three attended private undergraduate and public law schools. Thus, the dominant pattern appears to be education in a Nuevo México university and a private law school, particularly one in the Washington, D.C. area. In recent years a new trend from graduates of Nuevo México undergraduate and law schools has modified this pattern. Surprisingly while Chicano Nuevo México attorneys sought undergraduate and law school educations throughout the Midwest, Southwest, and East, only two attended undergraduate schools in California and none in neighboring Texas and only one graduated from a California Law School and none from one in Texas. There is no record of any Nuevo México Chicano now practicing ever having graduated from Hastings College of Law, Boalt Hall, U.C.L.A. Law School, The University of Southern California Law School, Loyola University of Los Angeles Law School or Southwestern University (all in California) nor from the University of Texas or St. Mary's University. Furthermore, Chicanos are extremely selective of a law school in any given area. For example, twenty-seven Chicanos graduated from four different law schools in the Washington, D.C. area but none graduated from Catholic University. Why Georgetown and not Catholic University?

Age is a second indicator of socialization. There is a six year difference in average age between private and public attorneys, with the latter, the older group. (See Table 6). This is accounted for by the fact that judges and district attorneys are usually older members of the bar. (See Table 7). In Nuevo México, this factor is not overcome by the young age of assistant district attorneys. Among the five known assistant district attorneys, only Benny Flores is under fifty years of age.

Table 6
Average Age of Attorneys by Private
and Public Practice

	Average Age	(N)
all attorneys	49.50 years	82
all private attorneys	48.01 years	62
all public attorneys	54.25 years	20

Table 7
Average Age of Private
Law School Graduates, Judges and District Attorneys

Private Law Schools	Average Age	N
Georgetown University	52.77	9
Other Private Law Schools	55.66	6
Total all Private Law Schools	54.94	15
Judges*		
With Luján†	65.8	5
District Attorneys**	53.25	8
Judges* and District Attorneys**	58.07	13

*Although not listed as judges by *Martindale-Hubbell*, David Chávez, Jr. was Chief Justice of the New Mexico Supreme Court, Roberto L. Armijo was a justice on an appellate Court, and Santiago E. Campos was a District Court Judge.

**Not included is Alfonso G. Sánchez who unsuccessfully prosecuted Reies López Tijerina. Mr. Sánchez is no longer in public office.

†Eugene D. Luján is listed as a public attorney. Actually he is a retired Supreme Court Justice.

Chicano judges have the oldest average age of any group. (See Table 8). The next group in age are the district attorneys and assistant district attorneys whose average age of 53.25 years is slightly below the average age for public attorneys.

Table 8
Comparison of the Average Age of Judges and Other
Public Attorneys

Average Age of:	Average Age	N
Judges		
Including Luján†	65.8	5
Without Luján	61.0	4
All Eight**	62.37	8
District Attorneys*	53.25	8
University of New Mexico Law		
School Graduates	44.0	3
All public law school graduates	52.0	4
Georgetown Law School graduates	52.77	9

*Not included is Alfonso G. Sánchez who unsuccessfully prosecuted Reies Tijerina. Mr. Sánchez is no longer in public office.

**Although not listed as judges by *Martindale-Hubbell*, David Chávez, Jr. was Chief Justice of the New México Supreme Court, Roberto L. Armijo was a justice on an appellate Court, and Santiago E. Campos was a District Court judge.

†Eugene D. Luján is listed as a public attorney. Actually he is a retired Supreme Court Justice.

The graduates of the University of New Mexico Law School were the youngest group by ten years. (See Table 8 and 9). This may be because the University of New México did not have a law school until after World War II. Georgetown graduates closely parallel in age *all* public attorneys since Georgetown graduates account for nearly fifty percent of all public attorneys. (See Table 9). One judge, district attorney, assistant district attorney, and U.S. Attorney are graduates of the University of New México Law School.

Table 9
Average Age of
University of New Mexico Law School Graduates

	Age	N
Attorneys in Private Practice	42.7	20
Attorneys in Public Practice	44.0	3

Table 10
Average Age of
Georgetown University Law School Graduates

	Age	N
Attorneys in Private Practice	50.38 years	13
Attorneys in Public Practice	55.0 years	9
All in Public and Private Practice	52.26 years	22

Finally, it should be noted that there is a significant difference in age between all private attorneys and all public attorneys of six years and between private attorneys and judges of thirteen to seventeen years. There is also a significant difference between the average age of all attorneys, public and private, and all judges of twelve to sixteen years.[26] When one compares public and private attorneys it is immediately clear that attorneys in private practice are much younger than their counterparts in public practice. (See Tables 11 and 12).

There are twenty graduates from the University of New Mexico Law School and twenty who have graduated from private law schools, except Georgetown, and there is a difference of eight years in the average age between these two groups. The much younger age of attorneys who have graduated from the University of New Mexico readily points out that the University of New Mexico may significantly alter the degree to which Chicanos enjoy the benefits of counsel in the future. It may also eventually lead to a break in the pattern of elite

273

domination by those who could afford to go to school out of state. However, one must be cautious before asserting major changes in the social structure. The fact that Georgetown Law School graduates average fifty years of age would seem to indicate that this group still has an advantage for at least the next decade in securing positions in the public sector of law practice. Another surprise is that the average age of out-of-state public law school graduates is the highest among all the groups.

Table 11
Average Age of
Private Law School Graduates

	Average Age	N
Private Practice - all	50.15	33
Georgetown University	50.38	13
Other Private Law Schools	50.0	20
Public Practice - all	54.94	15
Georgetown University	52.77	9
Other Private Law Schools	55.66	6
Catholic Law Schools		
Public Practice	56.20	10
Private Practice	50.10	19
all attorneys	55.65	29
University of Denver		
Public and Private Practice	45.4	5
George Washington University — all attorneys	60.33	3

Table 12
Age Of
Private Practice Attorneys

	Average Age	N
All attorneys	49.50	82
All Private Attorneys	48.01	62
All Private Attorneys who graduated		
from out-of-State Public Law Schools	52.83	6
Georgetown Law School Grads. —		
Private Practice	50.38	13
Non-Georgetown Private Law School		
Graduates	50.0	20
Private Attorneys who graduated from		
Univ. of New Mexico Law School	42.7	20
Private Attorneys who graduated from		
State Schools in- and out-of-state	45.0	26

There is another method by which age and education can be analyzed. Attorneys are divided according to generation rather than solely by average age. Four generational groupings are made here: (1) The Depression generation (born 1912 and earlier); (2) The World War II generation (born 1913-1922); (3) The "Forties" generation (born 1923-1932); and (4) The Young Generation (born (1933 - present).

The oldest generation includes those attorneys sixty years of age and older. (See Table 13). It could easily be named the Depression Generation. Ten of these twenty individuals passed the bar during the Depression years 1930-1941. It is highly improbable any of them entered undergraduate school any later than 1932. These individuals most likely came from families of some financial means since only three matriculated at public law schools. Even public law schools, however, cost a great deal of money.

For this generation the University of New Mexico is the most popular undergraduate school and Georgetown University is the most popular law school. Of ten attorneys who studied at Nuevo México undergraduate schools, seven graduated from the University of New Mexico. Undergraduate information is known on nine of thirteen private attorneys. Seven of the nine graduated from Nuevo México universities, including five from the University of New Mexico. Three of the six public attorneys also received their undergraduate education at Nuevo México universities and their legal education at Georgetown.

A criticism of this specific generational division is that there are really two generations listed. There are ten attorneys 60 to 69 years of age and there are another ten attorneys 70 years of age or older. In the older grouping no two individuals attended the same law school. In addition, there is no law school information on three individuals indicating that perhaps there existed for the older groups a different pattern for obtaining a legal education. On the other hand, some of these facts may be explained in terms of age. In the oldest groups many classmates may have died already. However, the only satisfactory explanation is that all divisions are somewhat arbitrary. The only justification for the present division is that grouping individuals 60 years of age and over is quite common and an easy division with which to work.

Table 13

Depression Generation
(born 1912 and earlier)

Name	Age 1973	Year Passed Bar	Age At Time Passed Bar	Undergraduate School	Law School Attended
1. Private Attorneys					
M. A. Otero, Jr.	80	1915	23	No information	Washington & Lee University
Manuel A. Sánchez	78	1925	31	N. Mexico Institute of Mining & Technology	No information
Charles T. Flota	76	1919	25	Not listed	Kent College of Law
Gilberto Espinosa	75	1921	24	University of New Mexico	No information
David Chávez, Jr.	74	1922	24	University of New Mexico	Georgetown University
Louis C. Luján	72	1937*	37	Notre Dame University	Notre Dame University
Jośe E. Armijo	71	1928	27	University of Michigan	University of Michigan
Hilario Rubio	71	1929	28	No information	No information
Isidore Gallegos	65	1932*	25	N. Mexico Highland Univ.	St. Louis University
Benjamín Osuna	64	1934**	26	University of New Mexico	University of Michigan
Joe L. Martínez	63	1943**	32	University of New Mexico	Georgetown University
Marcelino P. Gutiérrez	60	1934*	22†	No information	George Washington University
Maurice Sánchez	60	1939*	27	University of New Mexico	Northwestern University
2. Public Attorneys					
Eugene D. Luján	85	1925	38	No information	George Washington University
John B. Sánchez	76	1934*	38	Nebraska Central College	University of Colorado
J. V. Gallego	68	1930*	25	St. Louis University	St. Louis University
Filo Sedillo	64	1933*	25	St. Louis University	No information
E. E. Chávez	62	1944**	34	Western N. Mexico Univ.	George University
Paul F. Larrazolo	62	1937*	27	University of New Mexico	Georgetown University
Tibo Chávez	60	1939*	27	University of New Mexico	Georgetown University

*Passed bar during Depression years 1930-1941.
**Passed bar during World War II.
†Youngest Chicano to ever pass bar in Nuevo México

The next generation of attorneys was born in time to have received both undergraduate and law degrees before World War II, but the overwhelming number appear to have postponed their legal schooling until after World War II. (See Table 14). This generation is the oldest of the four generations at the time it passed the bar. (See Table 17). One would have expected the Depression to have had a greater effect on schooling than World War II. Such is not the case. Tables 12 and 13 reveal that thirteen Chicanos passed the bar between 1930 and 1941 but only three passed the bar between 1942 and 1945. Only one Chicano from this generation passed the bar during World War II and only three others passed the bar immediately prior to World War II.

It is within this generation that the popularity of Georgetown University Law School reaches its highpoint. Eight, (44.4 percent), of the total number of Georgetown graduates, including 60 percent of those in public practice, attended Georgetown during this period. In the post-war group one also finds the first graduates of the University of New Mexico Law School. Only one, Patricio Sánchez, is in public practice.

The generation of those in their forties, having to face neither a great Depression nor a great war, produced the largest number of attorneys. (See Table 15). There is nothing which particularly stands out about this group. They were an average two years younger than the previous generation at the time they passed the bar. Ten are graduates of the University of New Mexico Law School, demonstrating that school's increasing influence in providing a legal education for Chicanos. Another six received law degrees from Georgetown.

Table 14

World War II Generation
(born 1913-1922)

Name	Age 1973	Year Passed Bar	Age At Time Passed Bar	Undergraduate School	Law School
1. *Private Attorneys*					
Albert T. Gonzáles	59	1940	27	Western N. Mexico University	Georgetown University
Lorenzo A. Chávez	58	1944**	30	University of N. Mexico	Georgetown University
Richard C. Civerolo	55	1950†	33	University of N. Mexico	University of N. Mexico
B. C. Hernández	55	1949†	32	University of N. Mexico	De Paul University
Reuben E. Nieves	54	1949†	31	Unlisted	University of Oklahoma
Pedro R. Melendez	52	1950†	30	Indiana University	Indiana University
Arturo G. Ortega	52	1951†	31	Georgetown	Georgetown University
Claude S. Sena	52	1951†	31	University of N. Mexico	Georgetown University
Edward J. Apodaca	51	1950†	30	University of N. Mexico	Georgetown University
Ruben Rodriguez	51	1952†	31	University of N. Mexico	University of N. Mexico
Albert A. Anella	50	1956†	36	Syracuse University	University of N. Mexico
Robert J. Armijo	50	1949†	27	N. Mexico Highland Univ.	Vanderbilt University
Avelino V. Gutiérrez	50	1950†	28	University of N. Mexico	University of N. Mexico
2. *Public Attorneys*					
Joe Angel	57	1958	43	N. Mexico Highland Univ.	University of Denver
Joseph M. Montoya	57	1939*	24	Regis College	Georgetown University
Samuel Z. Montoya	56	1941*	25	University of N. Mexico	Georgetown University
Patricio S. Sánchez	53	1954†	35	N. Mexico State University	University of N. Mexico
Lotario D. Ortega	50	1952†	30	Georgetown University	Georgetown University

*Passed bar during Depression years 1930-1941.
**Passed bar during World War II.
†Probably participated in World War II.

Table 15
The "Forties" Generation
(born 1923-1932)

Name	Age 1973	Year Passed Bar	Age At Time Passed Bar	Undergraduate School	Law School Attended
1. Private Attorneys					
Ramón López	49	1951	28	University of N. Mexico	University of New Mexico
Daniel Sosa, Jr.	49	1951	28	N. Mexico State University	University of New Mexico
Manuel García, Jr.	48	1954	30	University of N. Mexico	University of New Mexico
Tito N. Quintana	48	1957	33	University of N. Mexico	University of Denver
Matías L. Chacón	47	1951	26	Indiana University	University of New Mexico
Anthony F. Avallone	46	1956	30	Hamilton College	Columbia University
Santiago E. Campos	46	1953	28	University of N. Mexico	University of New Mexico
Eliu E. Romero	46	1955	29	University of N. Mexico	University of Denver
M. L. Armijo, Jr.	45	1950	23	University of Wisconsin	University of Wisconsin
A. T. Montoya	45	1954	27	Regis College	Georgetown University
Albert Rivera	45	1954	27	American University	Georgetown University
Matías A. Zamora	45	1956	26	University of N. Mexico	Georgetown University
Leon J. García	44	1954	26	Creighton University	Creighton University
Reginald J. García	44	1957	29	University of Loyola of New Orleans	University of New Mexico
Alfonso G. Sánchez	44	1957	29	No information	University of New Mexico
Lalo Garza	43	1956	27	University of N. Mexico	University of New Mexico
Walter K. Martínez	42	1955	25	University of N. Mexico	University of New Mexico
Roquier E. Sánchez	41	1960	29	Loyola University of Los Angeles	Georgetown University
Lorenzo E. Tapia	41	1962	31	N. Mexico Highlands University	American University
2. Public Attorneys					
Donald A. Martínez	49	1953	30	N. Mexico Highlands University	Georgetown University
Edison C. Serna	49	1950	27	N. Mexico State University	Tulane University
John J. Sánchez	47	1959	34	University of N. Mexico	Georgetown University
Charlie W. Chávez	44	1953	25	No information	University of New Mexico

There are twenty-one attorneys in the Youth Generation. (See Table 16). During the Youth generation there was a sharp decline in Georgetown Law School graduates. Only three, or half the previous Generation total and only 37.5 percent of the World War II Generation total, graduated from Georgetown. However, one must be cautious in making generalizations. Two of the Georgetown graduates belong to elite families. There is a slight decline in University of New Mexico Law School graduates from a high of ten to eight. This may be a result of what appears to be matriculation at a greater variety of law schools. Perhaps an unconscious search for a new elite school is underway. On the other hand, it may simply be a consequence of the Chicano Movement's opening up new legal educational opportunities. More attorneys than in any previous generation received both undergraduate and law degrees at the University of New Mexico. Generally, undergraduate schooling has been at one of the State universities but there has not been such a heavy concentration at the University of New Mexico.

Table 16

The Young Generation
(born 1933-present)

Name	Age 1973	Year Passed Bar	Age at Time Passed Bar	Undergraduate School	Law School Attended
1. *Private Attorneys*					
Frank Bachicha, Jr.	39	1963	30	University of N. Mexico	University of Denver
Felix Briones, Jr.	39	1958	25	University of N. Mexico	University of N. Mexico
Stephen Carnas	38	1960	26	Harvard University	Harvard University
J. E. Gallegos	37	1961	26	University of N. Mexico	University of N. Mexico
Theodore R. Montoya	37	1961	26	Georgetown University	Georgetown University
Joseph F. Baca	36	1965	29	University of N. Mexico	George Washington Univ.
James E. Casados	35	1965	28	University of N. Mexico	University of N. Mexico
Peter G. Prima	34	1967	29	Brigham Young University	University of Chicago
David R. Sierra	34	1964	26	Drake University	University of N. Mexico
R. S. Apodaca	33	1964	25	N. Mexico State University	Georgetown
Owen M. López	31	1968	27	Stanford University	Notre Dame University
Nicolas R. Pica	31	1969	28	University of N. Mexico	University of N. Mexico
Raymond G. Sánchez	31	1968	27	University of N. Mexico	University of N. Mexico
Carlos B. Sedillo	31	1964	23	University of Arizona	University of Arizona
George E. Pérez	30	1967	25	Creighton University	Creighton University
John P. Salazar	29	1968	27	University of N. Mexico	Northwestern University
Patrick S. Vellella	29	1968	25	University of N. Mexico	University of N. Mexico
2. *Public Attorneys*					
Victor R. Ortega	39	1959	26	Harvard University	Harvard University
Frank R. Martinez	37	1967	32	University of N. Mexico	University of N. Mexico
Ernest E. Valdez	37	1963	28	University of N. Mexico	University of Denver
Benny E. Flores	32	1968	28	N. Mexico Highlands University	Georgetown University

Table 17 summarizes the average age trend by generation at the time they passed the bar. Except for the World War II generation, the average age of those who pass the bar keeps getting younger. This may be due largely to schooling trends. It may also be related to the absence of a national crisis which diverts individuals away from a legal training. The average age of public attorneys is consistently older than that for private attorneys. Part of the explanation may be that in every generation there are one or two individuals who take up the law as a second profession and end up in public practice. The average age of judges is not significantly different from that of public attorneys.

Table 17
Average Age of Attorneys at Time Passed Bar by Generation

Generation	All Attorneys	N	Public	N	Private	N
60 yrs. and Over	28.25	20	30.57	7	27.0	13
50-59 yrs.	30.77	18	31.4	5	30.53	13
40-49 yrs.	28.30	23	29.25	4	28.21	19
39 yrs. and Under	26.85	21	28.50	4	26.47	17

Another important factor in the socialization processes is family background. Every major study on the social background of influential groups in society traces family ties to elite families. The case is no different in Nuevo México. (See Table 18). Information on family background indicates that at least forty-six attorneys (56 percent) are members of elite families.[27] The data also reveals that six of the eight known judges are members of elite families with long histories of political and judicial backgrounds. For example, Judges Luján, Montoya, Armijo, Gallegos, Chávez and Larrazolo have some combination of governors, state, and national legislators in their family backgrounds. Judges Montoya, Armijo and Chávez are known to come from family backgrounds which include members of the judiciary. All six are members of identified elite families which go back at least into the Eighteenth Century. These are not simply old families but elite families who participated in governing Colonial, Mexican, and U.S. Nuevo México. Thus, the bar is an elite profession and the judiciary represents the elite among the elite.

Table 18

Elite Family Attorneys

Name	Position	Law School
Eugene D. Luján	Retired Nuevo México Supreme Court Chief Justice	George Washington U.
Louis C. Luján	Private Attorney	Notre Dame U.
Manuel Luján, Jr.	U.S. Representative; Father, Mayor of Santa Fe	
Joseph M. Montoya	U.S. Senator	Georgetown
Samuel Z. Montoya	Associate Justice, Nuevo México Supreme Court	Georgetown
A. T. Montoya	Private Attorney; Member, State Senate	Georgetown
Theodore R. Montoya	Private Attorney	Georgetown
[Theodosious] Nestor Montoya	U.S. Representative (1921-1923); Member, State Constitutional Convention; Member, Territorial Legislature for 20 years; Regent, University of N. México	
Don Diego de Montoya	1st ranking Alcalde (Judge of first instance) of Santa Fe c. 1810	
Miguel A. Otero, Jr.	Private Attorney; Served in State House of Representatives	Washington & Lee U.
Don Miguel Otero II	Territorial Governor; Treasurer	Either in St. Louis Mo. or Washington, D.C.
Don Miguel A. Otero	Attorney; Secretary of Nuevo México; Delegate to U.S. Congress	Either in St. Louis, Mo. or Washington, D.C.
Don Marian Sabino Otero	Member, Territorial Leg.; Delegate, U.S. Congress	Either in St. Louis, Mo. or Washington, D.C.
Don Antonio José Otero	Judge, Territorial Supreme Court	
Don Vincent Otero	Alcalde; family goes back to 1776	
B. C. Hernández	Judge, Court of Appeals	De Paul University
Benigno C. Hernández	U.S. Representative (1915-1921)	
Gilberto Espinosa	Private Attorney; Brother-in-law of late Sen. Dennis Chávez; author of a number of books including *A History of New México*. Son may be taking bar exams.	No information

Table 18 (cont.)

Name	Position	Law School
Tobia Espinosa	M.D.; brother of Gilberto: served two terms in State Senate	
Aurelio Macedonio Espinosa	Brother of Gilberto; Chairman, Dept. of Romance Languages, 1932-1947, Stanford University. Aurelio's son teaching at Stanford University	
Capt. Marcelo Espinosa	Original settler, 1598	
Carmen Espinosa	Sister of Gilberto, educator and author	
José E. Armijo	Private Attorney	U. of Michigan
M. L. Armijo, Jr.	Private Attorney	U. of Michigan
Robert L. Armijo	Appellate Court Justice	Vanderbilt U.
Manuel Armijo	Mexican Governor	
Joseph F. Baca	Private Attorney	George Washington U.
Donald A. Martínez	District Attorney for San Miguel, Guadalupe and Mora counties; Democratic political boss of same three counties; defended Reies López Tijerina for a time.	Georgetown U.
José A. Baca IV	Major, U.S. Air Force	
José A. Baca II	Rancher; Banker; Governor — died in office; wife — Secretary of State	
Don Luis María de Baca*	Recipient of Vegas Grande Land Grant	
*Not to be confused with Don Filadelfo Baca family of Socorro County.		
R. S. Apodaca	Private Attorney	Georgetown U.
Edward J. Apodaca	Private Attorney	Georgetown U.
Lorenzo A. Chávez*	Private Attorney	Georgetown U. undergraduate at U. of N. México
Tibo Chávez	State Senator; co-author with G. Espinosa of *A History of New Mexico*	Georgetown U. undergraduate at U. of N. Mexico
E. E. Chávez	Assist. District Attorney	Georgetown U. undergraduate at Western N. México
David Chávez, Jr.	Chief Justice, Nuevo México Supreme Court; brother of Late U.S. Senator Dennis Chávez; ran for governor same year Dennis first ran for U.S. Senate	Georgetown U. undergraduate at U. of N. México
Charlie W. Chávez	Attorney Veteran's Administration	U. of N. México

288

Table 18 (cont.)

Name	Position	Law School
*The name Chávez is common in Nuevo México. Basically there are two consanguine family lines. The oldest family line is that founded in 1692 by Don Fernando Durán de Cháves, Alcalde of Bernalillo and San Felipe. This family line has primarily a military background. Don Bernardino Durán de Cháves was a General in the Spanish Army and Don Manuel Antonio de Cháves was a Colonel in the Mexican Army and a Lieutenant Colonel in the New México Volunteers during the U.S. Civil War. The exception in this family line is Don Amado de Cháves who was Speaker of the Territorial Assembly. The other Cháves family line was founded in 1780 by don Francisco Xavier Cháves. This family line includes three Mexican governors and one Delegate to the U.S. Congress who had previously been a member of the Territorial Legislature. While distinct consanguine family lines, these family are nevertheless related, more so in the contemporary period.		
Lotario D. Ortega	Attorney, Bureau of Indian Affairs	Georgetown U.
Victor R. Ortega	U.S. Attorney; Great Grandfather or Grandfather served in State Senate in 1899; brother, Bob Ortega, president or manager of a Nuevo México bank and serves on a Selective Service Board.	Harvard University
Arturo G. Ortega	Private Attorney; Member, State House of Representatives; Regent, U. of Nuevo México.	Georgetown U.
J. E. Gallegos	Private Attorney; 1972 Democratic candidate for U.S. Representative. He challenged Rep. Manuel Luján Jr.	U. of N. México
J. V. Gallegos	District Court Judge; may have served in State House of Representatives	St. Louis U.
Isidore F. Gallegos	Private Attorney; may be son of J. V. Gallegos. There is a 25 yr. difference in age.	St. Louis U.
George Pérez	Private Attorney; Member, State House of Representatives; father was coach at Santa Fe High School; this is an 18th Century elite family which declined in power and status toward the end of the 19th century.	Creighton U.
Paul F. Larrazolo	District Court Judge	
A. O. Larrazolo	Gov.; U.S. Senator; unpopular governor because he raised the "race" issue, i.e., spoke of the plight of and injustices toward the Hispanos.	Georgetown U.

Table 18 (cont.)

Name	Position	Law School
Albert González	Private Attorney; blind, one of Reies López Tijerina's first attorneys but withdrew; served in 16th Nuevo México Legislature; U.S. Senator Montoya (also Georgetown) was Best Man at González' wedding; Son Albert González, Jr., was on Sen. Montoya's Washington staff. Earned law degree at Georgetown while in Washington.	Georgetown U.
Manuel García, Jr.*	Private Attorney; father may have served in State House of Representatives.	U. of New México
Reginald J. García	Private Attorney	U. of New México
León García, Jr.	Private Attorney	Creighton U.
*García is a common Spanish-surname in Nuevo México. In 1810 there is a historical reference to Don Miguel García and to don José García de la Mora as being included in a committee which was composed of "the alcaldes and other honorable persons who enjoyed the confidence of the public."		
Owen M. López*	Private Attorney	Notre Dame U.
Ramón López	Private Attorney	U. of New México
*López is a common Spanish-surname in Nuevo México. In 1846 there is an historical reference to don Juan López as one of "the prominent men of New México who were related by blood or marriage."		
John J. Sánchez*	Attorney, Office of Economic Opportunity	Georgetown U.
Patricio S. Sánchez	Assistant District Attorney	U. of New MéMéxico
John B. Sánchez	Assistant District Attorney	U. of Colorado
Maurice Sánchez	Private Attorney	Northwestern U.
Raymond G. Sánchez	Private Attorney; Member, State Senate	U. of New México
Roquier E. Sánchez	Private Attorney	Georgetown U.
Alfonso G. Sánchez	Private Attorney; former District Attorney	U. of New México
Manuel A. Sánchez	Private Attorney	
*Sánchez is a common Spanish-surname in Nuevo México. There is a historical reference to a José María Sánchez as one of "the prominent men of New México" in 1846.		
Joe L. Martínez*	Associate Justice, Nuevo México Supreme Court	Georgetown U.
Donald A. Martínez	District Attorney; related to Baca family	Georgetown U.
Frank R. Martínez	Attorney, Dept. of Public Health and Welfare	U. of New México
Walter K. Martínez	Private Attorney; Member, State Senate	U. of New México
*Martínez is a common Spanish-surname in Nuevo México. May be related to a number of historical figures including: Felix Martínez, Vice President of Portland Cement Company and Member of the Territorial Legislature; Mariano Martínez, Member, Mexican Territorial Council; Antonio José Martínez, Priest and educator; Santiago, Pascual, and Vicente Martínez, all prominent men in 1846; Martín Serrano Martínez, General in the Spanish Army c. early 17th Century.		

The fourth indicator of socialization is prior political or judicial background. Over half of all Chicano attorneys in the State of Nuevo México have engaged in political activities, been in public practice, and/or come from political families. At least forty-eight Chicano attorneys have engaged in public practice; nineteen have been judges, ten have been prosecutors, fifteen have been members of the Legislature, and four are employed in public agencies. The thirty-four judges and legislators are elected officials as are the three district attorneys. Thirty-nine of eighty-two attorneys are known to have directly engaged in formal political activity. Forty-seven attorneys come from elite political families. Twenty-one of these forty-seven are in addition to those already mentioned above. In summary, sixty-nine of the eighty-two Chicano attorneys are or have been in public practice, are or have engaged in formal political activities, and/or are members of elite political families.

What role religion has played in the socialization of Chicano attorneys is difficult to assess. Perhaps Chicanos matriculated at Catholic Law schools from a sense of security. Perhaps Catholic law schools facilitated scholarships to prospective Chicano law students before it became the fashion. Only further research can answer these questions.

Lastly, what role does ethnic perception play in the socialization of Chicano attorneys? One profile of the successful "ethnic" politician is one who can bridge the "gap" between oppressor and oppressed sectors of society. The same profile can be applied to judges, prosecutors, and other members of the legal system. Sociologist Fernando Peñalosa devised a typology which identifies an individual's cultural predisposition or cultural orientation:

> At one extreme are those who acknowledge the fact of their Mexican descent but for who this fact constitutes neither a particularly positive nor a particularly negative value, because it plays a very unimportant part in their lives and their self-conception. At or near the middle of this putative continuum are those for whom being of Mexican ancestry is something of which they are constantly conscious and which looms importantly as part of their self-conception. Their Mexican descent may constitute for them a positive value, a negative value, or more generally an ambiguous blend of the two. At the other end of the continuum are those who are not only acutely aware of their Mexican identity and descent but are committed to the defense of Mexican American subcultural values, and stive to work actively for the betterment of their people. Tentatively I would like to suggest, without any implication as to their "correctness," that the terms "Americans of Mexican ancestry," "Mexican-Americans," and "Chicanos," are sometimes used for those who closely resemble the three types suggested.[28]

The question is whether the system of legal training has selected and socialized Americans of Mexican descent, Mexican Americans, or

Chicanos? What effect is the selection from predominantly one group having on the administration of law?

Conclusion

A profile of the Chicano legal profession in Nuevo México emerges. A fourth to a third of all attorneys are engaged in private practice. However, most at some time in their life engage in public practice. Attorneys are a distinct elite. They have either held state elective office, judicial positions, been prosecutors or they are members of old line elite families. Those who are incumbents in public office are older than those who do not hold office. Many have been to law school out-of-state but the old line family elites have either studied at St. Louis University or in the Washington, D.C. area, especially at Georgetown. Many have gone to Catholic law schools after taking an undergraduate degree at a Nuevo México university. Whether that indicates strong religious attitudes, family influences, or just elite concepts of a "good education" mixed with appropriate social and political contacts is not clear. Self-perception of ethnic identity is known least. It may be important whether an individual considers himself an American of Mexican descent, Mexican American, or Chicano.

The pattern among the judiciary of the various states is less clear because the definition of what kinds of judges to include in a study is difficult. Nevertheless, there are strong indications of patterns. The schooling of the judges in each state is different, but each group has one or two schools which clearly stand out. There is little venturing into another Southwestern State's law school. The preference is a school outside the region. Age is related to political power. In states where Chicanos have held some political power the judiciary tends to be markedly older. In California where the Chicano is just breaking into the political arena, the judiciary is rather young. Catholic schools are important in terms of providing a legal education, except in California. Finally the judiciary is overwhelmingly male.

The real need in this area is for more research to verify this data and expand many of the points only briefly mentioned. The first need is to find out who are all of the Chicano judges. A second need is to analyze the legal professions in each state. A third need is to see if the Chicano judiciary sentences any differently than Anglo judges.

Notes

1. United States Commission on Civil Rights, *Mexican Americans and the Administration of Justice in the Southwest* (Washington, D.C.: March, 1970), pg. 84.
2. Tergney T. Segerstedt, *The Nature of Social Reality: An Essay in the Epistemology of Empirical Sociology* (Totwa, New Jersey: The Redminister Press, 1966), pp. 1-150.
3. Gabriel A. Almond and Sidney Verba, *The Civic Culture: Political Attitudes and Democracy in Five Nations* (Boston: Little, Brown and Co., 1963), pg. 270.
4. Michael Curtis, *Comparative Government and Politics: An Introductory Essay in Political Science* (New York: Harper and Row, Publishers, 1960), pp. 25-26.
5. Joel B. Grossman, "Judicial Selection and the Socialization of Judges," in *The Federal Judicial System: Readings in Process and Behavior*, Thomas P. Jahnige and Sheldon Goldman, eds., (New York: Holt, Rinehart and Winston, Inc., 1968), pg. 7.
6. Gordon S. Black, "A Theory of Professionalization in Politics," *The American Political Science Review*, Vol. 64 (September, 1970) pg. 865.
7. Leo Grebler, Joan W. Moore, Ralph C. Guzmán, et. al., *The Mexican-American People: The Nation's Second Largest Minority* (New York: The Free Press, 1970), pg. 575.
8. Edgar Litt, *Ethnic Politics in America: Beyond Pluralism* (Glenview, Illinois: Scott, Foresman and Co., 1970), pp. 1-75.
9. Flaviano Chris García, "Political Socialization of Mexican-Americans" (Ph.D. dissertation, University of California, Davis, 1972). This work is not yet held by the UCSB Library, thereby preventing the use of García's findings.
10. See, for example, Florence Rockwood Kluckhohn, "Cultural Factors in Social Work Practice and Education," *Social Services Review*, (March, 1951) pp. 39-44, and William Madsen, *Mexican-Americans of South Texas* (New York: Holt, Rinehart and Winston, Inc., 1954).
11. V. O. Key, Jr., *Southern Politics* (New York: Vintage Press, 1949), pg. 272.
12. Edward Banfield, *Big City Politics* (New York: Random House, 1965), pg. 70. Compare with Carlos Muñoz, "Toward a Chicano Perspective of Political Analysis," *Aztlán — Chicano Journal of the Social Sciences and the Arts*, Vol. 1, No. 2, pp. 15-26. Also Charles Ornelas, "Book Review: The Mexican-American People: The Nation's Second Largest Minority," *El Grito*, Vol. 4 (Summer, 1971), pg. 17.
13. Octavio Ignacio Romano, "The Anthropology and Sociology of the Mexican-American: The Distortion of Mexican-American History," *El Grito*, Vol. 2 (Fall 1968), pp. 13-26.
14. Ruth Tuck, *Not With the Fist: Mexican Americans in a South West City* (Harcourt and Brace Co., 1946). See Mario Barrera, Carlos Muñoz and Charles Ornelas, "The Barrio as Internal Colony," in *People and Politics in Urban Society: Urban Affairs Annual Review*, Harlan Hahn, ed., (Beverly Hills, California: Sage Publications, 1972), for a critique of these two and other studies.
15. Sister Francis Jerome Woods, *Mexican Ethnic Leadership in San Antonio Texas* (Washington, D.C.: The Catholic University of America Press, Inc., 1948).
16. Commission, op. cit., pg. 84.
17. *California Roster of Federal, State, County and City Officials*, compiled by H.P. Sullivan, Secretary of State (Sacramento, California, 1970).
18. *Martindale-Hubbell's Law Directory*.
19. Sheldon Goldman and Thomas P. Jahnige, *The Federal Courts as a Political System* (New York: Harper and Row, Publishers, 1971), pg. 67.
20. Grossman, op. cit., pg. 7.
21. Kenneth N. Vines, "Federal District Judges and Race Relations Cases in the South," in Jahnige and Goldman, *The Federal Judicial System*, op. cit. pg. 134.
22. Grossman, loc. cit.
23. Commission, op. cit., pg. 58.
24. The name, date of birth, date of passing the bar, and schooling of the members of the Nuevo México legal profession were obtained from *Martindale-Hubbell's Law Directory*. Family ancestry, where it is known, was obtained from UCSB Political

Science Graduate Student Carlos Ramírez. We also made the effort to obtain the political background of as many members of the Chicano bar as possible. The extent of information on the Nuevo México Chicano bar would have been much less substantive without the continuing help of Mr. Ramírez. Mr. Ramírez is a descendant of a family which goes back to the original settlers of 1598. His contacts as well as his interests are extensive. In addition, his family is also helping out. His father and mother are sending a list of those who just passed the last bar examination as well as personal notes on family background whenever it is known.

25. The total of twenty Chicano attorneys in public practice is rather low for the period in question. This indicates three weaknesses in the data. First, in 1968, there was one member on the State Supreme Court, three at intermediate appellate courts, and fourteen district court judges, for a total of 18 judges. Yet *Martindale-Hubbell* listed only four Chicano judges plus one retired Supreme Court justice. Three more judges were identified through other sources. Thus, the directory listing is incomplete. Second, at least one non-incumbent Chicano prosecutor was not counted and probably others. Alfonso G. Sánchez, the District Attorney who prosecuted Reies López Tijerina, has since left public office. Third, only State Senator Tibo Chávez is listed as a legislator when in fact there were six Chicano attorneys serving in both Houses in 1968. Depending on which figures one employs about Spanish-surnamed Nuevo México attorneys, between 24.39 percent and 45.85 percent are public officials. The latter figure however is conservative. Two intermediate appellate court judges, nine district court judges, a retired Supreme Court justice and a non-incumbent prosecutor not identified were included in the count. Not included were nine individuals who had previously served in the state legislature and are not now incumbents. With these nine to be included then 59.75 percent of the known Chicano attorneys have served in public practice. There is no data available on individuals who have served in the past in public agencies. Given the normal turnover in the judicial, legislative and executive agencies, it is quite conceivable that in Nuevo México as high as eighty to ninety percent of all Chicano attorneys at one time or another engage in public practice. Therefore, with all its limitations, for purposes of consistency this paper will use the figure of 20 public attorneys.

26. Even if one removes Luján and Chávez from consideration one still finds that age difference between judges and the rest of the bar to be significant. The average age of judges is 58.0 years.

27. All of the historical material is taken from Carlos Ramírez, "Hispanic Elites in New Mexico," (unpublished paper), pp. 3, 10, 14-15, 18-24 and 26-27.

28. Fernando Peñalosa, "Toward an Operational Definition of the Mexican-American," *Aztlán*, Vol. 1, No. 1, (Spring 1970) pg. 4.

ACKNOWLEDGMENTS

I would like to thank Susan Halci, Sheryl Jimenez, Jonlyn Martinez, Roberta Marquez and Debbie Garcia for their research assistance. Debbie Garcia was funded by the Center for Regional Studies. I appreciate the Center's support for this project.

Duran, Tobias. "Francisco Chávez, Thomas B. Catron, and Organized Political Violence in Sante Fe in the 1890s." *New Mexico Historical Review* 59 (1984): 291–310. Reprinted with the permission of the University of New Mexico. Courtesy of Yale University Sterling Memorial Library.

Trujillo, Larry D. "'La Evolución del "Bandido" al "Pachuco"': A Critical Examination and Evaluation of Criminological Literature on Chicanos." *Issues in Criminology* 9 (1974): 43–67. Reprinted with the permission of *Issues in Criminology*. Courtesy of Yale University Law Library.

Garza, Hisauro. "Administration of Justice: Chicanos in Monterey County." *Aztlan* 4 (1973): 137–46. Reprinted with the permission of *Aztlan*. Courtesy of Yale University Sterling Memorial Library.

Carter, David L. "Hispanic Interaction with the Criminal Justice System in Texas: Experiences, Attitudes, and Perceptions." *Journal of Criminal Justice* 11 (1983): 213–27. Reprinted with the permission of Pergamon Press, Inc. Courtesy of Yale University Law Library.

Carter, David L. "Hispanic Perception of Police Performance: An Empirical Assessment." *Journal of Criminal Justice* 13 (1985): 487–500. Reprinted with the permission of Pergamon Press, Inc. Courtesy of Yale University Law Library.

Mirandé, Alfredo. "The Chicano and the Law: An Analysis of Community-Police Conflict in an Urban Barrio." *Pacific Sociological Review* 24 (1981): 65–86. Reprinted with the permission of JAI Press, Inc. Courtesy of Yale University Social Science Library.

Mirandé, Alfredo. "Fear of Crime and Fear of the Police in a Chicano Community." *Sociology and Social Research* 64 (1980): 528–41. Reprinted with the permission of the University of Southern California. Courtesy of Yale University Social Science Library.

Holmes, Malcolm D., and Howard C. Daudistel. "Ethnicity and Justice in the Southwest: The Sentencing of Anglo, Black, and Mexican Origin Defendants." *Social Science Quarterly* 65 (1984): 265–77. Reprinted from *Southwestern Social Science Quarterly,* by permission of the authors and the University of Texas Press. Courtesy of Yale University Sterling Memorial Library.

Hernández, Tanya Katerí. "Bias Crimes: Unconscious Racism in the Prosecution of 'Racially Motivated Violence'." *Yale Law Journal* 99 (1990): 845–64. Reprinted by permission of The Yale Law Journal Company and Fred B. Rothman & Company. Courtesy of Yale University Law Library.

LaFree, Gary D. "Official Reactions to Hispanic Defendants in the Southwest." *Journal of Research in Crime and Delinquency* 22 (1985): 213–37. Reprinted with the permission of Sage Publications Inc. Courtesy of Yale University Law Library.

Bondavalli, Bonnie J., and Bruno Bondavalli. "Spanish-Speaking People and the North American Criminal Justice System." In R.L. McNeely and Carl B. Pope, eds., *Race, Crime, and Criminal Justice* (California: Sage Publications, 1981): 49–69. Reprinted with the permission of Sage Publications. Courtesy of the authors.

Erlanger, Howard S. "Estrangement, Machismo and Gang Violence." *Social Science Quarterly* 60 (1979): 235–248. Reprinted from *Southwestern Social Science Quarterly,* by permission of the authors and the University of Texas Press. Courtesy of Yale University Sterling Memorial Library.

Dannefer, Dale, and Russell K. Schutt. "Race and Juvenile Justice Processing in Court and Police Agencies." *American Journal of Sociology* 87 (1982): 1113–1132. Reprinted with the permission of the University of Chicago Press, publisher. Courtesy of Yale University Sterling Memorial Library.

Safford, Joan Bainbridge. "No Comprendo: The Non-English-Speaking Defendant and the Criminal Process." *Journal of Criminal Law & Criminology* 68 (1977): 15–30. Reprinted with the permission of the *Journal of Criminal Law & Criminology.* Courtesy of Yale University Law Library.

Padilla, Fernando V. "Socialization of Chicano Judges and Attorneys." *Aztlan* 5 (1974): 261–94. Reprinted with the permission of *Aztlan*. Courtesy of Yale University Sterling Memorial Library.